SECOND EDITION

PERSUASIVE
COMMUNICATION

EDITED BY
KRISTIE SIGLER

Kendall Hunt
publishing company

Author's content is identified with brackets (⌐⌐) throughout.

www.kendallhunt.com
Send all inquiries to:
4050 Westmark Drive
Dubuque, IA 52004-1840

Published in the United States of America

BRIEF CONTENTS

CONTENTS

INTRODUCTION

This book is organized into three sections: Persuasion Theory and Research, Persuasive Writing, and Persuasive Presentations. Chapters in the Persuasion Theory and Research section provide a foundation of persuasive concepts, models, and theories supported by current research. The second section, Persuasive Writing, devotes attention to a discussion of academic writing and information about finding and using credible sources to support a persuasive argument. Finally, chapters in the Persuasive Presentations section focus on public speaking, listening, and critiquing speeches. Sections two and three provide writing and speaking instruction to encourage the immediate application of material presented in section one.

Questions provided at the beginning of each chapter guide your reading and make connections with information you already know. Following each chapter, you are asked to answer a few questions without looking back through your text. These questions help you practice retrieving information from memory, a skill necessary to demonstrate the understanding of material and apply it to other contexts. Additional questions require you to review key concepts and terms from the chapter. Finally, discussion questions encourage critical thinking, active listening, and the application of material to course goals and assignments. The last question in each chapter addresses ethics which is essential to any discussion of persuasion.

PERSUASION THEORY AND RESEARCH

This section includes chapters about persuasive concepts, theories, and models supported by current research. You will learn the definition of persuasion and the importance of attitudes, beliefs, and values. A chapter on classical rhetoric leads to the next two chapters that explore source factors and message factors in persuasion. This section concludes with a comprehensive overview of four persuasion theories: social judgment theory, cognitive dissonance theory, the theory of reasoned action, and the elaboration likelihood model.

As you read each chapter, keep your final presentation in mind. How can you apply what you are learning to your writing assignments and speeches? Use the questions included with each chapter to guide you. The material in this section is about theory and research, all of which are relevant to you and the work you will be doing for the course.

CHAPTERS

THE CONCEPT OF PERSUASION

BEFORE YOU READ

Respond to the following questions **before** you read the chapter.

1. How would you define persuasion? Is it positive or negative?

2. Describe an example of persuasion that you've encountered in the last week.

3. What benefit is there in learning about persuasion? How might it help you in your personal or academic life right now and in your professional life in the future?

Shekera, a 20-year-old female and a full-time student at a state university, is sitting in her nutrition class with Dr. Kalibo listening to her explanation on how complex carbohydrates are broken down into simple carbohydrates. Shekera loves the class and feels she has learned so much about food, diet, and health. Since the beginning of the semester, Shekera has almost quit drinking soda, has started eating vegetables every day, and has quit adding cream to her coffee.

Jake and Melinda have been dating for 2 years and have lived together for the past 8 months. Melinda regrets moving in with Jake and has decided to move out. This evening Melinda broke the news to Jake.

LEARNING OBJECTIVES

- DEFINE PERSUASION AND DIFFERENTIATE IT FROM OTHER FORMS OF INFLUENCE.
- DESCRIBE THE KEY CHARACTERISTICS OF PERSUASION.
- DESCRIBE SITUATIONS IN WHICH PERSUASION IS COMMONLY USED.
- CONSIDER THE ROLE OF ETHICS IN PERSUASION.

Jake responded with complete rage and began breaking things. Melinda yelled and pleaded with him to stop, and then Jake saw the fine porcelain Lladro figurine that her beloved grandmother had brought to her from Spain. Jake grabbed the Lladro, held it over his head and said, "Tell me you won't move out. Promise me you'll stay and I won't break it. If you leave, I break it." Melinda agreed to stay.

Nick is an 18-year-old male in his first year of college. On his way to class one day, he sees a flyer for the rowing club. It looks like fun, and Nick decides to go to the informational meeting that evening. At the meeting several members of the club spend a few minutes describing their experiences with the club, how much fun it is, and how many fun people they have met. By the end of the meeting, Nick can't wait to sign up. As he fills out the membership form, the club members congratulate him and welcome him to the rowing club.

So which of these situations involve persuasion? Is Shekera persuaded by her instructor to change her diet? Does Jake persuade Melinda to stay in the relationship? Is Nick persuaded to join the rowing club? All three of these situations involve influence, but are these examples of persuasion? One of these situations is clearly persuasion. Most scholars would agree that one situation is not persuasion, and one situation could be persuasion, but we need more information about the situation to know for sure. Let's begin discussing some of the characteristics of persuasion so that you can determine which of these situations are good examples of persuasion and which are not.

DEFINING CHARACTERISTICS OF PERSUASION

Persuasion has been defined in numerous ways, as is illustrated by the five definitions shown in Figure 1.1. Before we provide the definition to be used in this text, let's discuss some key characteristics that will help you understand why we define persuasion the way we do. First, **persuasion involves symbolic interaction using a shared symbol system**. Language and nonverbal behaviors are symbols, which means that communication between people involves symbolic interaction. Therefore, persuasion involves verbal and nonverbal communication. Four of the five definitions in Figure 1.1 refer

BOSTROM (1983)

"Persuasion is communicative behavior that has as its purpose the changing, modification, or shaping of the responses (attitudes or behavior) of the receivers" (p. 11).

PETTY AND CACIOPPO (1981)

"...any instance in which an active attempt is made to change a person's mind because the word is relatively neutral and because one person's propaganda may be another person's education" (p. 4).

LARSON (2013)

"...the process of dramatic co-creation by sources and receivers of a state of identification through the use of verbal and/or visual symbols" (p. 20).

PERLOFF (2010)

"...a symbolic process in which communicators try to convince other people to change their attitudes or behaviors regarding an issue through the transmission of a message in an atmosphere of free choice" (p. 12).

O'KEEFE (2002)

"A successful intentional effort at influencing another's mental state through communication in a circumstance in which the persuadee has some measure of freedom" (p. 5).

FIGURE 1.1 Definitions of persuasion.

to communication. The one definition that does not directly refer to communication does imply communication. Persuasive messages can be verbal and involve language (e.g., English), be nonverbal with symbols that have shared meanings (e.g., a smile, a picture of a flag), and are transmitted from a sender to a receiver. All three of the influence situations described above clearly involve communication and a shared symbol system, so all three have at least one characteristic of persuasion.

Second, **persuasion requires intent**. Without this requirement, we could argue that all communications are persuasive; however, only three of the five definitions in Figure 1.1 refer to intent in some way. When someone walks across campus and says "hello" to you, it is possible to interpret that as a persuasive intent to convince you that he or she is a friendly person and/or to convince you to respond in a friendly manner but, most often, it is nothing more than a greeting. A definition that doesn't require persuasive intent on the part of the sender doesn't help us distinguish persuasion from other related terms such as communication. The intent requirement means that persuasion focuses on messages that are intended to persuade the receiver. The second and third situations above clearly involve intent. Jake clearly intends to influence Melinda, and the rowing club clearly wants to influence Nick to join. But does Dr. Kalibo intend to influence Shekera to change her eating habits? Maybe. Assuming Shekera's teacher is like most other teachers, she wants Shekera to learn specific information about nutrition and dispel myths and misconceptions about food and diet. But that doesn't mean Dr. Kalibo intends to change Shekera's eating habits, particularly the changes that Shekera made. We would really need to ask Dr. Kalibo if she intended to change her students' eating habits. If that indeed was her intention, then the situation would have the second characteristic of persuasion. If Dr. Kalibo simply wanted students to learn the content, and she left it up to the students to decide what to do with that information, then we would likely conclude that this really is not persuasion. Education and persuasion overlap in numerous ways, and the similarities and differences are further discussed later in this chapter.

Third, **persuasion involves two or more persons**. There has to be a sender and a receiver for persuasion to occur. Some have considered whether nonhuman animals can be involved in persuasion, whether individuals can persuade themselves through intrapersonal communication, and/or whether inanimate objects (e.g., a tree) can be persuasion agents. Although each of these arguments has supporters, the persuasion discussed in this textbook (and in most persuasion research) refers to persuasion attempts between at least two persons. All three of the influence situations involve at least two persons, so they all have this characteristic.

Finally, we need to consider the outcomes of persuasion. Miller (1980) argues that persuasion is intended to shape, reinforce, or change the responses of the receiver, and all of the definitions in Figure 1.1 refer to some type of change. We generally expect persuasive messages to involve attempts to **change** the beliefs, attitudes, and/or behavior of the receivers. For example, you have probably heard and seen numerous public service campaigns that want people to avoid texting while driving. In our situations, we can see a change in behavior. Shekera changes her eating habits; Melinda stays rather than moves out; and Nick signs up for the rowing club. We also assume that Shekera's beliefs about her diet changed, which led to a change in her behavior. It's hard to say whether Melinda's beliefs about moving out changed, but her intended behavior was altered. We can also assume that Nick developed positive beliefs about the rowing club; otherwise, he wouldn't have signed up. Therefore, all three situations share this characteristic of persuasion.

Not all persuasive messages try to invoke change, however. Some attempt to **reinforce** currently held beliefs or attitudes and/or current behavioral practices. For example, Pepsi wants current Pepsi drinkers to remain loyal to the product. Political candidates speaking to members of their own party want members to remain loyal to the party and vote along party lines. Typically, speeches at the Republican and Democratic National Conventions focus on their supporters and use persuasive messages designed to reinforce current political views. Check out the 2020 convention speeches online to examine their focus. Another example is antismoking campaigns targeted at teens. Such campaigns are focused more on encouraging them *not* to start smoking than on altering current behaviors. Much of the persuasion surrounding us is attempting to reaffirm current beliefs, attitudes, and/or behaviors. The image in Figure 1.2 reinforces the benefits of running.

Additionally, some persuasion tries to shape responses. These are messages targeted toward receivers who have not developed an attitude toward an object and who often lack knowledge on the issue. For example, when a company introduces a new product, it tries to shape positive responses to that product. When Procter and Gamble introduced Febreze®, a product targeted at removing odors from fabric, the company needed to inform consumers and wanted them to think positively about such a product. Because receivers had no prior knowledge of this product, the company wasn't trying to change anything and there was nothing there to reinforce. ⌈Persuasion often involves large audiences such as those involved in advertising and public health campaigns.⌋ Thus, depending on the situation, the intended outcome for persuasion may be change, reinforcement, or shaping of receiver responses. ⌈When the coronavirus was identified in 2020, government and health officials needed to shape responses to this new and different type of virus. Over time, messages transitions from shaping behaviors like social distancing to reinforcing them.⌋ Thus, depending on the situation, the intended outcome for persuasion may be changing, reinforcing, or shaping of receiver responses.

FIGURE 1.2 Public service announcement.

You may be wondering what is meant by "receiver responses." Depending on the situation, the desired response from the receiver may involve attitudes, beliefs, and/or behaviors. For example, at times, attitude change is desired. A political candidate may want voters to share favorable attitudes toward key campaign issues. A religious organization may want to target beliefs in receivers so that they are in alignment with the particular religion. Many times, however, behavior is the ultimate target of persuasion attempts. Advertisers ultimately want products to be purchased. Political candidates want votes and/or financial contributions. Social issue organizations often want to persuade the public about acceptable behavior (e.g., not smoking, wearing seat belts, adopting healthy exercise and eating patterns). We often expect attitudes and/or beliefs to be the basis for behavior, so targeting attitudes and beliefs may be an avenue to influence receiver behavior. As a result, when considering receiver responses, we need to consider attitudes, beliefs, and behaviors. We examine attitudes, beliefs, and behaviors in more depth in Chapters 2 and 3.

Thus, when all of these criteria are taken into account, we come to the following definition of persuasion, which draws on the multiple perspectives represented earlier: **Persuasion involves symbolic communication between two or more persons with intent to change, reinforce, or shape attitudes, beliefs, and/or behaviors of the receiver.**

At this point, we have discussed the situations presented at the beginning of this chapter in relation to the key characteristics of persuasion, but we really haven't answered the question of which of these is persuasion and which is not. We determined that Shekera's change of eating habits might not be a result of persuasion if Dr. Kalibo did not intentionally try to influence her eating habits. However, the other two situations seemed to have all of the characteristics of persuasion. The second situation, involving Jake and Melinda, brings up another issue in distinguishing persuasion from other forms of influence—coercion. **Coercion** is a social influence that involves force or threat of force. Jake uses a threat to force Melinda to stay. For this reason, this situation is a better example of coercion than it is of persuasion; however, the difference between coercion and persuasion is not always clear. Perloff's (2010) and O'Keefe's (2002) definitions of persuasion in Figure 1.1 refer to the receiver having free choice or freedom. Think of free vs. forced choice as a continuum as illustrated below.

Free choice _____ Forced choice

Having a gun pointed at your head with a demand for your laptop is clearly a forced choice. Or, in Melinda's case, the threat of a smashed treasured object is clearly a forced choice. In the third situation, Nick chose to become a member of the rowing club. No one forced or threatened Nick to sign up. Melinda's behavior was a result of force, whereas Nick's behavior was a result of choice. However, not all circumstances easily fit into one end of the continuum or the other. Consider the class you are in. The teacher controls the awarding of grades. Instructors set grading policies, work and attendance expectations, and so on. Students may choose to complete the work or not; however, there is a consequence in terms of the grade received for choosing not to complete the work. Is that a free choice, or is there an element of threat in this situation? Is the public service announcement in Figure 1.3 an example of persuasion or coercion? Are you being threatened? Do you have free choice when it comes to wearing a seat belt? Situations that fall toward the forced-choice end of the continuum are considered more coercion than persuasion, whereas situations that offer more free choice are considered more persuasion. However, where choice ends and force begins is not clear, making many situations ambiguous.

WHY STUDY PERSUASION?

The question of why we study persuasion is one that students may ask advisers and that researchers ask themselves. There are three major reasons people have for wanting to know more about persuasion. The most common reason students have given us for taking a class in persuasion is a very practical one. We all engage in persuasion in multiple contexts in our lives, and many want to study persuasion in order to be **more successful persuaders** themselves. That desire for mastery of the art of

We are bombarded by advertisements when we are on social media, streaming movies, listening to music, and doing almost any other online activity. Advertisements are also still central to traditional media such as radio, television, and print media. But not all persuasion involves advertising. Think about your interactions with friends, family, teachers, work colleagues, food servers, delivery people, etc. Many of these interactions involve persuasive messages. Our daily lives involve persuasion in interpersonal and small-group contexts.⌐ Students try to persuade parents to support them financially and emotionally. Roommates try to persuade each other to clean living quarters and to respect each other's privacy. Students try to convince faculty to grade them more positively. Group projects involve persuasion about meeting times, locations, and the division of labor. ⌐The people around us as well as media of all sorts surround us with messages constantly.⌐ It is hard to imagine a lack of persuasion in daily interactions for most people.

⌐Not all persuasive messages are clearly labeled as such. In traditional print media, advertisements are formatted to clearly differentiate them from journalistic content. Similarly, YouTube advertisements are clearly labeled as such. However, there are a number of messages that are not advertisements but are intended to persuade receivers. Some YouTube videos are disguised as educational when the true intent is to get us to buy a product. You may rely on reviews before making a purchase. Some reviews are written by the sellers of the product rather than the users, and in some cases are outright fraudulent. A 2018 article by consumer advocate, Christopher Elliott, explicitly says that we should not trust online reviews. Not only will companies plant positive reviews of their own products, but they also plant negative reviews of their competitors' products. Deception is unfortunately all too common in persuasive messages.

Public relations professionals practice the art of persuasion professionally and involve a broad range of activities such as media relations, special events, crisis management, grassroots lobbying, and more. Some of these activities are not clearly labeled as persuasion. For example, PR professionals regularly send press releases to news organizations with the intent to influence the news coverage of their clients. These messages are not necessarily dishonest or unethical but are often biased and influence the nature of the information that is presented as "news." Similarly, lobbyists regularly provide research reports and technical information related to congressional bills to influence the direction of public policy. These forms of persuasion are less explicit than advertisements and sometimes appear to be simply informational. However, public relations professionals and lobbyists have a persuasive goal and intend to influence decision-makers, therefore messages that may be labeled as "information" qualify as persuasive messages according to the characteristics of persuasion.

Promotional events are a common form of persuasion in marketing and public relations. For example, for years McDonald's has held an annual Monopoly game. Consumers are encouraged to purchase McDonald's products to collect Monopoly game pieces for a chance at a variety of prizes, including a million dollars. Although the odds against winning are great, McDonald's does great business during the promotion. Promotional events can be both big and small. Free T-shirts and other small items are popular promotional items. You likely have several pens, coffee mugs, and T-shirts that promote various universities, programs, and businesses. Promotional activities can be big, extravagant events such as New York Fashion Week or the notorious failed Fyre Festival which was supposedly intended to promote the Fyre app for booking musical talent. With promotional events, receivers are typically well aware of the persuasive intent and understand they are the target of the influence attempts.

Health promotion is another area where persuasion is used extensively. The Center for Disease Control (CDC) is continuously developing large campaigns to influence Americans to engage in healthy behaviors such as getting annual flu shots and cancer screenings. There are also many non-profit organizations that promote healthy behaviors such as the American Cancer Society and the American Diabetes Association. Communication scholars often team up with public health professionals in the development of campaigns to change attitudes, beliefs, and behaviors about health, disease, and wellness. If you take a health communication class, you will likely find a significant portion of the class is devoted to persuasion and social influence.

Another major context where persuasion is used extensively is the political arena. Our democratic society is built on the belief that the best ideas emerge from the debate of ideas. Political campaigns use persuasion to promote both specific candidates and their party platform. The United States Congress relies on persuasive speeches and debates to influence members of Congress as well as the American public. Lobbyists work to influence members of Congress and other government officials, as well as the American public, on policy and matters of law.

Persuasive messages take many forms and occur in many contexts. The purpose of this text is to examine principles of persuasion, tactics, and theories that both help us understand persuasion across contexts as well as to engage in a variety of persuasive activities across contexts. On the surface, persuasion in social media looks quite different from persuasion in a public speech, but once we get below the surface there are many similarities.

PERSUASION AS ONE OF MULTIPLE FORMS OF INFLUENCE

We have used the terms influence and persuasion, and we have used them somewhat differently. At this point we want to clarify how persuasion is different from influence as well as to clarify some related terms. Influence is a very general term that refers to a power that affects something. Persuasion, as we have discussed, is the use of communication to intentionally change, reinforce, or shape another's attitudes, beliefs, and/or behaviors. Clearly, persuasion is a form of influence. Coercion is also a form of influence that we discussed that involves force. Persuasion doesn't rely on force, although persuasion may involve pressure to change. Another term is propaganda. Propaganda is a term we often use to refer to persuasion attempts by those we do not agree with. When we are engaged in influence attempts, we call it persuasion. But when others are engaging in influence attempts that we disagree with, we often label that propaganda. This reflects the negative connotative meaning propaganda has for many people. Propaganda has been defined as a type of persuasion that involves mass audiences with the purpose of achieving the goals of the persuader. It often involves emotional appeals, concealment of purpose, and a lack of sound support, which all involve ethical issues.

Education is another form of influence that can be distinguished from persuasion. A teacher's intent is an important factor. If the source intends to change the receiver's

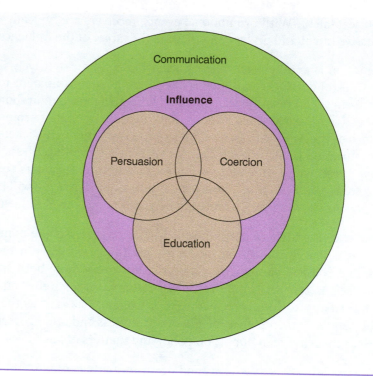

FIGURE 1.4 Venn diagram.

attitudes, beliefs, or behavior (or to reinforce or shape receiver responses), it would be considered persuasion. ⌈In general, the purpose of education is to help students prepare for life, including careers and further education. Learning is the primary outcome of interest. Teachers, particularly at the college level, focus on sharing information and leave it up to students to decide what to do with that information. For example, a political science teacher would expect students to understand different political perspectives but would not try to influence which perspective a student feels is best.⌋ In the case of Shekera and her nutrition class, it is quite likely that sharing of information was Dr. Kalibo's primary intent. It would be rare, however, for educators not to care about how that information is used. Most educators want their students to adopt the information and use it in their lives, and that runs pretty close to shaping, reinforcing, and changing responses. Dr. Kalibo might well have been pleased by the changes in Shekera's diet. Certainly public health campaigns have the intent of doing more than sharing information. Those campaigns want to affect how receivers think about health issues, and most want specific health behaviors to be the result. Many education efforts have persuasive elements, so education and persuasion are not always easy to distinguish from one another.

⌈Persuasion was defined as involving communication but how is communication similar and different from persuasion?⌋ Communication is a broad term that encompasses a variety of messages, including those that influence people. Communication has been defined in a variety of ways; however, our preferred definition was put forth by McCroskey and Richmond (1996), who define **communication** as "the process by which one person stimulates meaning in the mind(s) of another person (or persons) through verbal and nonverbal messages" (p. 3). The definition of persuasion used here refers to persuasion as a type of communication, and influence attempts involve communication. Thus, a hierarchy of terms would include communication as the umbrella term, influence next, with persuasion, coercion, and education being types of influence that overlap with one another. The Venn diagram in Figure 1.4 illustrates the relationships among communication, influence, persuasion, coercion, and education.

THE ROLE OF ETHICS IN PERSUASION

Up to this point, we have simply described types of social influence without making judgments about the appropriateness of using them. As the situation with Jake and Melinda at the beginning of the chapter illustrates, ethical implications should be considered in using and analyzing persuasion. Persuasion is a tool that can be used in an ethical or an unethical manner, and it can be employed to achieve ethical or unethical ends. Although what can be done with persuasion and what has been done with persuasion are discussed throughout the book, you shouldn't lose sight of the question of what *should* be done with persuasion. Just because you *can* doesn't mean you *should*. Jake successfully influenced Melinda to not move out, but was that ethical?

Throughout history and across societies, ethical issues involving social influence have been raised. For example, con artists use persuasion to bilk money from vulnerable people. Hitler used persuasion to attempt world domination and to support plans to eradicate large segments of certain populations in the Holocaust. Persuasion has been used to sell faulty products. Most people would find persuasion to be unethical in all of these cases. At the same time, persuasion has been used to help the public stop smoking and wear seat belts. Persuasion has been used to promote the sale of useful products that benefit consumers, and persuasion is the cornerstone of our democratic system of government. Most would argue that these are important and generally ethical uses of persuasion. Persuasion is a tool, like most other tools, that can be used to benefit others or to harm them. The ethical standards of the source often determine whether persuasion is ethical or unethical.

Throughout this text, as we lay out the processes involved in persuasion and develop concepts, theories, tactics, strategies, and methods for engaging in successful persuasion, ethical implications will be considered. Questions will be raised as the book progresses. After you have studied all the different approaches and methods you can use to persuade, it is important that you consider the ethical implications of your choices. Key perspectives on ethics are developed, and central questions are discussed. Discussion questions are provided at the end of each chapter and always include at least one question of ethics to consider. Should there be absolute standards in ethics? Are there guidelines (e.g., don't lie) that would be appropriate for every situation, or are ethics relative? Do the ends (e.g., a good outcome) justify any means (e.g., false evidence)? Is deceiving the receiver ever appropriate? Should the source of the message bear primary responsibility for ethics, or should the receiver share that responsibility (e.g., buyer beware)? You should be considering these questions as you read the rest of this book.

SUMMARY

- Persuasion is a common occurrence in everyday life.
- Key concepts in the definition of persuasion include the use of symbolic interaction; intent on the part of the source of the message; two or more persons; and the intent to shape, reinforce, or change the responses of the receiver.
- Persuasion involves symbolic communication between two or more persons with intent to change, reinforce, or shape the attitudes, beliefs, and/or behaviors of the receiver.
- Persuasion is studied so that we can be more successful in persuasion attempts, be better consumers of information, and better understand what is happening around us.
- Persuasion occurs in interpersonal, small-group, and mass media settings as well as in advertising, marketing, public relations, public health issues, social issues, and other contexts of society.
- Communication is an umbrella term that includes influence. Persuasion is a type of influence along with education and coercion.
- Ethics play an important role in persuasion and should be considered throughout this book.

KEY TERMS

Coercion—a social influence that involves force or threat of force.

Communication—the process by which one person stimulates meaning in the mind(s) of another person (or persons) through verbal and nonverbal messages.

Education—a form of influence that overlaps with persuasion.

Influence—a general term that refers to a power that affects something.

Persuasion—symbolic communication between two or more persons with an intent to change, reinforce, or shape the attitudes, beliefs, and/or behaviors of the receiver.

Propaganda—a type of persuasion that involves mass audiences with the purpose of achieving the goals of the persuader, and it often involves emotional appeals, concealment of purpose, and a lack of sound support.

QUESTIONS FOR REVIEW

Respond to the following questions **without** reviewing the text or your notes. These questions are provided to help you practice retrieving information and reflect on your reading.

A. How would you define persuasion?

B. Did you agree or disagree with anything you read? Explain.

C. What did you learn that was new to you?

D. What concepts, if any, were confusing to you?

Respond to the following questions. You may reference your text or notes to help you.

1. What are the four key characteristics of persuasion?

2. What are the three possible outcomes of persuasion? How do they differ?

3. What is the difference between persuasion and coercion? Why are these concepts a continuum?

4. Why is it important to study persuasion?

5. When and where does persuasion take place?

1. Before reading this chapter, you wrote a definition of persuasion. How does your definition compare to the definitions of other students in your class or group? To the definition provided in your text? Pay special attention to the four key characteristics of persuasion.

2. Identify examples from advertising or health and social campaigns that attempt to change, shape, or reinforce beliefs or attitudes and/or behaviors. Who is the target audience? What "receiver response" is desired by the persuader?

3. According to this chapter, "education is another form of influence that can be distinguished from persuasion." When considering higher education, do you agree or disagree? Does your response differ if you consider the type of institution or specific class? Or if you consider the statement from different perspectives, such as a college president, faculty, staff, students, or even parents of students?

4. This chapter provided several reasons for studying persuasion, and you were asked to list some before you began reading. Now that you have read the chapter, let's revisit those questions and consider if your answers have changed or remained the same. What benefit is there in learning about persuasion? How might it help you in your personal or academic life right now and in your professional life in the future?

5. Discuss the ethical questions provided at the end of the chapter:
   • Are there guidelines (e.g., don't lie) that would be appropriate for every situation, or are ethics relative?

   • Do the ends (e.g., a good outcome) justify any means?

- Is deceiving the receiver ever appropriate?

- Should the source of the message bear primary responsibility for ethics, or should the receiver share that responsibility (e.g., buyer beware)?

REFERENCES

Bostrom, R. N. (1983). *Persuasion*. Englewood Cliffs, NJ: Prentice-Hall.

Elliott, C. (November 21, 2018). This is why you should not trust online reviews. *Forbes*. https://www.forbes.com/sites/christopherelliott/2018/11/21/why-you-should-not-trust-online-reviews/#332690c12218

Freese, J. H. (1991). *Aristotle: The art of rhetoric with an English translation by John Henry Freese*. Cambridge, MA: Harvard University Press.

Larson, C. U. (2013). *Persuasion: Reception and responsibility* (13th ed.). Boston, MA: Wadsworth, Cengage Learning.

McCroskey, J. C., & Richmond, V. P. (1996). *Fundamentals of human communication: An interpersonal perspective*. Prospect Heights, IL: Waveland Press.

Miller, G. R. (1980). On being persuaded: Some basic distinctions. In M. Roloff & G. Miller (Eds.), *Persuasion: New directions in theory and research* (pp. 11–28). Beverly Hills, CA: Sage.

O'Keefe, D. J. (2002). *Persuasion: Theory and research* (2nd ed.). Thousand Oaks, CA: Sage.

Perloff, R. M. (2010). *The dynamics of persuasion: Communication and attitudes in the 21st century* (4th ed.). New York, NY: Routledge.

Petty, R. E., & Cacioppo, J. T. (1981). *Attitudes and persuasion: Classic and contemporary approaches*. Dubuque, IA: Wm. C. Brown.

CHAPTER 2

ATTITUDES AND BELIEFS

BEFORE YOU READ

Respond to the following questions **before** you read the chapter.

1. What do you think is the difference between an attitude and a belief?

2. ⌐You probably have strong attitudes about certain foods, movie genres, or rival teams. How and when do you think those attitudes were formed?

3. What are your most important values? Do you think you share any values with other students in your class? If so, which values might be similar?⌐

*She has **attitude**!*

*What's your **attitude** about the war?*

*He needs an **attitude** adjustment.*

*She has a bad **attitude**.*

LEARNING OBJECTIVES

- DEFINE ATTITUDE AND DESCRIBE THE CHARACTERISTICS OF ATTITUDE.
- EXPLAIN HOW ATTITUDES, BELIEFS, AND BEHAVIORS ARE SIMILAR AND DIFFERENT.
- DESCRIBE AND EXPLAIN THE FUNCTIONS OF ATTITUDE.
- EXPLAIN HOW ATTITUDES AND BELIEFS CAN BE FORMED THROUGH CLASSICAL CONDITIONING, OPERANT CONDITIONING, MERE EXPOSURE, AND SUBLIMINAL INFLUENCE.

*Persuasion involves symbolic communication between two or more persons with intent to change, reinforce, or shape **attitudes**, beliefs, and/or behaviors of the receiver.*

Each of these sentences uses the term *attitude,* and the word means something a little different in each sentence. What does the term *attitude* mean to you? Is it something you can observe? We use the term *attitude* frequently in everyday life and in a variety of ways; however, the term has a specific meaning in the persuasion context. As we discussed in Chapter 1, persuasion is often about change—changing beliefs, behaviors, and attitudes. At times we also want to reinforce those things rather than change them. But before we can do either of those things, we need to understand what we are trying to influence. In this chapter we focus on those things we are most often trying to change through persuasion: **attitudes**, **beliefs**, **behaviors**, and **behavioral intentions**.

Courtesy of Ann Frymier

The definition of attitude is important within the study of persuasion. In just about every definition of persuasion, attitude appears as part of the desired outcome. Persuasion theories are often referred to as attitude change theories, and a great deal of research examines the relationship between attitudes and behavior. People often believe that our attitudes influence our behavior, so understanding attitudes can help us understand and control persuasion. Thus, it is important to have a clear understanding of the concept of "attitude" before further exploring the field of persuasion. As with the term *persuasion,* there are multiple definitions of **attitude**. Take a moment to read through the definitions of attitude presented in Figure 2.1. As you can see, all the definitions refer to the evaluation and favorableness/unfavorableness of some objects. Before we fully examine the definition of attitude, let's discuss some key characteristics of attitudes so that the definition will be more meaningful for you.

FIGURE 2.1 Definitions of attitude.

CHARACTERISTICS OF ATTITUDES

The definitions of attitude in Figure 2.1 indicate important characteristics of attitudes. First, attitudes involve **evaluation**. This means attitudes involve likes and dislikes as an evaluative response as opposed to a cognitive or a knowledge-based response. These evaluative responses involve feelings, likes, and dislikes and are reflected in statements that use the terms *like* or *dislike*. For example, the sentences "I like country music" and "I can't stand country music" reflect attitudes toward country music. The evaluative component is key in distinguishing attitudes from beliefs and is discussed later.

Second, attitudes are always **tied to an object**. **Objects** can refer to any item, event, person, concept, or idea. We don't hold likes or dislikes in general. Instead, we link them to objects. A person could like BMWs, dislike Star Wars, or like her relationship with her parents. Since attitudes are always linked to an object, it is important to understand the specific object in order to understand the attitude. For example, someone who dislikes Japanese food has a different attitude than someone who dislikes sushi. The more specific the object, the better we will understand the attitude.

⌈The third characteristic is that attitudes **vary in direction and intensity**. Attitudes range from positive to negative, which refers to direction. When we describe the direction of an attitude, we are describing it as on a continuum from positive to negative. Attitudes also vary in **intensity**. Some attitudes are held more strongly, or in other words we are more certain in our evaluation of some objects.⌋

The fourth characteristic is that attitudes also are **related to behavior** or, in other words, attitudes can influence behavior and behavior can influence attitudes. Early researchers believed attitudes directly caused behavior, but we know today that the relationship is not that straightforward. Also we know that behavior sometimes influences attitude formation. Several persuasion theories assume that attitudes guide behavior even though other things influence behavior too. Several things influence the way we behave, such as our genetic makeup, the situation we are in, and other people around us. However, attitude also influences behavior. For instance, if a person evaluates chocolate positively (positive attitude), he or she is likely to eat chocolate (behavior). However, your experience (behavior) with a new food (think samples in the grocery store) is often the basis of your attitude toward that food. If it tasted good, you developed a positive attitude toward it.

The fifth characteristic of attitudes are that they can be explicit and implicit. **Explicit attitudes** are those attitudes that you are aware of and can easily describe. For instance, you are probably well aware of your attitude toward ice cream. Whether you like it or not, if someone asks you to evaluate ice cream, you know how you view it. **Implicit attitudes** are those attitudes that you are not aware of or conscious of (Greenwald & Banaji, 1995) and result in automatic evaluations. Implicit attitudes are forgotten evaluations that still exist in our cognition and can influence our behavior.

The final characteristic is that attitudes are **learned**. Attitudes are not characteristics that people are born with. Attitudes can be learned in more than one way. Sometimes attitudes are explicitly taught by parents, teachers, peers, or significant others. If parents tell their children that dogs are nasty creatures, chances are that the children will adopt a negative attitude toward dogs. It is in this manner that many prejudices are passed on from parents to children. In addition, some attitudes can be learned from direct experience. If a person tries peas and finds them distasteful, then he or she is likely to have a negative attitude toward peas. Sometimes, attitudes are learned from observations of others. This may include the influence of mass media as well as the direct observation of those around us. If we see others eating sashimi and appearing to enjoy it, we may then hold a positive attitude toward sashimi. Similarly, many advertisements show people who purchase a particular product (e.g., toothpaste) having great experiences often involving being attractive to the opposite sex. This scenario is designed to lead viewers to hold positive attitudes about the product being featured in the advertisement.

ATTITUDE DEFINED

There are many definitions of attitude, but as illustrated in the definitions in Figure 2.1, all definitions involve "evaluation." In this text, we will rely on Fishbein and Ajzen's (2010) definition of attitude, which states that an attitude is a "latent disposition or tendency to respond with some degree of favorableness or unfavorableness to a psychological object" (p. 76). The phrase "latent disposition" refers to the idea that attitudes can influence beliefs and behavior even if we are not consciously aware of them. As discussed, attitudes are tied to objects and a "psychological object" can be an idea, a person, a place, etc. A key characteristic of attitude expressed in this definition is that an attitude is an evaluation.

BELIEFS AND BEHAVIORS

Our discussion of persuasion has involved several concepts. Persuasion means changing or shaping attitudes, beliefs, and behaviors. Although we frequently hear the terms *attitudes, beliefs,* and *values* used together, these are three different concepts. We need to understand the differences and similarities among these concepts before we continue with our discussion of persuasion. A primary similarity among attitudes, beliefs, and behaviors is that they are learned. We learn attitudes, beliefs, and behaviors from our parents, peers, media, teachers, and our community.⌟

Beliefs are often confused with attitudes. Beliefs deal with the cognitive or informational dimension, whereas attitudes deal with the evaluative or liking dimension. **Beliefs** "link an object to some attribute" (Fishbein & Ajzen, 1975, p. 12). Often, what people say they know as truth actually reflects a belief. ⌜"Faith in the existence of God" is a belief that connects the object of God to the attribute of existence. A belief that "fire is hot" connects the object of fire to the attribute of hot.⌟ Beliefs reflect our way of thinking about the world and are related to attitudes and behavior. "Fire is hot," reflects a belief. Not liking to be burned reflects an attitude. Avoiding fire is a resulting behavior.

Fishbein and Raven (1962) proposed two classes of beliefs: beliefs-in and beliefs-about. **Beliefs-in** refers to beliefs in the existence of a concept. It could refer to beliefs in the existence of God, global warming, or the Tooth Fairy. **Beliefs-about** refers to beliefs about characteristics of a concept. For example, believing in God is a "belief-in" type of belief, and believing that God is all-powerful is a "belief-about" type of belief. Fishbein (1967) argued that beliefs-about involve a relationship "between the object of the belief and some other object, concept, value, or goal" (p. 259).

Some beliefs-about are *prescriptive*. When people say that school (object) should be required (attribute) for all children, they are expressing a prescriptive belief. Prescriptive beliefs generally indicate that something should or should not occur. Secondly, some beliefs-about are *descriptive*. An example of a descriptive belief is that the sky (object) is blue (attribute). Descriptive beliefs describe the characteristics of the object. Third, some beliefs-about are *evaluative*. ⌜If someone says that Mary (object) is a good citizen (attribute), this is a belief that Mary has met the criteria for being a good citizen. Descriptive beliefs are relatively objective and may represent facts in some cases, where evaluative beliefs are more subjective.⌟

Beliefs can be held with varying levels of strength or importance. **Peripheral beliefs** tend to include issues that are less important to a person. For example, fashion often involves peripheral beliefs. Hairstyles and clothing choices that are believed to be fashionable one year may be totally rejected the next year. Core beliefs are the opposite of peripheral beliefs. **Core beliefs** tend to be strongly held and hard to change. They are often formed early in life and are part of an individual's sense of self. These beliefs are hard to change because of either constant reinforcement or a total lack of experience. If a child grows up in a religious family, attends services regularly, and is part of social groups in that religious organization, then those religious beliefs are being constantly reinforced. Similarly, someone who was raised to be prejudiced toward an ethnic group and has had no interactions with members of that group will have beliefs that have never been challenged by actual experience. When considering beliefs, it is important to consider how strongly they are held. Very strongly held core beliefs and values are harder to change, whereas peripheral beliefs are generally much easier to change.

Core beliefs are sometimes referred to as **values**. Rokeach (1968) defined values as "an enduring belief that a specific mode of conduct or end-state of existence is personally and socially preferable to alternative modes of conduct or end-states of existence" (p. 160). Examples of values are "people should take initiative" (mode of conduct) and "the best people are well educated" (end-state of existence). Values are types of beliefs generally closely linked to our identities and our sense of self. For example, most educators value education, as it represents core beliefs that are interwoven with their life choices. To have that value overturned would lead to serious questions about their life, so it would be difficult to persuade them to alter that value. Values tend to be broad core beliefs that offer the foundation for many other beliefs and attitudes. Figure 2.2 depicts the relationship between values, core beliefs, and peripheral beliefs. Imagine an onion with many layers. The core of the onion represents values and core beliefs. As you move to the outer rings, each layer is less central to your identity and easier to change. Peripheral beliefs are found in the outer layers of the onion.

Behavior refers to overt physical actions on the part of an individual and is often linked to attitude. ⌜However, behaviors are not necessarily good indicators of attitude or beliefs. We can directly observe behavior, but we cannot directly observe attitudes and beliefs. Attitudes and beliefs are psychological in nature and held inside the mind of each individual. We often infer attitudes from behavior; however, behavior is complex and is influenced by a lot of things besides attitudes and beliefs. Behavior is related to attitude and beliefs, but the relationship is complicated.⌟

Related to behavior is the concept of **behavioral intention**. Fishbein and Ajzen (1975) proposed this concept as a step between the psychological construct of attitude and overt behavior. They describe behavioral intention as "a person's intention to perform various behaviors" (p. 12). ⌜Much of our behavior is intentional, making behavioral intention a useful concept in persuasion. For example, we often measure people's intention to vote for a particular candidate in an effort to evaluate campaign messages as well as to predict the outcome of an election. It's typically much easier

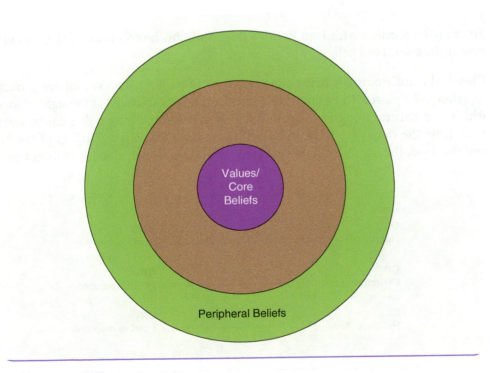

FIGURE 2.2 Core beliefs and peripheral beliefs.

to measure people's intention to behave than their actual behavior.⌐ We discuss the concept of behavioral intentions again in relation to the theory of reasoned action.

Attitude, behavioral intention, behavior, belief, and *value* are all terms used throughout this text. An understanding of these terms is an important foundation for understanding persuasion theories and research, as well as to the practice of persuasion.

THEORIES OF ATTITUDE, BELIEF, AND BEHAVIOR FORMATION

Where do attitudes and beliefs come from? Attitudes and beliefs are often learned just as we learn behaviors. Persuasion in general focuses on changing attitudes, beliefs, and behaviors; however, there are times when we want to form new attitudes, beliefs, and behaviors rather than change existing ones. To be an effective persuader, we need to be able to influence the formation of attitudes, beliefs, and behaviors as well as change existing ones. Traditional persuasion theories (such as those discussed in Chapters 6–9) focus on changing attitudes, beliefs, and behavior rather than on forming new ones. ⌐The theories discussed in the following section help us understand how attitudes, beliefs, and behavior are formed. The first two theories, classical conditioning and operant conditioning, are learning theories that were originally developed to explain how we learn behaviors, but are useful in explaining attitude and belief formation as well. Mere exposure theory describes how attitudes are formed passively. Subliminal influence is an intriguing approach to attitude formation that is greatly misunderstood and surrounded by myth.⌐

CLASSICAL CONDITIONING

Go to YouTube and search for "Classical Conditioning Ivan Pavlov" to learn more about Ivan Pavlov and how he discovered the conditioning phenomenon.

You may be familiar with Ivan Pavlov's dogs and how he conditioned them to salivate at the sound of a bell.

Classical conditioning is based on the concept of **pairing**. Two stimuli must occur together to be paired. In Pavlov's experiments, the dogs salivated at the sight of food, which is a natural thing for dogs to do. This is not something a dog has to learn. Each time the dogs were to be fed, a bell was rung. After a few pairings of the bell and the food, the dogs would salivate at the sound of the bell alone. In this example,

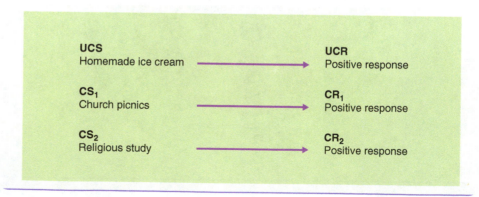

FIGURE 2.3 Higher-order classical conditioning.

food is the **unconditioned stimulus** and salivating is the **unconditioned response**. These are labeled "unconditioned" because they were not learned; it is just the natural response to salivate at the sight of food. The bell is considered the **conditioned stimulus** because it was paired with the food. When the dogs salivated upon hearing the bell, the salivating was considered the **conditioned response** because the salivating was now a learned response to the sound of the bell. Therefore, the unconditioned response and the conditioned response are the same behavior (salivating), but salivating as a conditioned response is caused by different stimuli than the unconditioned response.

Once a behavior is conditioned, it can act as an unconditioned stimulus and be paired with yet another stimulus as is shown in Figure 2.2. This is known as **higher-order conditioning** and is how attitudes are frequently conditioned. The example in Figure 2.3 illustrates higher-order conditioning. Homemade ice cream is frequently served at church picnics and typically elicits a positive response. By serving homemade ice cream at church picnics, the unconditioned stimulus (UCS) of homemade ice cream is paired with church picnics, the conditioned stimulus (CS). After one or more pairings, church picnics elicit the same positive response as homemade ice cream. The positive response is considered the conditioned response (CR) because it is elicited by the church picnic rather than by the ice cream. Church picnics may then be paired with religious studies. After a few pairings, religious studies now elicit a positive response just as church picnics and ice cream did. There is no limit to the number of "levels" in higher-order conditioning.

Staats and Staats (1958) were some of the first to demonstrate that attitudes could be conditioned. In this study, they recruited 93 college students who were then arranged into 2 groups. Both groups were told that their task was to learn lists of words, with one list presented visually and the other orally. Students were told that the experiment focused on visual learning versus oral learning. The words presented visually were national names—German, Swedish, Italian, French, Dutch, and Greek—and were presented 18 times in random order. The oral words presented immediately after the words *German*, *Italian*, *French*, and *Greek* were neutral with no systematic meaning (e.g., with, chair, twelve). For one group of students, the word *Dutch* was always followed by a negative word (e.g., ugly, bitter, failure) and *Swedish* was always followed by a positive word (e.g., gift, sacred, happy). For the other group, it was just the opposite; the word *Dutch* was paired with positive words and the word *Swedish* was followed by negative words. Following the word presentations, students were asked how they *felt* about the words. Seventeen students indicated they were aware of the systematic word pairings and were excluded from the data analysis. The results are shown in Table 2.1 and indicate that Staats and Staats successfully conditioned students to have a positive attitude toward the word *Swedish* and a negative attitude toward the word *Dutch* or vice versa, depending on the group. As you can see in

TABLE 2.1 *ATTITUDE MEANS FOR STAATS AND STAATS (1958) STUDY*

	DUTCH		SWEDISH	
	MEAN	STANDARD DEVIATION	MEAN	STANDARD DEVIATION
Group 1	2.67	0.94	3.42	1.50
Group 2	2.67	1.31	1.83	0.90

Table 2.1, Group 1, which heard positive words paired with the word *Swedish*, had a more positive attitude toward *Swedish* than the word *Dutch* (attitude was measured on a 7-point scale).

Classical conditioning is a rather simple way of forming a positive attitude. As a persuader, you simply pair your object of interest with something positive. You just have to make sure that the unconditioned stimulus elicits a positive response in your audience. Numerous examples of classical conditioning can be found in advertising, such as many perfume ads. These types of advertisements show a beautiful, sexy woman—something that tends to elicit a positive response from both men and women—and the perfume. No other information about the perfume is generally provided. The product is simply paired with an image that is likely to elicit a positive response. Advertisers hope you are exposed to the ad enough times for the conditioning to occur. Classical conditioning is often very useful, but some objects are too complicated for conditioning to work effectively. Therefore, we need additional strategies.

Look for advertisements for high end consumer products. What kinds of stimuli do they pair their product with?

OPERANT CONDITIONING

The basic premise of **operant conditioning** is that learning occurs as a result of reinforcement and punishment. If reinforcement follows a behavior, the behavior will be learned and repeated. If punishment or no response at all (extinction) follows a behavior, the behavior will occur less frequently or disappear completely. An attitude can be formed or learned in a similar manner. For example, if a child expresses a negative view toward spiders and receives some form of verbal praise or attention for not liking spiders, the child is likely to develop a negative attitude toward spiders.

Insko (1965) demonstrated the relative ease with which attitudes can be formed using verbal reinforcement. Insko had some of his graduate students contact by phone 72 students from his Introductory Psychology course. Students were asked to strongly agree, agree, disagree, or strongly disagree with 14 statements regarding the creation of a Springtime Aloha Week at the University of Hawaii (where the experiment took place). Half of the students were verbally reinforced for indicating a positive attitude, and half were reinforced for indicating a negative attitude. The verbal reinforcement came in the form of the graduate student saying "good." Insko's graduate students were able to successfully influence students' attitudes toward Aloha Week. Students receiving a reinforcement for expressing a positive attitude had a significantly more positive attitude than students reinforced for expressing a negative attitude. To further test the reinforcement, a week after the phone interview, the students completed a Local Issues Questionnaire on which one item, about two-thirds through the questionnaire, asked about the Springtime Aloha Week. Once again, students who had received a reinforcement for a positive attitude had a more positive attitude toward Aloha Week than did those students receiving a reinforcement for expressing a negative attitude. Therefore, the reinforcement successfully formed an attitude, and the attitude continued beyond the initial experiment.

One interesting thing about the Insko (1965) study is that the reinforcement was a simple "good" coming from a complete stranger. ⌜When you talk to a salesperson, you may notice that the sales person reinforcing (or at least trying to reinforce) your positive responses. Operant conditioning may be one of the strategies used to get you to say yes to their offer. For instance, the sales person may initially ask you a question such as, "Would you like to save some money?" Most people will say yes. The sales person⌐ follows your response with a, "Good, good. Most people do." Insko's study demonstrates how easy it is for a researcher or a polling firm to influence the audience's attitude. Such tactics may explain why different groups doing essentially the same poll can come up with such different results. This is why understanding *how* data were collected is necessary to understanding what the final results mean.

Operant conditioning is frequently used when new products are introduced. Companies often offer a variety of rewards for trying their products. Rewards may be coupons, entry into a drawing, or free samples. Reward programs are used extensively by companies such as Starbucks to keep customers coming back. Parents and teachers also frequently use operant conditioning to influence children's beliefs and behaviors. Think back to when you were in elementary school. What types of rewards were used? Were they effective? Punishment can also be used to influence attitudes and behavior, although punishment is generally less effective than reward. Punishment, being negative in nature, is generally avoided by advertisers and other persuaders.

⌐Classical and operant conditioning are established learning theories that help us to both understand and influence how people form new attitudes, beliefs, and behaviors. However, researchers recognized that people sometimes held attitudes that did not appear to be a result of either classical or operant conditioning. Mere exposure theory explains another way in which attitudes can be formed.

MERE EXPOSURE THEORY

Do you like familiar things more than unfamiliar things? Do the latest fashions "grow" on you after a while? Sometimes people develop positive attitudes toward things simply because they are familiar. In 1968 Robert Zajonc published an experiment where he exposed research participants to unfamiliar foreign language words and symbols (Turkish words and Chinese characters). Participants were told the experiment was about foreign language learning, but the real purpose was to see if greater exposure would result in more favorable attitudes toward unfamiliar words and symbols. Participants were exposed to the unfamiliar words and characters either 0, 1, 2, 5, 10, or 25 times during the experiment. After the exposure, participants were told the words/symbols were adjectives and asked to guess if the word/ symbol was a positive or a negative adjective on a 7-point scale (good–bad). The results were clear and consistent. The more participants were exposed to the unfamiliar words or symbols, the more positive their evaluation of them. Participants had no information or logical reason to evaluate some words more positively than other words. No conditioning had occurred. It appeared that positive attitudes developed simply because of exposure. Zajonc (1968) drew the conclusion that merely being exposed to a neutral stimulus resulted in positive evaluations and the **mere exposure theory** was born.

Go to YouTube and search for "Mere Exposure Brain Game" to learn more about the mere exposure effect.

In a more recent test of mere exposure, Courbet, Fourquet-Courbet, Kazan, and Intartaglia (2014) examined the impact of pop-up ads on websites. They created a website on diet and health geared toward students and four pop-up ads for a fake brand of mineral water called Lomis. One pop-up ad contained the brand logo only, a second contained the logo plus an image of the product, a third contained the logo plus the words "mineral water," and the fourth pop-up contained a filler brand and was used as a control condition. Research participants were exposed to a pop-up for 3 seconds each time they opened a new web page. Research participants were students enrolled at a French university and were told the French Ministry of Health was conducting a poll on student's diet and health and were directed to consult the website just as they would in normal everyday life when looking for information. Half of the participants were contacted a week later by a different researcher supposedly conducting market research on new brands, where the fake Lomis brand was one of them. Participants completed a survey on the brands that included a series of timed evaluation ratings on the brands. The other half of the participants were contacted 3 months after the initial experiment to participate in the fake market research survey. None of the participants remembered seeing the pop-up ads for Lomis water, indicating the pop-up ads did not result in an explicit attitude. However, exposure to the brand logo with either an image or the name of the product did result in participants having faster positive responses. This result was found for the groups contacted 1 week and 3 months after the experiment. The best explanation for the findings is that the pop-up ads created a positive implicit attitude, which allowed for faster responses by participants. Courbet and his colleagues concluded that, "Internet pop-ups processed at a low attention level and later forgotten can have long term effects" (p. 288). However, they did not assess whether the implicit attitude actually impacted buying behavior.

Mere exposure to brand names, brand images, and logos does not increase brand recall. We are not conscious of our familiarity with the image, but the familiarity predisposes us to evaluate it more positively. Interestingly, the mere exposure effect applies to visual stimuli, but not auditory stimuli (Montoya, Horton, Vevea, Citkowicz, & Lauber, 2017). The mere exposure effect is also greater when receivers are highly involved in the content and have little knowledge of persuasion. Matthes, Schemer, and Wirth (2007) investigated product placement in a TV magazine program and manipulated the frequency of product placement. Research participants who viewed the video with more product placement incidents, who had high involvement in the content, and had little understanding of persuasion tactics, had the most positive attitudes toward the product, although their brand recall did not increase. Participants in the high exposure and low involvement condition who had a greater understanding of persuasion tactics had the most negative attitude toward the product. Presumably, this group had a greater recognition of the product placement, recognized the persuasion tactic, and reacted with greater resistance and perhaps annoyance. Those with greater persuasion knowledge were more apt to remember the brand name as placement increased and were more apt to evaluate the brand negatively.

These two studies (along with many similar studies) demonstrate that when we are repeatedly exposed to a stimulus, we can form an attitude toward it, even when we don't remember the stimulus. The mere exposure effect only occurs with neutral stimuli. Mere exposure does not change existing positive or negative attitudes. Mere exposure helps us understand attitude formation, but it does not help us understand how to change existing attitudes. Nor does it help us understand how to change beliefs and behaviors. Additionally, as demonstrated in the Montoya et al. (2017) study, when people are aware of the exposure tactic, they are apt to respond with resistance. Sometimes mere exposure is confused with subliminal influence, but the two are not the same.

SUBLIMINAL INFLUENCE

What does the word subliminal mean to you? Many people associate this word with sex, unethical advertising, mind control, or other such tactics, but these are all inaccurate. **Subliminal** simply means below consciousness. In other words, if something is subliminal, you are not conscious of it. A subliminal message is a message that is present but not within your conscious awareness. Compare this to a **supraliminal** message, which is a message within your conscious awareness. The words on this page are a supraliminal message; you are conscious of seeing them. The stimuli used in the mere exposure studies discussed previously used *supraliminal stimuli*—the pop-up ads and product placements were clearly visible. This is the key difference between mere exposure and subliminal messages. Mere exposure explains the formation of an attitude toward a supraliminal stimulus that we don't necessarily remember seeing. Subliminal influence describes phenomena of attitude formation toward stimuli that are below conscious awareness.

Subliminal messages and advertising first came into the public eye in the 1950s when James Vicary claimed to have flashed the words "EAT POPCORN" and "DRINK COKE" throughout the movie Picnic at a drive-in theater (McConnell, Cutler, & McNeil, 1958). Vicary claimed that the theater experienced higher than usual popcorn and Coke sales and that the increase was a result of the subliminal messages. There are three things to note about Vicary's experiment. He did not have a control group (a group that was not exposed to the subliminal message for comparison purposes), he did not indicate popcorn and Coke sales for other showings of the same movie, and the findings have never been replicated (research findings are generally not accepted until they have been repeated by different researchers). Also, consider the movie in which these messages were inserted. The movie Picnic showed people eating and going on a picnic. You don't suppose watching people eat could have influenced popcorn and Coke sales, do you?

Despite the numerous problems with Vicary's experiment, people quickly began believing that advertisers frequently used subliminal messages in advertisements. This belief was further encouraged by a book written by Wilson Bryan Key (1972) that identified numerous advertisements that supposedly had subliminal messages embedded in them. Adding fuel to the fire, many accused Disney of inserting subliminal messages into their movies. In a 2015 article, former Disney animator Tom Sito "explained that adding inside jokes into older films wasn't considered a big deal," (Bradley, 2015), but it was an inside joke, not a subliminal influence. For example, many have accused Disney of inserting the word "sex" in "The Lion King." Sito explained that it doesn't say "sex," it says special effects, abbreviated SFX—a shout out to the special effects department. As a result of all of the controversial attention, a great deal of research has been conducted on subliminal messages and subliminal influence.

Two conclusions can be drawn from the research. First, subliminal messages can influence attitude formation under very specific laboratory conditions. Second, subliminal messages do not influence attitudes under normal conditions and do not change existing attitudes, beliefs, and behaviors. Let's begin the discussion with how subliminal messages can influence attitude formation. Krosnick, Betz, Jussim, and Lynn's (1992) research is a good example. In this study, 34 students from Ohio State University were recruited and came to a laboratory. They were seated in front of a screen and asked to "keep your eyes on the center of the screen" (Krosnick et al., 1992,

p. 155). Students were shown a series of nine photographs of a woman doing a variety of normal activities (e.g., getting into a car, grocery shopping, studying, sitting in a restaurant). Each photograph was shown for 2 seconds (these were the supraliminal stimuli). Immediately preceding each photo, half of the participants were shown a positive-affect-arousing photo (e.g., a bridal couple, a young ring bearer, a group of people playing cards, a group of smiling friends), whereas the other half of participants were shown a negative-affect-arousing photo (e.g., a skull, a werewolf, a face on fire, a dead body). These positive- and negative-affect-arousing photos were shown for 13 milliseconds and were the subliminal stimuli. After viewing the photos, participants were asked to rate the woman in the photos. Krosnick et al. report that not a single participant was aware of the affect-arousing photos (subliminal stimuli) and that, when told of the true nature of the study, all participants expressed surprise or disbelief. Krosnick and his colleagues' findings were surprising. Participants who had been exposed to the negative-affect-arousing subliminal photos rated the woman much more negatively than did the participants who had been exposed to the positive-affect-arousing subliminal photos. The participants were not even aware of the fact that the images influenced their attitude toward the woman in the photos. Krosnick et al. conducted a second study with a shorter exposure time to the subliminal message (9 milliseconds) and with stricter controls and found the same results. This and other studies have demonstrated that subliminal messages really can influence how we evaluate something.

The laboratory conditions present in Krosnick et al.'s study are common to most studies of subliminal influence that have been successful. One procedure that was important for the subliminal message to have an effect was that there be a minimum amount of supraliminal stimuli. One characteristic of the Krosnick et al. study was that the only supraliminal stimuli were slides. No video, no sound, just still pictures. The second important characteristic of the study was that the receivers were asked to devote a great deal of attention to the message. Recall that the participants were instructed to keep their eyes on the center of the screen. This focus was necessary so that the receivers didn't miss the subliminal message (remember, the subliminal message lasted for less than a quarter second—you blink and you miss it). The subliminal effect has only been found in controlled settings where other stimuli are minimized and receivers focus attention on the stimuli. Additionally, the research participants did not know the woman they rated; or in other words, this research tested attitude formation. Now, let's consider applying these results to the real world. In real-world settings, such as when you're watching television at home or online, are these characteristics present when you see advertisements? If you're like most people, the answer is no. More often than not, we are doing two or more things at once, and there are multiple distractions—people are talking, dogs are barking, and so on. There is a great deal of supraliminal stimuli. We don't focus our attention closely on the advertisements. Our real-life is not at all similar to the laboratory conditions necessary for the subliminal influence to occur. But, of course, researchers weren't satisfied. They wanted to see if subliminal messages can work in the "real world." One such real-world situation is self-help audio programs that use subliminal messages.

Subliminal audio programs that promise to help you lose weight, improve your memory, improve your self-esteem, stop smoking, and other behaviors appeal to many looking for a quick and easy way to improve themselves. Do these programs really work? Pratkanis, Eskenazi, and Greenwald (1994) conducted a study to determine the effectiveness of two subliminal programs—one to improve memory and one to improve self-esteem. To test the effectiveness of the programs, Pratkanis et al. recruited 78 students and community members who were interested in improving their memory or self-esteem. Participants were pretested and then given a set of subliminal audiotapes, either self-esteem or memory programs. Half of the tapes were mislabeled so that half of the participants who thought they were receiving the self-esteem program were actually receiving the memory program and half of the participants who thought they were receiving the memory program were actually receiving the self-esteem program. Participants were asked to listen to the programs at least once per day and were also asked to keep a listening log.

As part of the pretest, participants were asked about their beliefs regarding subliminal self-help programs, and 77 of the 78 participants expressed a strong belief in the effectiveness of subliminal programs. After listening to the subliminal programs every day for a month, participants completed a self-esteem and memory posttest. Results indicated that participants' self-esteem and a memory improved regardless of which program they listened to. In other words, participants' memories and self-esteem improved because they wanted it to, not because of the subliminal messages embedded in the programs. There was no relationship between increases in self-esteem or memory and what program had been listened to. Pratkanis and his colleagues concluded that self-esteem and memory were unaffected by either of the subliminal programs.

Although the idea of subliminal messages hidden in advertisements and music to control people's thoughts is very enticing and makes for good science fiction, there is no credible evidence to indicate that subliminal messages are at all useful in changing attitudes, beliefs, and behaviors. Hal Shoup, executive vice president of the American Association of Advertising Agencies, said about subliminal messages, "Those of us who practice this business find it an enduring challenge to affect the conscious, much less try to worry [about] the subconscious" (Galvin, 1996). There are two basic conclusions you should draw from the research on subliminal influence. First, subliminal messages can influence attitude formation in very specific laboratory-controlled circumstances. Second, subliminal messages are not useful in real-world persuasion situations like advertising, public relations, and public health campaigns. If advertisers or other sources do use subliminal messages, you have little to fear because they'll have no impact on you.

To summarize, classical and operant conditioning help us to both understand and influence attitudes, beliefs, and behaviors. We can see these theories used in advertising and marketing campaigns. Mere exposure theory and subliminal influence help us understand that attitude formation can occur even when we are not particularly aware of the stimulus. It's important to understand that this attitude formation process is very different than the persuasion process required to change people's existing attitudes, beliefs, and behaviors. Humans are not as malleable as the mere exposure and subliminal research suggests.

THE FUNCTIONS OF ATTITUDES

Why do people hold attitudes? Those who want to be successful persuaders can be more effective if they understand the functions that attitudes serve for message recipients. If we understand why an attitude is held and how it serves the receiver, then we can better understand how to alter those attitudes and know better how to leverage those functions to achieve persuasive outcomes. As we explore each type of function, we can understand how to design persuasive appeals that would target each type.

Katz (1960) launched this line of investigation and argued that attitudes serve multiple *functions* or purposes. The first is the **ego-defensive function**. These are attitudes that are held to help people protect their sense of self and prevent the need to face unpleasant realities. For example, Ashley might value academic achievement over sports achievement as a way to make herself feel better about her lack of athletic ability. Others might look down on a particular ethnic group or sexual orientation in order to make them feel better about their own ethnicity or sexual preference. These attitudes are tied to the individual's sense of self.

Knowledge is another function of attitudes. These are attitudes that help people understand the world around them. For example, believing that social workers are poorly paid and have bad working conditions leads to questions about why people would be social workers. To understand why someone would work for such low wages, an explanation is required. Viewing social workers as good, altruistic people helps explain social workers' willingness to work for low pay in poor working conditions. Our evaluations (attitudes) often help us bring understanding to the world around us, and clever persuaders offer that information in a manner designed to favor their outcomes.

The third function of attitudes is **utilitarian**. This refers to attitudes that benefit us by allowing us to avoid negative consequences and achieve positive outcomes. For example, students may like extra credit because it benefits them personally. Faculty may like tenure because they see personal benefit from it. These attitudes are tied closely to the individual's sense of rewards and costs.

The fourth function of attitude is the **value-expressive function**. This function refers to attitudes that allow people to express values important to them. For example, a person who values the environment might feel positively about hybrid vehicles and solar energy. These attitudes are held as a way of expressing values.

Smith, Bruner, and White (1956) proposed an additional function of attitudes. They suggested that attitudes serve a **social-adjustive function**. These attitudes are held to help us better fit in with and relate to those around us. Many people adopt attitudes that reflect those of their peer groups to better fit in with those groups. A teenager may like rap music if most of his or her friends do and if it is a frequent topic of conversation. Similarly, a teen may dislike smoking if his or her peers view it negatively. Someone may begin viewing *Ozark* as a good television show because everyone else is talking about it. Holding attitudes consistent with those of one's peers can help a person fit in socially.

Persuaders who understand how their audience uses attitudes can better understand how to persuade those individuals. The social-adjustive and value-expressive functions have received the most attention and have been the focus of a **functional matching** approach to persuasion. The idea here is that if an attitude serves a social-adjustive function for an individual, that person will be more receptive to social adjustive messages that emphasize how others view the attitude object and how holding a particular attitude helps one fit in. If an attitude serves a value-expressive function, that person will be more receptive to messages that emphasize expressing and attaining one's values. Lavine and Snyder (1996) demonstrated the effectiveness of functional matching in an experiment. They identified people whose attitude toward voting served a social-adjustive function, and they identified people whose attitude toward voting served a value-expressive function. They then created two sets of messages about voting: (1) a *value-expressive message* that argued that voting provides a way for people to express their support for values such as freedom and democracy; and (2) *a social-adjustive message* that informed participants that the majority of their peers were voting in an upcoming election and that voting enhanced a person's popularity and attractiveness. Half of each group received a social-adjustive message and half received a value-expressive message. Those who received a message that matched their attitude function perceived the message as higher quality, had a more positive attitude toward voting, and were more likely to vote than those who received a message that did *not* match how their attitude functions.

Thus, if we understand how an attitude functions for an individual or a group we can more easily create a message to influence that attitude. You may not always know how an attitude functions for a group of people. One way to deal with this is to incorporate both value-expressive and social-adjustive messages into the same message. An example of this approach is Rock the Vote campaign. These messages appeal to the democratic values of free speech, inclusion, and participation in the democratic process. But these messages also make it cool and desirable to vote, and portray it as the "in" thing to do. Lavine and Synder (1996) tested this approach by including a *mixed message* (one that incorporates multiple attitude functions) in their experiment. They found that mixed messages were not as effective as *pure messages* (ones that completely matched the attitude function); however, mixed messages were more effective than messages that did not match. So, matching your message to how the attitude functions for a person is most effective, but when this isn't possible, creating a mixed message is an effective alternative.

Go to YouTube and search for "Rock the Vote." What attitude functions do you think they are appealing to?

How might you go about using the functional matching approach? Imagine you are creating an advertisement for cars. What kind of information and images would you include for people whose attitude toward cars serves a value-expressive function as compared to those who held a social-adjustive attitude?

SUMMARY

- The six key characteristics of attitudes are evaluative, tied to an object, related to behavior, can be explicit or implicit, and learned.
- Attitude is defined as a latent predisposition or tendency to respond in a consistently favorable or unfavorable manner with respect to a given object.
- A belief links an object to some attribute.
- Beliefs-in refers to believing in the existence of an object. Beliefs-about refers to believing that an object has some characteristics.
- Beliefs about objects can be prescriptive, descriptive, or evaluative.
- Values are core beliefs that serve as a foundation for many other beliefs and attitudes.

- Behavior is an overt physical action and behavioral intention is a person's inten-tion to perform a behavior.
- Attitudes can be formed through classical conditioning in a process of pairing an unconditioned stimulus with a conditioned stimulus.
- Attitudes are frequently conditioned through a process of higher-order conditioning.
- Attitudes can be formed through operant conditioning with the use of reinforcement.
- ⌈Attitudes toward neutral stimuli can be formed through mere exposure such as pop-up ads and product placement.
- Subliminal stimuli are stimuli below a person's consciousness. Supraliminal stimuli are stimuli above a person's consciousness.
- For subliminal messages to be effective, supraliminal stimuli must be kept at a minimum and the receiver's attention must be focused on the message.
- Subliminal messages are not useful for changing existing attitudes and beliefs.⌋
- Attitudes can serve five functions: ego-defensive, value-expressive, knowledge, utilitarian, and social-adjustive.
- Functional matching is a persuasive strategy of matching the message with the attitude function.
- Attitudes can be formed through modeling, which involves four steps: atten-tion, retention, motor reproduction, and motivation.

KEY TERMS

Attitude—a learned predisposition to respond in a consistently favorable or unfa-vorable manner with respect to a given object.

Behavior—an individual's overt physical actions.

Behavioral intention—a psychological concept best described as an expectation or a plan. An intention is a plan for how you are going to behave.

Belief—a belief links an object to some attributes.

Beliefs-about—beliefs about characteristics of a concept.

Beliefs-in—beliefs in the existence of an object.

Conditioned response—a learned response.

Conditioned stimulus—a new stimulus that is paired with an unconditioned stimu-lus until it elicits the same response as the unconditioned stimulus.

Core beliefs—beliefs that are strongly held and hard to change.

Ego-defensive function—attitudes that are held to help people protect their sense of self and prevent the need to face unpleasant realities.

Evaluation—a key characteristic of attitude that indicates that attitudes involve like and dislike.

Explicit attitude—an attitude that a person is consciously aware of and can accurately report if asked.

Functional matching—when the persuasive message is matched to the function the relevant attitude serves for the audience.

Higher-order conditioning—when a conditioned stimulus acts like an unconditioned stimulus and can be paired with another stimulus.

Implicit attitude—an attitude that a person is not consciously aware of or may deny, but affects their evaluation of related objects.

Intensity—the strength of an attitude.

Knowledge function—attitudes that help people understand the world around them.

Mere exposure theory—repeated exposure to a neutral stimulus results in positive evaluations

Object—the target of an attitude; can be an idea, a person, a place, an event, a physical object, or a concept.

Pairing—a key concept of classical conditioning and refers to two stimuli being presented to the receiver at the same time.

Peripheral beliefs—beliefs about issues that are less important to a person.

Social-adjustive function—attitudes that are held to help us better relate to those around us.

Subliminal—when stimuli are perceived at below the level of consciousness.

Supraliminal—when stimuli are perceived at the conscious level.

Unconditioned response—an automatic or natural response (one that is not learned).

Unconditioned stimulus—a stimulus that elicits an unconditioned response.

Utilitarian function—attitudes that benefit individuals by allowing them to avoid negative consequences and achieve positive outcomes.

Value-expressive function—attitudes that allow people to express values that are important to them.

Values—enduring beliefs that specific modes of conduct or end-states of existence are personally and socially preferable to alternative modes of conduct or end-states of existence.

QUESTIONS FOR REVIEW

Respond to the following questions **without** reviewing the text or your notes. These questions are provided to help you practice retrieving information and reflect on your reading.

  A. How would you define attitude?

  B. Did you agree or disagree with anything you read? Explain.

  C. What did you learn that was new to you?

  D. What concepts, if any, were confusing to you?

Respond to the following questions. You may reference your text or notes to help you.

  1. What are the six key characteristics of attitudes?

  2. How is an attitude formed through classical conditioning, operant conditioning, and mere exposure?

  3. What are the five attitude functions? Give an example of each function.

  4. What are the similarities and differences between attitudes, beliefs, and values? How do these terms relate to each other?

1. Before reading this chapter, you wrote about the difference between attitudes and beliefs. How does your explanation compare to the explanations of other students in your class or group? To the definitions of attitudes and beliefs provided in your text? Pay special attention to the relationship between these concepts.

2. What did you learn about subliminal messages? Were you surprised by what the research says? Why or why not?

3. At the beginning of the chapter, you thought about strong attitudes toward certain foods, music genres, or team rivals. Now that you have read the chapter, let's focus on one of those attitudes and consider possible reasons for your strong attitude. What function does your attitude serve? How does this compare to the attitude functions of other students in the class? Why is this information useful for persuasion?

4. With your group, brainstorm a few items that would help you measure the attitudes and beliefs of your audience about your group's topic. When you are finished, discuss the process. What items were relatively easy to develop and what items were difficult to develop? Why were they easy or difficult?

5. Discuss the ethical questions provided at the end of the first chapter. What ethical considerations are relevant to the information in this chapter about attitudes, beliefs, attitude functions, values and beliefs, and attitude measurement?

   - Are there guidelines (e.g., don't lie) that would be appropriate for every situation, or are ethics relative?

   - Do the ends (e.g., a good outcome) justify any means?

- Is deceiving the receiver ever appropriate?

- Should the source of the message bear primary responsibility for ethics, or should the receiver share that responsibility (e.g., buyer beware)?

REFERENCES

Albarracin, D., Zanna, M. P., Johnson, B. T., & Kumkale, G. T. (2005). Attitudes: Introduction and scope. In D. Albarracin, B. Johnson, & M. P. Zanna (Eds.), *The handbook of attitudes* (pp. 3–19). Mahwah, NJ: Lawrence Erlbaum.

Bradley, B. (2015). Finally, the truth about Disney's 'hidden sexual messages' revealed. *Huffington Post.* https://www.huffingtonpost.com/2015/01/14/disney-sexual-messages_n_6452666.html

Courbet, D., Fourquet-Courbet, M., Kazan, R., & Intartaglia, J. (2014). The long-term effects of e-advertising: The influence of internet pop-ups viewed at a low level of attention in implicit memory. *Journal of Computer-Mediated Communication, 19,* 274–293.

Eagly, A. H., & Chaiken, S. (1993). *The psychology of attitudes.* Fort Worth, TX: Harcourt Brace Jovanovich College Publishers.

Fishbein, M. (1967). A consideration of beliefs, and their role in attitude measurement. In M. Fishbein (Ed.), *Readings in attitude theory and measurement* (pp. 257–266). New York: Wiley.

Fishbein, M., & Ajzen, I. (1975). *Belief, attitude, intention, and behavior: An introduction to theory and research.* Reading, MA: Addison-Wesley.

Fishbein, M., & Ajzen, I. (2010). *Predicting and changing behavior: The reasoned action approach.* New York: Psychology Press.

Fishbein, M., & Raven, B. H. (1962). The AB scales: An operation definition of belief and attitude. *Human Relations, 15,* 35–44.

Galvin, K. (1996, September 20). Put subconscious out of your mind. *The Cincinnati Enquirer.*

Greenwald, A. G., & Banaji, M. R. (1995). Implicit social cognition: Attitudes, self-esteem, and stereotypes. *Psychological Review, 102,* 4–27.

Insko, C. A. (1965). Verbal reinforcement of attitude. *Journal of Personality and Social Psychology, 2,* 621–623.

Katz, D. (1960). The functional approach to the study of attitudes. *Public Opinion Quarterly, 24,* 163–204.

Key, W. B. (1972). *Subliminal seduction.* New York: Signet.

Krosnick, J. A., Betz, A. I., Jussim, L. J., & Lynn, A. R. (1992). Subliminal conditioning of attitudes. *Personality and Social Psychology Bulletin, 2,* 152–162.

Lavine, H., & Snyder, M. (1996). Cognitive processing and the functional matching effect in persuasion: The mediating role of subjective perceptions of message quality. *Journal of Experimental Social Psychology, 32,* 580–604.

Mathes, J., Schemer, C., & Wirth, W. (2007). More than meets the eye: Investigating the hidden impact of brand placements in television magazines. *International Journal of Advertising, 26,* 477–503.

McConnell, J. V., Cutler, R. L., & McNeil, E. B. (1958). Subliminal stimulation: An overview. *American Psychologist, 13,* 229–242.

Montoya, R. M., Horton, R. S., Vevea, J. L., Citkowicz, M., & Lauber, E. A. (2017). A re-examination of the mere exposure effect: The influence of repeated exposure on recognition, familiarity, and liking. *Psychological Bulletin, 143,* 459–498.

Perloff, R. M. (1993). *The dynamics of persuasion.* Hillsdale, NJ: Lawrence Erlbaum.

Pratkanis, A. R., Eskenazi, J., & Greenwald, A. G. (1994). What you expect is what you believe (but not necessarily what you get): A test of the effectiveness of subliminal self-help audiotapes. *Basic and Applied Social Psychology, 15,* 251–276.

Rokeach, M. (1968). *Beliefs, attitudes, and values: A theory of organization and change.* San Francisco: Jossey-Bass.

Smith, M. B., Bruner, J. S., & White, R. W. (1956). *Opinions and personality.* New York: John Wiley.

Staats, A. W., & Staats, C. K. (1958). Attitudes established by classical conditioning. *Journal of Abnormal and Social Psychology, 57,* 37–40.

Zajonc, R. B. (1968). Attitudinal effects of mere exposure. *Journal of Personality and Social Psychology, 9* (2, Pt.2), 1–27

CHAPTER 3

CLASSICAL RHETORIC

BEFORE YOU READ

Respond to the following questions **before** you read the chapter.

1. What is rhetoric?

2. What do you know about Plato and Aristotle?

3. How would you define ethos, pathos, and logos? Which one tends to have the greatest impact on you? Why?

Classical rhetoric is the foundation upon which both **argumentation** and **rhetoric** stand. Rhetoric has been part of the academic training of educated persons for thousands of years: it is one of the most ancient academic fields. In medieval Europe, for example, rhetoric, grammar, and logic formed the *Trivium*, the subjects students were taught first. Argumentation was born, via Aristotle, from rhetoric.

Within this chapter, you will learn the major concepts of classical rhetoric. The chapter develops the subject historically, examining the ideas of major thinkers, with a focus on the ideas of Aristotle.

From *Contemporary Argumentation and Rhetoric,* Second Edition by Michael Korcok and Andrea Thorson. Copyright © 2014 by Michael Korcok and Andrea Thorson. Reprinted by permission of Kendall Hunt Publishing Company.

LEARNING OBJECTIVES

- WHERE AND WHEN THE STUDY OF RHETORIC BEGAN.
- HOW RHETORIC WAS DEFINED AND REGARDED DURING CLASSICAL TIMES.
- THE MAJOR CONTRIBUTIONS OF ARISTOTLE.

THE BEGINNING: CORAX AND SOPHISTS

A man named Corax in 465 B.C.E. at the Greek colony of Syracuse, Sicily, created the first recorded written rhetoric in our Western world. During this time the government had undergone a change and land disputes were rampant. Corax came to realize that the person who was able to dispute their side best would ultimately be the "winner" or owner of the land. Therefore, it seemed that power resided in the person who could plead the more plausible, logical, and overall effective case. Given this realization, Corax created a system of argumentation that would lead people to win their cases and thus their land. Corax's theory on argumentation and rhetoric soon spread to Athens and many other cities.

In Athens, citizens spoke for themselves; there was not the legal form of refutation we are familiar with today in terms of legal representation. This meant each citizen's probability of winning their case relied greatly on the quality of their speech and the delivery of their arguments. The wealthier families were able to pay for speechwriters to help them construct arguments, as well as to have access to the best educators. In short, they were able to hire today's version of lawyers or consultants. Until Corax, the ability for the average citizen to have access to quality argumentation was all but impossible.

In 490 B.C.E., a group of educators traveled city by city offering educational courses to citizens for a price. These roaming educators were called Sophists. Their goal was to make their students into *good* citizens. In their teachings, they emphasized forms of persuasive expressions, such as the art of rhetoric, which provided pupils with skills useful for achieving success in life, particularly in public life. Although rhetoric was taught often, Sophists also taught subjects like grammar and art.

At the time, access to education was a privilege afforded to those with birthright. In contrast, primarily, the Sophist educators of the time, sought to educate those who could pay for their services—regardless of their status in society. This approach angered many aristocracies. The Sophists did not make education available to all citizens, but they did educate a great many people who without their teachings would never have had access to such an education. Unlike other educators at the time, the Sophists centered their teachings purely on usable knowledge, that is, the knowledge that citizens could use in the social and political realms of their everyday lives, and thus it was highly useful and advantageous to acquire.

The Sophists also taught a delivery style that enhanced the language. Their delivery was engaging and performance-like. Delivery was taught as a central element of rhetoric, not cast aside as an unimportant consideration like so many other teachers of this time. Fundamentally, the Sophists did not claim that they had an ultimate truth or that they could teach someone to come to know the truth of something. Instead, they claimed that rhetoric helps us see the reality the speaker tries to create through language and they could help others craft useful rhetoric. The rhetoric the Sophists disseminated focused on practicality—how could this be useful in real life—instead of on the philosophical theory. The focus on delivery was a primary reason. Plato criticized the Sophists and claimed that the Sophists were teaching mere flattery. He did not like the Sophists because they did not focus on absolute truth, they focused on delivery, and they offered teaching of this art to people who normally would not have had access to it.

Given that political careers were the most popular ambitions at the time, the Sophists spent much, if not most, of their time teaching rhetoric. Politicians from distant cities would come to take in a lecture from the famous Sophists in an attempt to increase their ability to present arguments effectively. Perhaps one of the most controversial and notable beliefs these first teachers of rhetoric held was their disinterest in absolute truth; they did not believe in an absolute truth, only **probable truth.** Traditionally, society had valued the idea of coming to the "real" truth of matters, not to the best-argued position.

The Sophists were relativists. **Relativism** is the idea that "truth" is not absolute; rather, it is relative to the person or persons who hold the belief in question. Relativists, like the Sophists, believed humans are incapable of achieving absolute truth because the nature of the mind is limited. They also believed that understanding the power of language is crucial to the exploration of knowledge and is an essential tool to harness, control, and apply. Unlike others of the time, Sophists humanized philosophy. Before the Sophists, philosophy was often formulaic and prescriptive; by putting the person at the center of the argument process, the Sophists added a new component to the philosophy. Unlike Plato, who will be discussed later, the Sophists were not concerned with arriving at the ultimate "truth"; rather, they were interested in teaching people how to win an argument. They created a series of arguments that they claimed would always win. The Sophists controversially asserted that a person need not know an area well in order to defend or refute it; you must merely have the right rhetoric. Some of their techniques include manipulations, entrapping their opponents, large fiery language to intimidate, and even attempts to confuse, but they also used elements of logic and reasoning. Clearly, the Sophists did not always teach rhetoric from the most moral standpoint, which would ultimately lead to their demise.

FIGURE 3.1 Corith, Greece.

The Sophists taught their students to examine multiple sides of a given issue and deal in probabilities based on knowledge. Some, like Plato, criticized the fact that Sophists did not believe in a nominal world where transcendent forms of knowledge and truth exist, but rather focused more sharply on existential realities. The divergence in both sides' views of rhetoric can be summarized as contention between existentialism and transcendence. **Existentialism** can be understood as a philosophical approach that highlights the existence of a person as a free entity who determines their own development.

The Sophists believed rhetoric was good for civic virtue—the training of people to be good citizens. They also felt strongly that humans control their own destiny. Major criticisms of the Sophists were that they were naive relativists—that they believed that knowledge is relative to the limited nature of the mind and the conditions of knowing. They taught the use of language to create illusions to convince an audience, instead of using rhetoric to uncover illusions.

The period from 50 A.D. through 400 A.D. became known as the Second Sophistic, a time that marked the transition from the classical to the British period of rhetorical history. The Second Sophistic was a period that concentrated on the delivery and style of speech and less on the actual subject matter. It was a time where rhetoric became an "art of giving effectiveness to the speaker." It was a time that marked the final years of the Roman Empire, which was known for great political unrest. Oratorical and rhetorical theory had to adapt to the political and social style and delivery that were appropriate to this new time.

Some contended that the Sophists were not educators, but money-hungry men who taught others how to manipulate and deceive. Although they were not centered on what was right or wrong, they did teach people the basic tools of argumentation which became the groundwork for other philosophers and rhetoricians like Aristotle. Sophists also provided education to people who did not have access to those particular arts before. Perhaps most significantly, the Sophists illustrated the usefulness and advantage of passionate delivery.

PLATO

One could not discuss important contributions in rhetorical theory regarding truth without mentioning two key players: Plato and Aristotle. Contrary to the Sophists, Plato was primarily concerned with arriving at a given truth of a situation or an issue. You may have heard instructors, or others, discuss "ultimate truths." This concept comes from Plato's obsession with discovering what is termed the *ultimate truth*.

The Sophists were not concerned with whether the side they argued was correct; rather, they focused on the goal of getting others to accept the speaker's position. Plato, on the other hand, sought to find the absolute truth in a given situation and believed that the ethical use of rhetoric could aid in the discovery of truth. Plato argued that people like the Sophists taught and used **false rhetoric** for the pursuit of personal interests over the interest of finding the ultimate truth.

In today's world you could compare the idea of "false rhetoric" to a car salesperson. A family needs a car and a salesperson helps them find one. The family needed a car so they benefited from the sale, but the salesman also benefited. In Plato's sense of rhetoric, both the customer and salesperson should try to arrive at the ultimate truth regarding the worth of the car (as if there were a universal and perfect truth for a car). Naturally, the person buying the car does not want to spend any more than

© Dimitrios, 2014. Used under license from Shutterstock, Inc.

FIGURE 3.2 Plato founded the Academy in Athens, the first known institution of higher learning in the Western World. He was a noted philosopher, writing 36 dialogues, many of which were devoted to the subject of rhetoric.

necessary—even if spending less might hurt the salesperson's income. Do not forget the salesperson also has personal motives to sell the vehicle (money and sales for the month). The salesperson will sell the car at a price that may not be the true worth of the vehicle because it would benefit them to do so. Therefore, both people are trying to persuade the other to accept a specific price for the car—even if the offer is not the "true" worth of the car, and with no effort to "discover" the actual, true worth of the car. Plato would call this **false rhetoric** because it would not lead to the ultimate truth (the worth of the car). In the end, the better persuader or arguer will win this argument, which really means the Sophistic method will win out. The buyers will walk away with their great deal or be smoked by the salesperson, but no "truth" will be revealed. Plato feels rhetoric should be used to unveil the truth, not as a means to deceive or just persuade.

Plato's concern with "ultimate" or "transcendent" truth led him to believe that before humans are born their souls exist in a place that has access to absolute truths. When humans are born, they forget the truths their souls had once absorbed. Plato believed that now, in order for humans to arrive at truth, a series of questions, or rather the correct question(s), must be asked. We use this idea nowadays, when we use a series of questions to arrive at "truth" in our courts of law, or even when a loved one comes home far too late one night and you bombard them with questions to arrive at the truth of where they were.

Initially, Plato claimed that rhetoric was not a means of arriving at truth. Rather, he believed rhetoric was audience-centered, concerned with persuasion, and not always a virtuous endeavor. Eventually, Plato did come to appreciate rhetoric and acknowledge that rhetoric has the power to produce knowledge, but stressed that rhetoric can only provide ways of *conveying* truth. Plato believed that in order to arrive at the ultimate truth, one must engage in dialectic. **Dialectic** would allow humans to separate the truth from the false through questioning. His dialogues, *Gorgias* and *Phaedrus*, discussed false and true rhetoric in depth. Socrates, a character in Plato's dialogues, argues that human souls exist with the "form of the good" which refers to justice and knowledge. For a true and full understanding of Plato and these ideas you should consult his primary works. Generally, Plato disagreed with the Sophistic notion that an art of persuasion (rhetoric) can exist apart from dialectic, claiming that the Sophists appeal only to the probable rather than to that which is true. In the end, Plato argued that Sophists did not focus on bettering the audience, but flattering them.

Plato's *Gorgias* focused on the idea of false rhetoric. Plato's primary purpose was to use two characters in a debate to show the flaws in the ideas of the main character, Gorgias. Gorgias was a famous Sicilian sophist who introduced probability-based argumentation. Plato uses the arguments progressed by *Gorgias* as an opportunity to dismantle the ideas he asserted. The character he used to dismantle these arguments was Socrates. One of Socrates' primary arguments was that rhetoric was not an art. One of the more famous accusations in the *Gorgias* is when Socrates professes that rhetoric is a form of "cookery." Cookery in today's terms would mean something that was cooked up or contrived; it lacks real substance, something that is fake, selfish, and performance-based. Plato's *Phaedrus* focuses on "true rhetoric." This work employs an allegory to discuss the art of speaking. This time, the main idea of the dialogue focuses on what is good and true rhetoric, unlike the *Gorgias* which focuses on deliberating what is false or bad rhetoric. Plato asserts the ideal speaker is one who is moral and truthful.

According to Plato, rhetoric is, "A kind of influencing of the mind by means of persuasion." Plato considered rhetoric to be a psychological form, believing that one can only be truly healthy if one understands how the mind responds to various persuasions. He discussed the idea of adapting to audiences based on various criteria. He specifically discussed sex, area of residence, and age. The most common definition of rhetoric attributed to Plato is rhetoric as the "art of winning the soul by discourse."

He believed that men and women should be appealed to through similar means when he stated, "There is no special faculty of administration in a state which a woman has because she is a woman, or which a man has by virtue of his sex, but the gifts of nature are alike diffused in both; all the pursuits of men are the pursuits of women." Plato spent much time on the thought of persuasion by means of the mind, but his student, Aristotle, would spend even more time deciphering the links among rhetoric, persuasion, dialectic, and the mind. He warned that young audiences are usually unable to grasp more complex ideas and are overly concerned with the way they are perceived by others.

OTHER FAMOUS QUOTES COMMONLY ATTRIBUTED TO PLATO

"Wise men speak because they have something to say; fools because they have to say something."
"People are like dirt. They can either nourish you and help you grow as a person or they can stunt your growth and make you wilt and die."

FIGURE 3.3

ARISTOTLE

Aristotle synthesized two polarizations set forth by the Sophistic and Platonic worldviews. It was the intersection of these two paradigms that inspired the work of one of the most influential thinkers in the history of philosophy. Aristotle has long been considered the most distinguished student of Plato and the greatest contributor to rhetorical theory and analysis. The Sophistic notion that rhetoric was an art helped inspire Aristotle's famous argument of "audience adaptation." Aristotle was more enthusiastic about rhetoric than Plato and developed two definitions. The first is "Rhetoric is the counterpart of dialectic." The second definition offered by Aristotle is, "So let rhetoric be defined as the faculty of discovering in the particular case what are the available means of persuasion." Many theorists today still struggle with interpreting Aristotle's words, especially in this last definition. However, from what we understand and can interpret, Aristotle deems persuasion as an essential part of the rhetorical process and views rhetoric as a moral and practical art. The most common definition of rhetoric attributed to Aristotle is the rhetoric is "the faculty of discovering in any particular case all the available means of persuasion."

Aristotle classified discourse into three areas. First, he had **forensic** discourse. This discourse dealt with the past and criminality, such as, in a court of law. Second, **epideictic**, dealt with blame and praise; what you might hear at a special occasion like a funeral or a dedication. The third form was **deliberative**, which dealt with future

© Panos Karas, 2014. Used under license from Shutterstock, Inc.

FIGURE 3.4 A famous Greek philosopher, Aristotle is best known for contributing canons and proofs to the field of rhetoric. Aristotle established the library of Lyceum, was the pupil of Plato, taught Alexander the Great, and published numerous books.

policy and will be a primary focus of this text. Deliberative discourse has been one of the main focuses of American academic debate since the mid-1920s. Regardless of which you use, Aristotle contended that there needed to be four parts to any discourse: an introduction, a clear statement, an argument, and a conclusion.

He specialized in observing all things living and nonliving and in formulating the data from his observations in a form that others could then study and practice. His specialties were not only limited to merely the sciences, but also encompassed law, drama, and ethics. While Plato believed in transcendent truth, Aristotle was more concerned with **empirical truth.** Aristotle believed logic and scientific demonstration allow humans to arrive at truth, asserting rhetoric should be a more pragmatic endeavor than that articulated by Plato. In contrast to his teacher Plato, Aristotle believed rhetoric was the counterpart of dialectic. In this belief, Aristotle admits dialectical methods are necessary to find truth in theoretical discussion, but rhetorical methods should be used to find truth in practical experiences (legal conditions such as in a court of law). Aristotle articulated four distinct reasons for studying, practicing, and understanding rhetoric:

1. To uphold truth and justice and play down their opposites
2. To teach in a way suitable to a popular audience
3. To analyze both sides of a question
4. To enable one to defend oneself

PROOFS: ETHOS, PATHOS, AND LOGOS

One of the elements to persuasion, according to Aristotle, are proofs, which he terms **ethos, pathos, and logos**. Aristotle claimed that you could support and defend your ideas with these proofs. **Ethos** is described as those proofs that depend on the speaker's ability to be believable. **Pathos** are proofs designed to affect a listener's feelings. **Logos** uses reasoning to convince the hearers. "Of the modes of persuasion furnished by the spoken word there are three kinds. The first kind depends on the personal character of the speaker; the second on putting the audience into a certain frame of mind; the third on the proof, or apparent proof, provided by the words of the speech itself."

ETHOS

"Persuasion is achieved by the speaker's personal character when the speech is so spoken as to make us think [them] credible. We believe good [people] more fully and more readily than others: this is true generally whatever the question is, and absolutely true where exact certainty is impossible and opinions are divided… [the speakers] character may almost be called the most effective means of persuasion he possesses."

Ethos is an appeal to the audience's sense of honesty and character. Ethos is how the rhetoric convinces the audience that the speakers are credible and qualified to speak on the subject as well as convince the audience that they have good intentions toward them. Aristotle believed that ethos comprises three main things: goodwill, good sense, and credibility (intelligence and virtue). Ethos is created by the rhetor, displayed in the message, and dependent on the audience's perception of the character of the rhetor. For Aristotle, ethos was central to the speaker's persuasive potential. He believed ethos should be generated during the course of a speech and not be based on a previous reputation with the audience (1356). Today, however, when we discuss ethos we recognize both the speaker's perceived character during the speech and the speaker's credibility *before* the speech as well.

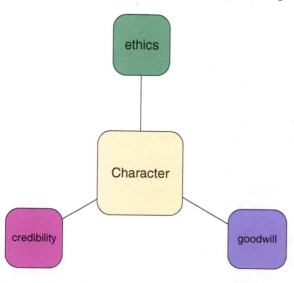

Before we can expect to convince an audience we must first be seen as a credible speaker in the eyes of the audience. When people are convinced that a speaker is knowledgeable, trustworthy, and has their best interests at heart they will be more likely to believe the speaker and accept and even act on their arguments. Keep in mind, ethos reflects the audience's perceptions of a speaker, not necessarily the "truth" of the speaker's credibility. So, then, how exactly do we manage to be perceived as credible? There are many aspects to creating your ethos as a speaker. Aristotle first articulated these ideas and we still use them today. Rhetors should ask themselves:

Does the audience believe I am a good person with good intentions?
Do they think I am a person of authority on the topic?
Do they think I am honest and good-natured?

PATHOS

"Persuasion may come through the hearers,
when the speech stirs their emotions."

Aristotle felt a study of emotion was essential to the systematic process of public speaking. He asserted **pathos** was "putting the audience in the right frame of mind," arguing that pathos was the component of speech that affects judgment and stimulates emotions (as cited in Stevenson, 2000, Book II Part 1). There are methods speakers can be taught in an effort to enhance the likelihood pathos attempts will work; however, Aristotle also warns us that the power to get your audience to receive your ideas by playing to their emotions like pity, fear, pain, and hostility can become unethical if your efforts result in an audience left unaware of potential harms and consequences. The corruption of an audience for one's own personal gain is not a virtuous act and should be avoided.

Pathos is the Greek word for "suffering" and "experience." When speakers use pathos they are attempting to inspire empathy or an emotional response, in hopes of changing attitudes, behaviors, and/or beliefs. In simple terms, pathos, is the speaker's appeal to the audience's emotions. Speakers use pathos when they want to make the audience feel what the speaker wants them to feel. Pathos is the artistic, expressive, passionate layer of a given speech. It is the moment(s) of a speech in which the speaker attempts to move the audience to action, to inspire, to motivate, to create an emotional climate among his/her listeners.

CLASSICAL FIGURES OF SPEECH USED TO INCREASE PATHOS

adhortatio: A commandment, promise, or exhortation intended to move one's consent or desires.
adynaton: The expression of the inability of expression—almost always emotional in its nature.
aganactesis: An exclamation proceeding from deep indignation.
apagoresis: A statement designed to inhibit someone from doing something.
aposiopesis: Breaking off suddenly in the middle of speaking, usually to portray being overcome with emotion.
apostrophe: Turning one's speech from one audience to another, or addressing oneself to an abstraction or the absent—almost always as a way of increasing appeal through emotion.
cataplexis: Threatening/prophesying payback for ill-doing.
conduplicatio: The repetition of a word or words in adjacent phrases or clauses, either to amplify the thought or to express emotion.
deesis: The vehement expression of desire put in terms of "for someone's sake" or "for God's sake."
descriptio: Vivid description, especially of the consequences of an act, that stirs up its hearers.
diacope: Repetition of a word with one or more between, usually to express deep feeling.

ecphonesis: An emotional exclamation.
enargia: Enargia, or vivid description, can be inherently moving, especially when depicting things graphic in nature.
epimone: Persistent repetition of the same plea in much the same words, a direct method for underscoring the pathetic appeal.
epitrope: A figure in which one turns things over to one's hearers (often pathetically).

FIGURE 3.5

LOGOS

"Persuasion is effected through the speech itself when we have proved a truth or an apparent truth by means of the persuasive arguments suitable to the case in question."

Logos refers to the appeal to logic. Logic is a rhetor's ability to present solid and rational reasoning on a given matter to a given audience. This was Aristotle's most stressed of the three proofs, yet logos alone will not win an argument; all the proofs are important.

Logos can be divided into inductive and deductive logic. Logos means "word" in Greek and is primarily concerned with the consistency of the rhetor's message, the clarity of their logic, reasoning, and claims. Deductive and indicative logic as well as syllogisms and enthymemes are primary components of this proof, which will be discussed in depth in upcoming chapters. In the meantime, you can absorb the idea that logos is an appeal to an audience's sense of reasoning. This is usually accomplished through reasoned argumentation, analysis, and evidence.

FAMOUS QUOTES COMMONLY ATTRIBUTED TO ARISTOTLE

"It is the mark of an educated mind to be able to entertain a thought without accepting it."

"Love is composed of a single soul inhabiting two bodies."

"We are what we repeatedly do. Excellence, then, is not an act, but a habit."

FIGURE 3.6

ARISTOTLE'S FIVE CANONS OF RHETORIC

Aristotle also contributed to what is now termed the five **canons of rhetoric:** invention, arrangement, style, memory, and delivery. Rhetoric was divided into these categories and is currently the most acceptable template for rhetorical education and pedagogy. Rhetorical treatises through the centuries have been drawn from these categories. At different points in time different areas were considered more important than others. For instance, at first, delivery was not considered as important, but some time later rhetoric was almost purely defined as style and delivery. Now rhetoricians accept all areas as equally important and recognize the importance of having each one in a given rhetorical act. We will briefly touch on the five areas.

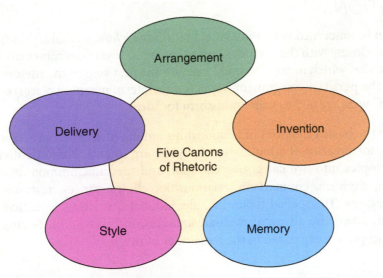

The Five Cannons of Rhetoric

Introduction	• the start of a speech, where the orator announces the subject, purpose, and persuasion in an attempt to gain credibility.
Statement of facts	• the speaker provides a narrative of what the current situation is and explains the nature of the case including a summary of the issues and/or a statement of the charge.
Division	• the speaker outlines what will come and reviews what has been said, or the point at issue in the case. This can be easily understood as a preview and review of points and basic organizational structure.
The proof	• this is where the speaker appeals to logic and rationality.
Refutation	• is where the speaker answers the counterarguments of her/his opponent.
Conclusion	• is the summary of the issue and main points and conventionally includes an appeal to pathos.

FIGURE 3.7

INVENTION

Invention is concerned with *what* is said rather than *how* it is said; thus invention is associated closely with the rhetorical appeal of logos. Invention comes from the Latin word *invenire,* which means "to find," because the first step in the rhetorical process is to find the persuasive argument. *Topoi* (a Greek term meaning places) or "topics of invention" were created to help brainstorm for ideas.

Topoi are the basic categories of relationships among ideas and they serve as simple templates for creating the foundation for your arguments. Aristotle divided these *topois* or topics into two categories: common and special. Common topics include: definition, division, comparison, relationship, circumstances, testimony, notion, and conjugates. The special topics include: judicial (justice vs. injustice), deliberative (good, unworthy, advantages, disadvantages), and ceremonial (virtue and vice). These concepts are expanded in the remainder of this text.

ARRANGEMENT

Arrangement dictates how a speech or writing should be organized. Originally, in ancient rhetoric, an arrangement was concerned only with oration. Now we have broadened rhetoric to include the written form as well. When you learn about a formal **debate** in the coming chapters you will be taught the various arrangements that are ideal for each type of debate and debate speech. The **classical** arrangement of oration is:

FIGURE 3.8 Stylistic evidence is the vivid, textured, artful expression of ideas that produce images in the mind of your audience.

STYLE

Style is the artful expression of ideas. There are seven pure types of style: clarity, grandeur, beauty, rapidity, character, sincerity, and force. Style is concerned with how something is said. Style is meant to align the appropriate verbal expression for the orator's given intentions. Two of Aristotle's students, Theophrastus and Demetrius, originally developed "virtues" of style. The rules are quite simple, but very necessary. For instance, one virtue is correctness. **Correctness** refers to the idea that a speaker/writer must adhere to specific and complete grammar and syntax rules. The speaker must employ good and competent **language** as well. In short, the speaker must display high ethos through the use of impressive language. The speaker must also be **clear and simple.** It is essential that one's audience understand the message if they are to be persuaded by it. This virtue of style stresses the importance of clarity over complexity.

Evidence is the next virtue of style. Evidence is not like the supporting evidence used in court cases or scholarly journals used to reinforce an argument. In its original form, evidence referred to the use of effective pathos as accomplished primarily through vivid language. Evidence, otherwise known today as vivid language, is a language that is colorful, concrete, and appeals to the senses. Vivid language choices help paint a picture in the mind of the audience. As the artist (speaker) your brushes and color palette are the tools with which you construct your argument, imagery, and purpose. The audience should be able to feel and see what the speaker is saying and vivid language choices are a great way to accomplish that task.

© Ramona Kaulitzki, 2014. Used under license from Shutterstock, Inc.

FIGURE 3.9 Good speechmaking will encompass many varying tonal changes. Monotone speakers cause their audience to lose interest and sometimes no amount of logos can bring them back.

- **Onomatopoeia**—the use of words that sound like what you are describing.
- **Conduplicatio**—the repetition of words or phrases at the start of successive phrases.
- **Repetition**—the repeating of a word for poetic effect, impact, or draw attention to that idea.
- **Polyptoton**—the repeating of words that come from the same root.
- **Hyperbole**—the use of wild exaggeration for impact or humor.
- **Alliteration**—the repeating of the same sound by words close in proximity. Sometimes alliteration can be as simple as repeating the same consonant letter.
- **Assonance**—the repeating of the same vowel sound.
- **Superlative**—the declaration that something is the best or worst of its kind
- **Epistrophe**—the repetition of the same word or series of words in a sentence, a clause, or a phrase.
- **Climax**—a figure that builds intensity in the speech by repeating words or phrases while increasing their power or significance.
- **Anagnorisis**—a statement designed to keep your audience from doing something. It is often used in conjunction with hyperbole and cause-and-effect language strategies.
- **Parallelism**—the use of like structures in two or more different clauses.

FIGURE 3.10

The next virtue, although common sense like the others, is too often ignored these days and that is the virtue of **propriety**. The term propriety seems like a term out of a 1950s family film, but it really is important still today. The virtue of **propriety** is basically the idea that speakers must be cognizant of what is appropriate given the occasion, audience, and timing.

And the final virtue, but certainly not the least important virtue, is called ornateness. **Ornateness** is a fancy way of saying the speech needs to be pleasant and interesting and it needs to be managed to maintain the audience's attention. This is accomplished through the use of a tonal variation of the speaker's voice, ensuring the rhythm of the speech is pleasing and diverse enough to keep the audience interested, as well as the use of various figures of speech. Above you will find a quick table of several figures of speech used today; this list is certainly not complete, as there are a great number of figures of speech a rhetor could choose. Classical rhetoric divided figures of speech into **tropes** (changes in the meaning of words) and **schemes** (changes in the pattern of words).

MEMORY

The degree to which an orator remembers their speech is the primary understanding of memory. Memory as a canon also considers the methods a speaker uses to ensure the audience retains the speech's primary teachings and persuasions. Mary Carruthers (1990) states, "To help recall something we have heard rather than seen,

FIGURE 3.11 Memory is a cannon in which an orator recalls their speech. There are many techniques speakers use to aid help them store their speech information. How will you store your information?

we should attach to their words the appearance, facial expression, and gestures of the person speaking as well as the appearance of the room. The speaker should therefore create strong visual images, through expression and gesture, which will fix the impression of his words. All the rhetorical textbooks contain detailed advice on declamatory gesture and expression; this underscores the insistence of Aristotle, Avicenna, and other philosophers, on the primacy and security for the memory of the visual over all other sensory modes, auditory, tactile, and the rest" (pp. 94–95). One of the most well known for their focus on memory was a famous Greek poet, Simonides of Ceos, who declared that should anyone want to train their memory they must "select places and form mental images of the things they wish to remember and store those images in the places, so that the order of the places will preserve the order of the things, and the images of the things will denote the things themselves, and we shall employ the places and the images respectively as a wax writing tablet the letters written upon it."

DELIVERY

Delivery is essential to appealing to the audience's emotions (pathos) and is critical in establishing a speaker's credibility (ethos). Delivery deals primarily with verbal utterances and emotional impact but with also body language, gestures, and tonal fluctuations. Because this canon is especially important to understand the mastery of rhetoric as an art, we have discussed it in greater detail below. Delivery in the Classical Era is much the same as today's understanding. Movement, body, face, and voice are all components the canon of delivery centered on long ago and it is still important today. We have managed over the years to dedicate a more specific examination of the delivery canon that is useful.

Much of the population thinks communicating effectively is a formula of words and sequence. However, effective communication means making sure one's body language and tone of voice are consistent with the content of the speech. Tone can add "music" to a speech, affect selling ability, and thrust an audience toward expressing a full continuum of emotions.

Delivery has been considered an integral part of communication, argumentation, and debate for centuries. Hellenistic and Roman treaties gave delivery significant deliberation, as did Aristotle. Aristotelian thought considers the following in terms of delivery: manner of presentation, mode of presentation (impromptu, extemporaneous, memory, and manuscript), body language, posture, gestures, movement, eye contact, vocal skills including articulation, and ultimately how the physical characteristics of a given rhetor affect the audience.

The Sophists, Cicero, Quintilian, and even Plato dedicated much of their discussion on rhetoric to the concept of delivery. In the 4th and 5th centuries, the Sophists taught the importance of eliciting emotional change in the audience partly through one's acoustic control (Golden, Berquist, & Coleman, 2000; Johnstone, 2001; Hikins, 1996). Cicero claimed delivery was the most important skill a rhetor could ever possess. "A moderate speaker with a trained delivery can often out do the best of them" (Cicero, 1959, III.11.19; Johnstone, 2001, p. 124). Quintilian agreed, saying, "A mediocre speech supported by all the power of delivery will be more impressive than the best speech unaccompanied by such power" (Cicero, 1959, XI.3.5-6; Johnstone, 2001, p. 124).

Delivery includes verbal and nonverbal elements. The major components of delivery that you need to be aware of and master in order to be a fully effective rhetor, arguer, or debater are: articulation, enunciation, pronunciation, tone, pitch, speech rate, pausing, expressions, and eye contact. For a more rounded and full understanding of how to master the art of delivery you should consider taking a public speaking course.

Someone who articulates well is a speaker who puts words together well and is able to convey meaning in a clear, straightforward yet, relatively sophisticated and educated manner. **Articulation** has components of enunciation and pronunciation. Generally, articulation reflects the speaker's credibility, perceived level of intelligence, and vocabulary.

Enunciation is the manner of speaking clearly and concisely. Speech and debate instructors often give their students a series of exercises to ensure they utter the sounds of each letter in a clear and precise manner in order to better their enunciation. The opposite of good enunciation is mumbling or slurring.

Pronunciation is a part of enunciation and therefore articulation. Pronunciation is to pronounce the sounds of words correctly. Various cultures pronounce words differently. For instance you may have heard people refer to "tomatoe versus tomahtoe"—it is the same word, just pronounced differently within different dialects. You want to try to use the dialect of your audience or at least be aware that if your dialect is different you risk misunderstandings.

Tone on the other hand is not as easily described, as its qualities are difficult to define. Tone incorporates subtle cues of the rhetor's attitude, emotions, and persuasive efforts understood as "the quality of voice." Given this, the quality of delivery in the utterance of words can significantly amplify or distort the purpose or rhetorical attempts of a given speech. Tone displays a wide range of emotions, energies, and descriptors. It carries social information, such as in a sarcastic, condescending, or subservient manner of speaking. Tone adds meaning and emotion to actual chosen words. Although tone is often identified with the implied or underlying meaning of a word, tone is much more subtle and delicate and occurs with the actual vocal control of the speaker. Tone has the unique ability to capture the essence of emotion that other forms of language cannot.

Your topic or your subject determines much of your tone. If you are giving the formal introduction of a renowned individual at a conference, it is quite possible that your speech will be formal and your tone serious yet inspired. Your tone is going to be quite different in a speech congratulating the graduating class than if you are giving the eulogy at a funeral. Tone can convey hopefulness, sadness, regret, deep intrigue, and light and airy kindness. Given the proper commitment, practice, and authenticity you can manage just about any tone you like in a speech.

Pitch refers to the highness or lowness of the utterance itself, specifically, level, range, and variation. The pitch variation is very important. I'm sure you can recall a moment when you listened to someone speak with an annoying pitch and, although you may have tried to look interested, you heard absolutely nothing of what they had to say. Pitch cannot be underrated.

Rate refers to the speed at which the rhetor speaks. It can also be understood as the number of words spoken per minute. A speaker's rate of speech often increases when she/he is nervous. A fast rate of speech will signal to the audience that you lack confidence and are weak, unsettled, insecure, and incompetent. None of these perceptions are necessarily accurate, but the accuracy is unimportant; the perception is what matters. Be sure to control your breathing; do not run out of air when you speak, take moments that draw out your point by delivering it slowly and with a low tone, and then add a quickened pace for diversity and interest. Pauses are essential tools in speaking, pauses are intervals of silence between or within words, phrases, or sentences that add meaning, create drama, reflect emotion, and more. When pauses are planned they can create a great sense of movement and emotional display.

Movement includes the physical shifts in the speaker's body, whether that be through actual purposefully planned steps and shifts of weight or more distracting negative speaker behaviors such as swaying back and forth, kicking or shaking legs, shifting back and forth, nervous habits, etc. A speaker with confident powerful movements will win the audience's attention; as we know, gaining the attention of an audience is not always a simple task. Fail to move with confidence and your audience will surely divert their attention elsewhere. An amazing message is worthless if it is never truly heard. Gestures and facial expressions are valuable traits of a skilled speaker.

Movements in eyebrows, corners of the lips, and even the range of gestures can make all the difference.

Similarly, **posture** refers to the relative relaxation or rigidity and vertical position of the body. A rigid speaker who lacks a natural stance and gesture will reflect a lack of professionalism, preparation, and general credibility. You are always being judged when you are a speaker, your posture communicates to your audience whether or not you are credible and whether they should bother paying attention to you. The great orators and rhetors employed impeccable posture while they delivered their messages.

There are many more rhetoricians to mention, but those mentioned in this chapter provide the most foundational information you need in order to move forward. The contributions of the Sophists, Plato, Aristotle, Cicero, and Quintilian are still used in rhetoric to this day. In the pages to come we will introduce you to more contemporary rhetoricians and provide you with a diverse understanding of where rhetoric has been and where it is now.

KEY TERMS

Argumentation—the communicative process of advancing, supporting, criticizing, and modifying claims so that appropriate decision-makers may grant or deny adherence.

Arrangement—dictates how a speech or a writing should be organized.

Canons of rhetoric—invention, arrangement, style, memory, and delivery.

Corax—the man who has the first recorded written rhetoric.

Debate—a method of argumentation, debate is the process of inquiry and advocacy and the seeking of a reasoned judgment on a proposition.

Delivery—includes verbal utterances and emotional impact but also body language, gestures, and tonal fluctuations.

Dialectic—allows humans to separate the truth from the false through questioning. Is the pragmatic procedures of argumentation that allow humans to separate the truth from the false through questioning.

Ethos—the speaker's credibility.

False rhetoric—is used by individuals pursuing their own interests rather than arriving at truth.

Logos—refers to organization and logic.

Memory—the degree to which an orator remembers her speech and the methods a speaker uses to ensure the audience retains the speech's primary teachings and persuasions.

Pathos—arguments that are primarily based on appeals to emotions.

Relativism—knowledge is relative to the limited nature of the mind and the conditions of knowing.

Rhetoric—is concerned with argumentation as a process. Also widely known as the "art of persuasion."

Sophists—a group of educators who traveled the land city by city offering educational courses to citizens for a price.

Style—the artful expression of ideas.

Tone—cues to a rhetor's attitude and emotions; the quality of voice.

QUESTIONS FOR REVIEW

Respond to the following questions **without** reviewing the text or your notes. These questions are provided to help you practice retrieving information and reflect on your reading.

A. How would you define rhetoric?

B. Did you agree or disagree with anything you read? Explain.

C. What did you learn that was new to you?

D. What concepts, if any, were confusing to you?

Respond to the following questions. You may reference your text or notes to help you.

1. What did the Sophists believe about truth and rhetoric?

2. What did Plato believe about truth and rhetoric? How does this compare to the position of the Sophists?

3. What did Aristotle believe about truth and rhetoric? How does this compare to the positions of the Sophists and Plato?

4. Define ethos, pathos, and logos. Provide an example of each one.

5. Identify and describe Aristotle's five canons of rhetoric.

QUESTIONS FOR DISCUSSION

1. Before reading this chapter, you identified ethos, pathos, or logos as having the greatest impact on you in a persuasive argument. Now that you have read the chapter, respond to that question again. Poll the class to see who chose each proof. Discuss the choices and consider the implications for developing persuasive messages.

2. The Sophists, Plato, and Aristotle viewed truth and rhetoric very differently. Whose position do you find most agreeable? Why?

3. Find an example of ethos, pathos, and logos in advertising, health, and/or social campaigns. Share and discuss your examples with the rest of the class.

4. In your group, discuss the importance of Aristotle's proofs in your final pre-sentations and brainstorm a few examples. Which proof will be the easiest to incorporate? Which one will be the most challenging? How can you help each other balance the three proofs?

5. Discuss the ethical questions provided at the end of the first chapter. What ethical considerations are relevant to the information in this chapter about truth and rhetoric, Aristotle's proofs and canons of rhetoric?

   • Are there guidelines (e.g., don't lie) that would be appropriate for every situation, or are ethics relative?

   • Do the ends (e.g., a good outcome) justify any means?

   • Is deceiving the receiver ever appropriate?

   • Should the source of the message bear primary responsibility for ethics, or should the receiver share that responsibility (e.g., buyer beware)?

REFERENCES

Aristotle. (1954). *Rhetoric* (W. Phys Roberts, trans.). New York: The Modern Library, Random House.

Aristotle. (2007/1356b). *On rhetoric: A theory of civic discourse* (George A. Kennedy, trans., 2nd ed.). New York: Oxford University.

Carruthers, M. J. (1990). *The book of memory: A study of memory in medieval culture.* Cambridge University Press.

Cicero. (1959). *De Oratore* (E. W. Sutton, trans.). Cambridge, MA: Harvard University Press.

Classic figures of speech. http://rhetoric.byu.edu/Figures/S/synonymia.htm

Golden, J. L., Berquist, G. F., & Coleman, W. E. (1976). *The rhetoric of western thought.* Dubuque, IA: Kendall/Hunt Publishing Co..

Golden, J., Berquist, G., & Coleman, W. (2000). *The rhetoric of western thought.* Dubuque, IA: Kendall/Hunt Publishing Company.

Hikins, J. (1996). *Remarks on the development of rhetoric.* Dubuque, IA: Kendall/Hunt Publishing Company.

https://en.oxforddictionaries.com/definition/us/existentialism

Johnstone, C. (2001). Communicating in classical contexts: The centrality of delivery. *Quarterly Journal of Speech, 87*(2), 121143.

Jowett, Plato's Republic p. 179.

Nicholson, G. (1999). *Plato's Phaedrus: The philosophy of love.* West Lafayette, IN: Purdue University Press.

Plato. (1967). *Gorgias* (W.R.M. Lamb, trans.). Cambridge, MA: Harvard University Press, passim.

Quintilian. (1963). *The institution oratoria of quintilian* (H. E. Butler, trans., 4 vols.). Cambridge: Loeb Classical Library.

Stevenson, D.C. (2000). Rhetoric by Aristotle. The Internet Classics Archive. http://classics.mit.edu/Aristotle/rhetoric.2.ii.html

The Rhetoric of Western Thought. James L. Golden, Goodwin F. Berquist, William E. Coleman.

This webpage reproduces a section of *Institutio Oratoria* by Quintilian published in Vol. I of the Loeb Classical Library edition, 1920 page 305. http://penelope.uchicago.edu/Thayer/E/Roman/Texts/Quintilian/Institutio_Oratoria/2C*.html#21.

Thorson, A., Korcock, M., Staller, M. *Contemporary public speaking: How to craft and deliver a powerful speech* [eBook]. Dubuque, IA: Kendall Hunt.

CHAPTER 4

SOURCE FACTORS

BEFORE YOU READ

Respond to the following questions **before** you read the chapter.

1. How did Aristotle define ethos?

2. Make a list of two to three credible leaders, influencers, journalists, etc. What makes them credible? Be specific.

3. In addition to credibility, what characteristics of speakers make them effective persuaders?

It's the first day of school. You enter class, look around to see if you know anyone in the class, and wait for the instructor. A few minutes later a young woman walks in, introduces herself as Ms. Brown, the instructor, and states that she is a graduate student and this is the first class she has ever taught. What is your response? What expectations do you have for the class? How knowledgeable do you think Ms. Brown is? Do you assume she is competent or incompetent? Now, let's rewind and do this again. A middle-aged woman walks in, introduces herself as Dr. Brown, the instructor, and states that she is a professor and this is her 15th year of teaching. What is your response? How knowledgeable and competent do you think Dr. Brown is? You may have had experiences similar to these. Do you give more attention to your instructors who are experienced professors? Are you more likely to challenge your instructors who are graduate students and assume they don't know what they're talking about?

LEARNING OBJECTIVES

- DEFINE CREDIBILITY AND DIFFERENTIATE THE MODERN DEFINITION WITH ARISTOTLE'S DEFINITION.
- DESCRIBE FACTORS THAT INFLUENCE PERCEPTIONS OF CREDIBILITY.
- EXPLAIN HOW CREDIBILITY AFFECTS PERSUASION.
- EXPLAIN THE TYPES OF POWER.
- DESCRIBE MILGRAM'S RESEARCH ON OBEDIENCE AND AUTHORITY AS A SOURCE FACTOR.
- EXPLAIN HOW SOURCE SIMILARITY, ATTRACTIVENESS, AND LIKEABILITY AFFECT PERSUASION.

Compare your assessment of instructor credibility with how you assess the credibility of various media such as the Internet or social media. What makes a news report, a website, a YouTube video, an Instagram post, a blog, or other messages credible? Are you persuaded by more credible sources in these contexts? Does your decision about who is a credible source vary in these contexts, or do you rely on the same factors you used in the instructor example? Just as you may be more willing to listen to an instructor you perceive as credible, we are often more persuaded by sources we perceive as credible across contexts.

In this chapter we examine what makes a source credible and what impact that has on persuasion. Source credibility has received far more attention than any other source factor; however, there are other source factors to consider as well. This chapter examines the parts of the persuasion process (source, message, channel, receiver). Recall from Chapter 1 that persuasion is a communication process, so we draw on the basic communication model of a source sending a message through a channel to a receiver who responds with feedback to the source.

The **source** is the individual creating and/or delivering a message. The characteristics of a source are important to persuasion. If two different people delivered the same persuasive message, they would not necessarily be equally successful. There are a number of source characteristics that influence persuasion. Some of these source characteristics can be controlled, at least to some extent; others we have little control over. One important thing to keep in mind as you learn about source characteristics is that there are specific source qualities or behaviors, and there is how an audience *perceives* those qualities and behaviors. Just as two people delivering the same message may not be equally persuasive; two people listening to the same source will not have the same perceptions of the source.

CREDIBILITY

One of the most studied source factors is credibility. This concept will also make appearances in later chapters. A simple definition of **credibility** is that it is a perception of believability. If you are credible, you are believable. The concept of source credibility has been studied for thousands of years and there has been much disagreement and confusion about exactly what it means to be a credible source. To complicate matters, the concept of source credibility is not stable. Perceptions of a source's credibility can change during the course of a single message or from one message to another. For example, you may perceive your communication professor as highly credible when he or she is talking about persuasion theory. But if your professor gave you advice on what cell phone to purchase, your perception of his or her credibility may not be so high.

Let's first examine how perceptions of credibility can change over the course of a message. There are two types of source credibility: initial and derived. **Initial credibility** refers to the level of source credibility apart from any specific message—that is, the credibility of a source prior to the presentation of a persuasive message. **Derived credibility** refers to the level of source credibility during and after the presentation of a particular message. Although these two types of credibility may be the same at times, they are often different. For example, have you ever watched a YouTube video and, as a result of what you watched, perceived the source as more credible than you did initially? This is an example of derived credibility increasing as a result of the message. The reverse can also be true. Have you ever perceived someone as having less credibility after you watched his or her video? Thus, when we consider source credibility, we must also consider both initial and derived forms.

ARISTOTLE'S APPROACH

Although many of the currently held theories and much of what we know from social scientific approaches to persuasion were developed in the last century, the study of persuasion itself is more than 2,500 years old. As you read in Chapter 3, writings by ancient Greeks serve as the foundation for much of our current understanding of persuasion. In particular, Aristotle gave us great insight into how persuasion works, and he did so from observing human behavior at that time. Much has changed over the last two millenniums, but the basics of human response to persuasive messages appear to have some enduring characteristics, and the nature of source credibility is one that has lasted.

Aristotle argued that persuasion has three important components: ethos, logos, and pathos. **Ethos** refers to the nature of credibility of the source, and some current credibility researchers use the term *ethos*. **Logos** refers to the nature of the arguments and structure of the message, and **pathos** refers to the emotional appeals of the message. We will discuss logos and pathos in Chapter 5. In this chapter, we focus on ethos.

DIMENSIONS OF CREDIBILITY

Source credibility is a multidimensional concept. Three dimensions, or parts, make up what we perceive as the credibility of the source. We must understand these dimensions in order to clearly understand the concept of credibility. The notion of source credibility having multiple dimensions is not new. Aristotle in ancient Greece argued that source credibility or ethos was composed of three dimensions: **good character, goodwill,** and **intelligence.** Good character refers to the moral nature, honesty and goodness, of the source. Goodwill refers to the speaker's intent toward the audience. If the speaker has good intentions and has the receivers' best interest in mind, then the speaker has goodwill toward the audience. Intelligence refers to the knowledge base of the speaker, or, in other words, a source's expertise. To have the maximum level of credibility, a source would need to be perceived as having all three characteristics: good character, goodwill, and intelligence.

Aristotle identified these dimensions from observing human behavior and watching what it took for speakers to be perceived as credible by audiences at that time. These are also dimensions that Aristotle thought *should* be considered when evaluating speakers, and he taught those principles to his students. These three dimensions were assumed to be true for many years. Then in the 1960s, scholars began to question Aristotle's approach and used modern research and statistical methods to re-examine credibility. A statistical technique known as factor analysis was developed that was designed to identify the dimensions of a construct. Factor analysis is a statistical method that allows researchers to identify which items of a scale measure the same thing. Items that measure the same thing are called *factors* or *dimensions*. Wanting to develop a better understanding of credibility and to test Aristotle's conceptualization of credibility, researchers used factor analysis in several studies to identify the dimensions of credibility. Many items, usually in the form of semantic differential scales (see Chapter 2), were developed to measure credibility and, with the use of factor analysis, various dimensions of credibility were identified.

Unfortunately, this research that was intended to improve our understanding of credibility resulted in making things more confusing. Several other dimensions of credibility were identified such as dynamism, charisma, and safety. As a result, different scholars measured source credibility differently, making it difficult to compare results and draw conclusions. In 1981, McCroskey and Young published an article that reviewed the previous 30 years of research on source credibility and the methods used. They argued that these "new" dimensions of credibility were perceptions related to credibility, but not actual components of credibility. Additionally, they argued that Aristotle and other scholars had sufficiently conceptualized source credibility as consisting of intelligence, character, and goodwill. McCroskey and Young concluded that when measuring credibility, goodwill collapsed with character; therefore, character and intelligence were the two primary components of source credibility. But the saga continued. In 1999, McCroskey and Teven again examined the construct of source credibility, particularly the goodwill dimension. They drew on research on teacher caring and argued that the concept of goodwill was represented in the caring construct. McCroskey and Teven conducted a study with 783 participants who reported on 1 of 10 sources. Using factor analysis, they were able to successfully identify goodwill, in the form of caring, along with intelligence and character, as dimensions of credibility, confirming Aristotle's original definition of credibility from 2,500 years ago. Over the years the term "intelligence" has changed to "expertise" to better reflect the idea that it is what a source knows rather than his or her ability to know. Similarly, the term "character" has changed to "trustworthiness" to better reflect perceptions of honesty and integrity. The scale developed by McCroskey and Teven to measure expertise, trustworthiness, and caring is shown in Figure 4.1 and is the most contemporary measure of credibility.

The debate about how to define and measure source credibility may or may not have concluded. However, because of this long debate about how to measure source credibility, credibility research has used many different measures. The problem is that, because different measures were used, drawing conclusions about the role of source credibility in persuasion is a bit like trying to conclude the color of apples when yellow, red, and green varieties are included in the sample. In the following paragraphs we review research on source credibility. Keep in mind that much of the research on source credibility was conducted before any kind of consensus was reached on how credibility should be measured.

From Communication Monographs, Vol. 66, 1999, by McCroskey and Teven.

Expertise

Intelligent	1	2	3	4	5	6	7	Unintelligent
Untrained	1	2	3	4	5	6	7	Trained
Inexpert	1	2	3	4	5	6	7	Expert
Informed	1	2	3	4	5	6	7	Uninformed
Incompetent	1	2	3	4	5	6	7	Competent
Bright	1	2	3	4	5	6	7	Stupid

Goodwill

Cares about me	1	2	3	4	5	6	7	Doesn't care about me
Has my interests at heart	1	2	3	4	5	6	7	Doesn't have my interests at heart
Self-centered	1	2	3	4	5	6	7	Not self-centered
Concerned with me	1	2	3	4	5	6	7	Unconcerned with me
Insensitive	1	2	3	4	5	6	7	Sensitive
Not understanding	1	2	3	4	5	6	7	Understanding

Trustworthiness

Honest	1	2	3	4	5	6	7	Dishonest
Untrustworthy	1	2	3	4	5	6	7	Trustworthy
Honorable	1	2	3	4	5	6	7	Dishonorable
Moral	1	2	3	4	5	6	7	Immoral
Unethical	1	2	3	4	5	6	7	Ethical
Phony	1	2	3	4	5	6	7	Genuine

FIGURE 4.1 McCroskey and Teven's (1999) measure of source credibility.

CREDIBILITY AND PERSUASION

So far, we have discussed how to define source credibility and its dimensions. We have not yet discussed the extent that credibility is useful when persuading someone. Your common sense probably tells you it is important. However, if you were to look at all the research conducted on credibility in persuasion, you would find that sometimes researchers concluded that credibility was very important and useful in changing receivers' attitudes. In other research, you would find that credibility seemed irrelevant to persuasive success. Finally, you would find in some research that credibility was actually a liability and inhibited persuasive success. Why the variation in results? In a nutshell, credibility functions differently in different situations. Fortunately, research and theory help us explain and understand the complexities of credibility. The elaboration likelihood model will help us better understand the inconsistent research.

PERSISTENCE OF SOURCE CREDIBILITY EFFECTS OVER TIME

In early credibility research, Hovland and his colleagues (Hovland, Lumsdaine, & Sheffield, 1949) observed a strange phenomenon. They conducted experiments comparing the persuasiveness of sources with high and low credibility. Their experiment involved exposing an audience to either a high or a low credibility source and measuring attitude immediately after hearing the message. They measured attitude again about a week later. Hovland and his colleagues found that the high credibility source was more persuasive initially—no surprise here. But when they measured attitude a week later, the receivers who had heard the low credibility source had a more positive attitude than the first time! They labeled this phenomenon the **sleeper effect**.

The sleeper effect describes the situation where receivers exposed to a low credibility source develop more positive attitudes over time, but when exposed to a high credibility source, receivers' attitudes become less positive over time. After enough time passes, the attitudes of those who heard the message from a high credibility source and those who heard the low credibility source tend to be the same. The sleeper effect is illustrated in Figure 4.2.

Kelman and Hovland (1953) tested the sleeper effect with a message advocating lenient treatment for juvenile delinquents. The high credibility source was a judge with experience with juvenile delinquents and who had authored several books on the topic. The low credibility source was a man off the street who appeared to be rather obnoxious and who had gotten into multiple problems as a youth. The topic was pretested with participants, and those in both the high credibility and low credibility conditions had similar views on the subject before being exposed to the message. When the participants were tested right after the message was presented, those exposed to the message from the highly credible source reported significantly more agreement with the message than did those exposed to the message from the low credibility source. However, when these same participants were asked their opinion about the topic (more lenient treatment for juvenile delinquents) 3 weeks later, both sets of attitudes had changed. Those who had been exposed to the message from the highly credible source reported attitudes that were less positive than right after the message. Those who had been exposed to the low

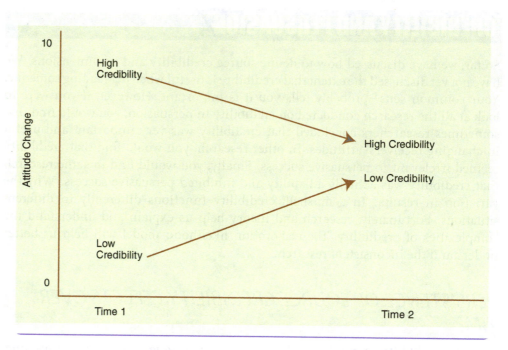

FIGURE 4.2 Sleeper effect. The impact of source credibility on attitude change wears off over time.

credibility source reported more positive attitudes than right after hearing the message 3 weeks earlier. This sounded like crazy talk! You know that researchers wanted to know more about this phenomenon.

The Discounting Model

The discounting model explains the sleeper effect phenomenon. It states that the effects of source credibility are temporary. The **discounting model** assumes that initial attitude change is a result of both source credibility and message content; however, permanent attitude change is based on message content (Allen & Stiff, 1998). After 3 weeks, the receivers remembered the content of the message, but not the source of the message. In other words, the effect of source credibility wore off after 3 weeks, and just the effects of the message content remained. To test this hypothesis, in another study, receivers were reminded of the credibility of the message source, and the sleeper effect was offset. The high credibility source generated a greater attitude change than the low credibility source with this reminder, but the attitude still decayed somewhat over time. Many of us remember information but often fail to remember where we read it or heard it. That lack of connection between source and message means that the effects of source credibility are temporary. However, a persuader can maintain the influence of source credibility by continuing to remind the target audience of the source supporting the message.

INTRODUCTIONS AND CREDIBILITY

Perceptions of credibility judgments are affected by the information the audience has about the source, such as the source's **education** and **experience**. When the introduction of a speaker includes information about the source's education and experience, perceptions of credibility are often increased. For example, in an early study of credibility conducted during the communist scare of the 1950s, Hovland and Weiss (1951) devised a message about atomic-powered submarines. The high credibility condition attributed the message to Robert Oppenheimer, a PhD physicist who directed the Manhattan Project, which led to the creation of the U.S. atomic bomb. In the low credibility condition, the message was attributed to *Pravda,* a Russian propaganda publication. As expected, Oppenheimer turned out to be a significantly more credible source, and the message attributed to him resulted in greater attitude change. Multiple studies have manipulated credibility using similar types of methods. A common manipulation is to describe one source as a university professor with years of experience in a topic area (high credibility manipulation) and describe the other source as a high school sophomore (low credibility manipulation) (Hewgill & Miller, 1965). ⌐Receivers use credentials to make judgments about a source's credibility. Some professions are generally trusted more than others. Nurses have been the most trusted profession for several years (see Table 4.2) and members of Congress and car salesmen are perceived as the least honest (Reinhart, 2020).⌐ These studies indicate that sharing relevant information about the source's credentials is a quite effective means of enhancing perceptions of credibility.

When posting information online in the form of tweets, comments on websites, and consumer reviews of products, you have the option of providing information about yourself or choosing a name that allows you to remain more anonymous. Although we know from prior research that how you introduce yourself matters, the question is what kind of credibility do we perceive for those who post with less personal information? Xie, Miao, Kuo, and Lee (2011) researched this question in the context of consumer online reviews of hotels. They found that those who included personal identifying information (their real name, where they lived, dates for the hotel stay) were rated as more credible than those who did not include this information (such as traveler@hotmail.com). In addition, the reviews with personally identifying information led to greater influence on behavioral intentions about staying at the hotel being reviewed than those who failed to include the aspects of source introductions. ⌐Experience includes all kinds of things and not just job experience. It may include personal experiences and lifestyle. For example, social media influencers often share information about their lifestyle as a means to promoting the products they are paid to sponsor. Thus, source information and experience matter across contexts and media platforms.⌐

Google "Most trusted professions" to see the latest reports of the most and least trusted professions

In most contexts, providing a source's education and experience to the receiver enhances perceptions of credibility to the extent that education and experience are positive qualities. What if the source doesn't have much education and lacks experience? It would be unethical to lie or mislead the audience about the source's background. So what do you do? As it turns out, the **timing** of the introduction *of the source* determines how much impact it has. If the audience is given the source's credentials first, that information has maximum impact on source credibility. If the source's credentials are given after the message is presented, the information has minimum impact on source credibility. When the credentials are introduced at the end of the message, high and low credibility sources are about equally effective. In this situation, the persuasive success or failure of the message is a result of other factors (Husek, 1965; O'Keefe, 1987). Thus, it is best for high credibility sources to establish their credentials at the beginning of the message, or certainly no later than the middle of the message. On the other hand, sources with low credibility are better off introducing their credentials at the end of the message and relying on message factors to persuade the audience. Why do you suppose this occurs?

When credibility manipulations are introduced *after* the message has been processed, the message has already been processed and information about the source will have little impact. Regardless of what factors of the message or situation affected the processing of the message, that process has already occurred before the credibility is introduced. If the receiver is paying attention and processing the message, the receiver is focusing on the content of the message without regard to the credibility of the source. Additionally, we tend to give strangers the benefit of the doubt and assume anyone speaking on a particular topic is at least moderately credible. It is probably a cultural characteristic that we have at least some trust in strangers, so this phenomenon may not be observed in other cultures. This assumption of at least moderate credibility enhances the persuasive effectiveness of low credibility sources when that lack of credibility is not introduced until the message has already been processed.

MESSAGE VARIABLES

Message variables refer to the content and structure of a message. Perceptions of credibility are based on characteristics and behaviors of the source, but what the source says (the message) also impacts perceptions of credibility. We will discuss message variables in greater detail in Chapter 5. At this point, however, we discuss how message variables interact with source credibility. A central variable is **message discrepancy**, which will be discussed again in an upcoming chapter. Message discrepancy refers to the difference between the advocated message and the receiver's position on a topic. For example, a source may advocate for making all abortions illegal, and the receiver's position might be that abortion should be legal during the first trimester—there is a discrepancy between the message and the receiver's position. You might think that highly credible sources could get away with more message discrepancy and this is true at least some of the time (Sternthal, Philips, & Dholakia, 1978). However, when a message was more discrepant and counter-attitudinal for receivers (a message that went against their attitude), highly credible sources were more persuasive than less credible sources. The opposite was true for pro-attitudinal messages (messages that support the audience's attitude) that were low in discrepancy. In this case, low credibility sources were more persuasive than high credibility sources (Chabet, Filiatraut, Laroche, & Watson, 1988; Harmon & Coney, 1982).

Humor is another variable affecting evaluations of source credibility, depending on how effectively it is employed in the message. Tamborini and Zillmann (1981) evaluated instructor use of humor in the college classroom. As with other researchers (e.g., Houser, Cowan, & West, 2007), they found that limited and appropriate use of humor could enhance receiver liking and trustworthiness of a source but not the expertise dimension. However, the type of humor must also be considered. Hackman (1988) found that the use of self-disparaging and other disparaging humor reduced perceptions of credibility. Wrench, Brogan, Wrench, and McKean (2007) found that religious leaders were perceived as more credible when they were also perceived to use humor. In another study, however, Wrench, Millhouse, and Sharp (2007) found that flight attendants who used humor in their preflight safety briefing were perceived as less credible. Humor is a complex variable that can be interpreted very differently by different people.

Humor can generate positive perceptions, but it can also very easily offend some members of the audience. In general, humor should be used with great caution in persuasive situations.

Not only can the content of the message affect perceptions of source credibility, but the **delivery of the message** can influence source credibility judgments as well. Speakers who are quite fluent in their speaking style are perceived as having more expertise than those who are less fluent (Burgoon, Birk, & Pfau, 1990; Engstrom, 1994). The rationale is that we assume fluency and knowledge go together. Objectively we know this is not necessarily true, but we still perceive speakers who are fluent and polished as more credible. Speakers who pause frequently, use fillers like "uh," or have more mistakes in delivery are assumed to be less knowledgeable, and therefore as less credible. Thus, improving your speaking patterns and eliminating unnecessary movements (e.g., shifting weight; fiddling with rings, watches, keys) can enhance perceptions of your credibility. This same principle applies in written messages as well. If your emails to colleagues and clients (and your professors) are poorly written and full of errors, your credibility will be reduced.

Some scholars have examined the message with regard to the source's best interest. Some evidence suggests that message incongruity with the source's interest interacts with source credibility. Messages that appear to go against the source's best interests tend to enhance the source's credibility overall and tend to win greater persuasive success (Walster, Aronson, & Abrahams, 1966). If we heard the head of the National Rifle Association arguing in favor of gun control or the leader of a labor union arguing in favor of reduced labor benefits, we would tend to believe them because these ideas are not what we would expect them to say to protect their own interests. This is particularly true for low credibility sources. If you have high credibility to begin with, using message incongruity doesn't help you. You can only be so credible. We tend to be more skeptical if people advocate for themselves, but we expect it to happen that way. When sources advocate against their own interests, we tend to believe them.

CHANNEL FACTORS

Not only do the characteristics of the message impact perceptions of source credibility, but the channel used to deliver the message does as well. Here we look at the credibility of the delivery channel. We know receivers trust some messages more than others due to the nature of the source and channel of delivery. What channels of information people trust have changed dramatically in recent years. Social media and Internet sources have surged in credibility, while traditional media have declined. However, the trust we have in a channel depends on the type of information we are seeking. As shown in Figure 4.3, when it comes to commercial brands, Americans trust Facebook as much as they do newspapers. Age also makes a difference. It comes as no surprise that younger Americans trust social media more than do older Americans. Additionally, people differ across the globe. Traditional media is trusted at differing levels around the world, and that trust changes over time.

Researchers have started examining the role of credibility in social media channels. For example, interest in credibility's role for tweets has increased as the popularity of Twitter has grown. Phelps (2012) reported the results of Microsoft research into

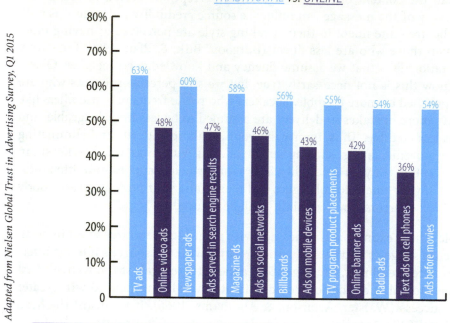

Adapted from Nielsen Global Trust in Advertising Survey, Q1 2015

PERCENT OF GLOBAL RESPONDENTS WHO COMPLETELY OR SOMEWHAT TRUST ADVERTISING FORMAT
TRADITIONAL vs. *ONLINE*

FIGURE 4.3

Twitter that identified factors associated with both low and high credibility tweets. High credibility was generally associated with sources that had expertise in the topic (as demonstrated on the Twitter bio), were influential (as assessed by a larger number of followers, retweets, and mentions by others), had a history on the topic (such as tweeting about the topic often, having posted material about the topic online outside of Twitter, or being in a location relevant to the topic of the tweet), and who had a reputation (being someone the receiver follows or has heard of). In addition, users who used a photo of themselves rather than a cartoon character or other avatar were considered more credible. The topic area of the tweets also made a difference. Those who posted about science were viewed as more credible than those who posted about politics or entertainment. Those whose Twitter names were more related to the topic were the most credible. For example, Phelps noted that "@AllPolitics" is more specific and thus more credible than "@Alex_Brown," which in turn is more specific and thus more credible than "@tenacious27." Johnson (2011) looked at how instructor tweets affected faculty credibility with students. Their study exposed students to social tweets, scholarly tweets, or a combination of social and scholarly tweets from a professor. Their results indicated that students who received the social tweets rated the professor higher on credibility, which suggests that social tweets may have increased perceptions of professor trust or caring. These studies suggest that in social media, like more traditional contexts, receivers develop perceptions of source expertise, trustworthiness, and caring based on the characteristics of the source, message, channel, and context.

Twitter is just one form of social media, and those in the influence business (e.g., public relations, advertising, strategic communication) have a great deal at stake in figuring out how credibility works in social media. A major public relations firm, Burson Marsteller, has noted that those who carry influence online carry a great deal of weight. "Representing 8% of the internet population (about 9 million users), this group influences more people on more topics than other online users. And, they are eight times more effective at communicating their views than Roper's traditional 'influentials'" (Kirwan, 2012, p. 6). It is important to consider the impact the channel has on a source's credibility and influence with the targeted receivers.

OTHER SOURCE FACTORS

Source credibility has received the bulk of research attention and is certainly an important factor in the persuasion process. But other source factors also affect the persuasion process. Persuaders such as advertisers make strategic choices about whom the source of the message should be in order to maximize the persuasive impact of their messages. These factors have received less research attention than credibility has, but they also contribute to our understanding of the persuasion process.

POWER

Power is the ability to get others to do what you want and is a broad-based concept that includes many ways of communicating. Sources who are perceived as powerful are influential, and receivers will often accept their messages because of the source's power. Power and credibility are sometimes linked, but not always. We may completely distrust someone in power, or perceive them as uncaring and incompetent. A commonly used description of power is the one provided by French and Raven (1959). They described five power bases: reward, coercive, legitimate, referent, and expert. **Reward power** is one's ability to use rewards to influence another's behavior. If your professor offers you 10 bonus points for attending a lecture, he or she is using reward power. **Coercive power** is the ability to use punishment to influence a person's behavior. If your professor said you would lose 10 points if you did not attend the lecture, it would be an example of coercive power. **Legitimate power** is the power one has because of his or her title or position. When your mom says, "Do it because *I* said so," she is using her legitimate power as your parent. This power base exists primarily because we believe that person has a right to tell us what to do. Referent and expert power are different from the three previous power bases. **Referent power** is based on the relationship between two persons. When people have referent power, others are willing to do what is asked of them because they like and/or respect that person. When your boss asks you to do something and you do it because you respect your boss, you are primarily influenced by referent power. Referent power is more implicit than reward and coercive power. Rarely do people with referent power actually refer verbally to the relationship when making requests. The power derived from the relationship is communicated implicitly. The last power base is **expert power**, which is based on how knowledgeable a person is. When our technology guru neighbor tells us to buy a specific router to solve our wireless problem, we do exactly as told because of the expertise we perceive our neighbor as having. Additionally, these power bases apply to not just our perceptions of individuals but also to our perceptions of groups, and organizations.

As you might guess, the power bases are not equal. Having power increases your ability to influence people, particularly short-term behavior. Coercive and reward power are generally effective at getting short-term behavior change, but not so good for changing attitudes and beliefs. For example, imagine a dishwashing dispute between two roommates, Fred and Barney. Barney wants Fred to wash his dishes after he eats and not just leave them in the sink. Barney might wield power by offering to drive Fred to class (reward power), and Fred may agree. However, this is not likely to change Fred's attitude about washing dishes or his beliefs about the importance of taking care of one's dirty dishes. Coercive and reward power are quite useful in gaining compliance from receivers. Referent and expert power are different matters. These two bases of power are developed over time as a result of how we conduct ourselves and are much more useful for influencing attitudes and beliefs. People are more apt to pay attention to sources (whether the source is an individual, group, or organization) when they are perceived as having referent or expert power, and these two power bases are closely linked to credibility. Referent power is linked to perceptions of caring and trustworthiness. Expert power is clearly linked to expertise. Legitimate power is a bit different than the other bases of power. Legitimate power has to do with your position and title. When we perceive someone as having legitimate power, we believe they have the authority or right to tell us what to do. Legitimate power is the reason people often "obey" authority figures such as police officers and teachers. The reasons people obey authority figures are not well understood; however, there is a great deal of evidence that people obey authority figures quite consistently.

AUTHORITY AND OBEDIENCE

On YouTube search for Milgram Obedience Study to see how the study was conducted.

In 1963, Stanley Milgram published a study on obedience that shocked the world. You may be familiar with this study. The procedure involved recruiting research participants to take part in an experiment on the effects of punishment on learning. On entering the experimental setting, the participant was told he (all participants were male) would play the role of teacher, and a confederate was introduced as another research participant who would play the role of learner. Electrodes were attached to the arm of the confederate, and the research participant was instructed to test the confederate on recalling word pairs. For each wrong answer, the participant was to administer a shock, with the first being 15 volts. With each wrong answer, the shock was increased by 15 volts, with 450 volts being the maximum. The confederate did not actually receive any shock but gave progressively more intense responses with increased voltage, such as progressively louder grunts, followed by asking for it to stop, screaming in pain, and claiming that his heart was bad, and finally being unresponsive. A researcher dressed in a white coat (authority figure) was present, and if the research participant expressed concern or a desire to stop, would urge the participant to continue. Milgram (1963) reported that 65% continued administering shocks until 450 volts was reached.

Milgram's (1963, 1974) research drew a great deal of attention for two reasons. First, because most people found it very unsettling to think that such a large proportion of normal people would obey the authority figure and administer electrical shocks. We like to think that only criminals or *bad people* would do such a thing. Second, the ethics of the research procedures were seriously questioned. Milgram put research participants into a difficult and stressful situation and reported that participants showed definite signs of stress, with three participants having seizures. As a result of the ethical concerns, this line of research was not continued. However, Milgram's study was replicated by Shanab and Yahya (1977) in Jordan with children. Shanab and Yahya replicated Milgram's procedures exactly with 192 children ranging from 6 to 16 years old. Shanab and Yahya reported that 73% of participants delivered shock until the last step, which is similar to that reported by Milgram (1963). Shanab and Yahya also reported no sex or age differences, meaning that sex and age did not influence whether the participants obeyed or not.

You may be thinking that a lot has changed since the 1960s, and even 1977, and that people are not as obedient now as they were back then. In response to such comments, Burger (2009) partially replicated Milgram's (1963) study. Burger created an experiment exactly like Milgram's except that it ended at 150 volts when the confederate yelled to stop and that his heart was bad. After observing whether the research participant was going to continue administering shocks or not, Burger stopped the experiment. Burger conducted extensive screening to ensure that all research participants were mentally healthy and free from previous experiences that might result in negative experiences for the participants as well as provided extensive debriefing with a clinical psychologist. Burger (2009) reported that 70% continued after the 150-volts point, whereas Milgram reported 83% continued beyond this point. Although this difference looks substantial, it was not a significant difference (was probably a result of chance rather than a real difference). Burger also reported no differences in obedience between male and female participants. ⌈He concluded that people in 2009 were just as likely to obey an authority figure as they were in 1963, and it is highly unlikely that anything has changed in the intervening years.⌋

Sources who have legitimate power are perceived as having authority and receivers are more likely to obey them, even when it goes against their better judgment. Sources with authority need to consider their legitimate power and understand the ethical implications of their power.

NORMATIVE INFLUENCE AND SIMILARITY

Are you more likely to be influenced by someone who is similar to you or different from you? Are you willing to go against the group? Do you look to those you admire for direction? We are referring to a set of related factors that include normative influence, identification, and similarity. Deutsch and Gerard (1955) introduced the **normative influence** concept when studying group influences and group dynamics theory. Deutsch and Gerard found that normative influences from group membership affected receivers' judgments, but only when the group was present and/or knew about the receivers' response. You might observe the impact of normative influence the next time you cross the street against the light. When a crowd is waiting to cross and one person starts off across the street against the light, do you and others follow? Lefkowitz, Blake, and Mouton (1955) used this situation to test normative influence. The norm is to wait until the light reads *walk* to cross the street (more so in cities than on college campuses). It is non-normative behavior to walk against the light (not to mention dangerous). Lefkowitz et al. found that more people crossed against the light when well-dressed confederates (a confederate is someone working with the researcher) crossed than when poorly dressed confederates crossed against the light. Although not involving a traditional persuasive message, this study did illustrate the power of normative influence to direct behavior in a natural setting. Similar to normative influence, Kelman (1961) described **identification** as a form of influence.

When we identify with an individual, we find that person more socially attractive and we are more willing to allow that person to influence us. We often identify with those in roles we value, such as the president of the United States, the CEO of a valued organization, an influencer, or a celebrity. With normative influence and identification, we are influenced because we associate ourselves with a group or an individual we value.

The perceived **similarity** of the source to the receiver is a source factor that enhances persuasion in some instances. We tend to think that we are more likely to be influenced by those similar to us, but the research on this idea is split. At times, similarity on the part of the speaker can lead to greater persuasive success (Brock, 1965), but, at other times, similarity reduces persuasive effectiveness (Infante, 1978) or seems to have no effect (Klock & Traylor, 1983). For similarity to enhance persuasion, the similarity must be relevant to the persuasive goal. For instance, Brock (1965) conducted an experiment with salespeople selling paint. Salespeople indicated they were either similar to the customer in terms of the type of painting they had done recently, or they were dissimilar in terms of the type of painting they had done recently. Brock found that similar sources were more successful at influencing the type of paint purchased by customers. If the similarity is irrelevant to the persuasive goal, such as noting a similarity in painting experience when trying to persuade someone to buy insurance, the use of similarity is generally ineffective.

Similarity also appears to influence our willingness to model a source's behavior. Anderson and McMillion (1995) illustrated this in a study of African American women's intentions to perform breast self-examination. The study used two educational videos on breast self-examination (BSE). One video was targeted at a broad audience and used a white male physician and women of various races modeling BSE. The other video was targeted at African American women and used an African American female physician and African American women modeling BSE. A third video was used with a control group. Anderson and McMillion found that the participants who viewed the similar videotape (African American physician and African American models) had greater intentions to perform BSE than those who viewed the diverse video or the control video. Participants also rated the African American female physician as more credible with regard to BSE than the white male physician. When a source is similar to the receiver in some relevant way, persuasion is often enhanced. Additionally, similar sources are often viewed as more credible. Advertisers and public health campaigns often choose spokespersons and models that look or sound similar to the target audience to help increase the credibility of their message. Similarity is another source factor that affects the persuasion process and is useful when you are involved in influence attempts.

PHYSICAL ATTRACTIVENESS

The **physical attractiveness** of the source is another source factor that plays a role in the persuasion process. Are physically attractive people more or less persuasive than unattractive people? If you spend a few minutes looking at the advertisements in any magazine, you'll conclude that only attractive models are used. Certainly, we prefer looking at attractive people more than unattractive people, particularly when they are strangers. But does physical attractiveness make you a more effective persuader? The answer, as with so many persuasion variables, is sometimes. Evidence suggests that physically attractive people are more effective persuaders in many situations (Chaiken, 1986). Widgery and Ruch (1981) had research participants read a persuasive message with a picture of the source attached to the message. Half of the participants read a message from an attractive source, the other half from an unattractive source. As expected, participants who read the message from the attractive source were more persuaded than those who read the same message from the unattractive source. Why would an attractive source be more effective than an unattractive source? Physical attractiveness may serve as a simple cue (Chaiken, 1986). By *cue* we mean a simple rule or shortcut for assessing a message. We tend to associate attractive things with good things. So the attractive source attached to the message served as a simple reason to believe the message. Source attractiveness is not so important when receivers devote a lot of attention and effort to the message. Additionally, physically attractive people are often perceived as more credible (Widgery, 1974). Therefore, attractiveness often contributes to perceptions of credibility. By itself, physical attractiveness probably has a small impact on persuasion, but because it contributes to perceptions of credibility, it becomes more important. Sources that are not physically attractive need to be aware of this fact and emphasize other qualities such as education, experience, trustworthiness, and caring to offset any negative effects of their physical appearance.

What are additional reasons for using physically attractive sources in persuasion? In order to influence someone, you have to have their attention. Physically attractive people tend to draw attention. A physically attractive model will draw attention to an advertisement. Getting the audience's attention is often half the battle in our advertisement-saturated environment. Besides drawing attention, we generally respond positively to attractive things, be they people, animals, art, or other objects. Pretty things elicit positive feelings and affect. Recall our discussion of classical conditioning in Chapter 2. By pairing a product, an organization, or an idea with a physically attractive source, the advertisement may result in the receiver being conditioned to have a positive response to the product, organization, or idea. ⌜Take a look at the most popular influencers on social media. How attractive are they? How are influencers using their attractiveness? To gain attention? As a simple cue? To enhance credibility?⌟

LIKEABILITY

A final source factor is the **likeability** of the source. Liking of the source has been related to trustworthiness in some research studies, and it makes sense that we would trust those we like more. Generally, sources we like are more effective than those we dislike, and generally liking is related to the trustworthy dimension of credibility. However, research has indicated that when liking and credibility come into conflict (e.g., when we like a source who has low credibility), then credibility outweighs liking. Wachtler and Counselman (1981) studied the size of damage awards in a personal injury lawsuit. Sources were portrayed as warm and friendly or cold and stingy. Participants were given messages attributed to one of the two sources who advocated a large award or a small award. Results indicated that participants liked the warm and friendly source more, but the cold and stingy source was rated as more credible and resulted in higher awards when advocating a large award. Advocating against one's best interest led to greater credibility attributions, and those outweighed the dislike for the source. Thus, liking the source can be a factor; however, it is not as important as source credibility and other persuasion factors.

⌜The source of a persuasive message is an important element in the persuasion process. Credibility is essential for persuasion. If we lack credibility, our audience does not believe our message—if they even pay attention to us. We discussed several source factors and they all affect credibility. Next, we will examine the other key components of the persuasion process including the message, channel, and receiver. In real-world persuasion these components all occur simultaneously, but for the sake of clarity, we will discuss each component separately. As we work through these components, keep in mind that, in practice, we have to bring them all together to be effective persuaders.

SUMMARY

- The two kinds of source credibility are initial credibility and derived credibility.
- Aristotle studied persuasion more than 2,500 years ago and focused on ethos, logos, and pathos. Ethos is the study of a source's credibility.
- Aristotle argued that good character, goodwill, and intelligence are the dimensions of source credibility.
- McCroskey and Teven (1999) developed a measure of credibility that included expertise, trustworthiness, and caring.
- The discounting model explains the sleeper effect phenomenon.
- The discounting model states that receivers forget the source of the message, but remember the content.
- Including a source's education and experience in an introduction enhances perceptions of credibility.
- The timing of the source introduction determines whether credibility will play a role in processing the message.
- Message variables that interact with source credibility include message discrepancy, use of humor, and delivery of the message.
- The channel of message delivery can affect source credibility and how credibility is established.
- Sources with greater levels of power are more influential. Referent and expert power are the most effective power bases.
- Milgram's (1963) study of obedience revealed the power of authority.
- Sources that are perceived as similar are sometimes more effective, particularly when the similarity is relevant to the persuasive goal.
- Attractive sources are sometimes more effective, because they may gain attention and be associated with good things through classical conditioning.
- The likeability of a source is important, with more likable sources being more generally effective than disliked sources.

KEY TERMS

Credibility—a perception of believability.

Derived credibility—the nature of the credibility of a source during and after the presentation of a particular message.

Discounting model—assumes that initial attitude change is a result of both source credibility and message content; however, permanent attitude change is based on message content.

Ethos—the nature of the source's credibility and composed of three dimensions: good character, goodwill, and intelligence.

Expertise—a primary dimension of credibility that refers to the perceived knowledge and intelligence of the source.

Identification—occurs when a target accepts influence from an agent because he or she wants to be associated with the agent.

Initial credibility—the credibility of a source prior to the presentation of a persuasive message.

Goodwill—a dimension of credibility that refers to the perceived caring on the part of the source.

Logos—the nature of the arguments and structure of the message.

Message discrepancy—the difference between the position being advocated by a message and the preferred position of the receiver.

Message incongruity—when a message goes against (is not congruent with) the source's interests or needs.

Normative influence—a factor that can influence perceptions of credibility; refers to the influence from group norms; also referred to as identification and similarity.

Pathos—the emotional appeals of the message.

Power—the ability to get others to do what you want.

Power bases—include five types of power: reward, coercive, legitimate, referent, and expert.

Sleeper effect—suggests that high credibility sources have a more persuasive impact immediately following the message than do low credibility sources but that, over time, the effects of credibility wear off.

Trustworthiness—a primary dimension of credibility that refers to receivers' perceptions of the source's honesty.

QUESTIONS FOR REVIEW

Respond to the following questions **without** reviewing the text or your notes. These questions are provided to help you practice retrieving information and reflect on your reading.

  A. List several source factors that influence persuasion.

  B. Did you agree or disagree with anything you read? Explain.

  C. What did you learn that was new to you?

  D. What concepts, if any, were confusing to you?

Respond to the following questions. You may reference your text or notes to help you.

  1. Derived credibility can increase or decrease as a result of a message. Provide an example of when this occurred for you.

  2. According to McCroskey and Teven, what are the three components of source credibility? How do these compare to the components identified by Aristotle?

  3. What message variables impact perceptions of credibility? When are low or high credibility sources more persuasive?

  4. Identify five power bases and provide an example of each one from your own life.

5. How do source factors including similarity, physical attractiveness, and like-ability influence persuasion?

QUESTIONS FOR DISCUSSION

1. Before reading this chapter, you listed several credible people. Discuss how your examples exhibit one, two, or all three components of credibility. Are any other source factors apparent in your examples?

2. In your group, discuss source credibility as an important factor in your final presentations. What information could you provide to establish your credibility as a speaker on the topic you have chosen? What else could you do to strengthen your ethos appeal? Keep track of ideas for each group member for future reference.

3. What channels of information do you trust? Why? The channels you trust likely differ from channels trusted by your parents. What implications does this difference have for persuasion?

4. Understanding authority as a source factor that influences persuasion can provide insight into a number of national scandals where authority figures were obeyed even though their actions were unethical or illegal. What examples can you provide? Can you justify obedience in these situations? Why or why not?

5. Discuss the ethical questions provided at the end of the first chapter. What ethical considerations are relevant to the information in this chapter about source credibility and other source factors?

- Are there guidelines (e.g., don't lie) that would be appropriate for every situation, or are ethics relative?

- Do the ends (e.g., a good outcome) justify any means?

- Is deceiving the receiver ever appropriate?

- Should the source of the message bear primary responsibility for ethics, or should the receiver share that responsibility (e.g., buyer beware)?

REFERENCES

Allen, M., & Stiff, J. B. (1998). An analysis of the sleeper effect. In M. Allen & R. W. Preiss (Eds.), *Persuasion: Advances through meta-analysis* (pp. 175–188). Cresskill, NJ: Hampton Press.

Anderson, R. B., & McMillion, P. Y. (1995). Effects of similar and diversified modeling on African American women's efficacy expectations and intentions to perform breast self-examinations. *Health Communication, 7*, 327–343.

Brock, T. C. (1965). Communicator-recipient similarity and decision change. *Journal of Personality and Social Psychology, 1*, 650–654.

Burger, J. M. (2009). Replicating Milgram: Would people still obey today? *American Psychologist, 64*, 1–11.

Burgoon, J. K., Birk, T., & Pfau, M. (1990). Nonverbal behaviors, persuasion, and credibility. *Human Communication Research, 17*, 140–169.

Chabet, J. C., Filiatraut, P., Laroche, M., & Watson, C. (1988). Compensatory effects of cognitive characteristics of the source, the message, and the receiver upon attitude change. *Journal of Psychology, 122*, 609–621.

Chaiken, S. (1986). Physical appearance and social influence. In C. P. Herman, M. P. Zanna, & E. T. Higgins (Eds.), *Physical appearance, stigma, and social behavior: The Ontario Symposium, Vol. 3* (pp. 143–177). Hilsdale, NJ: Lawrence Erlbaum.

Deutsch, M., & Gerard, H. (1955). A study of normative and informative influences upon individual judgment. *Journal of Abnormal and Social Psychology, 54,* 629–636.

Engstrom, E. (1994). Effects of nonfluencies on speaker's credibility in newscast settings. *Perceptual and Motor Skills, 78,* 739–743.

French, J. R. P., & Raven, B. (1959). The bases of social power. In D. Cartwright (Ed.), *Studies in social power* (pp. 150–167). Ann Arbor, MI: Institute for Social Research.

Hackman, M. Z. (1988). Audience reactions to the use of direct and personal disparaging humor in informative public address. *Communication Research Reports, 5,* 126–130.

Harmon, R. R., & Coney, K. A. (1982). The persuasive effects of source credibility in buy and lease situations. *Journal of Marketing Research, 19,* 255–260.

Hewgill, M. A., & Miller, G. R. (1965). Source credibility and response to fear-arousing communications. *Speech Monographs, 32,* 95–101.

Houser, M. L., Cowan, R. L., & West, D. A. (2007). Investigating a new education frontier: Instructor communication behavior in CD-ROM texts—do traditionally positive behaviors translate into this new environment? *Communication Quarterly, 55,* 19–38.

Hovland, C. I., Lumsdaine, A., & Sheffield, F. (1949). *Experiments in mass communication.* Princeton, NJ: Princeton University Press.

Hovland, C., & Weiss, W. (1951). The influence of source credibility on communication effectiveness. *Public Opinion Quarterly, 15,* 635–650.

Husek, T. R. (1965). Persuasive impacts of early, late, or no mention of a negative source. *Journal of Personality and Social Psychology, 24,* 125–128.

Infante, D. A. (1978). Similarity between advocate and receiver: The role of instrumentality. *Central States Speech Journal, 29,* 187–193.

Johnson, K. (2011). The effect of *Twitter* posts on students' perceptions of instructor credibility. *Learning, Media and Technology, 36*(1), 21–38.

Kelman, H. C. (1961). Processes of opinion change. *Public Opinion Quarterly, 25,* 57–78.

Kelman, H. C., & Hovland, C. I. (1953). Reinstatement of the communicator in delayed measurement of opinion change. *Journal of Conflict Resolution, 2,* 51–60.

Kirwan, P. (2012). Selected findings: How to measure your social media impact and ROI. Retrieved from http://usefulsocialmedia.com/impact/selected-findings.php.

Klock, S. J., & Traylor, M. B. (1983). Older and younger models in advertising to older consumers: An advertising effectiveness experiment. *Akron Business and Economic Review, 14,* 48–52.

Lefkowitz, M., Blake, R., & Mouton, J. (1955). Status factors in pedestrian violation of traffic signals. *Journal of Abnormal and Social Psychology, 51,* 704–706.

McCroskey, J. C., & Teven, J. J. (1999). Goodwill: A reexamination of the construct and its measurement. *Communication Monographs, 66,* 90–103.

McCrosky, J. C., & Young, T. J. (1981). Ethos and credibility: The construct and its measurement after three decades. *Central States Speech Journal, 32,* 24–34.

Milgram, S. (1963). Behavioral study of obedience. *Journal of Abnormal and Social Psychologist, 67,* 371–378.

Milgram, S. (1974). *Obedience to authority: An experimental view.* New York: Harper & Row.

O'Keefe, D. J. (1987). The persuasive effects of delaying identification of high- and low-credibility communicators: A meta-analytic review. *Central States Speech Journal, 38,* 63–72.

Phelps, A. (2012, March 16). Think fast: Is that tweet true or false? How we use credibility cues to make decisions. Nieman Journalism Lab. Retrieved February 23, 2013, from http://www.niemanlab.org/2012/03/think-fast-is-that-tweet-true-or-false-how-we-use-credibility-cues-to-make-decisions/?utm_source=feedburner&utm_medium=feed&utm_campaign=Feed%3A+NiemanJournalismLab+%28Nieman+Journalism+Lab%29.

Reinhart, R. J. (2020, January 6). *Nurses continue to rate highest in honest, ethics.* Washington, DC: Gallup World Headquarters. https:// news.gallup.com/poll/274673/nurses-continue-rate-highest-honesty-ethics.aspx

Shanab, M. E., & Yahya, K. A. (1977). A behavioral study of obedience in children. *Journal of Personality and Social Psychology, 35,* 530–536.

Sternthal, B., Philips, L. W., & Dholakia, R. (1978). The persuasive effect of source credibility: A situational analysis. *Public Opinion Quarterly, 42,* 285–314.

Tamborini, R., & Zillmann, D. (1981). College students' perceptions of lecturers using humor. *Perceptual and Motor Skills, 52,* 427–432.

Wachtler, J., & Counselman, E. (1981). When increased liking or a communicator decreases opinion change: An attribution analysis of attractiveness. *Journal of Experimental Social Psychology, 17,* 386–395.

Walster, E., Aronson, E., & Abrahams, D. (1966). On increasing the persuasiveness of a low prestige communicator. *Journal of Experimental Social Psychology, 2,* 325–342.

Widgery, R. N. (1974). Sex of receiver and physical attractiveness of source as determinants of initial credibility perception. *Western Speech, 38,* 13–17.

Widgery, R. N., & Ruch, R. S. (1981). Beauty and the Machiavellian. *Communication Quarterly, 29,* 297–301.

Wrench, J., Brogan, S., Wrench, J., & McKean, J. (2007, November). *The relationship between religious followers' functional and relational goals and perceptions of religious leaders' use of instructional communication.* Paper presented at the annual National Communication Association Conference, Chicago.

Wrench, J. S., Millihouse, B., & Sharp, D. (2007). Laughing before takeoff. Humor sex and the pre-flight safety briefing. *Human Communication, 10,* 381–399.

Xie, H., Miao, L., Kuo, P., & Lee, B. (2011). Consumers' responses to ambivalent online hotel reviews: The role of perceived source credibility and pre-decisional disposition. *International Journal of Hospitality Management, 30,* 178–183.

CHAPTER 5

MESSAGE FACTORS

BEFORE YOU READ

Respond to the following questions **before** you read the chapter.

1. How did Aristotle define pathos and logos?

2. Do you prefer to rely on statistics or stories and examples when you try to persuade someone? Are you more likely to be persuaded by statistics or stories and examples? Why?

3. Based on your topic and/or your group's topic, could you use fear or guilt to persuade your audience? Why or why not?

And so, my fellow Americans, ask not what your country can do for you; ask what you can do for your country. My fellow citizens of the world, ask not what America will do for you, but what together we can do for the freedom of man.

—John F. Kennedy, January 20, 1961

LEARNING OBJECTIVES

- DESCRIBE LOGICAL AND EMOTIONAL APPEALS.
- DESCRIBE THE EXTENDED PARALLEL PROCESSES MODEL AND HOW IT IS USED.
- EXPLAIN HOW EVIDENCE AND REASONING ARE USED TO PERSUADE.
- EXPLAIN HOW LANGUAGE CHOICES AFFECT PERSUASION.
- EXPLAIN HOW NONVERBAL MESSAGES AFFECT PERSUASION.

I have a dream that one day this nation will rise up and live out the true meaning of its creed: "We hold these truths to be self-evident; that all men are created equal."

I have a dream that one day on the red hills of Georgia the sons of former slaves and the sons of former slave owners will be able to sit down together at the table of brotherhood.

—Martin Luther King, Jr., August 28, 1963

What is it about these words, these messages that influenced millions of people? These messages were delivered more than 50 years ago and both men have long passed, yet the messages are still repeated and discussed and continue to influence people. In the previous chapter, we laid out the approach to organizing persuasion research by looking at the source, message, receiver, and channel factors. In this chapter, we examine the impact that message factors have on persuasive success. Message factors involve anything dealing with the content and structure of the message itself, such as the strategies or arguments being employed, the language used to frame the message, the evidence employed to support claims, and the structure of the message. Messages can be written or oral and involve both verbal and nonverbal elements. Watching a video of President Kennedy or Reverend King giving these famous speeches reveals that the nonverbal messages each used were as important as the verbal messages. In this chapter, we discuss some of the many choices one must make when constructing a persuasive message.

When constructing a message, you must make many decisions. One major decision is what content to include in the message. Obviously, the content is in part dictated by the topic of your message; however, you can never include everything about a topic, so you must choose what content to include and what to exclude. Other choices you must make are whether to use emotion, such as fear, in your message, to take a logical approach, or to use both.

EMOTIONAL APPEALS

Two general types of persuasive messages are based on logical appeals and emotional appeals. A **logical appeal** is a persuasive message that relies on logic and reasoning to be persuasive; an **emotional appeal** is a persuasive message that relies on emotion to be persuasive. Aristotle identified three means of persuasion—ethos (the nature of the source), pathos (the emotion of the audience), and logos (the nature of the message presented by the source) (McCroskey, 1997). We addressed ethos, or the nature of the source, in Chapter 4 when we discussed source characteristics such as credibility and attractiveness. Pathos and logos correspond with emotional appeals and logical appeals, respectively. Although these three means of persuasion are unique and distinguishable from one another, they often overlap somewhat. In other words, emotional appeals often contain logical elements, and logical appeals often contain emotion.

Both logical and emotional appeals can be effective, but the context or situation should be considered. For instance, Wilson (2003) recorded the logical and rational persuasive strategies students used while working in teams on class projects over a 3-month period. Students rated the effectiveness of these strategies using face-to-face and e-mail messages. Emotional strategies were perceived as slightly more effective than logical strategies in e-mail interactions, whereas logical strategies were perceived as more effective than emotional strategies in face-to-face interactions. Thus, the context of the interaction can play a crucial role in the effectiveness of the type of message used. Wilson did not examine what emotions were targeted in the messages the students constructed, which also needs to be considered. Similarly, advertisers make regular decisions about what images to use in messages. A study by Harris Interactive (2010) found that Americans reported that puppies tugged at their heartstrings most, with images of babies following as a close second. These results were more pronounced for women than men, and all ages seemed to respond to puppies, whereas those in the 35 to 54 age range were more affected by images of babies than other age groups. Thus, context and receiver characteristics must be considered to understand the impact of emotional and logical appeals.

Humans experience many emotions, and nearly all of these emotions could potentially be used in a persuasive message. An example of an emotional appeal is a story or picture of a deprived child being used to persuade an audience to give money to a charity or an organization that helps children in need. Many emotions can be targeted by persuasive messages, but three have been used frequently by persuaders and explored by researchers: humor, guilt, and fear.

HUMOR

Do you have a sense of humor? Do you like funny advertisements? Are you more likely to buy a product from or agree with someone who uses humor? Humor is used frequently in advertising (Cline & Kellaris, 1999) and in political communication such as political cartoons.

There are several definitions of humor and they tend to focus on two different aspects of humor. One approach to humor is appreciation and interpretation. This is a receiver-oriented approach to humor. Some people enjoy humor more than others. A second approach to defining humor emphasizes the source and humor production. This approach is most relevant to our discussion of humor as a message. Booth-Butterfield and Booth-Butterfield (1991) defined humor as "intentional verbal and nonverbal messages and other forms of spontaneous behavior that elicit laughter, chuckling and taken to mean pleasure, delight and/or surprise, in the targeted receiver" (p. 206). An emotional appeal that uses humor contains a message that is designed to elicit laughter, amusement, and a positive response.

Is humor an effective persuasion strategy? Humor is very effective at gaining an audience's attention (Cline & Kellaris, 1999; Weinberger & Gulas, 1992). Getting your audience's attention is an important first step in the persuasion process. With the thousands of messages that bombard us every day, it is a continuing challenge for persuaders to get our attention. Humor is most effective at gaining our attention when it is relevant to the

"We're not hibernating this year. Too much cultural change to keep up with."

FIGURE 5.1 Cartoon

topic (e.g., product, idea) of the influence attempt. If the humor is unrelated to the persuasive topic and goal, it may take attention away from the persuasive message. Research has provided few consistent findings about humor, but the one consistent finding is that humor must be relevant to the persuasive goal to be useful.

Humor generates positive emotions and tends to reduce negative reactions to being persuaded (Slaski, Tamborini, Glazer, & Smith, 2009). In other words, people often resist attempts to change their attitudes, beliefs, and behaviors and may feel annoyed or angry at the source. The positive emotion generated by humor can counter the negative reaction to being persuaded.

The positive emotion generated by the humor can also lead to an enhanced liking for the source (Weinberger & Gulas, 1992), and liked sources are perceived as more credible (Nabi, Moyer-Guse, & Byrne, 2007). But, as mentioned in Chapter 4, humor does not necessarily increase perceptions of credibility, and may even decrease them (Hackman, 1988). Being liked can help you be more persuasive, but being perceived as credible is probably more important. One problem with studying humor is its many forms—cartoons, jokes, puns, riddles, and so on—and genres—sexual, political, self-disparaging, other-disparaging, and so on. Because humor varies so greatly, it is difficult to study. As a result, research findings are often contradictory, making it difficult to make generalizations about the use of humor. Humor elicits positive feelings in receivers, which is why funny people are liked. However, humor can be very offensive too. We have all been offended by humor at one time or another. Humorous put-downs targeted at people we like or at groups we associate with are usually perceived as offensive.

The research on humor can be confusing, but we have three recommendations. *First*, know your audience before using humor so you can avoid offending them. Don't assume that you and your audience will find humor in the same things. *Second*, make the use of humor relevant to your persuasive goal. The humor needs to help your audience process the message and not distract them from it. And *third*; humor alone is not persuasive. It must be combined with other message and source factors to create a persuasive message.

GUILT

Not only are positive emotions such as humor used to persuade, but more negative emotions such as guilt are used as well. You may be very familiar with this emotion and its use as a persuasive tool. Some people rely on this strategy extensively to accomplish their goals. What we mean specifically by guilt in the persuasion context is when we believe that our behavior does not meet our own standards (O'Keefe, 2002). Like other emotions, guilt occurs on a continuum, so you may experience a little bit of guilt, a lot of guilt, and everything in between.

We often think our behavior doesn't meet standards and thus we feel guilty. Advertisers may attempt to take advantage of this guilt by offering products or services that help alleviate the guilt. A study by Huhmann and Brotherton (1997) found that over 5% of the ads in magazines contained guilt appeals. For instance, mothers working outside the home often feel guilty for not spending more time with their children and for not doing things "a good mother should." A cookie maker may use the guilt a mother experiences for not baking homemade cookies to sell expensive cookies that are "better than homemade." Buying these cookies may help working mothers alleviate some of the guilt they feel. As noted, guilt is not a positive emotion. It seems risky to use a negative emotion to influence people; they might get mad at the source. Coulter and Pinto (1995) conducted a study on this very issue. They examined three levels of guilt (low, moderate, and high) and measured participants' emotional responses as well as their attitudes toward the products: bread and dental floss. Coulter and Pinto found that advertisements with a high level of guilt resulted in anger and feelings of being manipulated. They concluded that moderate levels of guilt might be the most effective at both gaining the audience's attention and eliciting an acceptable level of guilt. When a guilt appeal is explicit, persuasion is usually reduced (O'Keefe, 2002). Guilt appeals that are implicit and elicit a low to moderate amount of guilt are probably the most effective.

In a similar study, Turner and Underhill (2012) tested high, moderate, and low guilt appeals in emergency preparedness messages. Turner and Underhill specifically examined whether participants felt angry with the source when exposed to a guilt appeal. Anger was the highest for the high guilt appeal. However, higher guilt was associated with perceiving emergency preparedness as important. So guilt appeals can be a double-edged sword. Receivers may be more influenced by higher levels of guilt, but they also are angrier at the source and situation.

Moderate levels of guilt are overall better than high levels. ⌜Since guilt is something that makes people feel bad, we should consider the ethics of using guilt appeals.⌟ Is it ethical to elicit guilt to persuade? The same question can be asked about another negative emotion that is frequently used to persuade: fear.

FEAR

One of the most widely used emotional appeals in applied settings, and certainly the most researched of all the emotional appeals, is fear appeals. A **fear appeal** is a type of emotional appeal that relies on fear to persuade the audience; however, fear appeals often have many qualities of logical appeals as well. Kim Witte (1994) provides a current and useful definition of fear appeals: "a persuasive message that attempts to arouse the emotion of fear by depicting a personally relevant and significant threat and then follows this description of the threat by outlining recommendations presented as feasible and effective in deterring the threat" (p. 114). The first portion of Witte's definition describes a fear appeal as a message that arouses the emotion of fear. This part of the definition is probably along the lines of what you were expecting. You may not have anticipated the second part of the definition that refers to an outline of recommendations that deter the threat. This second part of the definition reflects our current understanding of what an *effective* fear appeal is. There are many examples of messages that arouse fear (or at least are intended to arouse fear) but do not mention how to eliminate the threat. For example, for many years anti-drug campaigns have relied on fear to get their message across. These messages may or may not have aroused fear in you, but rarely do they provide specific recommendations on how to avoid drug use. Current research indicates that simply arousing fear in the audience is not sufficient to influence attitudes, intentions, or behaviors (Witte, 1992, 1994). Therefore, we are including recommendations that deter the threat in our discussion of fear appeals.

Web Activity: Go to YouTube and search for anti-drug commercials. How many generate fear?

Early research in fear appeals found that sometimes fear appeals worked, sometimes they didn't, and sometimes they had a boomerang effect (the audience did the opposite of what the source was advocating). In an attempt to understand why fear appeals worked sometimes and not others, Leventhal (1970) offered the **parallel response model**, which proposed that people had one of the two responses when they were exposed to a fear appeal. One response was described as a **fear control response**, which is an emotional response. For example, if you are the recipient of a fear appeal that makes you feel fearful, and you respond by focusing on how to reduce the fear, you are having a fear control response. Your focus is on the emotion you are experiencing and how to eliminate this unpleasant emotion (fear) so that you can feel better. The most common ways people reduce fear is to deny that they are really in danger and to downplay the threat. These strategies are quite successful at eliminating the fear, but these strategies don't eliminate the threat or the cause of the fear. For example, suppose you are a smoker. You hear a fear appeal targeted at getting you to quit smoking, and you have a fear control response. You downplay the threat of smoking and the likelihood that you'll be negatively affected by smoking. You are unlikely to take steps to stop smoking. A fear control response rarely, if ever, results in receivers changing their attitudes or behavior.

If after receiving the fear appeal you focus on eliminating the threat from your life, you are having a **danger control response**. A danger control response is considered a cognitive response (the fear control response was an emotional response), because you focus on assessing the threat and how to eliminate it. So, if you take a danger control response to a fear appeal on smoking, you focus on ways to quit smoking so that you can eliminate the threat to your health.

Leventhal's parallel response model provided a new level of understanding of fear appeals and provided an explanation for why fear appeals sometimes worked and sometimes did not. When the audience has a fear control response, they probably will not adopt the source's recommendations (e.g., quit smoking, wear their seat belts). When the audience has a danger control response, however, the fear appeal is more likely to be successful because the audience is more likely to adopt the source's recommendations as a means of eliminating the threat. Although Leventhal's parallel response model was very useful in explaining *why* and *how* fear appeals worked, it did not provide sufficient detail to predict *when* receivers would take a danger control response rather than a fear control response and hence limited the ability to elicit a danger control response from the audience.

EXTENDED PARALLEL PROCESS MODEL

Building on Leventhal's parallel response model and the protection motivation theory developed by Rogers (1975, 1983), Witte (1992) developed the **extended parallel process model (EPPM)**. The EPPM builds on the concept that people have either a danger control response or a fear control response when exposed to a fear appeal. Additionally, Witte (1992, 1994) specifically outlines the message components that are necessary for an *effective* fear appeal and explains how the audience's perceptions of the message differ with a danger control response and a fear control response. The improved explanation of the EPPM has led to a greater ability to predict when receivers will have a danger or a fear control response and provides guidance on how to construct a message that elicits the danger control response.

Web Activity: Google distracted driving. Do current messages that discourage distracted driving successfully convey severity and susceptibility to create perceived threat?

The EPPM is illustrated in Figure 5.2. An effective fear appeal must have these four components: severity, susceptibility, response efficacy, and self-efficacy. **Severity** refers to the grimness of the threat presented in the message. Imagine a message that shows the consequences of not wearing a seat belt. The message depicts a driver going through the windshield and being killed. This is pretty grim, pretty severe. An effective fear appeal must depict a threat the audience perceives as severe. Related to this is the second component, susceptibility. **Susceptibility** refers to how probable it is that the threat will affect the audience. In our seat belt fear appeal example, if you perceive that you are at risk for going through the windshield, you will feel susceptible to the threat. If you perceive the threat as unrealistic or not applicable to you, you will not feel susceptible to the threat. For fear to be elicited, you must perceive the threat depicted in the message as severe and you must perceive yourself as susceptible to the threat. If after appraising the message you believe that the threat is not severe *or* that you are not susceptible, then no fear is elicited and you are not likely to be motivated to process the message further or to take any action. In Chapter 4 we discussed source credibility. A threat is more effective if it is delivered by a highly credible source, in part, because high credibility sources make the threat appear more credible itself. Hearing a homeless person wander the streets and threaten that a terrorist attack is imminent has little credibility. However, having the secretary of state or the president of the United States holds a press conference and says that a terrorist attack is imminent will have much more impact and believability. Thus, a highly credible source can enhance the effectiveness of a threat.

For a fear appeal to be effective there must be more than just a threat. The third component of the EPPM is response efficacy. **Response efficacy** refers to how effective

Threat + Severity = Perceived Threat

Response Efficacy + Self-Efficacy = Perceived Efficacy

If Perceived Threat > Perceived Efficacy = Defensive Motivation = Fear Control Response

If Perceived Efficacy > Perceived Threat = Protection Motivation = Danger Control Response

Excerpt from "Putting the Fear Back Into Fear Appeals" by K. Witte, *Communication Monographs*, Vol. 59, 1992.

FIGURE 5.2 Witte's 1992 extended parallel processing model.

the recommended response is in eliminating the threat. The recommended response is what you want your audience to do, such as wearing a seat belt or refraining from using drugs. The audience also has to be convinced that the recommended response will be effective at eliminating the threat. Examine the message in Figure 5.3. The source provides five things parents can do to reduce the likelihood of their teens abusing prescription drugs. This is a good example of response efficacy. Going back to our earlier example, wearing a seat belt almost completely eliminates the threat of going through the windshield in the event of an accident. You must perceive the recommended response as effective in order for the fear appeal to be effective. If you perceive the recommended response as ineffective in eliminating the threat, you are unlikely to adopt the recommended response.

The fourth component of the EPPM is self-efficacy. **Self-efficacy** refers to the extent the audience believes they are capable of performing the recommended response. If your response to the seat belt fear appeal was "I could never stand to wear a seat belt all the time," your self-efficacy regarding the recommended response would be quite low. It is unlikely that you would begin wearing a seat belt (the recommended response). On the other hand, if your response was along the lines "It takes two seconds to wear a seat belt. What's the big deal? I can wear a seat belt," then you would have high self-efficacy and be very likely to begin wearing your seat belt. So when a person is exposed to a fear appeal containing these four components, the person first appraises the threat to determine the severity of the threat and his or her susceptibility. If the threat is perceived as moderate or severe, the person is motivated to assess the efficacy of the recommended response and his or her self-efficacy, or ability to perform the recommended response. The greater the perceived threat, the more motivated the person is to assess the efficacy of the recommended response. If the threat is perceived as trivial or irrelevant, the person will give little attention to the recommended response.

So when does a person have a danger control response and when does he or she have a fear control response? When the perception of efficacy (efficacy of recommended response and self-efficacy) is greater than the perception of threat, ⌜the audience is motivated to protect themselves (protection motivation), and the danger control process will dominate. The audience will focus on how to eliminate the threat (accept the recommended response).⌟ When the perception of the threat is greater than the perception of efficacy, ⌜the audience will be motivated to defend themselves (defensive motivation), and the fear control processes will dominate. The audience will focus on eliminating the fear (become defensive and deny he or she is at risk).⌟ Figure 5.2 summarizes these principles of the EPPM. The perception of the threat determines the intensity of the reaction to the fear appeal; the perception of efficacy determines

When teens want to get high
YOUR PRESCRIPTION IS AVAILABLE FOR PICK UP.

TEENS ARE ABUSING PRESCRIPTION DRUGS THEY FIND AT HOME.
HERE'S WHAT THEY ARE DOING—AND HOW PARENTS CAN STOP IT.

It can be medication left over from your last surgery. Maybe they're the pills you keep on the dresser or tucked inside your purse. Teens are finding prescription drugs wherever people they know keep them—and abusing them to get high. In fact, 70 percent of persons age 12 and older who abuse prescription painkillers say they get them from a relative or friend[1]—leading to several troubling trends:

- **Every day, 2500 kids age 12 to 17 try a painkiller for the first time.[2]**
- **Prescription drugs are the drugs of choice for 12 and 13 year olds.[3]**
- **Teens abuse prescription drugs more than any illicit street drug except marijuana.[4]**

What's also disturbing is they don't realize these drugs can be as dangerous as street drugs. So kids who would never try street drugs might feel safe abusing prescription drugs. Misperceptions about prescription drug abuse have serious consequences. In fact, drug treatment admissions for prescription painkillers increased more than 300 percent from 1995 to 2005.[5] Now that you know prescription drug abuse is a problem, here are ways parents can keep it from affecting their kids' lives:

- **Safeguard** all drugs at home. Monitor quantities and control access.
- **Set clear rules** for teens about all drug use, including not sharing medicine and always following the medical provider's advice and dosages.
- **Be a good role model** by following the same rules with your own medicines.
- **Properly conceal and dispose** of old or unused medicines in the trash.
- **Ask friends and family** to safeguard their prescription drugs as well.

Following these steps is a start. Let your teen know where you stand.
When you talk about drugs and alcohol, include prescription drugs in the conversation.
To learn more, visit **THEANTIDRUG.COM** or call **1-800-788-2800**.

Office of National Drug Control Policy.

1. 2006 National Survey on Drug Use and Health, SAMHSA, September 2007.
2. Ibid. 3. Ibid. 4. Ibid. 5. 2005 Treatment Episode Data Set, SAMHSA, 2007.

PARENTS.
THE ANTI-DRUG.

FIGURE 5.3 Response efficacy example.

whether fear control or danger control processes will be initiated (Witte, 1992). Therefore, for a fear appeal to be effective, the message must portray the threat as sufficiently severe and likely to occur so that the audience perceives the threat as substantial. The message must also convince the audience that the recommended response will effectively eliminate (or reduce) the threat and that the audience is capable of performing the recommended response.

USING THE EXTENDED PARALLEL PROCESS MODEL

The EPPM not only explains when and why an audience will have a danger control response versus a fear control response but also gives us specific guidance on how to create an effective fear appeal. Mark Morman (2000) applied the EPPM in developing messages to convince young men to perform testicular self-exams in order to increase early detection and decrease deaths due to testicular cancer. Testicular cancer is the most common malignancy among American white males between the ages of 24 and 34 and the second most common in other age groups of white males (Morman, 2000). (Rates of testicular cancer are much lower for African American, Hispanic, and Asian American males.) Additionally, testicular cancer is on the rise, up 51% from 1973 to 1995 (Morman, 2000). Morman's goal was to motivate young men to perform the testicular self-exam (TSE) regularly. Additionally, Morman wanted to test the EPPM and to examine whether a fact-based or a narrative-based message would be most effective.

First, Morman developed four versions of a fear appeal advocating the regular performance of TSE. One message used a fact-based approach and used high efficacy. The second message also used a fact-based approach but used low efficacy. The high-efficacy message explicitly states that performing a TSE reduces the threat of testicular cancer and gives specific information on how to perform the TSE. The low-efficacy message is much more vague and general in presenting the TSE as a means of reducing the threat of testicular cancer. The third message was a narrative-based approach that used high efficacy. The narrative approach was written as a personal story. The fourth message also used a narrative-based approach but had low efficacy.

Morman (2000) recruited 80 male students at a Midwestern university and a Midwestern community college. All participants were between the ages of 18 and 32 (men aged 15 to 35 are most at risk for testicular cancer). The men were told that the purpose of the study was to evaluate testicular cancer and TSE awareness materials in the early stages of development. The participants were then randomly assigned to read one of the four messages. After reading the message, the men were asked to respond to a variety of questions that assessed fear arousal, susceptibility, severity, response efficacy, and self-efficacy, along with other questions.

Morman (2000) found that the men who read the high-efficacy messages had greater intentions to perform the TSE than those men who read the low-efficacy messages. Men in the two groups reported an equal amount of fear in response to the severity of the message. The difference was in the response efficacy and self-efficacy communicated in the messages. The men who read the high-efficacy messages had a danger control response and therefore intended to perform the TSE. These men perceived their efficacy as greater than the severity of the threat, resulting in the danger control response. The men reading the low-efficacy messages had a fear control response and focused their energy on reducing the fear rather than developing intentions to perform the TSE. These men perceived the threat as greater than their efficacy in dealing with the threat, resulting in the fear control response. Morman was also interested in whether a fact-based or a narrative-based message would be more effective. Morman found that both message types were equally effective.

The EPPM has been employed in many contexts, and it has been integrated with specific individual factors that can affect the success or failure of persuasive messages based on the topic. For example, Wong and Cappella (2009) used Witte's EPPM in a study of antismoking messages in conjunction with smokers' readiness to quit. For smokers with a low readiness to quit smoking, threat and efficacy were critically important for influencing receivers' intention to quit smoking. However, for smokers with a high level of readiness to quit, efficacy was the most important factor. Those ready to quit did not require a high threat message because they had been convinced of the threat by prior messages. For them, messages directed at convincing recipients about their own ability to quit were most important.

Fear appeals are a useful means of persuasion and have been used a great deal with health topics. As we have discussed, fear alone is insufficient for an effective message. The fear-inducing components of the message (severity and susceptibility of threat) must be accompanied by response efficacy and self-efficacy information. The efficacy component of the message is necessary for the audience to be motivated to adopt the recommended response. If the efficacy component is missing, the audience will most likely focus on eliminating the fear (an emotional process) rather than on eliminating the danger (a cognitive process). Witte's extended parallel process model not only does a good job of explaining why fear appeals work but also provides specific guidelines for how to develop an effective fear appeal. Recent research has found that the EPPM also works when the fear appeal threat is directed toward others. Roberto and Goodall (2009) used the EPPM model to test doctors' intentions and behavior toward testing patients for proper levels of kidney functioning in response to threats to patient health from kidney disease in combination with efficacy messages about the role of early detection. Their research found that Witte's model works even when the receiver isn't the direct target of the threat.

Emotion is an important element when deciding what content to include in a message. ⌐In addition to pathos, Aristotle identified logos, or the nature of the message, as central to persuasion. The nature of the message includes evidence, reasoning, and whether one or both sides of an issue are addressed.⌐

LOGICAL APPEALS

A logical appeal relies on the reasoning and strength of the content. It appeals to an audience's logical side. In general, people want the world to be consistent, logical, and to make sense. Persuasive messages that are logical and make sense can be quite persuasive. When creating a logical appeal, we give particular attention to the type and quality of information we include. Specifically, we use evidence. Additionally, the logic and reasoning used to organize the content are quite important.

EVIDENCE

You may be most familiar with the use of evidence in court cases. We frequently hear about DNA evidence either being the basis for convicting someone of a crime or setting someone free who was wrongly convicted. DNA evidence is one form of physical evidence, but there are other forms of evidence as well. Evidence is an important element in logical appeals. McCroskey (1969) defined **evidence** as "factual statements originating from a source other than the speaker, objects not created by the speaker, and opinions of persons other than the speaker that are offered in support of the speaker's claims" (p. 170). DNA evidence would be considered an object not created by the speaker. Essentially, evidence is something created by someone else, and that *something* could be an opinion, a factual statement, or some type of object. Just because something is a piece of evidence does not mean it is necessarily "good evidence." Whether or not a piece of evidence is considered good or strong is largely a matter of opinion. At a minimum, however, the evidence must be *relevant* to the topic in order to be considered good evidence. If the evidence is irrelevant to the topic, it is clearly poor evidence.

Should you use evidence when creating your persuasive message? That depends. It depends largely on the source and nature of the evidence. McCroskey conducted a series of experiments on the impact of evidence on attitude change and on audience perceptions of source credibility. In summarizing more than 20 studies on evidence, McCroskey (1969) drew 5 conclusions about the use of evidence in persuasive messages.

The *first* conclusion was that the use of good evidence has little if any impact on attitude change or source credibility if the source has initial high credibility. In other words, if your audience perceives you as highly credible from the beginning, using evidence in your persuasive message isn't more effective than using your own opinions. If you are highly credible, including evidence will not enhance your persuasiveness with an audience. However, evidence may enhance your persuasiveness if your audience is really focused on your message rather than on you. If you have low to moderate initial credibility, using evidence helps increase your credibility, and thus helps you be more persuasive.

A *second* conclusion from McCroskey's research is that evidence has little impact on attitude change if the evidence is delivered poorly. If you stumble, lose your place, fidget, mumble, or perform other distracting behaviors, the audience is likely to disregard the good evidence you used in your message. Similarly, in a written message, if it has grammatical errors, misspelled words, or is poorly organized, the audience will likely dismiss your message. So, for evidence to be effective in changing an audience's attitude, the evidence must be well delivered.

A *third* conclusion is that evidence has little impact on attitude change or source credibility if the audience is familiar with the evidence. In other words, the evidence must be new to the audience. Why? The audience processed the evidence the first time they were exposed to it. At that point, either the audience was influenced by the evidence or they discarded it. In a sense, the influence of that evidence gets used up on the first exposure. In the second exposure, the evidence no longer has any influence left.

⌐McCroskey's (1969) fourth conclusion is that the use of good evidence increases sustained audience attitude change regardless of the source's credibility. This means that if you deliver a persuasive message containing evidence to an audience and influence their attitude, the audience's attitude change will more likely last than if you did not use evidence. This is consistent with the discounting model discussed in Chapter 4. Recall that the discounting model assumes that initial attitude change is a result of both source credibility and message content; however, permanent attitude change is based on message content (Allen & Stiff, 1998). Therefore, if you are interested in obtaining long-term attitude change in your audience, including evidence in your message is a good idea, even if you are a highly credible source.

The fifth and last conclusion drawn from McCroskey's program of research is that the mode of transmission—audio recording, video recording, or live—has no impact on the effectiveness of evidence. Evidence is equally effective regardless of which of these three channels of communication the source uses, as long as it is well-delivered. More recently, Reynolds and Reynolds (2002) concluded overall that persuaders who cite evidence are more effective than those who don't.⌐

Using good evidence in a persuasive message can enhance attitude change and increase source credibility when the source has moderate-to-low initial credibility, the evidence is delivered well, and the audience is unfamiliar with the evidence. ⌐Since people tend to remember the content and forget the source of a message, even highly credible sources benefit from using strong evidence.⌐

NARRATIVE VERSUS STATISTICAL EVIDENCE

We just concluded that using evidence is generally a good strategy when constructing a persuasive message, but what type of evidence should you use? Evidence can take several forms. As the definition describes, evidence can be in the form of factual statements, opinions, or physical objects. Two specific types of evidence are statistical evidence and narrative evidence. **Statistical evidence** refers to a summary of many cases that is expressed in numbers and is used to support a claim. An example of statistical evidence is telling an audience that 73% of people wearing a seat belt survived an accident compared to 44% of people who were not wearing a seat belt in the year 2000 (car-accidents.com). This information is based on many cases (all reported accidents within the United States) and is presented as a summary in the form of percentages.

Narrative evidence refers to case stories or examples used to support a claim. An example of using narrative evidence is providing a story of an individual who was wearing his or her seat belt and survived a terrible auto accident. Previously, we discussed Morman's (2000) study of fear appeals and his comparison of fact-based and narrative-based messages. The fact-based messages use statistical evidence (e.g., "96 percent of all testicular tumors are discovered by men performing the routine self-exam"). The narrative-based messages tell a story about a young man named Kyle who was diagnosed with testicular cancer and are examples of narrative evidence.

Narrative evidence is more vivid and personal than statistical evidence. However, narrative evidence is usually an example of one. In other words, it describes one incident that may or may not be representative of other cases. Statistical evidence is based on many cases and is relatively uninfluenced by exceptional cases. You may conclude from this discussion that statistical evidence is better than narrative evidence. Statistical evidence does provide more information about the issue than narrative evidence, but that does not necessarily mean it is more persuasive.

One strength of narrative evidence is that it tends to be more vivid than statistical evidence and may generate a more concrete image in the minds of the audience. Kazoleas (1993) found that participants exposed to a message containing narrative evidence retained greater attitude change 2 weeks later than did participants exposed to a message containing statistical evidence. Additionally, some audience members may not fully understand the meaning and implications of statistics, but do understand the meaning and implications of the narrative. Both narrative and statistical evidence have their strengths, so is one more persuasive? Allen and Preiss (1997) identified 16 studies that specifically compared statistical and narrative evidence. Of those, 10 studies found statistical evidence to be more effective, 4 studies found narrative evidence to be more effective, and 2 studies found no difference. Using a procedure call meta-analysis that summarizes the effects of several studies, Allen and Preiss concluded that statistical evidence was slightly more effective in terms of persuasion than narrative evidence. In another meta-analysis, Zebregs, Neijens, de Graaf, and van den Putte (2015) concluded that statistical evidence influences beliefs and attitudes more than narrative evidence; however, narrative evidence influenced audience intention to perform a recommended behavior more than statistical evidence.

There is no need to choose between narrative and statistical evidence. In most cases, the two forms of evidence can be combined in a single message. ⌜Combining narrative and statistical evidence is the most persuasive. This was demonstrated by Allen et al. (2000). Messages containing both narrative and statistical evidence were more persuasive than messages with only statistical evidence, which were more persuasive than messages with only narrative evidence or messages with no evidence. Statistical evidence contains information that influences beliefs. Narrative evidence creates an effective response that helps create the motivation needed to act on those beliefs. ⌟ Combining the two forms of evidence may allow the persuader to create a message that is vivid, memorable, and more persuasive than using either type of evidence alone.

REASONING

To create a persuasive message, the source has to do more than just string together pieces of evidence. Good evidence must be accompanied by sound reasoning to maximize persuasiveness. **Reasoning** is the process of drawing conclusions from evidence. Several forms of reasoning can be used by a source. Three common forms of reasoning are inductive, deductive, and causal reasoning. **Inductive reasoning** begins with a specific example and then draws a general conclusion. The following statement is an example of inductive reasoning: When Colorado legalized recreational marijuana, tax proceeds increased, so every state should legalize recreational marijuana to increase tax proceeds. The statement starts with a specific example, what happened in Colorado, and uses this to draw a conclusion about what all states should do.

Deductive reasoning begins with a general statement and then draws a specific conclusion and relies on factual statements. The following is an example of deductive reasoning: States rely on taxes to provide services to their citizens. Legal marijuana is heavily taxed. Therefore, states should legalize marijuana to increase tax proceeds. The first statement is about state taxes in general. The conclusion is specific to taxing legal sales of marijuana.

The third type of reasoning is **causal reasoning**, which involves connecting two or more events and concluding that one caused the other. An example of causal reasoning would be evaluating the legalization of marijuana and the rate of fatal crashes in Colorado. Colorado legalized the recreational use of marijuana in 2012. Between 2013 and 2016, there was a 40% increase in fatal crashes in Colorado. Legalization of rec-reational marijuana increases traffic fatalities. However, this reasoning needs addi-tional evidence to show that the increase in traffic fatalities was actually caused by the use of marijuana and not some other factor. Just because two things are associated does not mean one causes the other.

In our discussion of evidence, we said that evidence must be relevant to the persuasive goal. It is through the reasoning that we make the evidence relevant to our persuasive goal. You might think of using evidence and reasoning as constructing a path from where the audience is on an issue to where you want them to be. All three forms of reasoning can be effective. The available evidence and the conclusion you want to draw largely determine the form of reasoning you use.

ONE-SIDED VERSUS TWO-SIDED MESSAGES

Regardless of the topic of persuasion, there is almost always an opposing side. If you work for a political candidate, he or she will have an opponent; if you work in advertising, your product will have a competitor; if you work for a nonprofit organization, other nonprofit organizations will be competing for the same dollars you are. Your audience may or may not know a lot about your competitor. When you are constructing a persuasive message, one issue that arises is whether to address your competitor. For example, imagine you work for a political candidate who is running for the U.S. Senate and wants to abolish the death penalty. When constructing a persuasive message for the campaign, do you only provide reasons why the death penalty should be abolished, or do you also acknowledge or address the reasons why the death penalty should exist? If you choose to address only the reasons for abolishing the death penalty, you are constructing a one-sided message. A **one-sided message** only presents arguments in favor of a particular issue. A **two-sided message** presents arguments in favor of an issue but also considers opposing arguments. This should not be confused with a balanced presentation of the issues in controversy. A two-sided message in this context still clearly advocates for one side of the issue, but it acknowledges counter arguments and sometimes refutes them. If you choose to use a two-sided message, one issue that arises is how you should address the opposing arguments in your two-sided message. Do you just mention them and let the audience do with them as they wish? Or should you refute them? A two-sided message that presents opposing arguments and then refutes them is a **refutational two-sided message**. A message that simply mentions the opposing arguments but does not refute them is a **non-refutational two-sided message**.

So which type of message should you use? After reviewing and analyzing (using meta-analysis) 70 studies, Allen (1998) concluded that a refutational two-sided message was overall more effective than either a one-sided message or a non-refutational two-sided message. Allen et al. (1990) found further evidence of the superiority of the refutational two-sided message in an extensive study. Why is a refutational two-sided message more effective than the other message types? The theory that best explains this is the inoculation theory, which is discussed later. In addition to being more persuasive, sources of refutational two-sided messages are perceived as more credible than sources of one-sided and non-refutational two-sided messages (Allen et al., 1990). When a source provides reasons for his or her position and also discusses and refutes the opposition's arguments, he or she is displaying knowledge of the topic, which increases perceptions of expertise. As we discussed in Chapter 4, expertise is a key component of source credibility.

MESSAGE STYLE

In the preceding sections, we discussed the issue of what type of content to include in a persuasive message. Should we use evidence, should it be in the form of statistical or narrative evidence, and should we use fear-inducing content? These important issues dramatically affect the effectiveness of your persuasive message. However, in addition to the content you include in your message, the *style* of how you say it also affects the persuasiveness of your message. Style includes both language style and nonverbal behaviors. By **language style** we mean the types of words you choose to present your message. For example, let's take the statement "The university has an innovative diversity plan that will enhance the quality of education for students." If we change it to "The university has an ingenious diversity plan that will create an innovative and distinctive educational experience for students," we have not changed the logical meaning of the statement. We have changed the style of the message, however, and an audience would most likely interpret the two statements differently. There are two issues in language style we will discuss. One involves choosing words that communicate power rather than powerlessness. The second issue is language intensity.

POWERFUL VERSUS POWERLESS SPEECH

We discussed types of power in Chapter 4 and defined power as the ability to get others to do what you want. When a person has power, he or she is perceived as having status and is likely to also be perceived as credible. Among other factors, the words you choose contribute to whether you are perceived as powerful or not.

Several language features contribute to **powerless speech**. Four such features that have been studied include *hedges* or *qualifiers* ("sort of," "kinda," "I guess"), *hesitation forms* ("uh," "well, you know"), *tag questions* (". . . , don't you think?"), and *disclaimers* ("This may sound odd, but"). When a person's speech contains these features, he or she will likely be perceived as less credible and be less persuasive than if those features are not present (Burrell & Koper, 1998). **Powerful speech** is defined as the absence of hedges, qualifiers, hesitation forms, tag questions, and disclaimers. We sound confident, and therefore powerful, when we eliminate powerless features from our speech.

Johnson and Vinson (1990) wondered how a person would be perceived if he or she began with powerless speech but then switched to powerful speech. Would the switch to powerful speech overcome the negative effects of powerless speech? Similarly, they also wondered about the consequences of starting off with powerful speech but then switching to powerless speech. Johnson and Vinson designed an experiment that manipulated the number of hedges and hesitations in a transcribed testimony. They also manipulated whether the hedges and hesitations occurred at the beginning of the testimony, in the end, or throughout. In all, they had four conditions: powerful (no hedges or hesitations), powerless (hedges and hesitations throughout), powerful beginning (hedges and hesitations in the last third of the testimony), and powerful ending (hedges and hesitations in the first third of the testimony). They found that it did not matter where the powerless language was placed. All three groups of testimony that contained powerless language were less persuasive and were perceived as less credible than the powerful testimony.

In a second study, Johnson and Vinson (1990) wondered if a small number of powerless features would have a negative impact or if a person could get away with a few powerless features in her or his speech. Again, Johnson and Vinson created four conditions: a powerful condition (no hedges or hesitations), moderate power (10 powerless features), low power (19 powerless features), and powerless (39 powerless features). Their results indicated that even the small number of powerless features contained in the moderate power condition resulted in reduced persuasiveness.

These two studies are consistent with other research on powerless speech, and we should conclude that using powerless speech in the form of hedges, hesitations, disclaimers, and tag questions reduces persuasiveness and should be avoided. Powerless speech is usually only a concern in oral messages, such as when you are giving a persuasive speech or when you are in a one-on-one or small-group situation. It would be truly rare to find the powerless speech in formal written persuasive messages. For some people the use of powerless speech has become a habit. Spend a day listening to yourself and see how often you use powerless speech.

LANGUAGE INTENSITY

Language intensity refers to language characteristics that indicate the extent the source deviates from neutrality. Two language features determine whether language is intense or not. The first is **emotional intensity**, which is the amount of affect expressed in the language choices of the source. The word *incredible* is more emotionally intense than the word *good*; *catastrophic* is more emotionally intense than *terrible*, which in turn is more emotionally intense than *bad*. The second feature is **linguistic specificity**. Linguistic specificity is "the degree to which a source makes precise reference to attitude objects in a message" (Hamilton & Stewart, 1993). Words that are specific have more narrow meaning and are more precise. Words that are less specific are more vague, have broader meaning, and provide less precise information. Specific language is more likely to bring a vivid picture to mind. For example, describing an object as "6 feet wide and 8 feet tall" is more specific and vivid than describing an object as "quite large"; however, both descriptions are accurate. Combining specific language with emotional language creates intense language.

A study by Buller et al. (2000) tested different messages (high intensity vs. low intensity and deductive vs. inductive organization) and their effectiveness in influencing parents to protect their children and themselves from the harmful effects of sun exposure. Buller and his colleagues found that parents were most influenced by the deductive message that used intense language. They concluded that the intense message was more effective because it was more memorable. Intense language is more vivid because it is more likely to bring a specific picture to mind. It is easier to remember a message that we have associated a picture within our mind.

Research has suggested that high credibility sources can successfully employ more intense language, but that low credibility sources are less effective when they use intense language (Bradac, Bowers, & Courtright, 1979). This doesn't necessarily hold true for obscenity, which is a form of intense language; some evidence suggests that sex plays a role in this interaction. In general, males can successfully use more intense language than females, so care should be exercised in applying this principle too literally. Still, language choice is a message variable that interacts with source credibility in determining persuasive success.

Language intensity has also been explored in computer-mediated contexts. Andersen and Blackburn (2004) found that more intense language in an e-mail request to complete a survey resulted in a higher compliance rate. Andersen and Blackburn created two different e-mail requests—one with high-intensity language and one with low-intensity language. The response rate was 35% for the low-intensity message and 47.6% for the high-intensity message. This is an important finding because as persuaders we often need information from our target audience (audience analysis) and we often obtain that information by conducting surveys. Getting people to complete surveys is an ongoing battle for researchers of all stripes. Using more intense language appears to be more effective in getting people to complete those surveys.

Intense language is not always appropriate. Whether to use intense language and how intense to be are decisions you must make with the topic and the context of the message in mind. Some issues are so inherently emotional that using intense language with them could potentially be explosive. In other cases, using intense language may be perceived as being in poor taste or as manipulative. To be an effective persuader, you must constantly be considering the characteristics of your audience and the persuasive context as you decide how to construct your message.

NONVERBAL MESSAGES

In Chapter 4 we stated that sources who are attractive, powerful, liked, and perceived as similar to the receiver are more persuasive. The perception of these source qualities is largely a result of nonverbal behavior. The nonverbal messages used by sources have a big impact on whether they are perceived as attractive, liked, or similar. You might think of attractiveness as largely due to physical qualities; however, nonverbal behaviors have a big impact on how we perceive those physical qualities. Regardless of physical features, people are perceived as more attractive when they smile and make eye contact. Similarity and likability are judgments made based on what a source both says and does. We observe nonverbal behaviors to make inferences about the kind of person they are and make judgments about their similarity and likability.

Web Activity: Go to Ted Talks website (www.ted.com) and search for Amy Cuddy, "Your Body Language May Shape Who You Are." Consider the implications of her research on persuasion.

Nonverbal messages include all of the things people do that communicate that do not involve language. Recall the definition of communication in Chapter 1, "The process of stimulating meaning in the mind of another person with verbal and nonverbal messages." Both face-to-face and mediated communication include verbal and nonverbal messages. Nonverbal messages are estimated to stimulate between 65% and 93% of the total meaning of communication (Mehrabian, 1981). Nonverbal behaviors are categorized by type and include facial expression, eye behavior, touch, use of space, vocal qualities (including silence), physical appearance, movement, use of personal objects, and use of time.

When we communicate with a source (face-to-face or mediated), we observe their nonverbal behaviors to help us both understand the message and to determine what kind of person the source is. If the source uses nonverbal immediacy behaviors, we will likely perceive him or her as likeable, warm, and trustworthy. **Nonverbal immediacy behaviors** "simultaneously signal warmth, decrease psychological or physical distance between communicators, are interpersonally stimulating, and signal availability for communication" (Andersen, 2004, p. 165). Nonverbal immediacy behaviors include eye contact, physical closeness, smiling, open body position, positive gestures, and touch. A caveat here: appropriate use of these behaviors communicate immediacy. All of these behaviors can be used in aggressive and inappropriate ways. Only socially appropriate use of these behaviors creates perceptions of immediacy and enhances persuasiveness. Also, what is socially appropriate is culturally based.

What is appropriate in one culture is not appropriate in another. Here, we limit our discussion to U.S. culture. We generally communicate our emotions and feelings through our nonverbal behaviors. When we like someone and want to communicate with them, we naturally use more nonverbal immediacy behaviors.

Making eye contact invites communication, increases attractiveness and trustworthiness, and signals liking. Eye gaze is also associated with greater compliance with requests (Burgoon, Dunbar, & Segrin, 2002). We find it hard to trust someone who doesn't make eye contact and we associate deception with a lack of eye contact. Receivers are more likely to comply with a request if the source is perceived as trustworthy. Gaze and eye contact are also used to convey power and dominance. Those with power tend to make more eye contact while speaking than those without power; however, those with power make less eye contact while listening than those without power. Those with less power are expected to attend closely (gaze at) their superior when he or she speaks. Staring also communicates power, where gaze aversion signals submission. In addition to eye contact, facial expressions are very important nonverbal behaviors. Smiling is particularly important. Smiling and positive facial expressions create perceptions of liking and closeness. Of course, this is only true when we perceive the smile as authentic and not forced. When we listen to sources, we devote most of our attention to their face. Smiling combined with eye contact communicates liking and invites further communication.

Vocal Behavior is how we speak and includes volume, speed, inflection, tone, pronunciation, and accent. A monotone voice lacks variation and communicates boredom and lack of interest. When sources speak with vocal variety, they communicate interest, enthusiasm, and liking. Speaking relatively quickly with no long pauses, filled pauses, or hesitations, as well as pleasant warm voice qualities, are associated with greater attraction and compliance. Think of your most interesting teacher and your most boring teacher, and compare their vocal behavior (not what they say, how they say it). The interesting teacher probably uses a lot more vocal variety and sounds interested and enthusiastic about what he or she is saying.

When we communicate, we use our whole body—particularly our hands and face. Body movement includes our gestures, posture, and movement. An open body position invites communication and engagement and creates perceptions of liking. A closed body position communicates defensiveness and avoidance. Closer (but appropriate) physical distance communicates liking and invites communication. If someone you don't like initiates a conversation with you, you probably step back a bit to create more distance without even thinking about it. If you watch Ted Talks, notice the movement and posture of the speakers. They move around the stage and use gestures to engage the audience. Their movement is meaningful, not distracting offensive, or aggressive. They rarely if ever use a podium; rather they use movement to reduce the distance with the audience.

Physical touch is a powerful nonverbal behavior that when used appropriately, communicates affection and liking. Touch is highly regulated by social and cultural norms. Greetings often involve touch (e.g., handshakes, fist bumps, hugs). Inappropriate touch can be offensive, and it can communicate intimidation and aggression. Appropriate touch in persuasion contexts is usually brief and involves relatively public body parts such as our hands, lower arm, and shoulder. Crusco and Wetzel (1984) demonstrated the power of appropriate touch in a study with female servers in restaurants. In this study, three servers in two restaurants were trained to deliver a "fleeting touch" or a "shoulder touch" when returning change to a customer. A fleeting touch was defined as touching a diner's palm with her fingers for one-half second as she returned the diner's change. A shoulder touch involved touching the customer's shoulder for one to one-and-half seconds as she returned the change. After collecting payment for the bill, diners were randomly assigned to either a fleeting touch, a shoulder touch, or no touch. The percent of tip was noted for each customer. The percentage of tip was significantly higher for both the fleeting touch and shoulder touch than for the no touch condition. Crusco and Wetzel also examined the day of the week, weather, alcohol consumption, number of diners at the party, and sex of the customer to see if these factors could explain differences in tip percentages. Tips were higher on sunny days, at the end of the week, and with larger dinner parties. However, when these factors were controlled, touch still had a significant and positive effect on tip percentage.

Nonverbal behaviors are important aspects of persuasive messages. The role of nonverbal messages varies depending on the context and the media used. Several nonverbal messages are prominent in face-to-face and video interactions and attention should be given to these behaviors to maximize persuasion. In mediated contexts where nonverbal behaviors are restricted, receivers place more emphasis on the nonverbal behaviors that are present such as tone of voice, font style, pictures, and other design features. If the persuasion is occurring on a website or in an email, receivers use the "look" of the site and message to make judgments about the source.

Both the content and style of a persuasive message are important considerations when persuading an audience. In this chapter, we addressed several message factors that can be manipulated to enhance persuasion. At this point we want to again remind you of source factors. We have purposively separated source factors from our discussion of message factors to help you understand these concepts. However, in real persuasion, the source and the message are closely linked and the two interact. When constructing a persuasive message, the effective persuader considers both the message and who is delivering it.

SUMMARY

- Logical appeals rely on logic and reasoning to be persuasive.
- Emotional appeals rely on one or more emotions to be persuasive.
- Humor must be relevant, appropriate for the audience, and used with other persuasive strategies to be effective.
- Moderate guilt appeals are more effective than high guilt appeals.
- Leventhal's parallel response model explains two responses to fear appeals: a fear control response and a danger control response.
- Witte's extended parallel process model explains how an audience processes a fear appeal and identifies four components of an effective fear appeal.
- Perceived efficacy must be greater than perceived threat for the audience to have a danger control response.
- Evidence can enhance attitude change and source credibility when the source has low to moderate initial credibility, the evidence is delivered well, and the evidence is new and unfamiliar to the audience.
- Use of good evidence results in greater sustained attitude change.
- Both narrative and statistical evidence are useful, but combining the two forms is the most effective.
- Reasoning connects evidence to the claim. Three types of reasoning include inductive, deductive, and causal.
- Two-sided refutational messages are more effective than one-sided messages and non-refutational two-sided messages.
- Use of powerless speech in even small amounts reduces the persuasiveness of a speaker.
- Intense language is specific and emotionally intense. Messages that use intense language are more memorable than messages that use less intense language.
- Nonverbal messages are important for positive source perceptions of credibility, attractiveness, and similarity.
- Use of nonverbal immediacy behaviors enhances persuasion.

KEY TERMS

Causal reasoning—involves connecting two or more events and concluding that one caused the other.

Danger control response—a cognitive response to a fear appeal that focuses on how to eliminate the danger or threat that is causing the fear.

Deductive reasoning—begins with a general statement, draws a specific conclusion, and relies on factual statements.

Emotional appeal—a persuasive message that relies on emotion to be persuasive.

Emotional intensity—the amount of affect expressed in the language choices of the source.

Evidence—factual statements originating from a source other than the speaker, objects not created by the speaker, and opinions of persons other than the speaker that are offered in support of the speaker's claims.

Extended parallel process model (EPPM)—developed by Witte and describes the two ways receivers process fear appeals and how different responses result from different ways of processing.

Fear appeal—a persuasive message that attempts to arouse the emotion of fear by depicting a personally relevant and significant threat and then follows this description of the threat by outlining recommendations presented as feasible and effective in deterring the threat.

Fear control response—an emotional response to a fear appeal that focuses on how to eliminate the fear.

Guilt appeal—a persuasive message intended to stimulate the emotion of guilt, which is often experienced when a person thinks his or her behavior does not meet his or her own standards.

Inductive reasoning—begins with a specific example and then draws a general conclusion and relies on probability.

Language intensity—language characteristics that indicate the extent the source deviates from neutrality.

Language style—the types of words a person chooses to present a message.

Linguistic specificity—the degree to which a source makes precise reference to attitude objects in a message.

Logical appeal—a persuasive message that relies on logic and reasoning to be persuasive.

Narrative evidence—case stories or examples that are used to support a claim.

Non-refutational two-sided message—a message that mentions the opposing arguments but does not refute them.

Nonverbal immediacy behaviors—behaviors that communicate warmth, closeness, and availability for communication.

Nonverbal message—a message or part of a message that does not involve language.

One-sided message—a message that only presents arguments in favor of a particular issue.

Parallel response model—developed by Leventhal and proposes that people have one of two responses when exposed to a fear appeal.

Powerful speech—the absence of hedges, qualifiers, hesitation forms, tag questions, and disclaimers.

Powerless speech—the use of language features such as hedges or qualifiers, hesitations, tag questions, and disclaimers that create perceptions of little power.

Reasoning—the process of drawing conclusions from evidence.

Refutational two-sided message—a two-sided message that presents opposing arguments and then refutes them.

Response efficacy—how effective the recommended response is in eliminating a particular threat.

Self-efficacy—the extent the audience believes they are capable of performing the response recommended in a message.

Severity—the grimness of the threat presented in a message.

Statistical evidence—an informational summary of many cases that is expressed in numbers and used to support a claim.

Susceptibility—how probable it is that a particular threat will affect the audience.

Two-sided message—a message that presents arguments in favor of an issue but also considers opposing arguments.

QUESTIONS FOR REVIEW

Respond to the following questions **without** reviewing the text or your notes. These questions are provided to help you practice retrieving information and reflect on your reading.

A. List several message factors that influence persuasion.

B. Did you agree or disagree with anything you read? Explain.

C. What did you learn that was new to you?

D. What concepts, if any, were confusing to you?

Respond to the following questions. You may reference your text or notes to help you.

1. What are the three types of emotional appeals described in this chapter? Provide an example of each one.

2. Identify and define the four components that are necessary for an effective fear appeal.

3. What five conclusions did McCroskey make about the use of evidence in persuasive messages?

4. What is the difference between one-sided messages and two-sided messages? Which type is most effective in persuasion? Why?

5. Would you characterize your language style as one that typically uses powerful or powerless speech? How intense is your language style? Describe any changes you could make in your language style to be more persuasive. Keep these things in mind for your final presentation.

6. How do nonverbal behaviors affect persuasion?

QUESTIONS FOR DISCUSSION

1. What are examples of logos and pathos appeals used in advertising or health and social campaigns? Which type of appeal seems to be used more frequently? How does this compare to the discussion of statistical and narrative evidence in this chapter?

2. In your small group, find an advertisement or message from a health or social campaign that uses a fear appeal. Using the Extended Parallel Process Model (EPPM), discuss the components of the message and its overall effectiveness. Share your example with the rest of the class.

3. In your small group, discuss how you can incorporate pathos and logos in your final presentation. Which type of appeal do you think will be more effective for your audience? Why?

4. What section of this chapter is most useful to you as you consider your final presentation? Why? How will you use what you have learned to develop a more persuasive message?

5. Discuss the ethical questions provided at the end of the chapter. What ethical considerations are relevant to the information in this chapter about fear and guilt appeals, use of evidence in persuasion, language style, and nonverbal messages?

   - Are there guidelines (e.g., don't lie) that would be appropriate for every situation, or are ethics relative?

   - Do the ends (e.g., a good outcome) justify any means?

- Is deceiving the receiver ever appropriate?

- Should the source of the message bear primary responsibility for ethics, or should the receiver share that responsibility (e.g., buyer beware)?

REFERENCES

Allen, M. (1998). Comparing the persuasive effectiveness of one- and two-sided messages. In M. Allen & R. W. Preiss (Eds.), *Persuasion: Advances through meta-analysis* (pp. 87–98). Cresskill, NJ: Hampton Press.

Allen, M., Bruflat, R., Fucilla, R., Kramer, M., McKellips, S., Ryan, D. J., & Spiegel-hoff, M. (2000). Testing the persuasiveness of evidence: Combining narrative and statistical forms. *Communication Research Reports, 17,* 331–336.

Allen, M., Hale, J., Mongeau, P., Berkowitz–Stafford, S., Stafford, S., Shanahan, W., et al. (1990). Testing a model of message sidedness: Three replications. *Communication Monographs, 57,* 275–291.

Allen, M., & Preiss, R. W. (1997). Comparing the persuasiveness of narrative and statistical evidence using meta-analysis. *Communication Research Reports, 14,* 125–131.

Allen, M., & Stiff, J. B. (1998). An analysis of the sleeper effect. In M. Allen & R. W. Priess (Eds.), *Persuasion: Advances through meta-analysis* (pp. 175–188). Cresskill, NJ: Hampton Press.

Andersen, P. A. (2004). Influential actions: Nonverbal communication and persua-sion. In J. S. Seiter & R. H. Gass (Eds.), *Perspectives on persuasion, social influence and compliance gaining* (pp. 165–180). Boston, MA: Pearson & Allyn & Bacon.

Andersen, P. A., & Blackburn, T. R. (2004). An experimental study of language intensity and response rate in e-mail surveys. *Communication Reports, 17,* 73–84.

Booth-Butterfield, S., & Booth-Butterfield, M. (1991). The communication of humor in everyday life. *Southern Communication Journal, 56,* 205-218.

Bradac, J. J., Bowers, J. W., & Courtright, J. A. (1979). Three language variables in communication research: Intensity, immediacy, and diversity. *Human Communication Research, 5,* 257–269.

Buller, D. B., Burgoon, M., Hall, J. R., Levine, N., Taylor, A. M., Beach, B., et al. (2000). Long-term effects of language intensity in preventive messages on planned family solar protection. *Health Communication, 12,* 261–275.

Burgoon, J. K., Dunbar, N. E., & Segrin, C. (2002). Nonverbal influence. In J. P. Dillard & M. Pfau (Eds.), *The persuasion handbook: Developments in theory and practice* (pp. 445–473). Thousand Oaks, CA: Sage.

Burrell, N. A., & Koper, R. J. (1998). The efficacy of powerful/powerless language on attitudes and source credibility. In M. Allen & R. W. Preiss (Eds.), *Persuasion: Advances through meta-analysis* (pp. 203–216). Cresskill, NJ: Hampton Press.

Car-Accidents.com Get the Facts: Statistics. (n.d.). Retrieved February 12, 2003, from www. car-accidents.com/pages/stats/2000_seatbelts.html.

Cline, T. W., & Kellaris, J. J. (1999). The joint impact of humor and argument strength in a print advertising context: A case for weaker arguments. *Psychology and Marketing, 16,* 69–86.

Coulter, R. H., & Pinto, M. B. (1995). Guilt appeals in advertising: What are their effects? *Journal of Applied Psychology, 80,* 697–705.

Crusco, A. H., & Wetzel, C. G. (1984). The Midas touch: The effects of interpersonal touch on restaurant tipping. *Personality and Social Psychology Bulletin, 10,* 512–517.

Hackman, M. Z. (1988). Audience reactions to the use of direct and personal disparaging humor in informative public address. *Communication Research Reports, 5,* 126–130.

Hamilton, M. A., & Stewart, B. L. (1993). Extending an information processing model of language intensity effects. *Communication Quarterly, 41,* 231–246.

Harris Interactive. (2010, November 12). Do emotional images in advertising pull at heart strings? Harris Polls, retrieved from http://www.harrisinteractive.com/NewsRoom/HarrisPolls/tabid/447/mid/1508/articleId/627/ctl/ReadCustom percent20Default/Default.aspx.

Huhmann, B. A., & Brotherton, T. P. (1997). A content analysis of guilt appeals in popular magazine advertisements. *Journal of Advertising, 26*(2), 35–46.

Johnson, C., & Vinson, L. (1990). Placement and frequency of powerless talk and impression formation. *Communication Quarterly, 38,* 325–333.

Kazoleas, D. (1993). The impact of argumentativeness on resistance to persuasion. *Human Communication Research, 20,* 118.

Leventhal, H. (1970). Findings and theory in the study of fear communications. In L. Berkowitz (Ed.), *Advances in experimental social psychology* (Vol. 5, pp. 120–186). New York: Academic Press.

McCroskey, J. C. (1969). A summary of experimental research on the effects of evidence in persuasive communication. *Quarterly Journal of Speech, 55,* 169–176.

McCroskey, J. C. (1997). *An introduction to rhetorical communication* (7th ed.). Needham Heights, MA: Allyn & Bacon.

Mehrabian, A. (1981). *Silent messages: Implicit communication of emotion and attitudes* (2nd ed.). Belmont, CA: Wadsworth.

Morman, M. T. (2000). The influence of fear appeals, message design, and masculinity on men's motivation to perform the testicular self-exam. *Journal of Applied Communication Research, 28,* 91–116.

Nabi, R. L., Moyer-Guse, E., & Byrne, S. (2007). All joking aside: A serious investigation into the persuasive effect of funny social issue messages. *Communication Monographs, 74,* 29–54.

O'Keefe, D. J. (2002). Guilt as a mechanism of persuasion. In J. P. Dillard & M. Pfau (Eds.), *The persuasion handbook: Developments in theory and practice* (pp. 329–344). Thousand Oaks, CA: Sage.

Reynolds, R., & Reynolds, J. (2002). Evidence. In J. P. Dillard & M. Pfau (Eds.), *The persuasion handbook: Developments in theory and practice* (pp. 428–445). Thousand Oaks, CA: Sage.

Roberto, A. J., & Goodall, C. E. (2009). Using the extended parallel process model to explain physicians' decisions to test their patients for kidney disease. *Journal of Health Communication, 14,* 400–412.

Rogers, R. W. (1975). A protection motivation theory of fear appeals and attitude change. *Journal of Psychology, 91,* 93–114.

Rogers, R. W. (1983). Cognitive and physiological processes in fear appeals and attitude change: A revised theory of protection motivation. In J. T. Cacioppo & R. E. Petty (Eds.), *Social psychophysiology: A sourcebook* (pp. 153–176). New York: Guilford Press.

Skalski, P., Tamborini, R., Glazer, E., & Smith, S. (2009). Effects of humor on presence and recall of persuasive messages. *Communication Quarterly, 57,* 136-153.

Turner, M. M. & Underhill, J. C. (2012). Motivating emergency preparedness behaviors: The differential effects of guilt appeals and actually anticipating guilty feelings. *Communication Quarterly, 60,* 545-559.

Weinberger, M. G., & Gulas, C. S. (1992). The impact of humor in advertising: A review. *Journal of Advertising, 21,* 35–59.

Wilson, V. E. (2003). Perceived effectiveness of interpersonal persuasion strategies in computer-mediated communication. *Computers in Human Behavior, 19,* 537–552.

Witte, K. (1992). Putting the fear back into fear appeals: The extended parallel process model. *Communication Monographs, 59,* 329–349.

Witte, K. (1994). Fear control and danger control: A test of the extended parallel process model (EPPM). *Communication Monographs, 61,* 113–134.

Wong, C. H., & Cappella, J. N. (2009). Antismoking threat and efficacy appeals: Effects on smoking cessation intentions for smokers with low and high readiness to quit. *Journal of Applied Communication Research, 37*(1), 1–20.

Zebregs, S., Neijens, P., de Graaf, A., & van den Putte, B. (2015). The differential impact of statistical and narrative evidence on beliefs, attitude, and intention: A meta-analysis. *Health Communication, 30,* 282–289. doi:10.1080/10410236.2013.842528

CHAPTER 6

SOCIAL JUDGMENT THEORY

BEFORE YOU READ

Respond to the following questions **before** you read the chapter.

1. What is an attitude? Why is it important to the study of persuasion?

2. You have strong attitudes and weak attitudes about certain events, ideas, or people. Give an example of an idea or an issue about which you have a strong attitude.

3. Do you think students in your class have a strong or weak attitude about your group's topic? Explain your answer.

It's All Relative

Have you ever noticed that if you take a sip of coffee that is at room temperature it tastes *cold*, yet if you take a sip of a soft drink that is at room temperature it tastes *warm*. Why is this? The two beverages are at the same temperature. How we perceive something depends in part on what we are comparing it to. Therefore, whether we perceive something as warm or cold depends on to what it is being compared. The "something" that we compare an experience to is referred to as an *anchor*. If our anchor is 190° F, as it probably is for hot

LEARNING OBJECTIVES

- EXPLAIN THE CONCEPTS OF LATITUDE OF ACCEPTANCE, REJECTION, AND NONCOMMITMENT.
- EXPLAIN HOW ASSIMILATION AND CONTRASTING OCCUR.
- EXPLAIN HOW EGO-INVOLVEMENT AFFECTS THE JUDGMENT OF MESSAGES.
- DESCRIBE THE ATTITUDE CHANGE PROCESS FROM THE SOCIAL JUDGMENT PERSPECTIVE.

coffee, then tasting something that is 75° F seems pretty cold. If our anchor is 40° F, as it likely is for soft drinks, then 75° F seems pretty warm. Although it is possible to perceive something without comparing it to something else, human beings almost always immediately compare what they perceive to what they already know to help them make sense of the stimuli.

We make comparisons when understanding physical phenomena such as temperature, weight, brightness, loudness, and so on, but we also make comparisons when interpreting social phenomena. Similarly, whether we perceive the media as being "liberal" or "conservative" depends greatly on what has been referred to as our **attitudinal anchors**. An attitudinal anchor is the position on a particular issue that a person finds most acceptable (Sherif, Sherif, & Nebergall, 1965). Thus, someone whose preferred political stance is at the liberal end of the continuum would have been more likely to favor Hillary Clinton for president and probably would have viewed Fox News as being too conservative. Conversely, an individual with a more conservative attitudinal anchor who supported Donald Trump would more likely have rated Fox News as being fair and well balanced but see CNN as being too liberal. Muzafer Sherif and Carl Hovland (1961) applied these principles of psychophysical judgment to the domain of attitudes in persuasion and developed **social judgment theory**. It is one of the oldest theories of persuasion.

LATITUDES OF ACCEPTANCE AND REJECTION

A basic premise of social judgment theory is that an attitude toward an issue or an object can be thought of as a range of attitudes rather than as a single point along a continuum. With this theory, a person's stance on abortion would not simply be either pro-choice or pro-life, but it would encompass a range of positions that would be acceptable and/or unacceptable. For example, at one end of the continuum of possible attitudes toward abortion is the pro-life view, with the most extreme position being that abortion should not be legal under any circumstances. At the other end of the continuum is the pro-choice view with the most extreme position being that abortion should be available upon demand at any point during a pregnancy. Between these two extreme positions are more moderate positions, some of which are more pro-life and some of which are more pro-choice. Figure 6.1 illustrates an example of a continuum of possible positions on abortion, with the midpoint of the continuum representing a neutral attitude toward the issue. This continuum has nine positions, but there is no set number of positions. Imagine that your attitudinal anchor coincides with Position 2 in Figure 6.1, which indicates that abortion should be acceptable in most cases short of gender selection of babies. This is the position you agree with most strongly and support most fully. Although Position 2 is your most preferred position, you probably find other positions acceptable as well. Let's say that you also find Positions 1 and 3 acceptable even if they don't represent your most preferred position. This range of positions is referred to as your **latitude of acceptance (LOA)**, which is simply the range of positions a person finds acceptable.

If we continue to use abortion as an example, you probably also find one position the most unacceptable. Let's say that Position 9 in Figure 6.1, where abortion is unacceptable under any circumstances, represents your most unacceptable position. You probably find some other positions unacceptable as well. For example, these may be Positions 6, 7, and 8. These positions represent your **latitude of rejection (LOR)**, which is simply the range of positions you find unacceptable. To continue our example, let's say that Positions 4 and 5 represent positions you have no real opinion on or feel neutral toward. This range of positions is the **latitude of noncommitment (LNC)**.

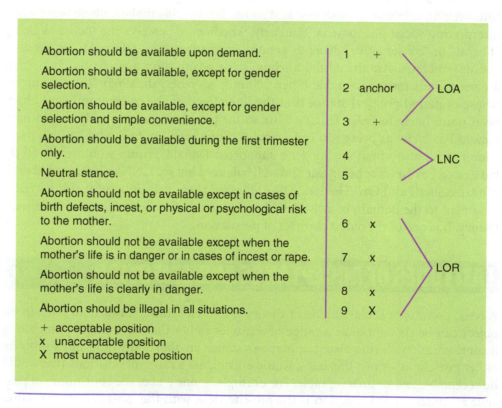

FIGURE 6.1 Latitudes of acceptance and rejection.

Social judgment theory proposes that each issue or attitude object has a range of positions that can be divided into the LOA (which contains the attitudinal anchor), LOR, and often (but not always) an LNC as well. The width, or a number of positions included in any given latitude, can vary. Depending on the topic, a person's latitude may be so narrow that it includes only one position. A latitude could also be split. For example, the LOR might include the extreme ends of the continuum, while the LOA includes moderate positions. The latitudes of acceptance, rejection, and non-commitment are important components of social judgment theory and are discussed further as we explore other aspects of the theory.

JUDGMENTS AND ATTITUDE CHANGE

A core assumption of social judgment theory is that your attitudinal anchor influences how you evaluate a persuasive message. This is illustrated in Figure 6.2. Let's say you are on the receiving end of a message based on Position 4 of Figure 6.2. You're likely to perceive this message as near your attitudinal anchor (Position 2). Because you perceive the message as similar to your views, you are assimilating the message. Assimilation means a person perceives a message as being similar to his or her attitudinal anchor and possibly closer than it really is from an objective point of view. When people assimilate a message, they are accepting the message. When people assimilate a message, they may distort it, perceiving it as being in agreement with their views when the message really may be quite discrepant. On the other hand, receivers may alter their anchor, essentially moving the anchor in the direction of the message. When assimilation occurs, receivers may perceive the message as closer to their anchor than it really is (a distortion of the message), move their anchor in the direction of the message, or some combination of the two. Therefore, a premise of social judgment theory is that assimilation facilitates persuasion.

Look once again at the continuum in Figure 6.2. If you perceived the message (based on Position 4) as being quite different from your attitudinal anchor, you would be contrasting the message. Contrasting occurs when a person perceives the message as being in opposition to his or her views. Like assimilation, contrasting often involves distortion, and where assimilation facilitates persuasion, contrasting inhibits persuasion. With contrasting, receivers perceive the message as being more different from their views than it really is. An objective bystander may judge the message as representing Position 3, but the receiver may distort the message and perceive it as representing Position 7 (falling in the LOR).

A third possible way of responding to a message is the process called the boomerang effect. Rather than assimilating or contrasting the message, receivers may actually move their anchor away from the intended direction of the message. We often think

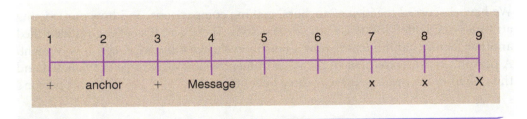

FIGURE 6.2 Assimilation and contrast effects.

that the worst thing that can happen if we pitch a persuasive message is that the listeners will simply fail to accept the message. The boomerang effect suggests that the message could actually be counterproductive; we could end up with receivers more opposed to our position than they were in the first place. In this case, the anchor is actually moved in the opposite direction of what we wanted.

An example of the boomerang effect can be found in politics. Rush Limbaugh was a popular conservative talk show host. He was opposed to a congressional proposal to require all health insurance coverage to include contraceptives. Although much of the prior debate centered on whether there should be exemptions for religious organizations, Limbaugh's most publicized criticism focused on the defense of the proposal by a law student named Sandra Fluke. His on-air comments included labeling her as a slut and a prostitute along with indicating that if public taxpayers were going to pay for her to have sex, he wanted her to post a video of it online so everyone could watch. Public outcry resulted from what was perceived to be a personal attack on a young woman, and public opinion became more favorable about insurance coverage of contraceptives. In this case, Limbaugh's message was not only rejected, but individuals' attitudinal anchors appeared to move in the opposite direction and away from the position advocated by his message. Thus, if a message is perceived as falling within the LOR, it will be rejected and the anchor may even move in the opposite of the intended direction.

Assimilation and contrasting are perceptual effects. Our preexisting attitudes and beliefs influence the way we perceive and interpret information. We selectively attend to and organize information on the basis of our attitudes and beliefs (as well as other factors). ⌜For example, let's take Dominic, a liberal Democrat, who believes the media is an extension of big business and capitalism. When Dominic watches the news, he is more likely to attend to comments and stories that support his view that the media is an extension of big business and capitalism. Where Aaliyah, a conservative Republican who believes journalists are bleeding-heart liberals, is more likely to attend to comments and stories that support her view that journalists are a bunch of bleeding-heart liberals.⌟

If the message is perceived as falling in the LNC, social judgment theory does not predict exactly how the message will be processed. Either assimilation or contrasting could occur. A few studies more recently have reported greater message acceptance when the message fell into the LNC; however, limited research supports this finding. Recall that prediction is a criterion of a good theory. Although social judgment theory helps us explain how people evaluate messages, it is limited in its ability to predict outcomes when messages fall into the LNC.

EGO-INVOLVEMENT

We have discussed the idea of anchors, making comparisons, and how our existing attitudes and beliefs influence our comparisons. Sherif and his colleagues identified another factor that influences how a person evaluates a message: ego-involvement. A person's ego-involvement in the issue influences how a message is evaluated and thus whether the message is assimilated or contrasted. Ego-involvement is a person's commitment to an issue and is related to a person's self-concept and self-esteem (Sherif et al., 1965). Ego-involvement is also called value-relevant involvement and is different from outcome-relevant involvement. A person is ego-involved when his or her attitude toward an issue is closely linked to his or her identity and self-concept. For example, students might have ego-involving attitudes toward grades. It is difficult to be objective in evaluating our own work if our grade and our sense of self-value are tied up in achieving a positive outcome. Although people likely have attitudes toward thousands of different objects/issues/people, only a few of those attitudes will be ego-involving.

Social judgment theory predicts that ego-involvement will affect the persuasion process in two ways. The first prediction is that ego-involvement affects the size of the LOR and LNC. Social judgment theory predicts that as ego-involvement increases, the width of the LOR increases (includes more positions) and the LNC decreases (includes fewer positions) or disappears. Therefore, let's say that Rose defines herself as pro-life and she is highly ego-involved in the abortion issue. Rose believes that abortion should be illegal but should be available to women who are victims of violent rape and young girls who are victims of incest and that abortion should only occur during the first 6 weeks of pregnancy. Rose has thought through the issue, and she believes she is right. As a result of this involvement with the issue, there are very few, if any, positions for which she is noncommittal, making her LNC very narrow (or even nonexistent). Another result of this involvement is that her LOR expands to include all the positions she may have previously been noncommittal on as well as any position that does not fall in her LOA. Originally Sherif and Hovland (1961) hypothesized that the LOA would also be affected by ego-involvement and would become much narrower. Research indicated, however, that the LOR and LNC were affected by ego-involvement but that the LOA was not (Eagly & Chaiken, 1993).

The second prediction is that ego-involvement is thought to increase contrasting and assimilation effects. An ego-involved person is more likely to either assimilate or contrast a message; in other words, a highly ego-involved person distorts a message more than does a person who is less ego-involved. If a person is ego-involved, he or she is committed to a position and has a personal stake in the issue. Also, the ego-involved person has probably considered various positions and concluded that his or her position is the *best*. As a result, the person tends to dichotomize the issue into the two extremes with no (or very little) middle ground. A result of this dichotomized view is that the receiver distorts (assimilates or contrasts) the message to make it fit into his or her LOA or LOR.

In an effort to demonstrate the impact of ego-involvement on message acceptance and rejection, Hovland, Harvey, and Sherif (1957) conducted a study that has become somewhat famous over the years. It took place in Oklahoma during the 1950s and, at this time, Oklahoma was a "dry" state (the sale of alcohol was prohibited). There had recently been a referendum on the issue (prohibition won), but it was still a hot topic of discussion. By drawing on statements made by various newspapers in the state, nine positions on the prohibition issue were identified and are shown in Figure 6.3. These nine statements were the basis for a measure developed by Hovland and his colleagues and referred to as an "ordered alternatives questionnaire." This measure consists of a set of nine positions representing the continuum of positions on an issue. This measure was used to assess the latitudes of acceptance, rejection, and noncommitment. Essentially, individuals were asked to mark on the questionnaire the statement they most agreed with (their attitudinal anchor), any other statements they agreed with, the statement they disagreed with most, and any other statements they disagreed with.

Hovland and his colleagues were particularly interested in examining the hypothesis that ego-involvement would increase assimilation and contrasting effects. To test their hypothesis, they identified people with established and publicly committed stands on the wet-dry issue. They recruited 183 members of the Women's Christian Temperance Union and the Salvation Army as having high ego-involvement in prohibition (the dry stand). Hovland et al. note that recruiting individuals with high ego-involvement in repeal (wet stand) was difficult; however, they were able to recruit 25 people personally known to the experimenters or their assistants as being committed to the repeal of prohibition. Additionally, 290 college students who represented a more moderate position on the issue were recruited.

To test their hypothesis, Hovland et al. prepared three messages based on arguments actually used by prohibition and repeal advocates during the referendum. One message represented an extreme "wet" position, one an extreme "dry" position, and one a moderate position based on Position F in Figure 6.3. The wet message was presented to the dry and moderate participants, the dry message was presented to the wet and moderate participants, and the moderate message was presented to all three groups. Approximately 3 weeks before hearing the audio-recorded message, participants indicated their latitudes of acceptance, rejection, and noncommitment regarding the positions shown in Figure 6.3. After listening to the message, participants once again indicated their latitudes of acceptance, rejection, and noncommitment on the issue. Hovland et al. were able to support their hypothesis. Participants whose view diverged greatly from that advocated by the message perceived the message as being more different from their own view than it actually was (contrasting effect). Those participants whose view was close to the position advocated by the message tended to perceive the message as being closer or more similar to their view than it really was (assimilation affect).

Hovland et al.'s (1957) study provided the first evidence that ego-involvement influenced how a message was evaluated and specifically demonstrated the assimilation and contrast effects. However, this study has also received a good deal of criticism. A primary criticism is that the participants were *presumed* to be highly ego-involved because of their group memberships. The researchers assumed that anyone who was a member of the Women's Christian Temperance Union would be highly ego-involved in the prohibition issue and that college students in journalism, speech, education, chemistry, and other classes would be only moderately involved in the issue. Furthermore, those who were recruited as wet were chosen on the basis of personal acquaintance. It is questionable whether or not Hovland et al. really examined different levels of ego-involvement. Later research, however, examined ego-involvement using different methods and found similar results: that persuasion was reduced when highly ego-involved participants were exposed to counter-attitudinal messages (Eagly & Chaiken, 1993). Therefore, it is fairly safe to conclude that ego-involvement influences how we interpret messages; however, the process and its finer points are not well understood.

(A) Since alcohol is the curse of mankind, the sale and use of alcohol, including light beer, should be completely abolished.

(B) Since alcohol is the main cause of corruption in public life, lawlessness, and immoral acts, its sale and use should be prohibited.

(C) Since it is hard to stop at a reasonable moderation point in the use of alcohol, it is safer to discourage its use.

(D) Alcohol should not be sold or used except as a remedy for snake bites, cramps, colds, fainting, and other aches and pains.

(E) The arguments in favor and against the sale and use of alcohol are nearly equal.

(F) The sale of alcohol should be regulated so that it is available in limited quantities for special occasions.

(G) The sale and use of alcohol should be permitted with proper state controls so that the revenue from taxation may be used for the betterment of schools, highways, and other state institutions.

(H) Since prohibition is a major cause of corruption in public life, lawlessness, immoral acts, and juvenile delinquency, the sale and use of alcohol should be legalized.

(I) It has become evident that man cannot get along without alcohol; therefore, there should be no restriction whatsoever on its sale and use.

From Journal of Abnormal and Social Psychology (Hovland, Harvey, & Sherif, 1957).

FIGURE 6.3 Ordered alternatives questionnaire.

CHANGING ATTITUDES WITH SOCIAL JUDGMENT THEORY

Social judgment theory proposes that attitude change is most likely to occur when the message is perceived to fall within the LOA. When a message is perceived to fall within the LOA, the position being advocated is assimilated, its content is positively evaluated, and attitude change may occur. On the other hand, if a message is perceived as falling within the LOR, contrasting occurs, the content is negatively evaluated, and the persuasion attempt fails. You may draw the conclusion that changing attitude is easy: all you have to do is make sure your message falls within your audience's LOA. Like most things that "seem easy," however, attitude change is not quite that simple. For one thing, your message may not fall within a person's LOA. The message you want your audience to accept may be highly discrepant from their initial position on the issue. We are often faced with these kinds of challenges in applied persuasion settings. A person advocating a liberal Democratic candidate for president is not likely to find many message positions that fall within the LOA of a conservative Republican.

The level of message discrepancy is a key issue in predicting attitude change within social judgment theory. **Message discrepancy** refers to the difference between the position being advocated by a message and the preferred position of the receiver. For example, let's say your audience's preferred position (anchor) is represented by Position B in Figure 6.3 (the sale and use of alcohol should be prohibited). If you present a persuasive message based on Position I (there should be no restriction on the sale and use of alcohol), your message would be much more discrepant than if you present a persuasive message was based on Position G (the sale and use of alcohol should be permitted with state controls and taxation). Social judgment theory makes the prediction that as message discrepancy increases, attitude change will also increase to the point where the message is discrepant enough to fall within the LOR. At this point, continuing to increase levels of discrepancy will result in reduced attitude change. This relationship between message discrepancy and attitude change is shown in Figure 6.4. With small amounts of message discrepancy, only small amounts of attitude change are likely. As the message becomes more discrepant, greater attitude change is possible; however, the possibility of the message being contrasted and rejected also increases.

A study by Siero and Jan Doosje (1993) found that messages that fell within the LNC were most persuasive. Siero and Jan Doosje presented three messages advocating using cars less in order to save the environment (this study was conducted with members of the Royal Dutch Tourist Association, which is similar to the American Automobile Association in the United States). All three messages advocated using cars less frequently but varied in their level of extremity. When a message was judged as falling within a person's LNC, attitude was most likely to change. However, little attitude change occurred when the message was judged as falling within the LOR.

A similar study was conducted on a college campus. Many universities are concerned about alcohol abuse on campus, and have searched for the most effective way to change student behavior. Smith, Atkin, Martell, Allen, and Hembroff (2006) drew on social norms surrounding drinking, and argued that messages using social norms falling in the LNC were most likely to be accepted. They researched how believable students found claims about different percentages of students on campus who had five or fewer drinks when they partied. Researchers found that respondents' belief that 60% to 70% of campus students had five or fewer drinks when they partied represented the LNC at the upper end of the scale. They then widely disseminated ads and posters on campus that included the LNC social norm of "most (63%) drink zero to five when they party" in the message. The results showed both a shift in social norms and a reduction in the number of reported drinks that occurred during partying on that campus. This applied research did not compare the LNC-based message to ones in students' LOA or LOR, so it is difficult to claim that messages in the LNC are superior to others, but it does support the concept that, in some cases, messages falling in the LNC can result in attitude and behavior change.

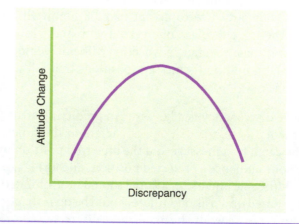

FIGURE 6.4 Discrepancy and attitude change.

Therefore, it is best to construct a persuasive message so that it falls within the receiver's LOA or LNC. If the message is judged to fall within the LOR, it will most likely be rejected. Thus, persuasion that seeks greater attitude change is not likely to occur with a single message. It would be necessary to target messages at the outer edges of the receiver's LOA or LNC in order to gradually drag the anchor toward the desired point. This process would have to be repeated over time to gradually move a receiver toward the ultimately desired goal.

MESSAGE DISCREPANCY AND ATTITUDE CHANGE

Three factors can influence the relationship between discrepancy and attitude change. These are ego-involvement, source credibility, and language intensity. When ego-involvement is high, the audience will tolerate relatively little message discrepancy before attitude change decreases. People with high ego-involvement have a larger LOR, so it takes relatively little discrepancy before the message will fall into the LOR and be rejected. The second variable is source credibility. The more credible the source is perceived to be, the more accepting the audience is of message discrepancy. In other words, the audience will give more consideration to messages from highly credible sources.

In Chapter 5 we discussed language intensity as a message factor. Recall that intense language is emotionally intense and specific. Language intensity also moderates the impact of message discrepancy on attitude change. Intense language enhances perceptions of message discrepancy. Messages that use intense language are interpreted as more extreme, so the distance between the receiver's position and the position being advocated by the message seems greater. Therefore, if the audience has low ego-involvement with the topic, increasing language intensity enhances attitude change, especially if the message is delivered by a credible source (Hamilton & Hunter, 1998). This is because the low involved person is less likely to reject the message, so greater discrepancy means the message has the potential to result in greater change. On the other hand, if the audience has high ego-involvement, increasing language intensity will probably reduce attitude change.

Influencing attitude from the perspective of social judgment theory requires the source to structure his or her message so that it is not too discrepant from the audience's attitudinal anchor. This leads to an incremental approach to persuasion. By incremental, we mean to slowly move your audience toward your position with a series of persuasive messages. Ideally, each message is assimilated, moving the anchor in the desired direction a little each time. An example of attitudes changing incrementally is Americans' attitude toward animal rights. In the early 1970s, the idea of animals having rights was quite foreign to most Americans. Many people perceived animals existing to serve humans, and little thought was given to the ethics of using animals for testing products for human consumption. Also, wearing fur coats was popular and viewed as a status symbol. We could describe Americans' attitudinal anchor as being against animal rights (on a continuum with animals having no rights at one extreme and with animals having rights equal to humans at the other extreme). Various groups have campaigned for animal rights and presented the American people with a variety of messages about animal rights and animal testing. Over the years, Americans' attitudinal anchor has gradually shifted toward animals having rights. Today there are cosmetic lines that tout their product testing as animal-free, fur coats are not nearly as popular (however, leather coats continue to be popular), and the number of vegetarians and vegans is increasing, all indicating the change in attitude toward animals among the American public.

When attempting to persuade audience members, their existing beliefs and attitudes will influence how they interpret your message. If they judge your message as being "on the other side," they are likely to disregard your message and you will be unsuccessful in your influence attempt. In fact, if the boomerang effect kicks in, the persuasive attempt could be counterproductive and move the receivers in the opposite direction from what you want. On the other hand, if they perceive your message as being "on their side," they are more likely to accept your message. If they perceive your message as falling within their LNC, then they may listen to you because they haven't made up their minds yet on these positions, and you have the opportunity to influence them. People who are highly ego-involved are very difficult to influence because they have essentially "made up their minds" and are therefore generally unwilling to accept a position that varies from their LOA.

APPLYING SOCIAL JUDGMENT THEORY

Let's consider how you might apply social judgment theory in constructing a persuasive campaign. For this process, we will work through a hypothetical example involving a challenging topic: passing death with dignity legislation in the state of Ohio. The first step in the process would be to identify the range of positions on assisted-suicide for voters in Ohio similar to what Hoveland et al. (1957) did with the wet-dry issue in Oklahoma. Using a sample of Ohio voters, we would need to learn what positions were in the LOA for the majority and what attitudes were in the LOR for the majority. We would want to know not only about the majority but also about the latitudes for certain groups such as Protestants and Catholics, professional and blue-collar workers, and the young and old. Some groups will be undecided. Others will hold moderate views, either in support of or in opposition to the legislation. Still other groups will feel very strongly about the topic. We would need to select representative samples of different groups and ask them to evaluate the continuum of all the possible positions.

We might expect members of the Catholic community to be strongly opposed to assisted-suicide, and the terminally ill to be in favor of such legislation. Both of these groups would likely be ego-involved in the topic. For the Catholic community, any message promoting assisted-suicide would likely be very discrepant and fall into their LOR. Finding a credible person to author a favorable message, such as a famous physician, would enhance our chances of gaining some movement with a larger message discrepancy. However, a message asking directly for support for this legislation would be expected to fail with the Catholic community because such a call would be squarely within the LOR regardless of the source of the message.

Google "Gay Marriage Timeline" to see a summary of how views of same sex marriage changed over the past 50 years.

Does this mean it is hopeless? No, not as long as we take a long-term view. Proponents of civil rights faced an uphill battle initially, and gradually barriers were broken down and attitudes toward racial rights were shifted. Similarly, attitudes toward same-sex marriage have changed dramatically over the past 20 years. Radical change will not occur overnight, but can happen slowly over time. In the case of death with dignity, attitudes have changed from being "unthinkable" to being supported by many Americans. To change attitudes toward assisted-suicide, we have to consider

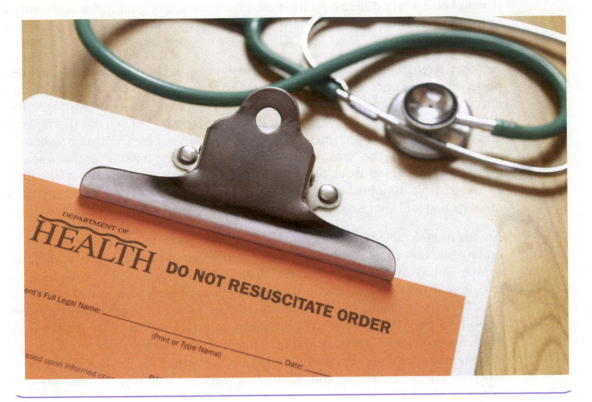

© Daisy Daisy/Shutterstock.com

FIGURE 6.5

how to tailor a message that can seek small, gradual changes toward the ultimate goal. We need to find where the edges of the LOA and/or LNC are for the groups not currently in favor of death with dignity laws and create messages targeted at those points in the attitude continuum. Given the size of the likely discrepancy between our message and the anchors of the target audience, finding highly credible sources would be important.

We also need to keep in mind that, with this topic, the opposition is also engaged in persuasive campaigns. Just as proponents are seeking gradual progress in legalizing assisted-suicide, the opposition is also engaged in campaigns to maintain the status quo and prevent the legalization of assisted-suicide. The American Medical Association has voiced strong opposition to the right to die initiatives. However, end-of-life directives and do not resuscitate orders have become common and represent a moderate position. These actions represent gradual steps toward legalizing assisted-suicide. Even in the absence of opposition, the movement toward social change is slow. In the presence of opposition, movement is even slower and at times is even reversed.

STRENGTHS AND LIMITATIONS

We use the criteria of explain, predict, and control for evaluating theory. We can use those three criteria to view the strengths and weaknesses of social judgment theory. One strength of social judgment theory is that it provides an *explanation* of how an attitudinal anchor can change over time. Slightly discrepant messages are assimilated, gradually changing the attitudinal anchor, until at some point the person holds a very different position than he or she did originally. Similarly, social judgment theory explains how and why some messages can backfire and result in a boomerang effect.

Another strength of social judgment theory is the implication it has for applied persuasion. Audience analysis is a central part of using social judgment theory effectively. The basic assumption of social judgment theory is that our existing attitudinal anchors influence persuasion. For this theory, the issue of message discrepancy and the importance of your message not being *too* discrepant from your audience's position are central concerns. The implication of these assumptions is that a source must know something about his or her audience. The source needs to know the audience's existing attitudinal anchors as well as their latitudes in order to construct a message that will not be contrasted.

An additional *explanatory* strength of social judgment theory is that it helps us understand how people process a persuasive message and why two persons holding similar initial attitudes (or attitudinal anchors) can respond to the same message in different ways. This strength of social judgment theory also leads to a limitation. We cannot predict how individuals will likely respond to a message unless we know how they evaluate the full continuum of positions. Just knowing the most preferred position or attitude toward the topic is not enough. In other words, social judgment theory is not very useful for *controlling* persuasion. Because of the enormous difficulty of applying and testing this theory, it has received relatively little research attention.

Another limitation of social judgment theory is that it does not provide a theoretical *prediction* for what happens when a message falls in the LNC. The theory predicts that a message will be assimilated if it falls into the LOA and contrasted if it falls into the LOR. Essentially, social judgment theory states that either assimilation or contrasting may occur if the message falls in the LNC, but does not specify the conditions necessary for either response, making it impossible to predict how people will respond in such a situation.

An additional limitation of social judgment theory is the ordered alternatives questionnaire. The theory is constructed with this attitude measurement device as its basis. If you examine the ordered alternatives questionnaire, it consists of a series of belief statements. ⌜The lack of distinction between attitudes and beliefs in social judgment theory contributes to the lack of prediction and control offered by this theory. Additionally, the ordered alternatives questionnaire was used to measure ego-involvement, which was an imprecise and questionable method for measuring ego-involvement.⌟ Another major weakness of social judgment theory is that it does not address how a message should be constructed. We know where we want it to be perceived on the attitude continuum, but no guidance is offered to help us figure out how to construct a message that can be placed so precisely. This also reflects a lack of good *control* for this theory.

Like all theories, social judgment theory has both strengths and limitations. It offers good explanatory power, but its predictive power is limited and our ability to control persuasion by using this theory is also quite limited. This theory offers some guidance in the design of messages, but its power in this area is less strong than other theories.

Strength in explanatory power is important enough to warrant understanding the theory and the unique contributions it has made to the study of persuasion, but the weaknesses in prediction and control make this a theory of less practical use overall.

SUMMARY

- We judge physical phenomena and communication events by comparing them to our previous experiences or attitudes. These are referred to as anchors.
- The latitude of acceptance (LOA) refers to those positions on an issue that we find acceptable. The latitude of rejection (LOR) refers to those positions on an issue that we find most unacceptable. The latitude of noncommitment (LNC) refers to those positions we have little or no opinion on.
- When we are exposed to a persuasive message, we compare it to our existing attitude (or LOA). If we judge the message as being similar to our attitude (even if it's not by objective standards), we are assimilating the message. If we judge the message as being dissimilar to our attitude (even if it's not by objective standards), we are contrasting the message.
- Creating clear and explicit messages can reduce assimilation and contrasting.
- Ego-involvement is a person's commitment to an issue and is closely linked to his or her identity and self-concept. Ego-involvement increases assimilation and contrast effects, and it affects the size of the LOR and the LNC.
- Message discrepancy refers to the difference between the position being advocated and the preferred position of the receiver. As message discrepancy increases, persuasion increases to a point at which attitude change begins to decrease.
- Ego-involvement, source credibility, and language intensity are three factors thought to influence the discrepancy-persuasion relationship.
- An important strength of social judgment theory is that it places emphasis on understanding the receiver. The application of social judgment theory requires a source to understand the existing attitudes of his or her audience.
- ⌈A limitation of social judgment theory is the lack of prediction for what happens when a message falls in the LNC.
- Another limitation of social judgment theory is the ordered alternatives questionnaire, which consists of belief statements and does not directly measure ego involvement.⌋

KEY TERMS

Assimilation—a person perceives a message as being similar to his or her attitudinal anchor and possibly closer than it really is from an objective point of view.

Attitudinal anchor—the position on a particular issue that a person finds most acceptable.

Boomerang effect—can happen during contrasting, when a person's anchor is moved in the opposite direction of the proposed message.

Contrasting—when a person perceives a message as being in opposition to his or her views.

Ego-involvement—a person's commitment to an issue and related to a person's self-concept and self-esteem.

Incremental Approach—slowly moving your audience toward your position with a series of persuasive messages.

Latitude of acceptance (LOA)—the range of positions along an attitude continuum a person finds acceptable.

Latitude of noncommitment (LNC)—the range of positions along an attitude continuum a person finds neither acceptable nor unacceptable.

Latitude of rejection (LOR)—the range of positions along an attitude continuum a person finds unacceptable.

Message discrepancy—the difference between the position being advocated by a message and the preferred position of the receiver.

QUESTIONS FOR REVIEW

Respond to the following questions **without** reviewing the text or your notes. These questions are provided to help you practice retrieving information and reflect on your reading.

   A. What are the LOA, the LOR, and the LNC?

   B. Did you agree or disagree with anything you read? Explain.

   C. What did you learn that was new to you?

   D. What concepts, if any, were confusing to you?

Respond to the following questions. You may reference your text or notes to help you.

1. Define these elements of social judgment theory: anchor, latitude of acceptance (LOA), latitude of rejection (LOR), and latitude of noncommitment (LNC).

2. Define assimilation, contrasting, and the boomerang effect. According to social judgment theory, which of these effects facilitates persuasion?

3. What is ego-involvement? How does it affect the persuasion process?

4. What three factors influence the relationship between discrepancy and attitude change? How does each factor influence the relationship?

5. If you were to apply social judgment theory to a persuasive message, what steps would you need to consider?

6. What are the strengths and limitations of social judgment theory?

QUESTIONS FOR DISCUSSION

1. In your small group, create a visual representation of social judgment theory. Be sure to include the key terms from the chapter. Compare your group's representation with other groups in the class.

2. In your small group, write down a range of positions about your group's topic going from one extreme to the other. How might this information help you use social judgment theory in your final presentations? Use the "Applying Social Judgment Theory" section in your text to guide your discussion.

3. Knowing your audience is essential in applying social judgment theory to a persuasive message. Let's assume your message falls within your audience's LOR. What are your options as a persuader? What would guide your decision about how to respond to this information about your audience?

4. At the beginning of the chapter, you were asked to identify an issue about which you have a strong attitude. You are ego-involved about that issue. How do you respond when someone tries to influence you on this issue? How does an understanding of social judgment theory provide insight about how you evaluate messages on this issue?

5. Discuss the ethical questions provided at the end of the chapter. What ethical considerations are relevant to the information in this chapter about social judgment theory?

   • Are there guidelines (e.g., don't lie) that would be appropriate for every situation, or are ethics relative?

   • Do the ends (e.g., a good outcome) justify any means?

   • Is deceiving the receiver ever appropriate?

   • Should the source of the message bear primary responsibility for ethics, or should the receiver share that responsibility (e.g., buyer beware)?

REFERENCES

Eagly, A. H., & Chaiken, S. (1993). *The psychology of attitudes*. Fort Worth, TX: Harcourt Brace Jovanovich.

Hovland, C. I., Harvey, O. J., & Sherif, M. (1957). Assimilation and contrast effects in reaction to communication and attitude change. *Journal of Abnormal and Social Psychology, 55,* 244–252.

Sherif, M., & Hovland, C. I. (1961). *Social judgment: Assimilation and contrast effects in communication and attitude change*. New Haven, CT: Yale University Press.

Sherif, C. W., Sherif, M., & Nebergall, R. E. (1965). *Attitude and attitude change: The social judgment involvement approach*. Philadelphia: W. B. Saunders.

Siero, F. W., & Jan Doosje, B. (1993). Attitude change following persuasive communication: Integrating social judgment theory and the elaboration likelihood model. *European Journal of Social Psychology, 23,* 541–554.

Smith, S. W., Atkin, C. K., Martell, D., Allen, R., & Hembroff, L. (2006). A social judgment theory approach to conducting formative research in a social norms campaign. *Communication Theory, 16,* 141–152.

CHAPTER 7

CONSISTENCY AND COGNITIVE DISSONANCE THEORY

BEFORE YOU READ

Respond to the following questions **before** you read the chapter.

1. What do you know about cognitive dissonance?

2. When have you made a decision that was inconsistent with one of your values? How uncomfortable were you as a result of your decision?

3. What did you do to make yourself feel more comfortable about the decision you made?

LUCIUS

⌐Lucius is a senior and an honors student at a prestigious university. He is involved in student government and takes great pride in his academic accomplishments and his integrity. He has one last general education requirement to meet: foreign language. He struggled through the first-level Spanish class. Despite his intelligence, Lucius finds learning a new language harder than anything else he has ever done. He needs to get an "A" on the final exam to get a "B" in his Spanish class. It's the night before the final exam and Lucius is studying

LEARNING OBJECTIVES

- EXPLAIN HOW DISSONANCE IS CREATED AND HOW IT IS REDUCED.
- DESCRIBE AND GIVE EXAMPLES OF THE CONTEXTS IN WHICH DISSONANCE OCCURS.
- EXPLAIN THE NECESSARY CONDITIONS FOR COGNITIVE DISSONANCE TO OCCUR.
- EXPLAIN THE STRENGTHS AND WEAKNESSES OF COGNITIVE DISSONANCE THEORY.

with Seth, an acquaintance from class. Seth offers Lucius an easy way to cheat on the test and ensure a grade of "A." Lucius goes home and contemplates the opportunity to cheat. What should he do? The next morning, Lucius takes the Spanish exam and gets an "A" thanks to Seth's cheating strategy. Upon seeing Seth, Lucius thanked Seth and celebrated his achievement.

Lucius' behavior is very inconsistent with his beliefs and attitudes. Lucius takes pride in his honesty, integrity, and academic accomplishment. He has never before cheated. This doesn't seem to make sense. How could Lucius cheat and feel good about the decision? Cognitive dissonance theory will help us understand this situation and the role of consistency in persuasion.

In Chapter 6, we described social judgment theory as a cognitive theory. By cognitive theory we mean a theory that examines how receivers process persuasive messages. In this chapter, we explore another cognitive theory that focuses on the human need for consistency. Cognitive dissonance theory proposes that humans are motivated to be consistent in their thoughts and behaviors. There is a great deal of support for this proposition, although alternative views are explored at the end of this chapter with a discussion of self-affirmation and self-perception theories. But first, we will discuss the role of consistency in persuasion.

CONSISTENCY

Social judgment theory was the first *cognitive theory* introduced. By cognitive theory we mean a theory that examines how receivers process persuasive messages. In this chapter we explore another cognitive theory that focuses on the human need for consistency. Cognitive dissonance theory proposes that humans are motivated to be consistent in their thoughts and behaviors. There is a great deal of support for this proposition, although an alternative view is explored at the end of this chapter with a discussion of self-perception theory. But first we will discuss the role of consistency in persuasion.

Fritz Heider (1946, 1958) was the first to examine consistency with the development of balance theory. Heider hypothesized that people desired consistency in their interpersonal relationships. Specifically, people want their friends to like the same things they do. For example, if I like Jeff and I like *Hamilton*, I want Jeff to also like *Hamilton*. Such a situation is balanced and comfortable. If Jeff doesn't like *Hamilton*, an imbalance is created and I become motivated to either like Jeff less or like *Hamilton* less to create balance. Some support was found for this theory but it never met the criteria for a good theory. During this same period, Osgood and Tannenbaum (1955) developed congruity theory that provided a more complex explanation of the human need for consistency. Congruity theory provided evidence that consistency was important, but it was not very good at predicting when attitude would change. However, the research on balance and congruity theories indicated that consistency was an important part of how people behaved and processed information. ⌈Cognitive dissonance theory provides a useful explanation for how consistency functions in the persuasion process.⌋

COGNITIVE DISSONANCE THEORY

Leon Festinger (1957) developed the most accepted consistency theory that still has adherents today: the **cognitive dissonance theory**. This theory is built on the knowledge generated by balance theory and congruity theory, and it has continued to be modified as more research is conducted. Festinger started with what he referred to as **cognitions**, or bits of knowledge that individuals have. Cognitions can be bits of knowledge such as "I ate pancakes for breakfast" or can be attitudes, beliefs, or values such as those discussed in Chapter 2. Think of the human mind as a vast network of cognitions.

Individual cognitions have one of three relationships with one another. A **dissonant relationship** involves two cognitions that are inconsistent with one another. ⌈In the example with Lucius, the cognition of "I cheated" is inconsistent, or dissonant, with the cognition "I'm an honest person."⌋ A **consonant relationship** involves two cognitions that are consistent with one another. In this case, "buying a power cord" would be consistent, or consonant, with the belief "I need an "A" on this exam." An **irrelevant relationship** involves two cognitions that a person perceives as unrelated. For instance, the cognition "I eat cheese" is most likely perceived as irrelevant to the cognition "I cheated on an exam." It is important to understand that the decision about what is dissonant, consonant, or irrelevant is up to the receiver. Each person gets to connect his or her own cognitions according to his or her own sense of what constitutes a consistent, inconsistent, or irrelevant relationship. When two cognitions have a dissonant relationship, cognitive dissonance occurs. **Cognitive dissonance** is an aversive motivational state or, in other words, it is unpleasant and people are motivated to eliminate it. When a person experiences cognitive dissonance, there is pressure to change one's cognitions and to regain ⌈consistency and equilibrium. We expect Lucius to feel cognitive dissonance about his cheating behavior and to be motivated to eliminate it and regain consistency. Before delving into dissonance reduction, we first need to discuss how much dissonance Lucius experienced.⌋

MAGNITUDE OF DISSONANCE

According to cognitive dissonance theory, a dissonant relationship between cognitions (or the perception of inconsistency) leads to pressure for change. However, not *all* dissonance results in a change. Festinger argued that the **magnitude of dissonance**, or the amount of dissonance, varies and that the magnitude of dissonance affects the pressure for change. Not all inconsistencies bother us enough to warrant changing our attitudes or beliefs. If Dahlia likes peas but finds out that her good friend Maddie does not, that finding probably will not make Dahlia feel uncomfortable enough to need to change how she feels about Maddie or peas. Of course, if Dahlia makes his living selling peas, that could be a different story. Festinger argued that the greater the magnitude or level of dissonance, the greater the pressure for change. So, did Lucius experience enough dissonance to experience pressure to change his attitudes, beliefs, or behaviors?

The magnitude of dissonance is a result of three key factors: the **importance** of the cognitions, the **ratio** of dissonant to consonant cognitions, and the degree of **cognitive overlap**. First, the more *important* the cognitive elements involved, the more dissonance that will likely be elicited. For example, a cognitive inconsistency related to a life-or-death question, such as driving when drunk, would generate more pressure to resolve the inconsistency than a conflict regarding vegetables. Again, the receiver determines the relationships, and the perception of importance is in the receiver's mind. ⌜Lucius believes strongly in honesty and values learning. These beliefs are inconsistent with his cheating behavior and it is quite likely that Lucius is experiencing a lot of cognitive dissonances.⌟

A persuader can try to raise the magnitude of dissonance by trying to raise the *importance* of the issue for the receiver. For example, antismoking campaigns have tried to increase the importance of the health hazards of smoking by emphasizing the damage done to children and family members around the smoker or the importance of the smoker being alive and healthy for loved ones. This is an effort to raise the importance of the issue. Once the magnitude or level of dissonance is large enough, the receiver feels pressured to reduce the dissonance in some way.

The *ratio* of dissonant to consonant elements also determines the magnitude of dissonance. Most of us have multiple cognitions, or pieces of information, about any given topic. ⌜Some of the cognitions are likely consonant and some are dissonant with one another. The greater the number of dissonant elements in comparison to consonant elements linked to the behavior in question, the greater the dissonance and the greater the pressure to change something to regain consistency.⌟

Let's take the example of smoking. Ernesto smokes cigarettes and has the cognition "I smoke cigarettes." On the consonant or consistent side with smoking Ernesto has cognitions such as "smoking keeps my weight down," "smoking calms me down," "smoking makes me more comfortable in social settings," "I need the nicotine," and "I like the flavor of cigarettes." On the dissonant side Ernesto has cognitions such as "smoking causes lung disease," "smoking causes cancer," "smoking offends other people," and "smoking is very expensive." This example has five consonant cognitions and four dissonant cognitions, a 5:4 ratio. Ignoring the importance of individual cognitions for a moment, the more consonant cognitions that are present, the less dissonance Ernesto will experience. The antismoking forces have developed as many arguments against smoking as possible with the hope of adding dissonant

Google "CDC Smoking Campaigns" to see some of the messages on anti-smoking. Are these messages likely to arouse dissonance in smokers?

cognitions to smokers' cognitive structures to increase the magnitude of dissonance to a level that requires action by the receiver. The Centers for Disease Control and Prevention (CDC) has launched several antismoking campaigns over the years, such as the "Tips from Former Smokers," that uses true images and stories of smokers. These public service announcements attempt to create dissonance by adding important dissonant cognitions.

The third factor that influences the magnitude of dissonance experienced is the degree of *cognitive overlap* between the choices facing the subject. *The lesser the cognitive overlap between the alternatives, the greater the dissonance experienced.* Cognitive overlap refers to the similarity of the choices available. The greater the similarity, the greater the cognitive overlap. Suppose you received an inheritance of $20,000. In deciding what to do with your inheritance, one option would be to replace your old car, an action that would be practical and greatly needed. Another option would be to splurge the bulk of the inheritance on a vacation through Europe, an action less practical that you don't necessarily need but would be wonderful. In this case, there is little similarity between buying a car and going to Europe, so there is little cognitive overlap. If you were choosing between these two options, you would likely experience a good deal of dissonance. On the other hand, if you were choosing between two different models of cars (e.g., a Toyota and a Honda), there is a great deal of cognitive overlap and therefore you would experience less dissonance than in the first example.

Persuaders often send messages to increase the magnitude of dissonance in order to increase the level of cognitive dissonance. The greater the dissonance, the more likely the target of the message is to feel pressured to do something to resolve the dissonance. Advertisers hope you will buy their products, and social movements such as Mothers Against Drunk Driving (MADD) hope you will support their cause. At other times, however, persuaders may try to help reduce the dissonance in order to prevent you from changing attitudes or behaviors. For example, the tobacco industry has tried to reduce dissonance about smoking with advertisements about smokers' rights and the danger of governmental control.

It should be noted that there is no magic level of dissonance that works for everyone. Each person has his or her own level of tolerance for inconsistency, and it is up to the receiver to decide how much dissonance is enough to warrant a change. Different people have different tolerances for dissonance, much as different people have different personality characteristics.

DISSONANCE REDUCTION

⌐When the magnitude of dissonance is greater than a person's tolerance, the individual becomes motivated to **reduce the dissonance**. What can we do to reduce dissonance? There are three basic ways of reducing dissonance. Individuals can (1) change their behavior, (2) change the importance of specific cognitions, and (3) add new cognitions. Changing behavior is often what persuaders want. Companies want consumers to buy their products, politicians want votes, charities want financial contributions, and social causes want action. **Changing behavior** or committing to change future behavior aligns our behavioral intention with our attitudes and beliefs, reducing dissonance and providing a sense of harmony.⌐

Our discussion of magnitude of the dissonance points toward the other two ways to resolve the dissonance. Recall that the importance of cognitions impacts the magnitude of dissonance. Therefore, the receiver can **change the importance** of certain cognitions to reduce dissonance. For example, deciding that the cognition about the cost of smoking is not so important after all would be one way to reduce dissonance without changing behavior. Changing the importance of cognitions can take different forms.

Robert Abelson (1959, 1963, 1968) ⌜described four modes of reducing dissonance, transcendence, differentiation, bolstering, and denial. Transcendence and differentiation are examples of changing the importance of cognitions. Transcendence refers to values that are more important than the issues causing the dissonance. The superior value transcends the lesser inconsistent attitude and is used to justify behaviors that to others appear to be very inconsistent. For example, in 1993, Michael Griffin shot and killed Dr. David Gunn who worked at an abortion clinic in Pensacola, Florida. Griffin and other protestors justified the murder by pointing out how many abortions Dr. Gunn had performed. The value of protecting hundreds of unborn children in the future by killing one doctor transcends the inconsistency for these individuals. Differentiation is the obverse of transcendence. Rather than finding a superior, encompassing value, differentiation involves splitting the cognitive element into acceptable or consistent parts and unacceptable or inconsistent parts. For example, Ruth experiences dissonance over engaging in environmentally unfriendly behavior. Ruth may differentiate pollution created by wastefulness and pollution created by living a productive life. Ruth reduces dissonance by focusing on her efficient use of electricity (she turns off lights), water (she takes short showers), and re-uses plastic bags.⌟

⌜**Adding new cognitions** is the third approach to reducing dissonance and involves linking new cognitions to the behavior that is creating dissonance. An individual may identify more reasons or cognitions that are consistent with his or her behavior to reduce the dissonance. This is also known as bolstering. Bolstering refers to adding consonant elements to reduce the ratio of dissonant to consonant elements. The more consonant elements, the less dissonance the receiver is likely to experience. A smoker who wants to continue to smoke might bolster his or her consonant cognitions by believing that smoking helps keep her weight down. Adding more positives helps counter the dissonance caused by inconsistent evidence. When bolstering is used, the individual is essentially strengthening beliefs and attitudes that support the individual's behavior or decision. This may represent an attitude shift. For instance, the individual could decide that smoking also enhances his or her concentration, creating a more consonant situation for the receiver. Again, cognitions are changed in order to reduce dissonance. Abelson (1959) identified bolstering as a specific example of adding new cognitions.

The fourth dissonance reduction strategy identified by Abelson is denial. Denial involves the receiver simply choosing to disbelieve or reject cognitive elements that create dissonance. For example, there is tremendous evidence that our climate is changing, but many people deny the validity of evidence as a means to reduce dissonance created by the inconsistency between their behaviors and their positive attitude toward maintaining an environment conducive to human existence. When individuals use denial to resolve dissonance, neither behavior nor attitude changes. Denial maintains the status quo. ⌟

When a person experiences cognitive dissonance, he or she is motivated to reduce the dissonance and uses one or more of the strategies we have discussed. Reduction of cognitive dissonance involves either changing one's behavior or changing one's cognitions. Changing one's cognitions is essentially changing one's attitudes and beliefs. As persuaders, we are interested in changing attitudes, beliefs, and behaviors. When we create situations in which receivers experience cognitive dissonance, we create an opportunity to influence the receivers' attitudes, beliefs, and/or behaviors.

COGNITIVE DISSONANCE CONTEXTS

⌈What kinds of situations lead to cognitive dissonance? As we discussed previously, dissonance occurs when we simultaneously hold two cognitions that are inconsistent with one another. How does that happen? In general, some event occurs that causes us to be mindful of the inconsistency between our cognitions. Keep in mind, that we often go about our day-to-day activities in a rather mindless manner; that is, we behave on autopilot with little thought. So something has to happen to make us mindful of what we are doing and its consistency with our attitudes and beliefs. ⌟Dissonance has been studied in four contexts or situations: induced compliance, hypocrisy, decision-making, and effort justification. Dissonance is not limited to these contexts, but the research on these contexts provides us with the key situational factors that create dissonance. ⌈If you understand why dissonance occurs in these contexts, you will be able to recognize other dissonance arousing contexts. ⌟Of course, when a theory explains what causes a phenomenon, we can better predict and control that phenomenon.

INDUCED COMPLIANCE

The initial study conducted by Festinger and Carlsmith (1959) is a classic example of **induced compliance** research. The researchers created a very boring task involving research participants—in this case undergraduate college students—putting spools on a tray and turning pegs for an hour. The research participants were told this was an experiment examining performance on the task. After the boring task, the researcher asked the participants for help with another part of the experiment. Participants were asked to tell a participant waiting to complete the study that the boring task they had just completed was enjoyable and interesting so future participants would have a positive expectation going into the experiment. The person posing as a waiting participant was really a confederate working for the experimenters. Half of the participants were offered $1 for performing this task; the other half were offered $20 (remember this is 1950s money). An additional group of students who completed the boring task but were not asked to talk to the waiting participant served as a control group.

Google "How much was a dollar worth in 1959" to see how much $1 and $20 was worth in 1959.

The task was considered to be a **counter-attitudinal behavior** and is a key characteristic of the induced compliance context. Counter-attitudinal behavior refers to individuals behaving in a manner that goes against their attitudes. In this case, the participants were well aware of how boring the task was, yet almost all of the participants (48 out of 51) agreed to tell the next participant that it was interesting. If we assume that most people see themselves as honest, telling a lie would be counter-attitudinal. In the induced compliance context, dissonance occurs as a result of a person performing a behavior that is inconsistent with his or her attitudes (counter-attitudinal behavior).

After the participants engaged in the counter-attitudinal behavior—lying to a person they believed to be the next participant—a researcher interviewed them about participating in departmental research projects. Mixed in with the survey items were questions asking the participants to rate how interesting and enjoyable the task had been. Those participants who had been paid only a $1 found the task to be significantly more interesting and enjoyable than those who had been paid $20. A control group also engaged in the boring task for an hour and was asked to evaluate how interesting and enjoyable the task was; however, they did not engage in the counter-attitudinal behavior. This group rated the experiment similar to those paid $20. Those participants who were induced to comply with a counter-attitudinal behavior developed a relatively positive attitude toward the task when paid $1 but not when paid $20. Is this what you expected?

Search for "A Lesson in Cognitive Dissonance" on YouTube to see how the experiment was conducted.

⌈Festinger and Carlsmith (1959) predicted that dissonance would be aroused for participants paid $1 but not for those paid $20.⌋ Why did the $1 group experience more dissonance for their counter-attitudinal advocacy? Those who were paid $1 experienced dissonance but could not use the money they were paid as a justification for their behavior. They had to convince themselves that they lied to other students because the task was not really that bad. ⌈Being paid $1 wasn't enough to justify their behavior. They had to find another reason for their behavior. The easiest justification was to tell themselves that the task was not really that bad, and so what they said to the other students wasn't really a lie.⌋ Those who were paid $20 could tell themselves they did it for the money so they experienced little dissonance. Thus, the group with the greater dissonance had to change their attitude in order to resolve the inconsistency.

Many studies of dissonance have involved inducing participants to perform a counter-attitudinal behavior. Perhaps the most interesting of these studies was conducted by Zimbardo, Weisenberg, Firestone, and Levy (1965) and involved convincing research participants to eat grasshoppers. In this experiment, half of the participants were exposed to a cold and unfriendly researcher who encouraged them to sample the grasshoppers. The other half was exposed to a warm and friendly experimenter who similarly encouraged the subjects to sample the grasshoppers. Then, those who had eaten at least one grasshopper, about half the participants, were asked to evaluate grasshoppers as food.

Cognitive dissonance theory predicts that those who ate the grasshoppers for the unfriendly researcher would rate the grasshoppers higher than those who ate them for the friendly experimenter. Why? Those who ate them for the unfriendly researcher experienced dissonance because they did not have a good reason for sampling the grasshoppers. They might tell themselves they ate the grasshoppers because they like to try new things and they like unusual foods. Those exposed to the friendly experimenter could convince themselves that they sampled the grasshoppers to please the experimenter. As a result, there would be less dissonance to resolve. With little or no dissonance to resolve, there would be no motivation to change one's beliefs about eating grasshoppers, and the grasshoppers would be rated unfavorably. This was exactly what the study results indicated. As with Festinger and Carlsmith's study, the smaller the incentive for the behavior, the greater the dissonance and the greater the attitude change. A second context, similar to induced compliance but opposite in some ways, is the hypocrisy context.

HYPOCRISY

Sometimes your target audience already has a positive attitude toward the issue of interest but does not behave in accordance with that attitude. In other words, they are being hypocritical. They say one thing but do another. The **hypocrisy** context involves ⌐pro-attitudinal behavior. **Pro-attitudinal behavior** is behavior that is consistent with or supportive of one's attitudes. In hypocrisy situations,⌐ individuals are reminded of their current attitude toward an issue and then reminded that their behavior is not consistent with the attitude they hold. In this case, we are more interested in changing their behavior than their attitude. An example of the hypocrisy context is that many young people believe that using condoms is an effective way to reduce the risk of contracting HIV and other sexually transmitted infections, but they do not actually use condoms and therefore put themselves at risk. A positive attitude toward condoms already exists, so messages about the benefits of condom use are not likely to be very effective. Stone, Aronson, Crain, Winslow, and Fried (1994) induced participants to feel dissonance about the inconsistency between their attitudes toward safe sex and their behavior.

Stone and his colleagues recruited 72 students who were sexually active and at risk for contracting HIV to participate in a study. Half of the participants were asked to develop a persuasive speech about HIV and safe sex targeted at high school students. These participants developed and videotaped their speeches. The real purpose of giving the speeches was for the participants to be reminded of their existing attitudes and beliefs about condom use as a means of preventing the spread of HIV. The remaining participants were asked to make speech outlines but did not actually give their speeches. Half of the participants who created and taped a speech and half of the participants who only made an outline were then given a list of circumstances that "might make it difficult to use condoms" (Stone et al., 1994, p. 119). Participants were asked to read the list and then to make a list of the circumstances surrounding their own past failures to use condoms. The purpose of making this list was to make participants mindful of their behavior that was inconsistent with their attitude toward practicing safe sex. The other participants were not made mindful of their past failures to practice safe sex. Finally, participants completed a questionnaire and had the opportunity to purchase condoms and obtain additional information on HIV (in the form of brochures).

Stone and his colleagues hypothesized that the group that made the public commitment and that was made mindful of past failures to practice safe sex would experience the greatest dissonance. In this situation, the easiest way to reduce dissonance would be to bring one's behavior in line with the existing attitude. In this case, buying condoms and intending to use them in the future allowed the participants to reduce dissonance. Stone et al.'s hypothesis was confirmed. Those participants in the hypocrisy condition (commitment and mindfulness) purchased the most condoms and also intended to practice safe sex in the future.

There are two key elements to using hypocrisy successfully. The first involves making the *attitude of interest salient*. Stone and his colleagues did this by asking participants to make a videotaped speech about safe sex. In another study, Dickerson, Thibodeau, Aronson, and Miller (1992) asked participants to sign a poster that would be displayed to make the attitude salient. ⌐The attitude must be made salient in an active way (Stone & Fernandez, 2008). In other words, recipients have to do something, not just read something or think about something; they have to take some action.⌐ The second key element is making *past failures* to behave in accordance with the attitude salient. Stone and his colleagues did this by having participants create a list of the circumstances surrounding the times they had failed to practice safe sex. The failures need to be associated with a *recent context* and should be *private rather than public*. When participants were publicly called out about their hypocrisy, they attempted to justify themselves and avoid changing their behavior. Therefore, to induce hypocrisy, you have to engage your audience ⌐in a set of activities that (1) makes their existing attitude salient, and (2) makes them privately contemplate their past failures to behave in a way that was consistent with their attitude.⌐

Stone and Fernandez (2008) reviewed research on hypocrisy and found considerable support that hypocrisy can generate behavior change in applied settings outside lab settings. ⌐In addition, Stone and Fernandez argued that hypocrisy works best with prosocial behaviors. People have a tendency to feel more dissonance over not performing positively valued activities than neutral or antisocial actions.⌐ Stone and Fernandez reviewed research that examined influencing consumer energy conservation, water conservation, and safer driving behaviors and found that hypocrisy approaches were effective across the board. In addition, they found evidence that this effect exists in other cultures. Research supporting the hypocrisy effect was reported in the United States, Canada, Australia, and Japan. This is a tried and true approach that works in the real world in multiple contexts.

The induced compliance context involved inducing the receiver to perform a *counter-attitudinal behavior*. Hypocrisy involves inducing the receiver to recognize that their *pro-attitudinal behavior*, is not consistent with their attitudes. Both the induced compliance and the hypocrisy contexts involve attitudes and behaviors that are inconsistent and result in dissonance. The dissonance creates pressure to change so that the attitude and behavior are in line with one another.

DECISION MAKING

An additional context for dissonance is **decision making**. When an individual makes a decision or choice, he or she is likely to experience dissonance. Lucius' decision to cheat on a final exam is a good example of the decision-making context. The decision-making context has four stages that are illustrated in Figure 7.1. The first stage is *conflict*. This is when the alternatives are being evaluated and information is being gathered. Before making the purchase, Larry and Marj compared the various types of computers and technology at the Apple Store. They also asked friends and acquaintances who were knowledgeable about technology. With the way the store displayed the various products, Larry and Marj could not avoid being exposed to the new technology and ways of using it. Being unable to avoid the alternatives, they experienced conflict about which alternative to choose—stick with what they have (a single desktop computer in their home office) or the new technology (and higher price). ⌐Before making the decision to cheat, Lucius considered his options and compared alternatives. He considered the consequences of doing poorly on the exam, the likelihood of being caught, and the ethics of cheating. As he considered his options, Lucius experienced conflict about what to do—should he do his best and trust his intelligence or cheat and risk getting caught.⌐ The second stage is the *decision*. At

Step 1–Conflict between alternatives

Step 2–Decision is made

Step 3–Cognitive dissonance is experienced

Step 4–Dissonance reduction occurs

FIGURE 7.1 Decision-making stages.

this point the decision is made—an alternative is chosen. Obviously, Lucius made a choice and the choice was to cheat on the exam. The third stage is *cognitive dissonance*. Once a decision is made, we often feel dissonance about whether we made the right choice. ⌐The reason we experience dissonance is that in choosing one option over another, we sacrifice all of the benefits of the unchosen option. Additionally, the chosen option is not likely perfect, therefore in choosing that option, we also choose its disadvantages. The advantages of the unchosen option and the disadvantages of the chosen option are dissonant with our decision, and thus generate dissonance.⌐

The fourth and final stage in the decision-making context is **dissonance reduction**. We seek supporting information to help us feel better about our decision, and our perception of our choice tends to become more positive than we perceived it initially. The dissonance reduction process helps us feel satisfied with the decision we made. ⌐Recall that Lucius was pleased with his decision. After making the decision, he experienced dissonance. The easiest way for him to reduce the dissonance was to change the importance of dissonant cognitions and add consonant cognitions. In the hours following the exam, he bolstered the cognitions about the importance of getting an "A" on the exam. He differentiated cheating in a class outside of his major from cheating in a major class. He added consonant cognitions by recalling all of the ways the teacher had been unfair and a poor teacher. Lucius denied the connection between cheating and his value for honesty. As Lucius considered each of these issues, his dissonance was reduced and he convinced himself that he made the right decision. Lucius could have also resolved the dissonance by concluding that cheating was a mistake, everyone makes mistakes, and vow never to cheat again.⌐

EFFORT JUSTIFICATION

Have you ever wondered why members of the military are so loyal and committed to the military ⌐when they have endured such difficult training and duties? Or similarly, why young men and women are committed to fraternities and sororities after enduring hazing? It doesn't seem to make sense that we would be so committed to a group that required so much from us.⌐ However, we observe this behavior in many ways. Hazing and initiation activities of various types and levels are common in fraternities, sororities, the military, and other organizations, yet these organizations typically have loyal members who willingly devote their time, energy, and money to the organization.

⌐Hazing and initiation are two different activities. Initiation is the process of meeting the standards and requirements of a group. For instance, initiation to be a firefighter involves demonstrating tremendous physical strength and endurance because the job of firefighting is physically demanding, and running upstairs carrying 75 lbs. is a real job requirement. The initiation activities are relevant to the group's purpose.

Hazing is the abuse of new or prospective members where the activities have no relevance to the group's purpose (Cimino, 2011). Activities such as forcing young men to wear diapers or to endure beatings to join a fraternity are irrelevant to the group's purpose. Rather these are examples of hazing and not initiation. When we expend great effort or endure great discomfort to obtain some desirable outcome, dissonance is aroused. This situation is referred to as the **effort justification** context. It is dissonant or inconsistent to perform a behavior that is unpleasant. The more unpleasant a behavior is, the more dissonance that is aroused. So, when an individual endures being forced to perform demeaning skits in public or engage in extreme forms of exercise in order to join a sorority (Roos, 2017), dissonance results. Dissonance is unpleasant, and we are motivated to reduce it. The easiest way to reduce dissonance in this type of situation is to increase the desirability of the outcome (sorority membership in this example). By believing that the sorority is very desirable with many wonderful benefits that will endure for a lifetime, the unpleasant behavior becomes justified. If you consider the group you are most committed to, you have probably put forth a good deal of effort for that group and have probably told yourself that it was worthwhile to do so. If you believed it was *not* worthwhile to put forth so much effort for the group, you would experience ongoing dissonance because it does not make sense to work hard for something that is not worthy of your time. It also does not make sense to endure abuse to join an organization.

Aronson and Mills (1959) were the first to study the justification of effort paradigm in a study that compared severe and mild group initiations. Aronson and Mills recruited 63 college women to join a discussion group on the psychology of sex. In the severe initiation group, the women had to read aloud in front of the experimenter sexual words and passages designed to be embarrassing for the women (remember, this was in the 1950s). In the mild initiation group, women had to read aloud in front of the experimenter passages and words that were related to sex but not sexually explicit. In a control group, women did not have to read anything to be allowed into the group. After completing the initiation, women were informed that they had "passed" and were allowed into the group. The women then listened to the group discussion that was designed to be as boring and banal as possible. After the discussion, the women rated the discussion and the participants. The women who experienced the severe initiation in order to be a member of the group evaluated the discussion and the participants significantly more positively than those women who experienced the mild initiation or those in the control group. This study provided the first evidence that greater effort to belong to a group resulted in more positive evaluations of that group. Research since this study has further supported this hypothesis and indicates that the process of reducing the dissonance generated by the initiation creates a positive evaluation of the group. Our commitment to a group is probably largely influenced by the amount of effort we have put forth to be a part of that group. However, we do not experience dissonance every time we do something that is inconsistent. Certain conditions are necessary for dissonance to occur.

NECESSARY CONDITIONS FOR COGNITIVE DISSONANCE

Much research has been conducted using cognitive dissonance theory, and part of that research has led to the identification of conditions necessary for cognitive dissonance to occur. One criterion is that receivers have to perceive the situation as involving **freedom of choice** rather than force. ⌐For example, if you observe a male colleague making sexual comments to his assistant and you don't report it to human resources, you will likely feel cognitive dissonance (assuming you find sexual harassment to be wrong). If, however, you feel certain you will lose your job (and therefore not able to support your family) if you make a report, you will likely feel you had no choice but to keep quiet. This is still a very unpleasant situation, but your lack of choice would likely subdue dissonance. Only when a person is engaging in the behavior by her own choice will those actions cause dissonance. You might be thinking that you would have a choice in this situation. Freedom of choice is not dichotomous; it is a continuum as discussed in Chapter 1. Your feelings of self-efficacy and perceived behavioral control (see Chapter 10) also influence how much freedom of choice you feel you have in a given situation. For example, some smokers say¬ they would like to quit, but they believe they are so addicted to nicotine that it is not within their power to quit. The dissonance-arousing messages against smoking will not be as likely to generate behavior change because the receivers do not believe they have a choice in the matter. ⌐In the dissonance studies discussed in the prior sections, participants were not coerced into performing the behaviors; they were free to decline. They had personal responsibility for their choices.¬

A second criterion for cognitive dissonance is that there must be **insufficient external justification** for the behavior. This means that the person needs to look internally to find the explanation for why he or she is engaging in the behavior that causes dissonance. If there is an external reason, then the behavior does not cause dissonance. For example, imagine Mary being very friendly to Sue even though Mary dislikes Sue. If Mary can point to an external reason for being friendly, such as being at a student organization meeting where social rules call for people to be friendly to everyone present, then Mary would experience no dissonance about behaving nicely to someone she disliked. However, if Mary and Sue were alone and Mary behaved in a friendly manner, Mary would experience some dissonance over the inconsistency between her attitude and her behavior. Persuaders who use cognitive dissonance theory try to create situations where there is no external justification for the target's behavior.

In the Festinger and Carlsmith (1959) experiment involving lying to others about the boring task, those in the $20 condition had an external justification for their behavior, whereas those who were paid just $1 for this task did not. Similarly, participants with a friendly experimenter in the grasshopper sampling experiment had an external justification of wanting to please a nice person as the rationale for eating the grasshoppers. Those with the unfriendly researcher had no external reasons to explain eating the grasshopper, so the explanation to resolve the inconsistency had to be that the grasshoppers were not so bad.

APPLYING COGNITIVE DISSONANCE THEORY

The earlier descriptions of the four contexts should have illustrated to some extent how cognitive dissonance theory is applied. The human motivation for consistency is central to cognitive dissonance theory and is a key factor in applied persuasion. As illustrated in the four dissonance contexts, when people become aware of an inconsistency in their behavior, attitudes, or beliefs, they are motivated to make a change and bring their attitudes, beliefs, and behavior into alignment. Applying the theory, persuaders can create situations where receivers are made aware of inconsistencies. ⌐One thing to note about the application of cognitive dissonance theory, is that it cannot be done in a mass-mediated message. Applying cognitive dissonance theory involves face-to-face interventions that engage receivers in activities.⌐ Persuaders can also take advantage of the dissonance reduction process by providing information that is consistent with the desired attitude or belief. For example, people will experience dissonance after making a big purchase such as a computer car. Providing new and positive information about the computer car will help the consumer reduce dissonance by concluding that they made a wise purchase.

⌐The hypocrisy context is particularly useful for health and safety interventions. Most of us are aware of health and safety behaviors that are good for us and that we should engage in, such as eating vegetables, wearing a seatbelt, exercising, and minimizing distractions while driving. But our behavior often doesn't match up with our beliefs and attitudes about these behaviors. Morrongiello and Mark (2008) used hypocrisy to design an intervention to reduce playground injuries among elementary-aged children and focused on reducing risky play behaviors on playground equipment. Following the key elements of hypocrisy, Morrongiello and Mark made students mindful of their past playground behavior by having the students make posters about behaviors students "should do" and "should not do" on the playground. Students were given pictures of low-risk, moderate-risk, and high-risk behaviors to arrange on the posters. Intervention students were also interviewed about their posters, made a list of risky playground behaviors, signed a poster advocating for safe play on playgrounds, and recorded a radio commercial directed at their peers on safe play behaviors. A month after the intervention, intention to engage in high-risk play behaviors were assessed by giving students a chance to revise what playground behaviors was shown on their "should do" and "should not do" posters. Students in the hypocrisy intervention were much less likely to show high-risk behaviors on their "should do" posters and less likely to intend to engage in high-risk behaviors as compared to students in the control group. Consistent with our earlier discussion, Morrongiello and Mark had students engage in activities that made their attitudes and beliefs about safe play behaviors salient and that encouraged them to reflect on their recent behavior (past failures). Additionally, the students had several choices, enhancing their freedom of choice and reducing opportunities for external justification.

Both induced compliance and effort justification can be observed in the typical car-buying process.⌐ If you have ever shopped for a car, one of the first things salespeople want you to do is test drive the car. Why? By taking the time to test drive the car, you are performing a behavior that has to be justified. The easiest way to justify it is to tell yourself that you are interested. After test driving the car, the savvy salesperson will elicit positive comments about the car from you by asking questions that almost require a positive response. Now you have not only taken the time to drive the car, but you have also made positive comments about the car—more justifications must be made. Next, the salesperson is likely to get out a contract and ask you for your address, where you work, and your social security number so that the dealer can begin to arrange financing, often under the guise of identifying the "best deal." Before you know it, you have invested over an hour of your precious time and started the paperwork necessary for buying a car. At this point, it would be rather inconsistent to say "No, I'm not interested in this car." Of course, if you are aware of the tactics being used, you can avoid feeling the pressure of cognitive dissonance and walk away. So, car dealers induce you to comply with simple behaviors such as test driving the car, voicing positive thoughts about the car, and giving them information to fill out the forms. Although no single behavior is that large, with each one you have more and more to justify. In a sense, using cognitive dissonance theory is like leaving a trail of breadcrumbs. Each crumb requires a small commitment. Although each is small, each must also be justified.

⌜Festinger (1957) considers cognitive consistency a basic need, similar to the needs for affection, food, and water. As humans, we are motivated to behave in ways that are consistent with our attitudes and beliefs. When our behaviors are inconsistent with our attitudes and beliefs, either we change our attitudes and beliefs, or we change our behavior. Persuaders take advantage of this basic need to create situations that either induce us to behave in ways that create dissonance or that cause us to acknowledge our inconsistent behavior.⌟

ALTERNATE EXPLANATIONS

A theory is an explanation for some phenomenon and a good theory explains, predicts, and controls that phenomenon. At the beginning of this chapter, a phenomenon of research participants paid $1 developing a more positive attitude toward a boring task than those paid $20 was presented. Festinger's (1957) cognitive dissonance theory explains why this happened. However, not everyone agreed that cognitive dissonance theory provided the best explanation for this phenomenon. The explanation for a phenomenon determines our ability to predict the phenomenon and our ability to control it, so we have to get the explanation right to make accurate predictions, and assert control over the process.

Several alternative explanations for the cognitive dissonance study effects have been put forth and tested. Two of these are worth mentioning. First, Claude Steele (1988) developed self-affirmation theory. The basic premise of **self-affirmation theory** is that situations that involve inconsistency threaten a person's need for integrity. Steele doesn't deny that inconsistency is a problem for people, but he argues that the problem with inconsistency is that it threatens our self-image. A basic premise of self-affirmation theory is that we are driven to maintain our sense of self as "adaptively and morally adequate, that is, competent, good, coherent, unitary, stable, capable of free choice, capable of controlling important outcomes, and so on" (Steele, 1988, p. 262). So, when we become aware of our inconsistent behavior, it threatens our self-adequacy and we engage in cognitive activity or behavior that affirms our sense of self as a good person. Our focus is on restoring our sense of our self as a good person, not on reducing inconsistency. Some support has been found for self-affirmation theory (Steele, 1988); however, Harmon-Jones (2002) argued that the nature of the methods used to test self-affirmation affected the importance placed on dissonant cognitions. Harmon-Jones (2002) concluded that cognitive dissonance theory explains the results of self-affirmation studies; therefore, self-affirmation theory does not provide a better explanation for the phenomena observed in cognitive dissonance studies.

A second alternative explanation for the cognitive dissonance study results has received more attention. Daryl Bem (1967, 1972) thought that Festinger and his

TABLE 7.1 *ATTRIBUTION SUMMARY TABLE*

	CONSENSUS	CONSISTENCY	DISTINCTIVENESS
High	External	Internal	External
Low	Internal	External	Internal

colleagues had it all wrong and proposed the **self-perception theory** as a better explanation of the induced compliance research results. He argued that the research participants made internal attributions about their behavior and it was these attributions that caused the results.

Self-perception theory is based on attribution theory. Attribution theory (Kelley, 1967) explains that how we relate to other people depends in part on what we think about them and why we believe they engaged in any given behavior. To make sense of other people's behavior, we create explanations for why they do things. The process of creating causal explanations for why things happen is referred to as **attributions** and the attributions we make determine the impressions we have of others. When we make attributions about others, we attribute their behavior to either internal or external causes. For example, if Trey is late to class, I might make an internal attribution and think the cause of Trey's tardiness is his disposition (he is lazy and inconsiderate). Or, I might make an external attribution and think the cause of Trey's tardiness is a result of the situation (the bus was late).

Bem argued that we not only make attributions about other people's behavior, we also make attributions about our own behavior. A basic premise of self-perception theory is that *we are observers of ourselves as we are observers of others.* According to self-perception theory, persuasion involves a person acting and then figuring out why he or she behaved in that way in order to understand his or her own attitudes. Bem advanced two postulates for self-perception theory. The first is that "individuals come to 'know' their own attitudes, emotions, and other internal states partially by inferring them from observations of their own overt behavior and/or the circumstances in which this behavior occurs" (Bem, 1972, p. 2). The second postulate is that "to the extent internal cues are weak, ambiguous, or uninterpretable, the individual is functionally in the same position as an outside observer, an observer who must necessarily rely upon those same external cues to infer the individual's internal states" (Bem, 1972, p. 2). In this case, if you are the target of a persuasive message and are unaware of any situational influences on your behavior, then you are likely to make an internal attribution about your behavior. In persuasion terms, that generally means you perceive your attitudes as being in line with your behavior.

Recall Festinger and Carlsmith (1959) induced compliance study involving the boring task for which participants were paid $1 or $20 to lie to others. Bem explains the results of this study using the two self-perception theory postulates. As the participants tried to decide how boring the task of putting spools on trays and turning pegs for an hour was, they were in the position of outside observers and looked to the situational cues to help them understand their internal states. Those who were paid $1 to lie to others saw a very weak situational cue for their behavior. Because the external cue was so weak, they needed to infer an internal reason for lying. In this case, it meant that participants saw their attitudes toward the task as more positive because there was no external explanation for their behavior.

Those who were paid $20 to lie to others, however, saw a situational cue that explained their behavior. They could infer that they were willing to lie for the researcher for the money (an external factor), and thus they had no reason to infer any internal reason for doing so. Those participants made a more negative evaluation of the task. If you were an outside observer, you would probably have drawn the same conclusions about another person's behavior. Thus, self-perception theory can explain the same research finding that was used to support cognitive dissonance theory. Research was conducted to support Bem's challenge to cognitive dissonance theory. To do this, research had to be designed that could demonstrate the usefulness of self-perception theory and simultaneously show the weaknesses of cognitive dissonance theory. Schachter and Singer (1962) conducted such a study that involved injecting participants with epinephrine (adrenaline). Participants were told that the study involved investigation of the effects of a vitamin mixture called "suproxin" on vision. They were then placed into four groups. Three of the groups received the epinephrine injection; the fourth was a control group. The control group was given a placebo injection of saline solution. The first epinephrine group was *informed* about the side effects to expect from receiving the injection, including an elevated heart rate, shaking hands, and warm or flushed faces. The second epinephrine group was *misinformed* about the effects of the injection; they were told that the expected side effects included numb feet, itching, and a slight headache. The final epinephrine group was left *ignorant* of the drug's effects and was told that it would cause no side effects at all.

Epinephrine is also known as adrenalin and is a hormone and medication. Side effects include shakiness, anxiety, sweating, and fast heart rate.

Each participant was asked to wait in the research room for about 20 minutes to let the supposed suproxin get into their system. During the wait a confederate posing as another research participant was brought into the room. The confederate was instructed to act either *euphoric* or *angry*. In the euphoric condition, the confederate doodled on paper, made paper basketballs and shot them at wastebaskets, made paper airplanes, shot paper balls with a rubber band, and used a hula hoop that was in the room. The confederate talked about his activities and invited the participant to join him. In the anger condition, the two students were asked to fill out a long questionnaire while they waited. The confederate complained about the injection, complained about the questions, and got angry about personal and insulting questions. Finally, the confederate ripped up the questionnaire and stomped out of the room.

According to self-perception theory, participants should base an evaluation of their own attitudes on observations of their own behavior and the situational cues surrounding that behavior. In the ignorant and misinformed conditions, the situational cues were weak or ambiguous about the true cause of the physiological arousal each participant experienced, so in these conditions participants used the confederate's behavior to infer how they felt. In the informed condition, the participants had been given a situational explanation for the arousal they experienced; thus, no further internal explanation attribution was needed.

Participants in the ignorant and misinformed condition were more likely to join in the behaviors of the confederate, and they were more likely to report either anger or euphoria based on the behaviors the confederate exhibited even though the physiological arousal was the same for both conditions. Thus, these participants were using situational cues that were more obvious (the behavior of the confederate) to explain their arousal because they had no other good explanation for what they experienced. Those in the informed condition were less likely to be influenced by the confederate's behavior because they had an explanation for the arousal (behavior) they observed in themselves.

The epinephrine results are not easily explained with cognitive dissonance theory because no cognitive dissonance was generated. This is an example of forming new attitudes because there were no prior attitudes about the behavior experienced after the drug injection. Bem argued that self-perception can explain and predict most of the classic cognitive dissonance theory results (such as the $1/$20 study) and explain research results that cognitive dissonance theory cannot. The research indicates that we make attributions about our own behavior and that we may use external cues to figure out how we feel. However, Eagly and Chaiken (1994) concluded that ⌜Bem's self-perception theory did not provide a better explanation than cognitive dissonance theory and that self-perception was less predictive of attitude change.

Cognitive dissonance theory has withstood several challenges. Both self-affirmation theory and self-perception theory provide interesting explanations for the phenomenon, but could not explain the diverse study results as well as cognitive dissonance theory. After more than a half-century of research and challenges, cognitive dissonance continues to give us a useful explanation for why people change their attitudes, beliefs, and behavior.⌟

STRENGTHS AND LIMITATIONS

⌜Cognitive dissonance theory is a valued perspective and endured many challenges. A primary strength is that it explains human behavior in many situations. It helps us explain how people manage contradictory behavior across many contexts. Secondly, it provides guidance on how to design experiences that result in greater commitment. For example, the induced compliance and effort justification contexts indicate that we *should not* offer big rewards and make entrance into a group too easy. People value things and experiences more when they have to work for them. However, cognitive dissonance theory should not be used to justify hazing rituals that harm people. There are a lot of ways people can work hard for something that results in benefits and no harm.⌟

This theory also has limitations. Broad explanatory power is a strength, but it is also a weakness. Because of the many ways to resolve dissonance, cognitive dissonance theory is difficult to disprove. If dissonance is successfully aroused and change occurs, the theory is supported. If change does not occur, the theory can explain that as well by indicating that the magnitude of dissonance was not sufficient or an alternative method of dissonance reduction such as denial was used. This breadth reduces *predictive* ability and *control* ⌜of persuasive outcomes. A weakness of cognitive dissonance theory is that it is difficult to predict what a person will change to reduce dissonance. We can predict they will change something, but not a specific attitude, belief, or behavior. This lack of prediction reduces control and our ability to design persuasive messages and situations that result in the attitude change we desire. In fact, cognitive dissonance is not useful for creating persuasive messages. It is useful in designing situations that will cause dissonance, but not persuasive messages.⌟

In short, cognitive dissonance is a well-regarded theory of persuasion that offers a strong basis for persuasion research and application. As other theories are developed, we will examine a broader view of persuasion.

SUMMARY

- Consistency theories are based on the human drive to be psychologically consistent with beliefs, attitudes, and behavior.
- Cognitive dissonance theory posits that cognitions have one of three relationships: dissonant, consonant, or irrelevant.
- The magnitude of dissonance refers to the amount of dissonance a person experiences. It is a result of the importance of the elements, the ratio of dissonant to consonant elements, and the degree of cognitive overlap.
- Dissonance can be reduced by changing the behavior, changing the importance and/or ratio of dissonant elements, or adding new consonant cognitions.
- The four major contexts in which cognitive dissonance occurs are: induced compliance, hypocrisy, decision making, and effort justification.
- Necessary conditions for cognitive dissonance to occur include freedom of choice and insufficient external justification for the behavior.
- ⌜Self-affirmation and self-perception theories challenged cognitive dissonance theory, but scholars conclude that cognitive dissonance provides the best explanation for the dissonance phenomenon.⌟
- Major strengths of cognitive dissonance theory include the breadth of explanatory power and guidance in creating situations that result in commitment.
- ⌜Major limitations of cognitive dissonance theory include the difficulty in disproving the theory, the difficulty predicting how dissonance will be resolved, and the limited ability to control the persuasion.⌟

KEY TERMS

Adding cognitions—one of three basic ways of reducing cognitive dissonance.

Attributions—the process of creating causal explanations for why things happen.

⌜**Changing behavior**—one of three basic ways of reducing cognitive dissonance.

Change importance of cognitions—one of three basic ways of reducing cognitive dissonance.⌟

Cognitions—bits of knowledge individuals have stored in their minds.

Cognitive dissonance—an aversive motivational state that people are motivated to eliminate.

Cognitive dissonance theory—a consistency theory that emphasizes consistency among cognitions.

Cognitive overlap—the similarity of the choices available. The greater the similarity, the greater the cognitive overlap.

Consonant relationship—two cognitions that are consistent with one another.

Counter-attitudinal behavior—a behavior that is counter, or against, the attitude one holds.

Decision making—a context for dissonance; after making a decision, people often experience cognitive dissonance.

Dissonance reduction—the process a person engages in to reduce cognitive dissonance that involves one or more of the following: change the behavior, change the ratio, change the importance, denial, bolstering, transcendence, and differentiation.

Dissonant relationship—two cognitions that are inconsistent with one another.

Effort justification—dissonance that results from enduring much or working hard to obtain a less than perfect outcome.

Freedom of choice—a necessary condition for dissonance to occur; the receiver needs to freely choose to engage in the dissonance-arousing behaviors.

Hypocrisy—situations in which an individual is reminded of his or her current attitude toward an issue and then reminded that his or her behavior is not consistent with the attitude he or she holds.

Importance of cognitions—one of the three factors that determine the magnitude of dissonance experienced.

Induced compliance—when dissonance results from being induced to perform a counter-attitudinal behavior.

Insufficient external justification—a necessary condition for dissonance to occur; there must be little external (as opposed to internal) reason for engaging in the dissonance-arousing behavior.

Irrelevant relationship—two cognitions that a person perceives as unrelated to one another.

Magnitude of dissonance—the amount of dissonance experienced.

Pro-attitudinal behavior—a behavior that is consistent with one's attitudes.

Self-attribution theory—a theory that provides an alternative explanation for cognitive dissonance research results that emphasizes the need for integrity.

Self-perception theory—a theory that provides an alternative explanation for cognitive dissonance research results that emphasizes self-attribution.

QUESTIONS FOR REVIEW

Respond to the following questions **without** reviewing the text or your notes. These questions are provided to help you practice retrieving information and reflect on your reading.

1. What are some key ideas about cognitive dissonance theory?

2. Did you agree or disagree with anything you read? Explain.

3. What did you learn that was new to you?

4. What concepts, if any, were confusing to you?

Respond to the following questions. You may reference your text or notes to help you.

1. What three factors influence the magnitude of dissonance? How does it increase? What role does it play in cognitive dissonance theory?

2. What are the seven options for dissonance reduction?

3. What is the hypocrisy context? What elements are necessary to use hypocrisy successfully? Why are these elements important?

4. Before you read this chapter, you were asked to identify a decision that resulted in cognitive dissonance. Identify and describe each stage of your decision. Identify and discuss the option(s) you used to reduce dissonance.

5. What is self-perception theory? What are its two postulates? ⌈What theories provide alternative explanations for dissonance theory research results?

6. What are the strengths and weaknesses of cognitive dissonance theory?⌋

QUESTIONS FOR DISCUSSION

1. In your small group, discuss how you might use cognitive dissonance theory in your final presentations. How can you make your audience aware of inconsistencies in their behavior, attitudes, or beliefs?

2. Both cognitive dissonance theory and self-perception theory can explain induced compliance. Which theory more effectively explains the research results? Why?

3. When you graduate from college, you will have decisions to make about what job to pursue and where to live. Imagine taking a job in a city far away from your family, even though you would prefer to live closer to home. What would influence the magnitude of dissonance you might feel? How might you attempt to reduce the dissonance?

4. Find an example of a health or social campaign message that is designed to create dissonance. Are the necessary conditions for cognitive dissonance present? Is the message effective? Why or why not?

5. Discuss the ethical questions provided at the end of the chapter. What ethical considerations are relevant to the information in this chapter about consistency and cognitive dissonance theory?

- Are there guidelines (e.g., don't lie) that would be appropriate for every situation, or are ethics relative?

- Do the ends (e.g., a good outcome) justify any means?

- Is deceiving the receiver ever appropriate?

- Should the source of the message bear primary responsibility for ethics, or should the receiver share that responsibility (e.g., buyer beware)?

REFERENCES

Abelson, R. P. (1959). Modes of resolution of belief dilemmas. *Journal of Conflict Resolution, 3,* 343–352.

Aronson, E., & Mills, J. (1959). The effect of severity of initiation on liking for a group. *Journal of Abnormal and Social Psychology, 59,* 177–181.

Bem, D. J. (1967). Self-perception: An alternative interpretation of cognitive dissonance phenomena. *Psychological Review, 74,* 183–200.

Bem, D. J. (1972). Self-perception theory. In L. Berkowitz (Ed.), *Advances in experimental social psychology* (Vol. 6, pp. 1–62). New York: Academic Press.

Cimino, A. (2011). The evolution of hazing: Motivational mechanisms and the abuse of newcomers. *Journal of Cognition and Culture, 11,* 241-267.

Dickerson, C. A., Thibodeau, R., Aronson, E., & Miller, D. (1992). Using cognitive dissonance to encourage water conservation. *Journal of Applied Social Psychology, 22,* 841–854.

Eagly, A. H., & Chaiken, S. (1994). *The psychology of attitudes.* Fort Worth, TX: Harcourt Brace Jovanovich.

Festinger, L. (1957). *A theory of cognitive dissonance*. Evanston, IL: Row, Peterson.

Festinger, L., & Carlsmith, J. M. (1959). Cognitive consequences of forced compliance. *Journal of Abnormal and Social Psychology, 58,* 203–210.

Harmon-Jones, E. (2002). A cognitive dissonance theory perspective on persuasion. In J. P. Dillard & M. Pfau (Eds.), *The persuasion handbook: Developments in theory and practice* (pp. 99-116). Thousand Oaks, CA: Sage.

Heider, F. (1946). Attitudes and cognitive organization. *Journal of Psychology, 21,* 107–112.

Heider, F. (1958). *The psychology of interpersonal relations*. New York: Wiley.

Kelley, H. H. (1967). Attribution theory in social psychology. In D. Levine (Ed.), *Nebraska Symposium on Motivation* (Vol. A5, pp. 192–238). Lincoln: University of Nebraska Press.

Morrongiello, B. A., & Mark, L. (2008). "Practice what you preach": Induced hypocrisy as an intervention strategy to reduce children's intention to risk take on playgrounds. *Journal of Pediatric Psychology, 33,* 1117-1128.

Osgood, C. E., & Tannenbaum, P. H. (1955). The principle of congruity in the prediction of attitude change. *Psychological Review, 62,* 42–55.

Roos, D. (November 22, 2017). *How hazing works.* Retrieved from https://people. howstuffworks. com/culture-traditions/national-traditions/hazing.htm

Schachter, S., & Singer, J. E. (1962). Cognitive, social and physiological determinates of emotional state. *Psychological Review, 69,* 379–399.

Steele, C. M. (1988). The psychology of self-affirmation: Sustaining the integrity of self. In L. Berkowitz (Ed.), *Advances in experimental social psychology* (Vol. 21, pp. 261-302). San Diego, CA: Academic Press.

Stone, J., & Fernandez, N. C. (2008). To practice what we preach: The use of hypocrisy and cognitive dissonance to motivate behavior change. *Social and Personality Psychology Compass, 2*(2), 1024–1051.

Stone, J., Aronson, E., Crain, A. L., Winslow, M. P., & Fried, C. B. (1994). Inducing hypocrisy as a means of encouraging young adults to use condoms. *Personality and Social Psychology Bulletin, 20,* 116–128.

Zimbardo, P. G., Weisenberg, M., Firestone, I., & Levy, B. (1965). Communicator effectiveness in producing public conformity and private attitude change. *Journal of Personality, 33,* 233–255.

CHAPTER 8

A REASONED ACTION APPROACH

BEFORE YOU READ

Respond to the following questions **before** you read the chapter.

1. If close friends invited you to a party on an evening when you need to study for a midterm, what would you do? What would influence your decision?

2. If you wanted to persuade a friend to study abroad for a semester, what would you say or do? Be specific.

3. Why is it important to know your audience when creating a persuasive message?

The theories we have discussed up to this point have focused on changing attitudes as a key component of persuasion. There are times, however, when we just want to change behaviors and we want to do that as quickly and efficiently as possible. AT&T launched a campaign to change people's behavior with regard to texting while driving. Several states such as Michigan and Ohio have banned texting while driving and are creating campaigns to change people's behavior.

State governments, AT&T, and other organizations want drivers to refrain from texting while driving. The campaigns particularly target young drivers; however, teens are not the only ones who text while driving. Apps have been created to block texts while we're driving or that automatically notify senders that we are

LEARNING OBJECTIVES

- GIVE EXAMPLES OF BEHAVIORS THAT ARE UNDER VOLITIONAL CONTROL.
- EXPLAIN WHEN BEHAVIORAL INTENTIONS ARE A GOOD PREDICTOR OF BEHAVIOR.
- DESCRIBE THE COMPONENTS OF THE THEORY OF REASONED ACTION AND HOW THEY RELATE TO ONE ANOTHER.
- EXPLAIN HOW BELIEF STRENGTH AND BELIEF EVALUATION CONTRIBUTE TO ATTITUDE TOWARD BEHAVIOR.
- EXPLAIN HOW NORMATIVE BELIEFS AND MOTIVATION TO COMPLY CONTRIBUTE TO SUBJECTIVE NORM.
- EXPLAIN HOW CONTROL BELIEFS AND PERCEIVED POWER OF CONTROL BELIEFS CONTRIBUTE TO PERCEIVED BEHAVIORAL CONTROL.
- DESCRIBE AND GIVE EXAMPLES OF THE STRATEGIES USED TO INFLUENCE ATTITUDE, SUBJECTIVE NORM, AND PERCEIVED BEHAVIORAL CONTROL.
- USE THE CRITERIA FOR GOOD THEORY (EXPLAIN, PREDICT, AND CONTROL) TO EXPLAIN THE STRENGTHS AND WEAKNESSES OF THE THEORY OF REASONED ACTION.

driving and will respond when it is safe. Parents of teens who died in car crashes caused by texting have appeared on *The Today Show* and other news venues, telling their stories and pleading for a change in behavior. These messages represent an approach to persuasion that focuses more directly on altering behavior—a challenge taken on by Ajzen and Fishbein (1980) in the development of the **theory of reasoned action** (TRA).

Search "Texting and Driving" on YouTube to find the messages intended to change our texting and driving behavior.

⌐The current theory of reasoned action (Fishbein & Ajzen, 2010) merges the original theory of reasoned action introduced by Ajzen and Fishbein in 1980 and the theory of planned behavior, which was introduced by Ajzen in 1985 as an extension of reasoned action. Ajzen (1985, 1991) addressed limitations of the theory of reasoned action by adding the construct of perceived behavioral control. When perceived behavioral control was greater, attitudes were better predictors of behavior. The addition of perceived behavioral control to the theory of reasoned action strengthened the ability to predict and control behavior.⌐

The reasoned action approach to influence takes a different approach to persuasion than the theories discussed in previous chapters. If you think of a theory as a map that directs you where to go and what to look for, the theory of reasoned action is a different kind of map than social judgment theory or cognitive dissonance theory. First, the theory of reasoned action focuses on behavior as the ultimate outcome rather than attitude change. Attitude change is still important and plays a substantial role in the theory; however, it is not the primary goal. Second, an underlying assumption of this theory is that human beings follow a fairly consistent and reasoned approach in their behavior. Icek Ajzen and Martin Fishbein, the developers of this theory, assume that people make reasoned decisions about how to behave, and that much behavior is under **volitional control**. If behavior is under volitional control, an individual has control over the behavior. Whether or not you get to class on time is, for the most part, something you control. To the extent that you depend on others (e.g., bus drivers), the less volitional control you have. You may be late to class because the bus broke down and you had to walk the rest of the way. In this situation, your behavior was less affected by the choices you made and more affected by circumstances beyond your control. Therefore, the theory of reasoned action is a map of how people make rational choices about what behaviors to engage in. This is not the map we want to use when trying to understand mindless or automatic behavior.

ATTITUDES ARE NOT ALONE

Up to this point, we have focused primarily on attitudes in our discussion of persuasion. ⌜We've discussed how attitudes influence behavior and the possibility of behavior influencing attitudes, but overall, we have focused on changing attitude as a goal of persuasion.⌟ Fishbein and Ajzen's (2010) theory of reasoned action (TRA) focuses on behavior change with attitude being one of the three factors that influence behavior. Attitude, social pressure (subjective norm), and behavioral control influence intention, which in turn influences behavior. As we discuss in more detail later, behavioral intention is proposed as being the best single predictor of behavior. So attitude is not the only kid on the persuasion block.

Before we discuss intentions, subjective norm, and behavioral control, let's briefly discuss Ajzen and Fishbein's (1980) approach to attitude. In Chapter 2, we defined attitude as a learned predisposition to respond in a consistently favorable or unfavorable manner to a given object. Within the theory of reasoned action, the object is always behavior—specifically, the behavior you are trying to influence—and is referred to as **attitude toward behavior**. So, if your persuasive goal is to get your fellow students to give blood at the blood drive this Friday, the only attitude of concern is your audience's attitude toward giving blood this Friday at the blood drive. This is a fairly specific attitude, as opposed to the more general attitude toward giving blood. A person might have a positive attitude toward giving blood but have a negative attitude toward giving blood this Friday because he or she has an important job interview at the same time the blood drive is going on. Attitude toward specific behavior is the focus in the TRA.

THE ROLE OF INTENTIONS

A person's intention to do something is the best predictor of whether he or she will actually perform the behavior. For example, if you raise your hand in class to answer a question (behavior), you probably intended to do so. **Behavioral intention** is a psychological concept best described as an expectation or a plan. An intention is a plan for how you are going to behave. As stated previously, intention is the best predictor of behavior in general; however, this is not always the case. Three factors influence the intention–behavior relationship. By **intention-behavior relationship** we mean the extent behavioral intentions influence behavior. The first factor has to do with **volition**. As mentioned previously, an assumption of Ajzen and Fishbein's is that behavior is under volitional control. If a behavior is not under volition, intention will not be a good predictor of behavior. For example, suppose that Mikhail intends to marry Natasha. But he does not have complete control over marrying her. Natasha has to say yes to Mikhail's proposal. So Mikhail's behavioral intention may not be a very good predictor of his behavior; Natasha may say no. Volition should be thought of as a continuum. At one extreme are those behaviors over which you have complete control (e.g., wearing underwear); at the other extreme are those behaviors over which you have no control (e.g., being late because the bus broke down); and in between are a whole range of behaviors influenced by both you and circumstances beyond your control. Intentions are a good predictor of behavior to the extent that it is under volitional control.

The other two factors affecting the intention-behavior relationship are related to how intentions are measured. You may be asking why we would want to measure intentions rather than direct behavior. There are two reasons we are concerned about measuring intentions and behavior. The first reason is that, to study persuasion, we have to be able to measure the variables of interest. If we think that intentions influence behavior and want to test the relationship, we have to measure it. The second reason concerns applied persuasion. In applied situations we frequently have to demonstrate the effectiveness of our messages and campaigns. We may ultimately want to influence people's behavior, but it is often much easier and less expensive to measure individuals' behavioral intentions. If we can measure behavioral intentions, and intentions are predictive of behavior, then we are relieved of the burden of measuring actual behavior. Also, in long-term campaigns, such as political races, measuring behavioral intentions may be a way of assessing the effectiveness of the campaign along the way. So, regardless of whether your interest is in research or applied persuasion, measuring intentions and behavior is relevant.

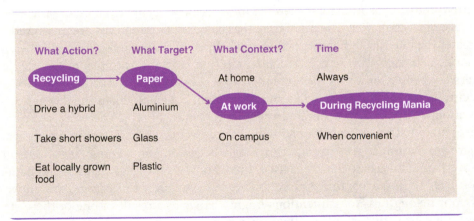

FIGURE 8.1 Example of attitude factors for predicting environmental behavior.

Intentions are a good predictor of behavior as long as the measures correspond to one another. The second factor that influences the intention–behavior relationship is correspondence. The measures of intention and behavior must correspond with one another, or, in other words, have the same dimensions. For intentions and behavior to correspond, they need to match in terms of *action, target, context,* and *time*. These factors are useful guidelines for the measurement of attitudes as well as behavioral intentions and behavior. Let's say you want to influence people to recycle where you work. You plan first to measure your colleagues' intentions to recycle and then their actual recycling behavior. Your measures of intention and behavior must measure the same action. In this case, *action* is recycling—or more specifically, putting recyclables into a recycling bin. The *target* refers to what you want people to recycle. Do you want them to recycle newspapers, bottles, aluminum cans, plastic (what type of plastic?), old tires, or motor oil? The list could go on. For your workplace campaign, you may focus on paper. This is the target, and both the measure of intention and the measure of behavior must focus on this target. *Context* refers to where you want people to recycle. Do you want people to recycle at home, at work, or in public places? In this case you're focusing on your specific workplace. Again, the measures of intention and behavior must focus on the same context. *Time* is the last element in correspondence. When do you want the behavior to occur? In our recycling example, you probably are interested in people doing this indefinitely; however, you may focus on a narrower time frame such as within the next month during the recycling mania campaign. If your measure of intention and your measure of behavior do not correspond to one or more of these elements, your measure of intentions will not predict behavior well.

For example, if we asked people if they intended to recycle within the next month, they may say yes because they intend to recycle bottles and cans at home. When we measure their behavior (recycling paper at work), they indicate that they did not do this. The measure of intention does not predict the measured behavior. Therefore, the four elements—action, target, context, and time—act as a guide for how to define the behavior we want to influence and how to measure both the behavior and the intention. These elements are useful in developing good measures but are also useful in helping clarify what specific behavior we want to influence. Intentions are a good predictor of behavior as long as the measures of each correspond with one another.

The third factor in the intention–behavior relationship is the amount of **time** between the measurement of intentions and the performance of the behavior. Intentions are a better predictor of behaviors when the measurement occurs right before the performance of the behavior. The more time that passes after intentions are measured, the greater the likelihood that something will happen to change intentions and therefore change behavior. During a presidential election year, for example, numerous pollsters ask people for whom they intend to vote. A poll taken in April is often not very accurate in predicting who will win the election, but a poll taken the day before the election is usually very accurate in predicting who will win. Therefore, we have to recognize that intentions can and will change over time. This is particularly true if there are a number of steps in performing a behavior. For example, if you intend to move from Chicago to San Francisco, there are several things that have to happen. You have to find a job, find a place to live, sell your place in Chicago, and move all of your belongings. Your intentions might change as a result of one of these steps, making your earlier intentions inconsistent with your final behavior.

SUBJECTIVE NORM

Earlier we stated that social pressure was one of the three things that influence behavioral intention. Social pressure from an important other is called a **subjective norm**. Important others are the people whose opinions you care about. Your subjective norm for a specific behavior such as refraining from texting while driving involves what you believe important others (people who are important to you regarding texting while driving) want you to do and how willing you are to comply with their wishes. So you may feel intense social pressure (high subjective norm) if your best friend (important other) really wants you to check a text while you're driving and you very much want to please your best friend.

PERCEIVED BEHAVIORAL CONTROL

In addition to your attitude toward the behavior and the social pressure you experience to perform (or not perform) a behavior, your beliefs about the level of control you have over the behavior determine your behavioral intention. **Perceived behavioral control** is the extent a person believes he or she is capable of performing a behavior and has control over whether it is performed or not (Fishbein & Ajzen, 2010). For example, do you have perceived behavioral control over texting? We're guessing that you feel capable of texting, but do you perceive control over whether or not you engage in texting? What would happen if you quit texting? Is that a choice you can make?

⌐We've discussed perceived behavioral control as a factor that affects whether we perform a behavior. TRA provides a more in-depth explanation of how and why perceived behavioral control influences behavior.⌐ Your perceived behavioral control along with your subjective norm for behavior and your attitude toward the behavior influences your intention to perform the behavior. TRA proposes that these three constructs are the primary factors in determining our behavior. Sometimes your attitude toward the behavior has a stronger influence on your intention, and sometimes your subjective norm or perceived behavioral control has a stronger influence on your intention, but these are the three factors that always influence your intention to perform a behavior.

THE MODEL

A visual representation of the theory of reasoned action is shown in Figure 8.1. Notice the arrow going directly from "Intention to perform behavior" to "Behavior." This arrow indicates that intention has a direct impact on behavior, just as we have been discussing. Arrows are also leading from "Attitude toward behavior," "Subjective norm," and "Perceived behavioral control" to "Intention to perform behavior." These arrows indicate that attitude and subjective norm have a direct impact on intentions. However, these three components do not necessarily have an equal impact on intention. Recall that sometimes attitude has a bigger influence on intention and sometimes subjective norm has a bigger influence, and sometimes perceived behavioral control dominates intention. Notice the factors contributing to attitude toward behavior, subjective norm, and perceived behavioral control. These concepts will be discussed in more detail in the following paragraphs. The model in Figure 8.2 is a visual way of describing the relationships hypothesized by TRA.

MEASURING AND PREDICTING ATTITUDE TOWARD BEHAVIOR

Earlier we discussed how Ajzen and Fishbein defined attitude and noted the similarities between their definition and the definition we presented in Chapter 2. In the TRA,

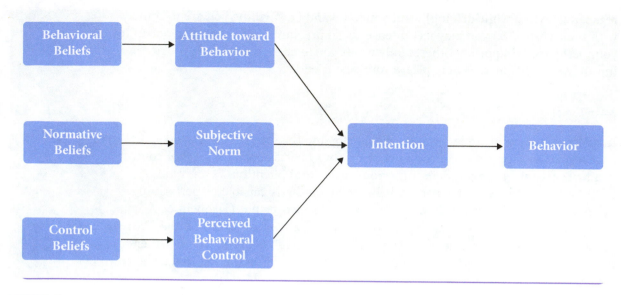

FIGURE 8.2 Theory of reasoned action.

Ajzen and Fishbein also specify the relationship between attitudes and beliefs and provide us with a formula for predicting attitudes. Ajzen and Fishbein state that attitude toward a behavior is a function of beliefs about the behavior. More specifically, a person's attitude is a result of the strength with which he or she holds those beliefs and how he or she evaluates those beliefs. The beliefs we have about the behavior are referred to as behavioral beliefs. Behavioral beliefs are beliefs about behavior that we view as most important. Behavioral beliefs frequently involve the consequences of performing a behavior. We may have dozens of beliefs about a particular behavior, but only some of them will be salient (important) at the time we are formulating an intention to perform or not perform a behavior. Ajzen and Fishbein estimate that we typically have six to nine behavioral beliefs about any particular behavior.

How do we find out what a person's behavioral beliefs are? The best way is to ask that person. When Strader and Katz (1990) wanted undecided students at a junior college to enroll in the nursing program, they first asked 120 students to list what they believe are the advantages and disadvantages of signing up for a career in nursing. Students expressed 407 beliefs. The most frequently listed beliefs would be considered the most salient for the students at the junior college. Ajzen and Fishbein (1980) recommend selecting about 10 behavioral beliefs. Strader and Katz identified the 11 most frequently mentioned beliefs:

1. Sense of accomplishment helping others
2. Good salary
3. Exposure to unpleasant sights and smells
4. Length of study program
5. Bad hours
6. Working with illness and death
7. Opportunities for the future
8. Relief that career decision is made

9. Meeting interesting people
10. Difficulty of study courses
11. Female profession

How strongly we hold a behavioral belief is referred to as **belief strength**. We may hold some beliefs very strongly, or, in other words, we believe beyond a doubt that the belief is true and likely to occur. For other beliefs, we may not feel as certain that the belief is really true. For example, you may believe that communication is a great major that will help you be successful in life; however, you may also have some doubts, making this belief weaker than your belief that the sky is blue. Belief strength is measured with a semantic differential scale that assesses how strongly an individual holds each behavioral belief. Below is an example of how Strader and Katz (1990) measured belief strength of the first behavioral belief listed above.

My signing up for a career as a registered nurse within the next month would mean I made a choice that gives me a sense of accomplishment in helping others.

Likely   +3   +2   +1   0   –1   –2   –3   Unlikely

If you are particularly astute, you may have noticed that, by definition, behavioral beliefs are strongly held beliefs, making the measurement of belief strength redundant. If you were to identify one person's behavioral beliefs, there is no question that all of his or her behavioral beliefs would have a high (+2 or +3) belief strength. However, if you have targeted a large group of people, such as all undecided students at a junior college, and have elicited behavioral beliefs from a sample as we discussed above, and have taken the 10 or so most frequently listed beliefs, you need to measure belief strength. The reason is that, when you use the most frequently listed beliefs (what Ajzen and Fishbein call modal behavioral beliefs), not everyone in your audience will hold these beliefs. These were simply the most commonly held beliefs. Some members of the audience may not hold these beliefs at all. So the measurement of belief strength becomes important for predicting attitude for a large group of people.

Belief evaluation refers to how we feel about each of our behavioral beliefs. Do we view the belief as being positive about the behavior or negative? For instance, a behavioral belief I have about visiting New York City is that a lot of people are there. I may see this as a positive thing. I may find all the people to be exciting, interesting, and invigorating. On the other hand, I may view the large number of people in New York City as a negative. I might think it is too crowded and feel overwhelmed or in danger because of all the people. Obviously, evaluating a belief negatively has very different consequences for attitude than evaluating a belief positively. Belief evaluation is also measured with a semantic differential scale. Again drawing on Strader and Katz's study, the item used to measure belief evaluation for the first behavioral belief is shown below.

How bad or good for you would it be to have a sense of accomplishment helping others?

Good   +3   +2   +1   0   –1   –2   –3   Bad

At this point, we have defined belief strength and belief evaluation and discussed how to measure each. You may be wondering "So what?" The usefulness of this information is that it allows us to understand how an attitude develops as well as to predict attitude. Theory helps us explain, predict, and control. Having information about the beliefs held by the audience not only helps us understand why they behave as they do but also helps us predict what they are likely to do. It also gives us the information we need to influence their behavior. You know what beliefs need to be changed and how they need to be changed in order to successfully change attitude.

Attitude toward a behavior is a function of the belief strength and belief evaluation of one's behavioral beliefs. Ajzen and Fishbein specify this relationship in a mathematical formula shown here.

$$A_B = \Sigma b_i e_i$$

The A_B refers to attitude toward the behavior. The sigma sign, Σ, is the statistical symbol for sum. The b_i refers to the belief strength for each behavioral belief, and e_i refers to the belief evaluation for each behavioral belief. This formula is telling us that attitude (A_B) is a result of how strongly a person holds behavioral beliefs about a behavior multiplied by the evaluation of those beliefs. The fact that the equation tells us to multiply belief strength and belief evaluation, rather than add them, is important. If you add them, each component is independent and carries its own weight individually. By multiplying, the components are interdependent, and it is the *interaction* of the components that influences attitude toward behavior.

This formula has theoretical and practical importance. On a theoretical level it tells us how these variables are related to one another. On a practical level it tells us exactly what information we need from our audience in order to understand their attitude. To calculate a person's attitude toward the behavior (A_B), you first multiply the belief strength (as marked on a scale like the one shown above) by the belief evaluation (as marked on a scale) for each behavioral belief. Once you have done this for each behavioral belief, you then sum (Σ) the products as is shown in Table 8.1. The result is a score that indicates the direction and intensity of the person's attitude toward the behavior.

TABLE 8.1 *PREDICTING ATTITUDE*

BEHAVIORAL BELIEFS	b_i	e_i	$b_i \times e_i$
1. Sense of accomplishment helping others	+2	+3	+6
2. Good salary	−2	+3	−6
3. Exposure to unpleasant sights and smells	+3	−3	−9
4 Length of study program	+2	−2	−4
5. Bad hours	+2	−3	−6
			−19

MEASURING AND PREDICTING SUBJECTIVE NORMS

Recall that the two factors that predict intention to perform a behavior are attitude toward the behavior and subjective norm. We have discussed the attitude toward behavior component; now let's discuss the subjective norm component. Above we defined subjective norm as the social pressure a person feels from important (salient) others to perform or not perform a behavior. Subjective norm is the result of two things: normative beliefs and motivation to comply. **Normative beliefs** are a person's beliefs about what salient others want him or her to do regarding the behavior in question. When Strader and Katz (1990) asked students to list the advantages and disadvantages of signing up for the nursing program, they also asked the students to list the persons or groups of persons who would influence their decision. This task provided Strader and Katz with a list of salient others that included mother, father, brother, sister, girlfriend, boyfriend, spouse, and friends. The normative beliefs were what the students thought those salient others wanted them to do regarding signing up for the nursing program. It's important to remember that normative beliefs are your audience's beliefs—not their salient others' beliefs. Normative beliefs are also measured with a semantic differential scale such as the one shown below.

My mother thinks
    I should   +3   +2   +1   0   –1   –2   –3   I should not
                sign up for a career in nursing within the next month.

To predict subjective norm, you need your audience's normative beliefs and their motivation to comply with their salient others. **Motivation to comply** simply refers to how willing your audience is to go along with what they think their salient others want them to do. For example, Alice may have the normative belief that her mother wants her to sign up for the nursing program, but she may not be at all motivated to comply with her mother's wishes. As shown below, motivation to comply is measured with a scale somewhat similar to those used to measure belief strength, belief evaluation, and normative beliefs.

How much do you want to do what your mother wants you to do regarding signing up for a career as a registered nurse within the next month?

_____ Not at all (0)   _____ Moderately (+2)

_____ Slightly (+1)   _____ Strongly (+3)

The motivation to comply scale does not contain negative numbers as did the scales for normative belief, belief strength, and belief evaluation. Ajzen and Fishbein (1980) state that it is unlikely people will be motivated to do the opposite of what their salient others think they should do, so therefore it is not necessary to measure how motivated they are to do what the salient others think they *should not* do.

Similar to the prediction of attitude toward behavior, Ajzen and Fishbein (1980) provide a mathematical formula for predicting subjective norm. As with the formula for attitude, this formula tells us the relationship among the variables and has both theoretical and practical importance.

$$SN = \Sigma NB_i MC_i$$

Similar to the formula for attitude, SN refers to the subjective norm, Σ is the statistical symbol for sum, NB_i refers to the normative beliefs the audience has regarding each salient other, and MC_i refers to the motivation to comply with each salient other. Similar to the formula for attitude, subjective norm results from normative beliefs and motivation to comply, and again these two variables are multiplied, not added. Again, by multiplying, the components are interdependent. To calculate the subjective norm, you multiply the normative belief for each salient other (as measured by a scale like the one shown previously) by the motivation to comply (as measured by a scale like the one previously), and then all of the products are summed. The result is a score indicating the degree of social pressure a person is experiencing to either perform or not perform the behavior.

MEASURING PERCEIVED BEHAVIORAL CONTROL

As in the case of attitudes toward behavior and subjective norms, perceived behavioral control is the result of two factors being combined according to the following formula:

$$PBC = \Sigma c_i p_i$$

Here, PBC refers to the level of perceived behavioral control over the targeted behavior. The two factors that are multiplied to find the perceived behavioral control are represented by the c_i and the p_i. The c refers to the control belief. **Control beliefs** are beliefs about specific factors that may facilitate or interfere with the performance of the behavior. For example, believing in one's ability to obtain a loan to pay tuition is a control belief. Getting a loan would facilitate enrolling in a nursing program. The p refers to the **perceived power**, which is the perceived ability of the control belief to facilitate or inhibit the performance of the behavior. For example, if we consider the control belief about getting a loan, perceived power is my perception that the loan will cover tuition. A summary of the formulas from TRA is shown in Figure 8.3.

A_B = $\Sigma b_i e_i$

SN = $\Sigma NB_i MC_i$

BhI = $A_{B(w1)} + SN_{(w2)} + PBC_{(w3)}$

BhI = behavioral intention

A_B = attitude toward behavior

b_i = belief strength for each salient belief

e_i = belief evaluation of each salient belief

SN = subjective norm

NB_i = normative belief for each salient other

MC_i = motivation to comply with each salient other

PBC = perceived behavioral control

Σ = statistical symbol for sum

i = is used to represent each individual belief

w_1 = the relative weight of the attitude toward behavior (A_B)

w_2 = the relative weight of the subjective norm (SN)

w_3 = the relative weight of the perceived behavioral control (PBC)

FIGURE 8.3 TRA formulas.

Control beliefs, like behavioral and normative beliefs, are identified by asking a sample of your target population a series of questions about the behavior in question. Once we have identified common control beliefs, we can assess the strength and power of each control belief. Strader and Katz did not measure perceived behavioral control; however, if they had, they would have had to first survey a sample to discover what factors students believed would either interfere with or facilitate them enrolling in a nursing program. Students may have had control beliefs about the ability to pay tuition, transportation to clinic sites, and the ability to work with blood and other bodily fluids. To measure this last control belief, the following question would be used:

How likely is it that you will be able to handle blood and other bodily fluids while training to be a nurse?

Extremely Likely   +3   +2   +1   0   –1   –2   –3   Extremely Unlikely

To measure perceived power for this control belief, the following question would be used:

My being able to handle blood and other bodily fluids while training to be a nurse would make it

Easier   +3   +2   +1   0   –1   –2   –3   More difficult for me to enroll in a nursing program

We could repeat these measures for as many control beliefs as existed and use the data to predict perceived behavioral control just as we used the data on individuals' strength and evaluation of behavioral beliefs to predict attitude toward behavior. In some research, scholars measure perceived behavioral control directly, rather than by measuring control beliefs and perceived power.

To summarize the relationships among the variables outlined in TRA, Fishbein and Ajzen provide the following formula:

$$BhI = A_{(w_1)} + SN_{(w_2)} + PBC_{(w_3)}$$

In this formula, BhI refers to behavioral intention, and the formula states that behavioral intention is a result of attitude toward behavior plus subjective norm, plus perceived behavioral control. The w_1, w_2, and w_3 refer to the relative weight placed on each of the three components, respectively. Recall from our previous discussion that sometimes attitude is more important and sometimes subjective norm or perceived behavioral control is more important in determining behavioral intentions. The relative weights are derived from a multiple regression analysis of the variables. Note here that attitude toward behavior, subjective norm, and perceived behavioral control are added together and not multiplied. The three components act *independently* on intention rather than interdependently.

STRATEGIES FOR INFLUENCE

At this point, we have reviewed how TRA explains human behavior. We have discussed the relationship between attitudes and beliefs and how the normative, attitudinal, and control components influence intention. As mentioned above, this information is useful not only for explaining but also for predicting how people will behave, and for developing persuasive messages for influencing their attitudes and behavior. In this section, we discuss how TRA directs us to approach a persuasive situation. One nice thing about TRA is that it provides some very specific strategies for constructing persuasive messages.

USING TRA TO CHANGE ATTITUDES

Attitude toward a behavior is a function of behavioral beliefs about the behavior. Change the beliefs and the attitude is likely to change. Notice that we said "beliefs," meaning more than one. If you were to change one or two behavioral beliefs, your attitude may not change in any significant way. There is no magic number of how many beliefs have to be changed, but a general rule is that the more beliefs you change the more likely that attitude will change in a significant and meaningful way. Specifically, there are three strategies for changing a person's attitude. First, you can *add a new behavioral belief*. This is equivalent to giving a person new information. For example, in their study, Strader and Katz (1990) could have added a behavioral belief about the shortage of nurses (assuming there was a shortage at the time) by telling students about this shortage and the need for nurses in a variety of specialties. Alternatively, Strader and Katz could have provided information about opportunities in nursing that students were unaware of. Whenever we learn new information, we develop new beliefs, so this strategy of adding a new behavioral belief is essentially providing your audience with new information. Second, you can *change the belief evaluation*. Strader and Katz used the following message to change the belief evaluation of the behavioral belief "bad hours."

> *Many students do not understand the flexibility nurses have with their hours. Most of your friends get up early in the morning, leave late in the evening, and have to fight rush hour traffic all of their life. Nurses are flexible and can choose whenever they want to work. Most nurses can choose the type of schedules that accommodate their life style. If you are a night person who likes basking in the sun during the day and wants to make extra money, nights may be for you. If you are a morning person, you can find a job in or outside the hospital on a day shift.*

This message is attempting to change how students evaluate their beliefs about the hours that nurses have to work. By changing the belief evaluation from negative to positive, the attitude toward becoming a nurse becomes a little more positive.

Third, you can *change the belief strength*. For example, a behavioral belief listed by the students in Strader and Katz's study was that there would be opportunities for the future. Assuming that the audience did not believe this very strongly, a message could be created to convince students that really good opportunities are available in the nursing field. Enhancing the belief strength of positive beliefs or, conversely, reducing the belief strength of negative beliefs leads to a more positive attitude.

USING TRA TO CHANGE SUBJECTIVE NORM

Subjective norm is the social pressure a person feels to perform or not perform a behavior and it influences intention. Subjective norm is based on normative beliefs about salient others and, therefore, to change the subjective norm, normative beliefs must be changed. Similar to attitude, there are three strategies for influencing subjective norm. First, you can *add new normative beliefs* about new salient others. This means suggesting to your audience that they should be concerned about the opinions of a particular person who is not currently a salient other. For instance, in the Strader and Katz study, teachers were not listed as salient others. Strader and Katz could have constructed a message telling students that their teachers think nursing is a good career choice and that the students should be concerned with what their teachers say.

Second, you can *change existing normative beliefs*. This strategy involves messages that attempt to convince the audience that their salient others want them to do something other than what they currently think their salient others want them to do. For example, in their study, Strader and Katz (1990) found that students believed their parents did not want them to sign up for the nursing program. A message based on changing normative beliefs would involve telling students that their parents really would be supportive of them signing up for the nursing program. This could be a tough sell depending on who the salient others are and the closeness of the relationship. Third, you can *alter motivation to comply* with salient others. This strategy involves creating messages that either encourage the audience to comply with salient others (who are supportive of the behavior) or discourage the audience from complying with salient others (who are not supportive of the behavior). Strader and Katz did not attempt to influence students' subjective norms. They thought that, with the limited information they had on parental beliefs, it would be unethical to attack either the normative beliefs or the motivation to comply with a parent. It is also questionable how successful such messages would have been. How many of us are going to believe a stranger telling us that what we think our parents or friends want us to do is not what they really want us to do? However, such a strategy may work in a more interpersonal persuasion situation such as when someone is persuading his or her significant other.

Influencing the subjective norm has ethical considerations. Is it ethical to attack or question salient others who are people the audience may love and depend on? It is generally considered ethical to influence a person's beliefs about objects or behaviors such as when we attempt to influence behavioral beliefs. Trying to influence how people feel and think about salient others may be quite ethical in some situations, but is likely to be unethical in other situations such as that encountered by Strader and Katz.

USING TRA TO CHANGE PERCEIVED BEHAVIORAL CONTROL

We can use perceived behavioral control to influence persuasive success in a manner similar to how we altered attitudes toward behavior and subjective norms. By altering the audience's perceptions of perceived behavioral control, we can alter their behavioral intentions. Recall that perceived behavioral control is based on control beliefs and perceived power. Therefore, messages targeted at control beliefs and perceived power could be used to alter perceived behavioral control. For example, if potential nursing students believed they could not handle blood and had low perceived power over this factor, their low perceived behavioral control would likely lead them to not choose nursing as their major. We could create a message that targeted this control belief and perceived power. However, sometimes extensive interventions are needed to change people's perceived behavioral control. For example, sometimes perceived power is based on real skills and abilities. No amount of messaging will change that. Rather, some type of training is needed to help people develop a skill set so that they have both real and perceived power over the factors preventing them from engaging in the behavior. Perceived behavioral control is of particular importance in certain situations. For example, a common barrier in getting people to stop smoking is that many smokers don't believe they actually *can* quit. Many smokers are well aware of the health hazards of smoking and are well aware of broad-based social disapproval for smoking. No change in behavior is likely to occur, however, unless the smokers are convinced that stopping smoking is actually within their control. Altering their perceived behavioral control by providing information about the effectiveness of nicotine patches, hypnosis, or other smoking cessation programs can alter the smokers' sense of perceived behavior control so that they can have stronger behavioral intentions toward quitting smoking. Perceived behavioral control is often applied in health situations such as sexual decision making among women (McCabe & Killackey, 2004) and condom use (Basen-Engquist & Parcel, 1992), as well as in other contexts such as hunting behaviors (Hrube, Ajzen, & Daigle, 2001).

CHANGING RELATIVE WEIGHT

An additional strategy revolves around the relative weight of the attitudinal, normative, and control components. Recall that sometimes attitude toward a behavior is more heavily weighted (has more influence on behavioral intentions), but at other times subjective norm has more weight. For instance if a person's attitude and subjective norm are in opposition, a strategy for influencing intention is to target the relative weights. For example, suppose Jane has a very positive attitude toward entering the nursing program, but she is also experiencing intense social pressure from her salient others to *not* enter the nursing program. If she places more weight on her attitude, she will most likely enroll in the nursing program. On the other hand, if she places more weight on her subjective norm, she is unlikely to enroll in the program. If Jane is placing more weight on the subjective norm and we want to influence her to enter the nursing program, a possible strategy is to convince her to place more weight on her attitude than on her subjective norm. A message such as "It's your life and your career; you should do what you want" is geared at increasing the weight placed on the attitudinal component. The same applies to perceived behavioral control. Sometimes this component is heavily weighted and is the primary reason a person does not engage in a behavior that they view positively and feel social pressure to perform.

When creating a persuasive message, TRA provides us with nine strategies: (a) add a new behavioral belief, (b) alter belief evaluations, (c) alter belief strength, (d) add a new salient other, (e) alter normative beliefs, (f) alter motivation to comply, (g) alter control beliefs, (h) alter perceived power, and (i) alter the relative weights. TRA specifies what kinds of things we need to learn about our audiences and what the message should target. Combining what we learned about the source, message, and channel factors in Chapters 4, 5, and 6 with the TRA theoretical framework allows us to create powerful and effective persuasive messages and interventions.

USING TRA TO CHANGE BEHAVIOR

To influence your audience's behavior, TRA directs you first to learn about your audience. An underlying premise of TRA is that you must understand a person's existing beliefs in order to influence their behavior. The TRA is similar to social judgment theory in this respect. That theory also directed the persuader to understand the audience. TRA specifically directs you to understand your audience's beliefs: behavioral beliefs, normative beliefs, and control beliefs. These beliefs serve as the basis for constructing persuasive messages to change beliefs, and ultimately behavior. If you're thinking that this sounds like a lot of work, you're right, it is; however, it is also quite effective.

To influence your audience's behavior, TRA directs you first to learn about your audience. An underlying premise of TRA is that you must understand a person's existing beliefs in order to influence their behavior. The TRA is similar to social judgment theory in this respect. That theory also directed the persuader to understand the audience. TRA specifically directs you to understand your audience's beliefs: behavioral beliefs, normative beliefs, and control beliefs. These beliefs serve as the basis for constructing persuasive messages to change beliefs, and ultimately behavior.

used the preliminary messages and focus group results to develop messages for the campaign. This group of students developed all branding related to the campaign, including the name, color scheme, tagline, mascot, and mission statement. Several messages were created to target behavioral beliefs and normative beliefs. The campaign became the Rethink campaign with the goal of reducing "prescription stimulant misuse on college campuses" (LaBelle et al., 2020) and occurred a week before midterm exams at Chapman University in Orange County, California. The tagline for the campaign was "Adderall Misuse: It's Nastier than You Think." To add a bit of humor to the campaign, a mascot was created: Addy, who looked like an Adderall pill. Two versions of Addy were created: Happy Addy and Angry Addy. Adderall is an important medication for people diagnosed with attention deficient disorder and other learning difficulties; therefore, LaBelle and her student wanted to support the prescribed, medical use of Adderall and used Happy Addy to represent legal use of Adderall. Angry Addy represents the problems with nonmedical use of Adderall.

Several messages were created using a variety of media. Traditional print media such as flyers and fact cards were distributed around campus. Cutouts of Addy the mascot were placed around campus. In addition to print media, a website (https://www.rethinkcampaign.org) was created, and messages were distributed on traditional media channels, such as the Dean of Students' weekly student newsletter. Several Rethink social media accounts were set up to send messages from Addy containing information about the misuse of Adderall. The Rethink campaign also included tabling sessions where student campaign members set up tables in the middle of campus to disseminate fact cards, have discussions with peers about misuse, take pictures with Addy, and encourage students to sign a petition to "rethink" misuse of Adderall and similar drugs, and hand out promotional items.

The messages directly addressed students' beliefs about taking Adderall. The message in Figure 8.3 targeted a common behavioral belief that there are no side effects to misuse of Adderall. The message in Figure 8.4 provides information about erectile dysfunction, a specific side effect that most people find undesirable. The outcome is that message recipients develop a stronger belief that negative side effects result from Adderall and this belief is evaluated negatively. Other messages, such as in Figure 8.5, addressed students' normative beliefs about the frequency and acceptability of using the prescription medication as study drugs. Specifically, that most peers (salient others) don't use Adderall as a study drug. The fact cards (see Figure 8.6) showed Addy giving information on health and legal risks that reinforced the messages in the flyers. Addy is portrayed as a peer giving helpful information. Portraying Addy as a trustworthy peer helped to increase the credibility of the messages.

Being good persuaders and researchers, LaBelle et al. (2020) not only implemented the campaign, but also evaluated it. To evaluate the campaign, they recruited 187 students from Chapman University where the campaign occurred and 64 students from a nearby university who served as a control and were not exposed to the Rethink campaign. Students from both universities completed the same measures 2 weeks before the campaign (pre-test) and 2 weeks after the campaign (post-test). All data were anonymous. LaBelle et al. measured students' attitudes toward four motives for using Adderall. Subjective norms for salient others were measured as was perceived behavioral control, and behavioral intention to misuse prescription stimulants. Finally, LaBelle et al. also asked students to self-report the frequency of their misuse of prescription stimulants.

Was the campaign effective? Yes. Students' attitudes toward the benefits of using stimulants to study became more negative at Chapman University, but not at the control university. Students' subjective norms also changed at the experimental site, but not at the control site. Students' norms regarding the frequency of others using stimulants decreased, or in other words, they changed their normative beliefs to most students do not use study drugs. However, there was no change in perceived behavioral control as a result of the campaign or in misuse of prescription stimulants. LaBelle et al. (2020) speculate perceived behavioral control did not change because these drugs are very easy to obtain from benevolent peers who have a prescription and there is no need to interact with a stereotypical drug dealer.

Perceived behavioral control was relatively high in the pre-test, meaning that students felt in control of obtaining study drugs or not. Also, promotion of not doing something is difficult. Perhaps in this situation, promotion of study behaviors that are more effective than study drugs would have increased behavioral control over alternative study aids.

"Designing and implementing the Rethink campaign has been one of the greatest joys of my teaching and research career. We have continued this campaign on Chapman's campus every semester since Spring 2017, and each group of students has found new and innovative ways to address the behavioral and normative beliefs surrounding prescription stimulant misuse. It is amazing to see TRA truly come to life in our campaign messages and events." —Dr. Sara LaBelle, Chapman University, https://www. chapman.edu/our-faculty/ sara-labelle

A caveat to these results is that just over 70% of the students in the study reported having heard of the Rethink campaign, and the number of messages students saw varied a great deal. Also, students' attitudes before the campaign were the biggest predictor of their post-test attitudes toward misuse. On the surface it appears that the campaign had a small effect. However, the campaign lasted just one week, and the more messages students saw, the more influenced they were. Therefore, it was quite effective. If the campaign had occurred throughout the entire semester it would likely have had an even bigger impact.

STRENGTHS AND LIMITATIONS

A major strength of the TRA from a communication point of view is that the model is receiver-oriented. The model focuses on the receiver's attitudes toward behavior, subjective norms, and perceptions of behavioral control and how these influence intention and behavior. Therefore, the model directs persuaders to understand their audience. Audience analysis becomes a requirement in the persuasion process. It's not just "what you say" to the receiver. Your message must be specifically directed at the receiver's beliefs and perceptions, both behavioral and normative. Another strength of the TRA approach is that it explains the relationship between attitudes, beliefs, and behaviors, as well as the relationship of attitudes and social pressure to perform a behavior that people experience. One important strength of the TRA is that it is well supported by research. TRA has successfully predicted individuals' behaviors. The TRA has been applied to a variety of behaviors, including voting, family planning, consumer purchases (Ajzen & Fishbein, 1980), seat belt use (Budd, North, & Spencer, 1984), eating in fast-food restaurants (Brinberg & Durand, 1983), seeking dental care (Hoogstraten, de Haan, & ter Horst, 1985), antipollution behavior (Hamid & Cheng, 1995), pediatrician recommendations for patients to get the human papillomavirus vaccination (Roberto, Krieger, Katz, Goei, & Jain, 2011), and AIDS prevention behavior (Cochran, Mays, Ciarletta, Caruso, & Mallon, 1992). The TRA approach is often applied in the health communication context, but has also been useful in predicting consumer behavior. A consequence of the ability of the TRA to predict behavior is that it allows us to have some measure of control over our audience's behaviors. The TRA provides specific strategies for influencing a person's beliefs and subsequent attitudes and subjective norms. Because the theory is described so specifically, it provides us with very clear and relatively simple strategies for developing a persuasive message.

Although the TRA has proved to be useful in a variety of situations, it has some limitations. One main criticism of the TRA approach is the emphasis on a specific behavior. Often, a behavior of interest is the culmination of several behaviors such as weight loss or obtaining a degree. Obtaining a college degree is a behavior, but it results from many other behaviors such as attending class, writing papers, reading books, and taking tests. To most effectively predict obtaining a college degree, we would need to understand the intention to perform each of the many underlying behaviors. This would be a mammoth task that few of us would be willing to undertake. However, because TRA does focus on specific behaviors, it can help us better understand the behaviors we are trying to influence. ⌜TRA is best suited for influencing the specific behaviors that go into earning a degree rather. However, because TRA does focus on specific behaviors, it can help us better understand the behaviors we are trying to influence.⌟

An additional limitation of the theory involves the relative weights component. To obtain the relative weights, one must have not only the person's attitudinal, normative, and perceived behavioral control data but also the person's behavioral intention to conduct the multiple regression analysis that provides the relative weights. In other words, there is no way for a practitioner to obtain the relative weights without also knowing a person's behavioral intention. This is a limitation in applied settings.

One last criticism of the TRA approach is that it does not include previous behavior in the model. A person's previous experience with a behavior has been found to influence both the intention to perform a behavior and the actual performance of the behavior (see Eagly & Chaiken, 1993, for a review). Recall that attitudes formed through direct experience are more predictive of behavior. Current behavior may be somewhat based on whether or not we have performed the behavior before. Fishbein and Azjen (2010) acknowledge the role of previous behavior and experience, but the theory does not specify (explain) exactly how it impacts the attitudinal, normative, and control components. In order to predict and control, a theory must provide a specific explanation of how components are related to one another. Previous behavior is a predictor of future behavior and shouldn't be ignored. When we look at efforts to change behaviors on which we would expect past behavior to have influence, such as losing weight and exercising, we find these efforts are often unsuccessful. The theory of reasoned action is a very useful theory of influence for such behaviors and increases our ability to influence such behaviors; however, it is not a magic bullet that will give you the ability to influence anyone at any time. Of course, no theory is a magic bullet.

SUMMARY

- The TRA explains how people make behavioral choices.
- Behavior change is the primary focus of the TRA.
- The best predictor of the behavior is intention to perform the behavior.
- Attitude toward behavior, subjective norm, and perceived behavioral control influence intention.
- The three situations for which intention to behave does not predict behavior are when behavior is not under volitional control, when the measure of intentions and the measure of behavior do not correspond with one another, and when too much time elapses between the measurement of intentions and the measurement of behavior.
- The social pressure a person experiences to either perform or not perform a behavior is referred to as subjective norm.
- The strength with which a person holds behavioral beliefs, along with how he or she evaluates those beliefs, determines attitude toward behavior.
- A subjective norm is determined by the normative beliefs a person holds about his or her salient others and how motivated he or she is to comply with those salient others.
- Perceived behavioral control is determined by an individual's control beliefs and perceived power.
- The three strategies for influencing attitude are to add a new behavioral belief, to change belief evaluation, and to change belief strength.
- The three strategies for influencing a subjective norm are to add new normative beliefs, to change existing normative beliefs, and to change the motivation to comply.
- An additional strategy for influencing behavioral intentions is to alter the relative weights of the attitudinal, normative, and control components.

- The TRA directs persuaders first to assess their audience's beliefs and then to develop persuasive messages based on those beliefs.
- Altering perceptions of behavioral control can alter behavioral intentions and ultimate behavior.
- Strengths of the TRA are that it is receiver oriented, it is able to explain the causes of behavior, it is able to predict behavior, and it provides persuaders with a measure of control over their audience.
- Limitations of TRA are a focus only on specific behaviors and not complex behaviors and the exclusion of previous behavior in the models.

KEY TERMS

Attitude toward behavior—an attitude toward a specific behavior.

Behavioral beliefs—beliefs about a behavior that we view as most important and that frequently involve the consequences of performing a behavior.

Behavioral intention—a psychological concept best described as an expectation or a plan. An intention is a plan for how you are going to behave.

Belief evaluation—how positive or negative we feel about each of our behavioral beliefs.

Belief strength—how strongly we hold a behavioral belief.

Control beliefs—beliefs about the likelihood of having the opportunities and resources necessary to perform the behavior and the frequency that a control factor will occur.

Correspondence—the measures of intention and behavior, which must be measured on the same dimensions (action, target, context, and time).

Intention-behavior relationship—the extent that behavioral intentions will influence actual performance of the behavior.

Motivation to comply—how willing individuals are to go along with what they think their salient others want them to do.

Normative beliefs—a person's beliefs about what salient others want him or her to do regarding a specific behavior.

Perceived behavioral control—an individual's perception of the level of control he or she has over a behavior.

Perceived power—the perceived ability of the control belief to facilitate or inhibit the performance of the behavior.

Subjective norm—the social pressure a person feels from salient (important) others to perform or not perform a behavior.

Volitional control—if a behavior is under volitional control, an individual has control over the behavior.

QUESTIONS FOR REVIEW

Respond to the following questions **without** reviewing the text or your notes. These questions are provided to help you practice retrieving information and reflect on your reading.

    A. What are some key ideas about the Theory of Reasoned Action (TRA)?

    B. Did you agree or disagree with anything you read? Explain.

    C. What did you learn that was new to you?

    D. What concepts, if any, were confusing to you?

Respond to the following questions. You may reference your text or notes to help you.

    1. What three factors influence intention to perform a behavior?

    2. Before reading this chapter, you discussed what would influence your decision to go out with your friends or study for a midterm. What factor most influenced you? Are you generally more influenced by the same factor? Why or why not?

    3. According to the TRA, what are the strategies for changing a person's attitude? Give an example of each one.

    4. According to the TRA, what are the strategies for changing subjective norms? Give an example of each one.

5. According to the TRA, what are the strategies for changing perceived behavioral control? Give an example of each one.

QUESTIONS FOR DISCUSSION

1. In your small group, discuss correspondence as a factor that influences the intention-behavior relationship. How does this factor apply to the goal of your final presentation? Be sure to discuss action, target, context, and time.

2. Both the TRA and social judgment theory direct the persuader to understand the audience. Why? Is one theory more useful in designing a persuasive message? How would you decide which theory to use?

3. In your small group, discuss how you could use the TRA as you prepare for your final presentation. How does the use of this theory compare to the use of other theories and concepts you have already discussed?

4. Do you tend to be more influenced by your attitude toward a behavior or subjective norms? Provide an example of a recent behavior to support your answer. Why are you more influenced by one or the other?

5. Discuss the ethical questions provided at the end of the chapter. What ethical considerations are relevant to the information in this chapter about using the TRA?

- Are there guidelines (e.g., don't lie) that would be appropriate for every situation, or are ethics relative?

- Do the ends (e.g., a good outcome) justify any means?

- Is deceiving the receiver ever appropriate?

- Should the source of the message bear primary responsibility for ethics, or should the receiver share that responsibility (e.g., buyer beware)?

REFERENCES

Ajzen, I. (1985). From intentions to actions: A theory of planned behavior. In J. Huhl & J. Beckmann (Eds.), *Action control: From cognition to behavior* (pp. 11–39). New York: Springer-Verlag.

Ajzen, I. (1991). The theory of planned behavior. *Organizational Behavior and Human Decision Processes, 50,* 179–211.

Ajzen, I., & Fishbein, M. (1980). *Understanding attitudes and predicting social behavior.* Englewood Cliffs, NJ: Prentice-Hall.

Basen-Engquist, K., & Parcel, G. S. (1992). Attitudes, norms, and self-efficacy: A model of adolescents' HIV-related sexual risk behavior. *Health Education Quarterly, 19,* 263–277.

Brinberg, D., & Durand, J. (1983). Eating at fast-food restaurants: An analysis using two behavioral intention models. *Journal of Applied Psychology, 13,* 459–472.

Budd, R. J., North, D., & Spencer, C. (1984). Understanding seat belt use: A test of Bentler and Speckart's extension of the "theory of reasoned action." *European Journal of Social Psychology, 14,* 69–78.

Cochran, S. D., Mays, V. M., Ciarletta, J., Caruso, C., & Mallon, D. (1992). Efficacy of the theory of reasoned action in predicting AIDS-related sexual risk reduction among gay men. *Journal of Applied Social Psychology, 22,* 1481–1501.

Eagly, A. H., & Chaiken, S. (1993). *The psychology of attitudes.* Fort Worth, TX: Harcourt Brace Jovanovich.

Fishbein, M. & Ajzen, I. (2010). *Predicting and changing behavior: The reasoned action approach.* New York: Psychology Press.

Hamid, P. N., & Cheng, S. (1995). Predicting antipollution behavior: The role of molar behavioral intentions, past behavior, and locus of control. *Environment and Behavior, 27,* 679–698.

Hoogstraten, J., de Haan, W., & ter Horst, G. (1985). Stimulating the demand for dental care: An application of Ajzen and Fishbein's theory of reasoned action. *European Journal of Social Psychology, 15,* 401–414.

Hrube, D, Ajzen, I., & Daigle, J. (2001). Predicting hunting intentions and behavior: An application of the theory of planned behavior. *Leisure Sciences, 23*(3), 165–179.

LaBelle, S., Ball, H., Weber, K., White, A., & Hendry, A. (2020). The Rethink cam-paign to reduce the normalization of prescription stimulant misuse on college campuses. *Communication Quarterly, 68,* 1-28.

McCabe, M. P., & Killackey, E. J. (2004). Sexual decision making in young women. *Sexual and Relationship Therapy, 19*(1), 15–28.

Roberto, A. J., Krieger, J. L., Katz, M. L., Goei, R., & Jain, P. (2011). Predicting pediatricians' communication with parents about the human papillomavirus (HPV) vaccine: An application of the theory of reasoned action. *Health Communication, 26,* 303–312.

Strader, M. K., & Katz, B. M. (1990). Effects of a persuasive communication on beliefs, attitudes, and career choice. *Journal of Social Psychology, 130,* 141–150.

CHAPTER 9

ELABORATION LIKELIHOOD MODEL

BEFORE YOU READ

Respond to the following questions **before** you read the chapter.

1. What do you know about the Elaboration Likelihood Model?

2. ⌜When you're shopping online, how do you decide what item to purchase? What factors do you pay attention to the most?

3. Name an issue that is important to you. Name an issue that you're personally involved in. Name an issue that is not particularly important to you.⌟

The theories we have discussed so far in this book have assumed that people are rational and carefully consider the persuasive messages they receive. How true do you think this assumption is? Social judgment theory, cognitive dissonance theory, and the theory of reasoned action all assume that people think rationally when receiving a persuasive message. These theories do a good job of explaining, predicting, and controlling persuasion in some situations, but other situations are beyond the scope of each theory. A good deal of research supports this rational approach, but a good deal of research also does not support it. For example, sometimes source credibility is an important factor and sometimes it is not. Sometimes including evidence in a message is effective and sometimes it is not. Petty and Cacioppo (1981, 1986) noticed these inconsistencies in research

LEARNING OBJECTIVES

- DESCRIBE ELABORATION.
- EXPLAIN THE TWO ROUTES TO PERSUASION AND HOW THEY ARE DIFFERENT FROM EACH OTHER.
- EXPLAIN HOW MOTIVATION AND ABILITY DETERMINE WHICH ROUTE TO PERSUASION IS TAKEN.
- DESCRIBE FACTORS THAT INFLUENCE MOTIVATION TO PROCESS AND ABILITY TO PROCESS.
- EXPLAIN HOW ATTITUDE IS INFLUENCED IN THE TWO ROUTES TO PERSUASION.
- EXPLAIN OBJECTIVE AND BIASED PROCESSING OF MESSAGES.

findings and the limited scope of each prior theory and developed the elaboration likelihood model to address these concerns.

TWO ROUTES TO ATTITUDE CHANGE

Petty and Cacioppo (1981, 1986) argued that people process information differently depending on the circumstances. Sometimes a **central route** is used to process persuasive messages. The central route involves *high elaboration,* or the receiver focusing on and thinking about the content of the message. This is active involvement that involves expending *cognitive energy* to think about and process the message. Theories that assume that receivers use rational thought and consider arguments in the message are most useful in understanding the central route to persuasion.

However, we do not always think carefully about each message directed at us. Indeed, it would be difficult to pay close attention to every message bombarding us from signs on buses and flyers posted around campus to Internet and television messages and speakers we are exposed to every day. Instead, we often use the **peripheral route** to process messages. The peripheral route involves low elaboration of the message, and rational thought does not play a key role here. When receivers are engaged in the peripheral route, there is little thinking about the content of the message or the arguments it contains and little cognitive energy is exerted. In fact, Petty and Cacioppo suggest that most of us are *cognitive misers* and choose to use as little cognitive energy as possible on most messages. When we employ the peripheral route and use a minimum amount of brainpower, we tend to rely on peripheral cues to help us decide how to respond to a message. **Peripheral cues** are factors that help us quickly decide how to process the message without having to engage in much elaboration. You can think of peripheral cues as shortcuts. Peripheral cues include things such as source credibility or the presence of evidence and are explained in more detail later in this chapter.

ELABORATION

The **elaboration likelihood model (ELM)** focuses on different ways people respond to persuasive messages. **Elaboration** refers to the amount of thinking the receiver devotes to the content of a message. Elaboration can be thought of as a continuum, ranging from no thinking at all about the content of the message to extensive thinking about the message. The theory is called the elaboration likelihood model because it makes different predictions depending on how likely it is that the receiver will elaborate on the message.

MEASUREMENT OF ELABORATION

A key issue with the development of any theory is being able to test the theory. Recall from Chapter 7 that to test a theory, a method must be designed, and the variables being studied have to be measured. Elaboration is a key issue in ELM, so to test the ELM, elaboration must be measured. If elaboration cannot be measured in a valid and reliable way, we can't test the theory. Multiple methods have been used to measure elaboration. One method is to ask research participants to **self-report** how much cognitive effort they put into evaluating a message (Petty, Harkins, Williams, & Latane, 1977). This is a simple approach, but we are not always conscious of how much thinking we put into messages. It is quite possible for self-reports to be in error; thus, this method has been used in few studies.

Argument recall has been used by some researchers as a measure of elaboration (Tyler, Hertal, McCallum, & Ellis, 1979). This has been more frequently employed as a measure of message comprehension and memory than elaboration. Recall is not an ideal measure of the elaboration engaged in by the receiver because it does not require participants to indicate personal thoughts. Just being able to re-create parts of the message does not necessarily mean that elaboration or personal thought occurred in response to the content of the message.

The most frequently used measure of elaboration is referred to as **thought listing** (Cacioppo & Petty, 1981; Cacioppo, Harkins, & Petty, 1981). With this method, research participants are asked to list what they were thinking about during the presentation of the persuasive message. By counting the different thoughts and evaluating the issue relevance of those thoughts, researchers can assess how much elaboration of the ideas occurred in the message. Receivers who generate the most issue-relevant thoughts are considered to have elaborated more and used the central route to process the message. Receivers who generate few issue-relevant thoughts are considered to have elaborated less and used the peripheral route to process the message.

WHY ONE ROUTE AND NOT THE OTHER?

ELM is different from the other theories we have discussed. Rather than assuming that persuasion works the same in all circumstances, ELM predicts two ways that persuasion works. One is the central route, and the other is the peripheral route.

Why do we use one route over another when exposed to a message? We need to be able to predict which route receivers will use in order for ELM to be a good theory. Knowing why people use a particular route to process the information also helps us explain and control the persuasive process.

Whether a person uses the central route or the peripheral route when processing a message depends on two characteristics: the levels of receiver *motivation* and the level of *ability* to process the information in the message. If the receiver is missing either of these characteristics, the receiver will use the peripheral route to process the message. A receiver must be both motivated *and* able to engage in elaboration to take the central route. **Motivation** refers to how much the receiver wants to elaborate on the message; **ability** refers to how capable the receiver is of elaborating on the persuasive message. If either motivation or ability is missing or low, the receiver will engage in the low elaboration or "peripheral processing." Thus, for central processing to occur, the receiver must have a reason to think about the content of the message (motivation) and must be capable of doing so (ability). Otherwise, peripheral processing is the result. Why are we motivated and able to process messages, or not?

MOTIVATION TO PROCESS

⌈Several factors affect motivation and ability processes.Let's start with motivation; however, keep in mind that the list of factors discussed in the following paragraphs is not exhaustive. Consider these to be examples. Four factors that⌟ affect **motivation to process** are discussed. One of the most important factors for motivation involves the level of **personal relevance** of the topic, sometimes referred to as the level of **personal involvement** with the topic. As you might predict, the more important the topic is to you personally, the more motivated you are to think carefully about the message and centrally process it. Conversely, the less important the issue is to you personally, the less motivated you are to think carefully about the message. When personal involvement is high, motivation to process is greater, and you are more likely to take the central route. We discussed the concept of ego-involvement as a factor in social judgment theory. The concepts of ego-involvement and personal involvement are defined somewhat differently. As we stated in our discussion of social judgment theory, ego-involvement refers to a person's commitment to an issue and is related to a person's self-concept and self-esteem (Sherif, Sherif, & Nebergall, 1965). Personal involvement refers to whether an issue or topic is relevant to the receiver's interests or goals. The terms "personal involvement" and "personal relevance" are used interchangeably because if we perceive something as relevant, we are more involved with the topic.

What does personal relevance look like? In one study, personal involvement was manipulated for college students by using the topic of coed visiting hours in residence halls (Petty & Cacioppo, 1979). To make this topic personally relevant, researchers told half of the participants that their own university was planning to implement either stricter or more lenient visitation hours. The other half of participants were in the low-relevance group and were told that a university halfway across the country was thinking about adopting either stricter or more lenient visiting hours. When an issue is affecting us directly, we are more personally involved in the issue and have greater motivation to think about it.

A second factor that affects motivation is the degree of **personal responsibility**, or, in other words, are you accountable for the message. If we think we are the only one responsible for the message outcome or consequences, we are more likely to centrally process the content than if we think others are also responsible. This factor has been examined in research by asking participants to evaluate the content or the quality of the message, with one group being told they were the only individuals asked to provide this service and the other group being told that numerous people would be providing the same evaluation (Petty, Harkins, & Williams, 1980). You probably have seen this phenomenon in editing group papers. When one person believes he or she is the only one editing a paper, that person tends to be more careful in seeking out typos and grammatical errors. However, when we believe all members of the group are doing the same editing, we tend to relax and assume others will catch errors if we fail to do so.

A third factor that affects motivation deals with the message content. When the message includes **incongruent information** the receiver has more motivation to centrally process the message and consider the content (Maheswaran & Chaiken, 1991). ⌈Incongruent information is information that is not consistent with what the receiver believes to be true. In other words, it is contradictory.⌋ This is in harmony with the cognitive dissonance theory. Because people tend to be uncomfortable with inconsistency, they are motivated to consider the content of the message to try to resolve that inconsistency when incongruent information is present; they become motivated to process the message.

Finally, the fourth factor is a personality characteristic that leads some people to more routinely centrally process information, and it has been labeled **need for cognition (NFC)** (Cacioppo & Petty, 1982; Cohen, Stotland, & Wolfe, 1955). Need for cognition refers to the desire or need to think and engage in information processing. Individuals who are high in need for cognition enjoy thinking about issues even when there is no personal relevance and their thoughts have no impact on the outcome. People high in NFC tend to centrally process most messages and think more about the content. It may be that these people find thinking about a message enjoyable in and of itself. A scale developed to measure levels of NFC among participants is included in Figure 9.1. Thus, different factors of each situation include the topic, the nature of the receiver, and the circumstances surrounding the message that need to be considered when evaluating the level of receiver motivation to process the message.

⌈To understand why a receiver is or is not motivated to process a message, several different factors must be considered. The message topic, the nature of the receiver, and the circumstances surrounding the message all influence motivation to process. These are also the factors we use to predict and control motivation to process.⌋

ABILITY TO PROCESS

Ability is the second characteristic that has to be present for central processing to occur. The receiver has to be able to comprehend the message in order to elaborate on the arguments. Similar to motivation, multiple factors affect a receiver's ability to process the message. Four factors are discussed.

How a message is structured and the words are chosen determine in part whether the audience will have the ability to process the message. The message has to be comprehensible to the audience before careful processing can occur. **Message comprehension** is the first factor and goes back to the second step in the Yale approach; it refers to how clear the message is to the receivers. The organizational pattern and language

EIGHTEEN-ITEM NEED FOR COGNITION SCALE

Adapted from Communication and Persuasion: Central and Peripheral Routes to Attitude Change by R. E. Petty and J. T. Cacioppo, 1986, Springer-Verlag.

Item Number	Item Wording

1. I would prefer complex to simple problems.

2. I like to have the responsibility of handling a situation that requires a lot of thinking.

3. Thinking is not my idea of fun.*

4. I would rather do something that requires little thought than something that is sure to challenge my thinking abilities.*

5. I try to anticipate and avoid situations where there is a likely chance I will have to think in depth about something.*

6. I find satisfaction in deliberating hard and for long hours.

7. I only think as hard as I have to.*

8. I prefer to think about small, daily projects to long-term ones.*

9. I like tasks that require little thought once I've learned them.*

10. The idea of relying on thought to make my way to the top appeals to me.

11. I really enjoy a task that involves coming up with new solutions to problems.

12. Learning new ways to think doesn't excite me very much.*

13. I prefer my life to be filled with puzzles that I must solve.

14. The notion of thinking abstractly is appealing to me.

15. I would prefer a task that is intellectual, difficult, and important to one that is somewhat important but does not require much thought.

16. I feel relief rather than satisfaction after completing a task that required a lot of mental effort.*

17. It's enough for me that something gets the job done; I don't care how or why it works.*

18. I usually end up deliberating about issues even when they do not affect me personally.

*Reverse scoring is used on this item.

Note: Subjects are asked to respond to the items on scales indicating their "agreement" or "disagreement," or to rate the extent to which the statements are "characteristic" or "uncharacteristic" of them (see Cacioppo and Petty, 1982).

FIGURE 9.1 Need for cognition scale.

choice affect message comprehension. We discussed message factors that influence persuasion, but here we are focusing on how clearly the message is presented. If the message is presented in a clear fashion with language appropriate for the audience, the audience is more likely to understand the content and is more able to think about the content. If the message is unclear and/or if the language used is at an inappropriate level for the audience, they will not be able to think about the content of the message. Consider a person with a fourth-grade reading level trying to read a *New York Times* opinion page commentary on economic policy. That person is not likely to be able to grasp the content of the message clearly enough to be able to give it careful and rational thought, even if he or she is motivated to process the message.

A second factor that influences the ability to process messages is **message repetition** (Alba & Marmorstein, 1987). The more often the information is presented, the greater the chance of comprehension. This is why many public speaking texts advise you to tell the audience what you are going to tell them with a pre-summary, tell them, and then tell them what you told them with a summary. The repetition of the key points helps increase the chances of comprehension. This is also why commercials are repeated. The more often they are presented, the more likely the target audience will comprehend them. The more complex the message, the more the need for repetition. We may be able to easily comprehend a simple message hearing it only once; however, we most likely need to hear a complex message multiple times to fully comprehend it.

A third factor that influences the ability to process is **distraction**. When receivers are distracted during the message presentation, their ability to process the message is lowered. Various types of distraction have been used in research, including having white noise play in the background while participants listen to the message, having background activities such as party sounds and laughter going on next door to where participants are reading the message, telling participants to focus on the quality of the tape recording they are listening to, or having an X appear on a screen to distract them from listening closely to the message content (Buller, 1986; Petty, Wells, & Brock, 1976). Heckling has also been used to distract audience members from thinking carefully about the content of the message they are listening to. For receivers to centrally process the message, they must be able to focus on the message content. The greater the distraction, the less able receivers are to process the message.

A fourth and final factor that influences the ability to process is **prior knowledge** of the topic. When receivers have greater prior knowledge of the topic, they have a greater ability to process the message. This idea also makes intuitive sense. If receivers already have some knowledge and understanding of a topic, then the information in the message fits into their existing framework of knowledge. If the topic is unfamiliar to them, then it is more difficult for them to make sense of the new information. ⌜For example, if you took a class with lots of terminology such as chemistry, not knowing the terminology inhibited your ability to understand the chemical characteristics and processes being discussed. If you entered the class having prior knowledge of some of the terminology, you were much more able to understand the lectures.⌟

As with motivation, the ability to process a message depends on the characteristics of the receiver, the nature of the message, and the circumstances surrounding the presentation of the message. Once these multiple factors are considered, we can better explain, predict, and control whether the receiver will centrally or peripherally process the persuasive message.

The diagram in Figure 9.2 summarizes the factors that determine whether a person processes a message centrally or peripherally. The model begins with an individual receiving a message. Let's say that individual is you. First, you assess the message and determine if you are motivated to process the message. The factors discussed previously influence whether you are motivated. If you are not motivated to process, you look for a peripheral cue and process the message via the peripheral route. If you are motivated to process, you must then assess your ability to process the message. If you are not able to process, again you look for a peripheral cue and process the message via the peripheral route. If you are both motivated and able to process, you engage in the high elaboration and centrally process the message. ⌜We are semi-conscious of assessing our motivation and ability to process and it happens very quickly. It's not something we spend time contemplating.⌟ Notice in Figure 9.2 that both central

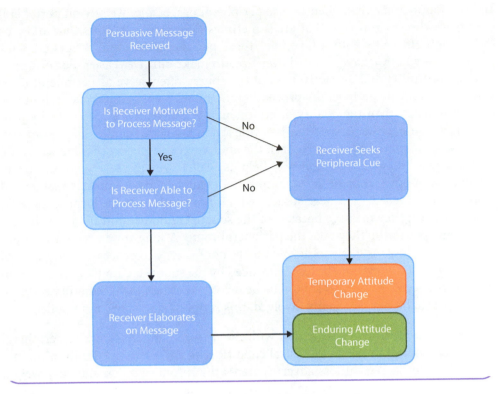

FIGURE 9.2 The elaboration likelihood model of persuasion.

processing and peripheral processing result in attitude change; however, one change is thought to be more stable and enduring, whereas the other change is temporary.

CENTRAL VERSUS PERIPHERAL ROUTES

Central route processing does not occur as often as peripheral route processing for most people most of the time. As we discussed earlier, we don't have the cognitive energy or even the time to think carefully about each of the thousands of messages that bombard us daily. However, many of the previously discussed persuasion theories focus on what ELM refers to as central route processing. For example, cognitive dissonance theory and the theory of reasoned action focus on rational judgments made by receivers who think about the content of persuasive messages they receive. Thus, we already have a good deal of understanding about how information may be processed in the central route. Because central route processing is rational in nature, the quality of the message is central to attitude change. When engaged in central route processing, the receiver is thinking through the message, analyzing the content, and evaluating the message. As you might expect, for the receiver to be persuaded, the message must contain high-quality information and well-constructed arguments. In Chapter 5, we discussed factors such as evidence that can be used to construct high-quality messages.

When a person engages in peripheral route processing, he or she engages in the low elaboration and exerts little effort to analyze the message. To assess the quality of the information and arguments takes effort, so this information is overlooked. The receiver looks for **peripheral cues** to use as a shortcut in assessing the message. Petty and Cacioppo argue that when we use peripheral processing, we rely on peripheral cues from the environment that are sometimes described as **scripts** that allow us to function efficiently with little effort. These peripheral cues and scripts are simple decision rules we have adopted over time to make our lives easier. For example, **source credibility** and **attractiveness** of the source often serve as peripheral cues. When receivers are peripherally processing the message, peripheral cues tend to be more important than the quality of arguments. When receivers are centrally processing, these peripheral cues are less important than the quality of arguments. When we are unmotivated and/or lack the ability to centrally process messages, we seek out cues like source credibility to help us evaluate the message without careful consideration of the content. For example, if a credible person indicates that a local school levy is needed, ⌜a college student who is not involved in the local school district may accept the message because of the source credibility and not consider the arguments put forth. They take the peripheral route. A long-time resident who has school-age children is likely to devote much more energy to process the arguments for and against the levy and be less influenced by the source credibility.⌟ A common script is that credible sources should be believed more than low-credibility sources. For a topic that is not personally involved, this script offers a shortcut for a decision.

Rewards or punishments associated with the message can also serve as peripheral cues. Recall our discussion of classical conditioning and operant conditioning theory in Chapter 2. Weight loss advertisements that promise quick and easy weight loss offer a reward for purchasing the products. This reward can serve as a peripheral cue. The fine print and arguments (or lack of them) in the message content may indicate flaws, but people who are peripherally processing tend not to pay attention to those specifics. Rather, a receiver uses the promised reward as a mental shortcut to determine that purchasing the weight loss product would be wise.

The **number of arguments** in a message can also serve as a peripheral cue regardless of whether the arguments themselves are strong or weak. For those engaged in peripherally processing, simply hearing a long list of arguments may cause attitude change without knowledge about the content of the arguments. For example, Petty and Cacioppo (1984) conducted several studies and found that when audiences with low involvement were peripherally processing, six arguments and nine arguments had more of a persuasive impact than did three, regardless of argument quality. However, the number of arguments had less impact with audiences who had high involvement and were centrally processing.

Others' reactions can also serve as a peripheral cue. When listening to a message in a group, we are typically aware of how others around us are reacting to the message. How the rest of the audience reacts to the message can serve as a cue to react either positively or negatively to the message. Axsom, Yates, and Chaiken (1987) demonstrated this principle in a study in which participants listened to an audiotaped persuasive message that included an audience's enthusiastic or unenthusiastic response. When participants had low involvement, and thus were processing peripherally, the audience responses influenced the participants' reactions to the message. When the participants had high involvement, and thus were processing centrally, the audience responses did not affect persuasion. Rather, argument quality influenced the receivers who were centrally processing the message. In this case, the response of the audience served as a peripheral cue for those engaging in the little elaboration and taking the peripheral route.

Similarly, some studies have suggested that for those who are peripherally processing, consensus can serve as a peripheral cue (Hazlewood & Chaiken, 1990; Kang, 1998). In these cases, simply having poll data or study results that claim many others support the position may be sufficient to generate a positive response in those who are peripherally processing the message. This is one reason why political campaigns promote polls that show their candidate or issue is ahead in public preferences and why advertisers try to claim they have the most popular product. What others are doing can serve as a simple cue for what we should do.

After our discussion in Chapter 5 of message factors, you might think **humor** would serve as a peripheral cue, and it might in certain situations. People enjoy humor and are motivated to consume humorous messages. Additionally, humorous messages are often very engaging. Therefore, humorous messages sometimes enhance motivation to process rather than serving as a peripheral cue. In a study, Nabi, Moyer-Guse, and Byrne (2007) concluded that humorous messages were deeply processed, but they were also discounted as "just a joke," which reduced persuasion. Nabi and her colleagues also found that participants liked funny sources more, which in turn enhanced perceptions of credibility. To the extent that humor enhances liking and credibility, it may serve as a peripheral cue. To the extent that humor gains attention and creates a positive effect on the message, it may enhance motivation to process the message. Again, as discussed in Chapter 5, sources need to be careful when using humor. Humor is a complex phenomenon that is difficult to explain, predict, and control.

Thus, a variety of factors can serve as peripheral cues depending on the situation. When either motivation or ability is low and receivers peripherally process a message, they will look in the message and the surrounding environment for a cue to help them assess the message and draw a conclusion without having to engage in much elaboration. However, when both motivation and ability are high, receivers engage in central processing and focus on the content of the message and ignore peripheral cues. Therefore, there are two distinct ways people process messages—peripherally or centrally—and the persuasive process differs significantly between these two routes.

ATTITUDE CHANGE IN CENTRAL AND PERIPHERAL ROUTES

Different processes are involved in attitude change with each processing route, but both can result in attitude change. Not all attitude change is equal. Attitudes formed through peripheral processing are more temporary, less stable, and are more susceptible to change or counter-persuasion. On the other hand, attitudes formed through central processing tend to last longer, be more stable, and be more resistant to change or counter-persuasion. In addition, attitudes formed via the central processing route tend to be better predictors of behavior than those formed through peripheral processing.

A receiver engaged in central processing is analyzing the message and carefully considering the information contained in that message. Flaws in the reasoning, incorrect information, or illogical conclusions will all be noticed. Therefore, the quality of the message content is critical when an audience engages in high elaboration. In Chapter 5 we discussed factors such as evidence, logic, language, and message structure as important in creating persuasive messages. Considering these factors along with accurate and relevant information is necessary when creating messages that will be effective for an audience engaged in high elaboration.

A receiver engaged in peripheral processing is looking for a shortcut, a way to quickly process the message with the least amount of effort. Once a shortcut is found, the receiver either accepts or rejects the message and moves on. Any flaws in reasoning, incorrect information, or illogical conclusions are not likely to be noticed. Source factors and message factors that make the message look good are important in creating a message that will be effective for an audience engaged in the low elaboration.

Thus, persuasion occurs differently in the two routes. Persuasion involving peripheral processing may be easier and a more common occurrence, but it is a more temporary form of attitude change. When long-term attitude change and resistance to counter-persuasion are needed, central route processing is more desirable. It may be more difficult to entice an audience to centrally process a message; however, the stronger and more stable attitude change that results often makes it worthwhile. Sometimes we seek long-term attitude change, such as in a political campaign or a social movement. On the other hand, sometimes short-term attitude change is sufficient. For example, if you are promoting a new frozen pizza by giving away free samples and receive a commission for each pizza sold, you probably are less concerned about long-term attitude change than you are with whether the consumer will buy a pizza today.

TESTING ELM

ELM is one of the most widely tested and used persuasion theories today. And, as is often the case, examining ELM research provides direction on how to use ELM in everyday persuasion situations. First, we examine some of the studies Petty and Cacioppo conducted to test the theory, and then draw on the methods used in these studies to discuss how to apply ELM to various persuasion situations.

In an early study, Petty and Cacioppo (1979) used personal relevance to test central and peripheral processing. They recruited college students and created persuasive messages that used the topic of requiring senior comprehensive exams. (A comprehensive exam is an exam given at the end of one's program that covers all main content areas of that program and must be passed in order to graduate.) This was expected to be a counter-attitudinal message for most students because it was expected that most would not embrace the idea of another hurdle to face before graduation. Petty and Cacioppo wanted some students to centrally process the message and some to peripherally process the message. To control this, they manipulated personal relevance. Recall that personal relevance influences motivation to process. One group of students was told that their own university was advocating the adoption of the comprehensive exam policy, effective immediately. Presumably, these students would see the issue as personally relevant and be motivated to centrally process the message. Message language was relatively simple so that everyone would have the ability to process. Therefore, students exposed to this version of the message were expected to engage in the high elaboration and centrally process the message. Another group of students heard the same message but were told that it was a policy being considered at a university across the country. Personal relevance would be low for this group, so the motivation to the process would be low, leading this group to engage in the low elaboration and peripheral processing. Half of the students in the high-relevance condition received high-quality arguments; the other half received low-quality arguments. Half of the participants in the low-relevance condition also received high-quality arguments; the other half received low-quality arguments. You may be wondering exactly what constitutes a *high-quality argument* as opposed to a *low-quality argument*.

The messages contained arguments that had been extensively pretested to ensure they were of high or low quality but were credible to the respondents. In a pretest using different participants, high-quality arguments generated 65% or more positive thoughts (in a thought listing process) about the topic and 35% or less negative thoughts about the topic. Low-quality arguments generated 35% or less positive thoughts and 65% or more negative thoughts among participants. In both cases, the messages were tested to ensure they were credible with college students and not considered totally unbelievable.

Students were told that the messages were editorials, and they were asked to assist the Journalism Department in evaluating the quality of each editorial. After hearing the 4-minute audiotaped message containing either strong or weak arguments about the topic, participants were asked to respond to questions about their attitude on the topic, to list their thoughts, and to report how much thought they put into evaluating the message, along with other measures.

Results supported the predictions made by the elaboration likelihood model. Those in the high-relevance condition (with the message relating to their own university) listed more issue-relevant thoughts and reported thinking more about the message, indicating they engaged in high elaboration (central route). Those in the low-relevance condition (with the message relating to a distant university) listed fewer issue-relevant thoughts and reported thinking less about the message, indicating they engaged in low elaboration (peripheral route). Thus, those in the high-involvement/personal relevance condition were more likely to centrally process the message while those in the low-involvement/personal relevance condition were more likely to peripherally process the message.

⌐Petty and Cacioppo (1986) also wanted to test the hypothesis that receivers who centrally processed strong arguments would be more influenced by the message and have a positive attitude toward comprehensive exams than would those who centrally processed weak arguments. Additionally, Petty and Cacioppo predicted that there would be no difference in attitude between strong and weak arguments when receivers engaged in peripheral processing.⌐ For participants in the low-relevance condition, whether they heard a message containing strong or weak arguments had little impact on their attitude toward comprehensive exams, just as predicted. For participants in the high-relevance condition, argument strength mattered. When strong arguments were heard, participants had a more positive attitude; when the weak arguments were heard, participants had a more negative attitude. Thus, when centrally processing, the subjects thought more about the arguments in the message and were more influenced by the strength of the arguments.

In the spring of 2009, Dr. Melissa Bekelja Wanzer, Professor in the Department of Communication at Canisius College in Buffalo, NY, taught a class on persuasion using this textbook. Working in groups, students created persuasive messages using the theories, models, and strategies they learned in class. One group of students created a set of messages that took on a life of its own. Megan Tremblay, Elyse Krezmien, Sara LaBelle, Ja'Nay Carswell, and David Jackson created a campaign titled "Check Yo Nutz" to raise awareness of testicular cancer among college age males, who have the highest incidence of this form of cancer. In September 2009, Dr. Wanzer and her students took the campaign to Roswell Park Cancer Institute in Buffalo. Administrators at Roswell Park were impressed with the students' work and agreed to collaborate with Dr. Wanzer and her students to implement a full scale campaign to increase the practice of testicular self-exams by young men and to increase awareness. In the spring of 2010, the Check Yo Nutz campaign was launched by Dr. Wanzer and her students with the help of a health communication campaign class taught by Dr. Catherine Foster at Canisius College.

The goal of the campaign was to influence college age males (*target*) to perform testicular self-exams (*behavior*) while showering (*context*) each month (*time*). Drawing on the *Yale* Model, students knew they had to get their audience's attention, so they created novel, bold, and humorous messages with a cheeky mascot named "Sammy the Squirrel" and the tag line "Check Yo Nutz." The mascot and tag line appeared on all of the message materials. The students also knew that message *repetition* was important for increasing the target audiences' *ability* to process, so a variety of materials (flyers, posters, brochures, shower cards, save the date postcards) were created and distributed using a variety of channels (social networking sites, videos, newspapers, website, mass media, and events). Drawing on the *theory of planned behavior*, students knew they needed to change young men's beliefs about testicular cancer and testicular self-exams (TSE) in order to motivate them to intend to perform the desired behavior. Information about the symptoms, incidence and outcomes of testicular cancer (TC) were provided in the materials, as well as how to conduct a TSE. Students also understood that to influence behavior, their audience needed to engage in *central route processing* of the messages. They focused on making the messages *personally relevant* to their audience of young men to increase their motivation to process centrally. In addition, the messages were *written*, *repeated*, and *straightforward* in an effort to increase the target audiences' ability to process messages. The team also planned several testicular cancer awareness events: "Don't Forget Your Buddies" where Nutty Buddy ice cream cones and TC information were handed out; "Dodge These Balls, Not Yours," a dodge-ball tournament for students, faculty and staff; and "The Check Now Luau," a faculty, staff, and student dance, with Sammy the Squirrel making appearances at each event.

Not only did Dr. Wanzer and her students design and implement this campaign, they also conducted research to evaluate the effectiveness of the campaign messages and strategies. Prior to the campaign they recruited a group of 272 college males at Canisius College and had them complete a pre-test survey assessing their knowledge and awareness of TC, their intention to perform TSE and seek information, and the frequency of performing these behaviors. Two weeks after the campaign events concluded, the same college males were asked to complete a post-test survey that assessed the same variables. Concurrently a control group of 52 males at another New York state school completed the same survey and these results were compared with the experimental site.

Overall, Dr. Wanzer and her colleagues found that the campaign was effective at increasing awareness of TC and increasing TSE among male students at Canisius College. There were significant increases in awareness, behavioral intention to perform TSE, and actual performance of TSE and information seeking behaviors when comparing males' responses to survey questions before and after the campaign. Also, participants at the experimental school showed statistically significant advantages over participants at the control school in all four measures of cancer awareness (i.e., exposure to TC information, knowledge of signs and symptoms, where to find TC information, and how to perform a TSE), and these effect sizes were large.

Males exposed to online campaign messages through the campaign website, Twitter, and Facebook were more likely to intend to discuss TC with a physician and perform a TSE in the next month (i.e., behavioral intent) than males who were not exposed to these same messages. Males who received a shower card reported greater awareness of TC and increased performance of TC behaviors (i.e., self-exams, search for TC information, etc.) than males who did not receive a shower card. One interesting outcome was that males who only read a brochure only reported greater awareness of TC, whereas males who attended one of the campaign events reported greater awareness and greater behavioral intent and actual behavior with regard to TSE.

Behavioral Intention to perform TSE measure
I will perform a self-examination for testicular cancer in the next month.

TSE Behavior measure
I perform a self-exam for testicular cancer every month.

Knowledge Questions
I have been exposed to information regarding testicular cancer.
I believe that I am not at risk for testicular cancer.
I know all of the warning signs and symptoms of testicular cancer.
I know how to perform a self-exam for testicular cancer.
I know where to go to find accurate information about testicular cancer.

A 5-point Likert Scale was used.

FIGURE 9.3 Integrating theory, research and practice at Canisius College.

APPLYING ELM TO INFLUENCE ATTITUDES

The elaboration likelihood model has been used in a variety of applied contexts. It has been used to design health communication campaigns (Slater, 1999), to influence beliefs of food risks (Frewer, Howard, Hedderley, & Shepherd, 1997), for eating disorder education (Keating, 2001), and for AIDS education (Dinoff & Kowalski, 1999). ELM has been applied to political advertising (Meirick, 2002) and social issues such as nuclear power (Katsuya, 2002) and attitudes toward rape (Heppner et al., 1995). It has frequently been applied in advertising and marketing (McCullough & Dodge, 2002; Petty & Cacioppo, 1983) and in the legal field examining jury decision-making processes (Frumkin, 2001). ELM has been used to understand how job candidates are evaluated (Forret & Turban, 1996; Larsen & Phillips, 2002) and to increase donations of blood (Hall, 1996) and organs (Skumanich & Kintsfather, 1996).

So, how does one go about applying this theory? If we go back to Petty and Cacioppo's (1979) study, they manipulated personal relevance in order to enhance motivation to process. If we consider the factors that influence *motivation* and *ability* to process, many of these can be manipulated by the source. The principles of ELM tell us we need to design into our message elements that will motivate our audience to process the message and make the message easy to process. We need to consider our audience's ability to process the message; what's easy for one person to process is difficult for another. Understanding our audience's existing knowledge and level of education are important to creating a message that is easy to comprehend. Additionally, channel characteristics should be considered and used to make the message easy to process. Of course you may conclude from your audience analysis that they are unlikely to engage in high elaboration.

If you successfully enhance motivation and ability to process, you must also have a really good message in terms of content that will hold up to audience scrutiny.

If you expect audience elaboration to be low, you need to be sure peripheral cues exist that your audience can use to quickly draw the conclusion you want. A practical approach is to design the message (or a series of messages) that contain peripheral cues for those engaged in peripheral processing AND that contain strong arguments that will be positively evaluated by those engaged in central processing. If you examine communication campaigns that contain several variations of the message, some versions are longer and contain more information (designed for central processing), and some are shorter with little content (designed for peripheral processing).

The principles of ELM can easily be combined with the principles from other theories and source and message concepts that were discussed in earlier chapters. Creators of communication campaigns rarely draw on a single theory. An example of a student-created campaign that used ELM as well as TRA, the Yale approach, and message factors such as humor is described in Figure 9.2. The students enrolled in Dr. Melissa Bekelja Wanzer's persuasion class took the concepts learned in the text to create a campaign targeted at young men to increase awareness of testicular cancer and to increase the practice of testicular self-exams. This campaign is a great example of applying theory and research to a real-life persuasive campaign (Wanzer et al., 2014).

STRENGTHS AND LIMITATIONS

⌐The elaboration likelihood model has several strengths. It has been researched in a variety of settings and has been able to predict and control persuasion in real-world arenas such as advertising, marketing, politics, and health. ELM can easily be used in conjunction with other theories as was demonstrated in the Check Yo Nutz campaign. A major strength of the theory is the explanation of the two ways people process messages and the identification of what kinds of messages are successful for receivers who are centrally processing and for those who are peripherally processing. This affords persuaders with a useful approach to message design. Another strength of ELM is that it can be used in a variety of contexts.⌐

Although the theory has advanced our knowledge about persuasion, there are some troubling aspects to the model and related research. Not all research has supported the ELM predictions. A central criticism of ELM was advanced by a meta-analysis conducted by Johnson and Eagly (1989). ⌐The meta-analysis involved looking at the results of multiple ELM studies and combining them for data analysis on a broader scale. The meta-analysis involved looking at the results of many ELM studies and combining them for data analysis. Johnson and Eagly found that research conducted by Petty and Cacioppo and their students was far more likely to support the ELM model than research conducted by others not associated with Petty and Cacioppo. The inability of other scholars to replicate findings was troublesome. Replication is a primary means of validating research findings.⌐

The central concept of argument quality was part of the difficulty other researchers had with replicating Petty and Cacioppo's work on ELM. Prior to the publication of their second book in 1986, Petty and Cacioppo had not clearly explained how they defined and measured argument quality. As explained earlier, they defined high-quality arguments as those that generated 65% or more positive thoughts in a thought listing process and 35% or fewer negative thoughts. Conversely, low-quality arguments were those that generated 65% or more negative thoughts and 35% or less positive thoughts. So what is a high-quality argument? An argument that elicits positive thoughts. How do you elicit positive thoughts? Write a strong argument. This definition of argument quality has received much criticism, especially from the communication discipline.

Psychology scholars like Petty and Cacioppo care little about message construction and message variables. Communication scholars, however, have a long history of seeking and recommending guidelines for building good arguments. The communication standards for argument quality did not always yield the same results as Petty and Cacioppo's approach. Once other scholars understood Petty and Cacioppo's approach to argument quality, and often borrowed messages tested by them (e.g., the comprehensive exam messages discussed previously), the results became more consistent. The inability to offer guidance to prospective persuaders about how to create high- and low-argument quality messages is a weakness of the theory.

Another limitation of ELM involves individuals with a high need for cognition (NFC). These individuals do not fall into the predicted patterns of central and peripheral processing advanced by the elaboration likelihood model. Because we don't know without testing which individuals are high in NFC, we don't know when individuals will fail to follow the predicted patterns.

Other scholars (Stiff, 1994) have questioned the single-channel premise that receivers process a message either centrally or peripherally. Is it possible to do both, a parallel-processing approach? Is it always a choice of central or peripheral processing, or can we choose to do some of both with a single message? This issue is raised in response to cues that have been found to function both in central processing and peripheral processing. Source credibility is a good example. According to ELM, source credibility is a peripheral processing cue and has the most impact on receivers who are peripherally processing. Yet, in some situations, source credibility may be a legitimate part of argument quality. Political advertising is an example. Credibility is often considered an important characteristic for a politician. Although credibility has often been observed functioning as a peripheral cue, a receiver thinking carefully about the message may look at the high credibility of the politician as evidence or a reason to support the candidate. In this case, the credibility serves as part of the strength of the arguments being made. Petty and Cacioppo and other scholars debate whether ELM can explain single and parallel processing, and this issue remains an open question about the theory. If the model can explain all responses to a message, it becomes difficult to disprove the theory.

Finally, as Petty and Cacioppo (1986) themselves note, the theory does not answer questions about why the parts of the model operate as they do. We have already noted the lack of knowledge about what constitutes high- or low-quality arguments. In addition, we do not know why some variables are peripheral cues or why others affect how we process the information. The model answers many questions, but many are still unanswered. New theoretical models are likely to build on this knowledge base and provide more answers (and probably more questions) to our understanding of persuasion processes.

SUMMARY

- Elaboration refers to thinking about the content and arguments of a message.
- ELM involves two routes of persuasion: a central route and a peripheral route.
- The central route involves high elaboration and expenditure of cognitive energy.
- The peripheral route involves low elaboration and the use of peripheral cues.
- Both motivation (how much the receiver wants to think about the message) and ability (how capable the receiver is of processing the message) are required for central processing to occur.
- Factors that influence motivation include the level of personal relevance or involvement with the topic, personal responsibility, incongruent information, and receivers' need for cognition (NFC).
- Factors that influence ability include message comprehensibility, message repetition, distraction, and receiver prior knowledge.
- Peripheral processing cues include source credibility/source attractiveness, rewards or punishments, number of arguments, and audience reactions.
- ⌈The primary way of measuring elaboration is the thought listing procedure.⌋
- Attitudes formed through peripheral processing tend to be more temporary, less stable over time, and more susceptible to change or counter-persuasion.
- Attitudes formed through central processing tend to last longer, be more stable, be more resistant to change or counter-persuasion, and be better predictors of behavior.
- Strengths of the ELM include broad research support, applicable to many contexts, identification of two ways messages are processed, and explanation of how to influence persuasion in both central and peripheral processing.
- Weaknesses of ELM include a lack of uniform support for the model through research, difficulty ⌈with replication of findings, problematic definition of message quality, inability to predict outcomes for high NFC individuals, and questions about single versus parallel processing.⌋

KEY TERMS

Ability to process—how capable the receiver is to elaborate on the persuasive message.

Argument recall—the ability to recreate parts of a message.

Central route—the receiver engages in the high elaboration and focuses on thinking about the content of the message.

Consensus—the perception that many or most people believe or behave a certain way.

Distraction—stimulus that distracts or diverts the receiver's attention away from the message.

Elaboration—the amount of thinking the receiver engages in about the content of a message. Elaboration can be thought of as a continuum ranging from not thinking at all about the content of the message to extensive thinking about the message.

Incongruent information—when information in a message is not consistent with what the receiver believes to be true.

Motivation to process—how much the receiver wants to elaborate on the message.

Need for cognition (NFC)—a personality predisposition that involves the need or desire to think about issues even when there is no personal relevance and their thoughts have no impact on the outcome.

Peripheral cues—simple decision rules and scripts people develop over time to allow for quick processing and decision making.

Peripheral route—the receiver engages in the low elaboration of the message.

Personal relevance/involvement—the extent to which a topic is important or of value to a receiver.

Personal responsibility—the degree to which the receiver is responsible for the message outcome or consequences, such as making a decision.

Prior knowledge—the knowledge about a topic that the receiver has before being exposed to a message on the topic.

Thought listing—a process in which research participants are asked to list what they were thinking about during the presentation of a persuasive message.

QUESTIONS FOR REVIEW

Respond to the following questions **without** reviewing the text or your notes. These questions are provided to help you practice retrieving information and reflect on your reading.

A. What are some key ideas about the Elaboration Likelihood Model (ELM)?

B. Did you agree or disagree with anything you read? Explain.

C. What did you learn that was new to you?

D. What concepts, if any, were confusing to you?

Respond to the following questions. You may reference your text or notes to help you.

1. What factors affect motivation to process a message?

2. What factors affect the ability to process a message?

3. What are examples of peripheral cues?

4. What is the difference between attitudes formed through the central processing route and those formed via the peripheral processing route?

5. How can ELM be used in generating persuasive messages?

6. What are the strengths and limitations of the ELM?

QUESTIONS FOR DISCUSSION

1. Before you read the chapter, you named an issue that is not important to you. You are likely to engage in peripheral processing when you encounter a persuasive message about those topics. What peripheral cues might influence you? Why?

2. Search online for an advertising, health, or social campaign that contains several variations of its message. Which messages are designed for central processing and which are designed for peripheral processing? How did you distinguish between the messages designed for central processing and those designed for peripheral processing?

3. In your small group, discuss how you might apply the ELM to your final presentations. Are you more or less likely to use this theory than the others you have discussed? Why or why not?

4. Do the strengths of the ELM outweigh its limitations? Why or why not?

5. Discuss the ethical questions provided at the end of the chapter. What ethical considerations are relevant to the information in this chapter about using the ELM?

- Are there guidelines (e.g., don't lie) that would be appropriate for every situation, or are ethics relative?

- Do the ends (e.g., a good outcome) justify any means?

- Is deceiving the receiver ever appropriate?

- Should the source of the message bear primary responsibility for ethics, or should the receiver share that responsibility (e.g., buyer beware)?

REFERENCES

Alba, J. W., & Marmorstein, H. (1987). The effects of frequency knowledge on consumer decision making. *Journal of Consumer Research, 14*(1), 14–25.

Axsom, D., Yates, S., & Chaiken, S. (1987). Audience response as a heuristic cue in persuasion. *Journal of Personality and Social Psychology, 53*(1), 30–40.

Buller, D. B. (1986). Distraction during persuasive communication: A meta-analytic review. *Communication Monographs, 53,* 91–114.

Cacioppo, J. T., Harkins, S. G., & Petty, R. E. (1981). The nature of attitudes and cognitive responses and their relationships to behavior. In R. Petty, T. Ostrom, & T. Brock (Eds.), *Cognitive responses in persuasion.* Hillsdale, NJ: Erlbaum.

Cacioppo, J. T., & Petty, R. E. (1981). Social psychological procedures for cognitive response assessment: The thought listing technique. In T. Merluzzi, C. Glass, & M. Genest (Eds.), *Cognitive assessment.* New York, NY: Guilford Press.

Cacioppo, J. T., & Petty, R. E. (1982). The need for cognition. *Journal of Personality and Social Psychology, 42,* 116–131.

Cohen, A., Stotland, E., & Wolfe, D. (1955). An experimental investigation of need for cognition. *Journal of Abnormal and Social Psychology, 51,* 291–294.

Dinoff, B. L., & Kowalski, R. M. (1999). Reducing AIDS risk behavior: The combined efficacy of protection motivation theory and the elaboration likelihood model. *Journal of Social and Clinical Psychology, 18,* 223–239.

Forret, M. L., & Turban, D. B. (1996). Implications of the elaboration likelihood model for interviewer decision processes. *Journal of Business and Psychology, 10,* 415–428.

Frewer, L. J., Howard, C., Hedderley, D., & Shepherd, R. (1997). The use of the elaboration likelihood model in developing effective food risk communication. *Risk Analysis, 17,* 269–281.

Frumkin, L. A. (2001). The effect of eyewitnesses' accent, nationality, and authority on the perceived favorability of their testimony. *Dissertation Abstracts International: Section B: The Sciences & Engineering, 61*(8–B), 4474.

Hall, M. M. (1996). Elaboration likelihood model in a field setting: The effect of individual factors on blood donating. *Dissertation Abstracts International: Section B: The Sciences & Engineering, 57*(2–B), 1501.

Hazlewood, D., & Chaiken, S. (1990, August). *Personal relevance, majority influence, and the law of large numbers.* Poster presented at the 98th Annual Convention of the American Psychological Association, Boston.

Heppner, M. J., Good, G. E., Hillenbrand-Gunn, T. L., Hawkins, A. K., Hacquard, L. L., Nichols, R. K., et al. (1995). Examining sex differences in altering attitudes about rape: A test of the elaboration likelihood model. *Journal of Counseling and Development, 73,* 640–647.

Johnson, B.T., & Eagly, A. H. (1989). The effects of involvement on persuasion: A meta-analysis. *Psychological Bulletin, 106,* 290–314.

Kang, M. (1998). The influence of public opinion polls on public opinion: The role of motivation and ability in the elaboration likelihood model. *Dissertation Abstracts International: Section A: Humanities & Social Sciences, 59*(2–A).

Katsuya, T. (2002). Difference in the formation of attitude toward nuclear power. *Political Psychology, 23*(1), 191–203.

Keating, M. C. (2001). The effects of eating restraint and speaker characteristics on the processing of a weight-related message. *Dissertation Abstracts International: Section B: The Sciences & Engineering, 62*(6–B), 2958.

Larsen, D. A., & Phillips, J. I. (2002). Effect of recruiter on attraction to the firm: Implications of the elaboration likelihood model. *Journal of Business & Psychology, 16*(3), 347–364.

Maheswaran, D., & Chaiken, S. (1991). Promoting systematic processing in low-motivation settings: Effects of incongruent information on processing and judgment. *Journal of Personality and Social Psychology, 61*(1), 13–25.

McCullough, T., & Dodge, H. R. (2002). Understanding the role consumer involvement plays in the effectiveness of hospital advertising. *Health Marketing Quarterly, 19*(3), 3–20.

Meirick, P. (2002). Cognitive responses to negative and comparative political advertising. *Journal of Advertising, 31*(1), 49–62.

Nabi, R. L., Moyer-Guse, E., & Byrne, S. (2007). All joking aside: A serious investigation into the persuasive effect of funny social issue messages. *Communication Monographs, 74*, 29–54.

Petty, R. E., & Cacioppo, J. T. (1979a). Effects of forewarning of persuasive intent and involvement on cognitive responses and persuasion. *Personality and Social Psychology Bulletin, 5*, 173–176.

Petty, R. E., & Cacioppo, J. T. (1979b). Issue-involvement can increase or decrease persuasion by enhancing message-relevant cognitive responses. *Journal of Personality and Social Psychology, 37*, 1915–1926.

Petty, R. E., & Cacioppo, J. T. (1981). *Attitudes and persuasion: Classic and contemporary approaches.* Dubuque, IA: Brown.

Petty, R. E., & Cacioppo, J. T. (1983). Central and peripheral routes to persuasion: Application to advertising. In L. Percy & A. Woodside (Eds.) *Advertising and consumer psychology* (pp. 3–23). Lexington, MA: D. C. Heath.

Petty, R. E., & Cacioppo, J. T. (1984). The effects of involvement on responses to argument quantity and quality: Central and peripheral routes to persuasion. *Journal of Personality and Social Psychology, 46*, 69–81.

Petty, R. E., & Cacioppo, J. T. (1986a). *Communication and persuasion: Central and peripheral routes to attitude change.* New York: Springer-Verlag.

Petty, R. E., & Cacioppo, J. T. (1986b). The elaboration likelihood model of persuasion. *Advances in Experimental Social Psychology, 19*, 123–205.

Petty, R. E., Harkins, S. G., & Williams, K. D. (1980). The effects of group diffusion of cognitive effort on attitudes: An information processing view. *Journal of Personality and Social Psychology, 38*, 81–92.

Petty, R. E., Harkins, S. G., Williams, K. D., & Latane, B. (1977). The effects of group size on cognitive effort and evaluation. *Personality and Social Psychology Bulletin, 3*, 579–582.

Petty, R. E., Wells, G. L., & Brock, T. C. (1976). Distraction can enhance or reduce yielding to propaganda: Thought disruption versus effort justification. *Journal of Personality and Social Psychology, 34*, 874–888.

Sherif, C. W., Sherif, M., & Nebergall, R. E. (1965). *Attitude and attitude change: The social judgment involvement approach.* Philadelphia: W. B. Saunders.

Skumanich, S. A., & Kintsfather, D. P. (1996). Promoting the organ donor card: A causal model of persuasion effects. *Social Science & Medicine, 43*(3), 401–408.

Slater, M. D. (1999). Integrating application of media effects, persuasion, and behavior change theories to communication campaigns: A stages-of-change framework. *Health Communication, 11*(4), 335–354.

Stiff, J. B. (1994). *Persuasive communication.* New York: Guilford Press.

Tyler, S. W., Hertal, P. T., McCallum, M., & Ellis, H. C. (1979). Cognitive effort and memory. *Journal of Experimental Psychology: Human Learning and Memory, 5,* 607–617.

Wanzer, M. B., Foster, C., Servoss, T., & LaBelle, S. (2014). Educating males about testicular cancer: Support for a comprehensive testicular cancer campaign. *The Journal of Health Communication, 19,* 303–320.

PERSUASIVE WRITING

This section includes chapters about academic writing. You will learn how to write in a concise, scientific manner appropriate for the study of communication. The first chapter of this section addresses common myths you may have about writing. The next two chapters provide information about finding, evaluating, and using credible sources in your writing assignments. You will learn strategies to improve your writing and critical thinking skills as you develop a strong persuasive message.

CHAPTERS

CHAPTER 10

ACADEMIC WRITING: MYTHS AND EXPECTATIONS

BEFORE YOU READ

Before you read the chapter, review seven common myths about academic writing. When you think about the writing assignments in this course, which myths do you tend to believe? Mark all that apply.

_____ 1. Writing is a talent that people are born with, and I do not have it.

_____ 2. I have to know everything I want to say before I can start writing.

_____ 3. My first draft should be as good as it can be, so I will only have to "clean it up" in revision.

_____ 4. I have one more source to read before I can start writing.

_____ 5. If I could just find the perfect source, I would understand exactly what to say about my topic.

_____ 6. There is nothing that can be done about "writer's block."

_____ 7. I cannot figure out my introduction, so I cannot write the paper.

LEARNING OBJECTIVES

● UNDERSTAND AND PUT ASIDE DEBILITATING BELIEFS ABOUT WRITING.

We must not be hampered by yesterday's myths in concentrating on today's needs.

—Harold S. Geneen

With a strong research proposal in hand, it is time to get started writing your paper. In this chapter we want to make your writing process easier and more effective by debunking some debilitating myths about writing, and ensuring that you understand what readers of academic research papers expect to see in them.

© L. Moore/Comet/Corbis

COMMON MYTHS ABOUT WRITING

The beliefs we hold about *research* can impede our ability to get our work done. That is why we debunked some counterproductive myths about research. Here we consider some widely held beliefs about *writing*. If you have any of the following beliefs, you will want to guard against letting them get in the way of your project.

MYTH 1: WRITING IS A TALENT THAT PEOPLE ARE BORN WITH, AND I DO NOT HAVE IT.

Writing is a skill that can be learned, and everyone can learn how to write. No matter what your current writing skills, you can learn to write better if you are willing to invest some time and effort. When people say, "I cannot write!" they often mean that they do not know how to engage in a specific type of writing and are intimidated by the prospect of looking foolish in front of their peers or teachers. The solution to this problem is not just to sit down and start writing with the hope of producing something that readers will expect. Instead, ask for (or find) samples of the kind of writing you must do and model your own writing on them. Later in this chapter, we will discuss what your teachers and readers of research essays expect to see in your paper. For now, be confident that no matter what your previous experience in writing research papers, you can write this one.

MYTH 2: I HAVE TO KNOW EVERYTHING I WANT TO SAY BEFORE I CAN START WRITING.

Many emerging writers wonder how they can get started writing if they do not know what they want to communicate. They fear that time spent writing without a clear sense of what is to be communicated is time wasted. So they spend time trying meticulously to plan everything they want to include so that they can write efficiently, only to find that they are no clearer on what they want to say than they were when they sat down to figure things out. Part of the problem is that preplanning tends to stifle the open-mindedness you need in order to forge connections among your sources. According to cognitive psychologists Dr. Veerle Baaijen and Dr. David Galbraith (2018), people who write with few expectations about final outcomes tend to enhance their personal understanding of the topic and develop ideas of their own far more often than do people who meticulously plan their writing. Baaijen and Galbraith explain that planners tend to use writing simply to express what they already know. Because of this, their understanding of the topic tends not to be developed or enhanced by the act of writing. To embrace an exploratory approach to drafting, you do not need to write fully crafted sentences and paragraphs. You can make concept maps, tables, index cards, sticky notes, or sketches. Whichever forms of exploration you choose, the important thing is that you spend time playing around with the ideas you have encountered in your research without the pressure to produce the final word.

MYTH 3: MY FIRST DRAFT SHOULD BE AS GOOD AS IT CAN BE, SO I WILL ONLY HAVE TO "CLEAN IT UP" IN REVISION.

People who want to plan their writing down to the last detail also tend to want their first draft to be as close to their final draft as possible for the sake of efficiency. In order to meet their goal, such writers sacrifice depth and complexity for efficiency. They tend to oversimplify the complicated issues at the heart of their research. But in order to meet the expectations of academic readers, you must wrestle with the complexities and nuances of a topic. Even experienced academic writers write multiple drafts, finding their ideas and analyses emerging as they write. You too should expect that your first draft will be messy, and that in subsequent revisions, you will add and subtract large chunks of text. For now, you should start thinking about revision as more than just cleaning and polishing your text. Expect to reconsider your ideas and arguments as your thinking develops through the work of drafting. If you start your first draft with the knowledge that much will change in revision, you free yourself to write whatever comes and find your best ideas.

MYTH 4: I HAVE ONE MORE SOURCE TO READ BEFORE I CAN START WRITING.

You may have only a short time to write your research paper, which means you need to start writing. Today. And you will need to continue writing tomorrow. And the next day. And the day after that. There is always going to be one more source you could read. But you cannot let the desire to find it interfere with your need to write. Start writing early in your research process and continue writing daily until you are done. Between your draft and your revision, you may well go read that source.

But because the only way to think effectively about your sources is to write about them, you cannot postpone writing until you have everything in hand and perfectly understood. In fact, it may be a good idea to set a time limit on your initial phase of research. Commit to the idea that at a certain point you will stop collecting research and start writing about it. Start writing with what you have and be willing to revise as you consider further evidence later in the process.

MYTH 5: IF I COULD JUST FIND THE PERFECT SOURCE, I WOULD UNDERSTAND EXACTLY WHAT I WANT TO SAY ABOUT MY TOPIC.

Many writers of research papers believe that there is one perfect source out there that will make everything fall into place, clear up every confusion, and enable them to breeze through the writing stage of the research project. This belief stems from the mistaken notion that their job as a researcher is simply to find and present information. However, your most important work is to make information meaningful by thinking carefully about what it tells you in regard to the problem you are trying to solve or the issue you are trying to resolve. Information only matters when you use it to advance the discussion about a topic. So, when you are confused and do not know what to think, do not go looking for a source. Instead, try writing about your confusion. Describe the source of your confusion. Do you not know the meaning of technical terms? Do you need help interpreting statistics? Is the relationship between ideas or data and conclusions not clear? Is the structure of the piece of writing unfamiliar? By explaining to yourself exactly what it is you do not understand, you can identify the strategies that you can try to overcome your difficulty. You may need to consult a specialized dictionary or get the help of someone who has an analytical skill that you do not yet have. Or you might just need to ask a question of your instructor or teaching assistant.

MYTH 6: THERE IS NOTHING THAT CAN BE DONE ABOUT "WRITER'S BLOCK."

Every writer periodically experiences moments when he or she struggles to get words on the page. When that happens, blinking cursors on empty pages seem to mock the writer's effort. But when you are writing a research paper in a short time, you cannot afford to give in to what is popularly known as writer's block. It can help to know that writer's block is partially a manifestation of fear and anxiety about completing an unfamiliar task. Studies of what researchers call "reluctance to write" indicate that it can be overcome by using many of the strategies that have been recommended to you in this book: committing to a schedule of work, measuring your output by word count rather than time spent, and using multiple writing techniques to relieve the pressure to produce perfect prose in early drafts.

MYTH 7: I CANNOT FIGURE OUT MY INTRODUCTION, SO I CANNOT WRITE THE PAPER.

It is true that the introduction is a particularly important part of the essay. It is the place where you introduce your reader to your topic and the questions driving research about it. It is the place where you identify the particular parts of the research conversation you find useful and problematic, and to which you want to respond. And

FIGURE 10.1 While you should not succumb to writer's block, you may be interested to hear that feeling stuck at first is common to many writers. Author Kurt Vonnegut is often thought to have said, "When I write, I feel like an armless, legless man with a crayon in his mouth."

it is the place where you define and justify your thesis. You need to have command of your research project to write an effective introduction. It is no wonder that writing an introduction at the start of your drafting process can be particularly daunting. If you can write your introduction, go ahead. But expect it to be highly provisional and subject to change. And do not struggle too much with it. If your introduction will not come, skip ahead and write a low-risk section of the body of your essay. Try describing and answering one of your supporting questions. Define and illustrate an important concept. Present the view of a writer whose ideas you want to build on or counter. In other words, start by writing small two- to three-paragraph chunks of your essay. When you have enough of these chunks, start stringing them together in an argument about your topic. Doing this kind of detailed work on the nuances of your topic enhances your understanding of what other researchers are saying, and helps you develop well-founded judgments about the uses and limits of their ideas and data. Do enough of it, and you will find yourself developing stronger opinions about the central questions of your topic, and your thesis and argument will become clearer. Having worked with the conceptual and informational materials of your topic long enough to decide what you think about it, you should be in a position to write a stronger, but still preliminary, version of your introduction.

Respond to the questions below.

   A. What did you learn about academic writing?

   B. Did you agree or disagree with anything you read? Explain.

   C. What did you learn that was new to you?

   D. Was any information or advice helpful or useful to you? Explain your response.

WEBSITES FOR FURTHER REFERENCE

http://owl.english.purdue.edu/owl/resource/567/1/
This Purdue University Online Writing Lab (OWL) web page details strategies to help alleviate any reluctance to write.

http://www.nwp.org/cs/public/print/resource/456
Having a writing ritual can ease anxiety and enable you to write more words more often. This National Writer's Project webpage discusses the "Who, What, When, and Where of Writing Rituals."

http://focuswriter.en.softonic.com/
With all their toolbars and abilities to launch you onto the Internet, modern word processors can be very distracting. It can be tempting to fiddle with fonts or look up a word in a dictionary or thesaurus. FocusWriter, a free text editor, removes all the distractions. Open FocusWriter and find nothing but your words on a gray background. FocusWriter also enables you to set time or word goals for your writing session, giving you the satisfaction of seeing yourself make progress on your writing task.

REFERENCES

Baaijen, V. M., & Galbraith, D. (2018). Discovery through writing: Relationships with writing processes and text quality. *Cognition & Instruction, 36*(3), 199–223. https://doi-org.proxy.lib. ohio-state.edu/10.1080/07370008.2018.1456431

CHAPTER 11

FINDING GOOD SOURCES

BEFORE YOU READ

Respond to the following questions **before** you read the chapter.

1. What is your group's topic? What is your subtopic?

2. What is your region? How familiar are you with this region?

3. What nonprofit organization have you chosen? Why did you choose this organization?

The answers you get depend on the questions you ask.

—Thomas Kuhn

During the second phase of your research, you will locate researchers working on the essential and supporting research questions you wrote in Phase I so that you can use their findings and ideas as evidence in an argument, as well as contribute to the conversation they are having.

If you have been working on Phase I, you already have some of the skills necessary to locate research conversations using Google Scholar and its "Cited by" and "Related articles" links. In Phase II, you will continue working with Google Scholar and also with more subject-specific databases available to you through your

LEARNING OBJECTIVES

- DISTINGUISH BETWEEN SCHOLARLY AND POPULAR SOURCES AND DECIDE WHEN AND HOW TO USE EACH TYPE.
- ANALYZE YOUR RESEARCH NEEDS USING A SIMPLE MNEMONIC: BEAM.
- WRITE AND ANALYZE A RESEARCH QUESTION THAT WILL MAKE IT MUCH EASIER FOR YOU TO FORMULATE SEARCH TERMS AND FIND THE BEST SOURCES FOR YOUR PROJECT.
- FIND, LOCATE, AND CHOOSE THE RIGHT RESEARCH DATABASES TO HELP YOU ANSWER YOUR RESEARCH QUESTIONS.
- SEARCH DATABASES EFFICIENTLY TO PRODUCE USEFUL RESULTS.

university or community library. We will work on database selection, search strategies, and search results analysis early in this chapter. Later in the chapter, we will discuss evaluating and working with the sources you find.

© Jupiterimages/BananaStock/Thinkstock

With a well-designed research project in hand, it is time to get down to the nuts and bolts of one of the most important elements of the research process: finding useful sources and working to understand them—and what you can *do* with them—once you have them. In this chapter, you will learn everything you need to know about library databases and search construction in order to find, understand, analyze, and use a coherent set of credible, relevant, reliable sources with which to work.

DISTINGUISHING BETWEEN SCHOLARLY, NEWS, TRADE, AND POPULAR SOURCES

As you start the work of the second phase of your research, it is important to understand the difference between two major types of sources: scholarly sources and news, trade, and popular sources. While each kind of source can contain useful information and interesting perspectives, they have different kinds of authority, which determine how you can use them in academic research.

FIGURE 11.1 Try to seek out reliable sources, such as those written by scholars or experts in a given subject area. Sir Isaac Newton's work in physics and mathematics has been a reliable source for many important scholars in the scientific field.

SCHOLARLY SOURCES

Scholarly sources are produced by professional researchers seeking to advance or evaluate knowledge, who submit their work for peer review. Peer review certifies the rigor of the research process and the reasonableness of the researcher's argument and interpretations. In order to be scholarly, both journal articles and books need to be peer-reviewed. Most databases of sources will provide you with the option to restrict your searches to scholarly sources. But if not, you can recognize scholarly sources by asking yourself the following questions:

1. Is the writer of the source a credentialed professional researcher writing in his or her field of expertise?
2. Has the source been successfully reviewed by peers?
3. Is the purpose of the source to advance or evaluate knowledge?
4. Does the source use an extensive citation system to document its own sources of evidence and its engagement with other researchers?
5. Is the source published in an academic journal or by an academic or university press?

If you answered "yes" to the questions on this list, then it is likely that the source is scholarly. If not, then likely you have a news, trade, or popular source.

NEWS, TRADE, AND POPULAR SOURCES

News, trade, and popular sources are produced by journalists, freelance writers, columnists, magazine writers, or practitioners of a trade. Unlike scholarly sources, they are not subject to scholarly peer review by credentialed experts, although they may be subject to editorial review or review by other industry practitioners. **News sources** tend to be published in newspapers or magazines such as the *Los Angeles Times*, *Time Magazine*, or *U.S. News & Weekly Report*. Written by journalists, their purpose is to report and analyze current events. **Trade sources** tend to be published in journals or magazines intended to be read by executives or practitioners working in a specific industry. For example, the trade magazine *R&D* is read by research and development executives, project managers, scientists, and engineers. While trade sources provide useful information to their readers, they tend to reflect the perspectives of the industry they serve, rather than seeking to advance or evaluate knowledge. **Popular sources** are written to educate or entertain, by writers who often are not experts in the field. They tend not to use specialized language or require any previous knowledge to read. Magazines such as *People* and *Reader's Digest* are examples of popular sources.

You will be able to recognize whether you are working with a news, trade, or popular source by asking yourself the following questions:

1. Is the writer a journalist, a freelancer, a columnist, a practitioner of a trade, or a magazine staffer?

2. Is the purpose of the source to report news or opinion; to earn money; to advertise a product or service; to educate a general audience; to persuade readers to hold an opinion, support a policy, or make a judgment; or to entertain?

3. Does the source make assertions without providing readers with a way to verify its sources for themselves?

4. Is the source a publication dedicated to news and opinion? A trade magazine or journal? A popular magazine?

If you answered "yes" to the questions on this list, then it is likely that the source is a news, trade, or popular source. Table 11.1 summarizes the main characteristics of each type of source.

Keep in mind that if you misidentify what type of source you have, you will undermine your credibility as a reliable researcher, you may misuse your source, and your arguments will be less persuasive.

USING SCHOLARLY AND POPULAR SOURCES

Now that you know how to distinguish between scholarly sources and popular sources, it is important to understand how to use each kind of source in your research. Whether scholarly or popular, sources need to be credible to be used in your research. Credible sources offer relevant evidence for their claims and are offered by well-informed people motivated to pursue the truth. Since scholarly sources are

TABLE 11.1 *SCHOLARLY AND POPULAR SOURCES*

	SCHOLARLY	NEWS, TRADE, OR POPULAR
WRITER	A credentialed professional researcher writing in his or her field of expertise.	A journalist, a freelancer, a columnist or pundit, a practitioner of a trade, or a magazine staffer.
PEER REVIEWED	Yes	No
PURPOSE	To advance or evaluate knowledge.	To report news or opinion; to earn money; to advertise a product or service; to educate a general audience; to persuade readers to hold an opinion, support a policy, or make a judgment; to entertain.
CITATION SYSTEM	Extensive. Used to document evidence and engagement with other sources.	Absent or minimal. Readers have no or minimal ways of verifying assertions.
PUBLICATION TYPE	Academic journal. Book published by an academic press.	News or opinion. Trade magazine. Popular magazine.

designed to be credible from the start, you are on firm ground using them in a variety of ways in your research. Be sure, however, to determine whether the researcher is writing about his or her field of special expertise. Someone who holds a PhD in history, for example, likely does not have the expertise to produce scholarly research on the environmental causes of Honeybee Colony Collapse Disorder. We will explore more sophisticated ways to use scholarly research later in this chapter. But for now, you should understand that they can provide you with the following:

- Authoritative information and data;
- Important concepts and methods to use to analyze and interpret data;
- Credible, valid, and reliable arguments to consider and to which to respond;
- Names of other scholars working in the fields and the titles of their publications; and
- Criticisms and evaluations of other researchers' published work.

In order for popular sources to be credible, you must assess whether they are biased or motivated by something other than the pursuit of the truth before you use them. You should not use sources that are written primarily to advertise a product or service or to entertain. Likewise, you should not use sources written by writers whose deeply held beliefs are affecting their ability to meet the scholarly standards of fairness, accuracy, open-mindedness, and, therefore, their ability to consider alternative explanations and points of view. If you do determine that popular sources are credible, you can use them in limited ways in your research, mostly at the beginning of your project, when you are trying to get up to speed in a new area of learning.

You can reasonably use popular sources to:

- Represent the conventional wisdom or popular view of a topic, which your research will evaluate and replace with a more scholarly view.
- Get a provisional overview of the issues involved in your topic, with the expectation that as you learn more, you will replace this overview with a better one drawn from your reading in scholarly sources.

- Get a provisional overview of any history or context that might be relevant to your topic, with the expectation that you will replace this overview with a better one drawn from your reading in scholarly sources.

- Locate the names of some expert researchers working in fields relevant to your topic.

- Learn which fields of study or academic disciplines are relevant to your topic.

- Learn some of the specialized vocabulary that researchers use to discuss your topic.

- Help you ask questions about your topic and determine what else you need to learn.

- Provide you with ideas about what kinds of statistics, data, or cases you might need to find to be qualified to write on the topic.

A final word on scholarly and popular sources: For the research project on which you are working, you will need to work extensively and critically with scholarly sources. As you learn more about your topic and start to think more carefully about the questions to which you are seeking answers, you should spend more time working with scholarly sources and less with popular sources.

BEAM: A COMMONSENSE WAY OF THINKING ABOUT SOURCES

In order to design the most useful set of sources for your project, you must have sources that will meet your needs as a writer, as well as ones that meet your information needs. Traditionally, students have been taught that they need "primary" sources and "secondary" sources. But, as Boston University writing professor Joseph Bizup (2008) argues, the traditional "primary" source/"secondary" source language is too abstract to tell new researchers very much about what to look for in sources. Bizup replaces primary and secondary source types with everyday terms that describe how writers use sources in their texts: to provide *background*, offer *exhibits*, engage in *arguments*, and describe *methods*. Bizup collects these uses in the mnemonic BEAM, shown in Figure 11.2.

BEAM is useful because it can help you assess your set of sources to see how well they meet your needs as a writer. Writers of research essays seek to persuade readers of the truth of a proposition by offering context-sensitive, evidence-supported claims, careful analysis, and plausible interpretations. You will need to assure your reader the following:

- You understand the larger context in which your work is situated.

- Your claims are well-supported by evidence.

- You have interpreted your evidence reliably using sound methods and relevant concepts.

- You have considered the views, analyses, and interpretations of other researchers working in the field.

Source: Adapted from Bizup, J. (2008). BEAM: A rhetorical vocabulary for teaching research-based writing. Rhetoric Review, 27(1), 72–86.

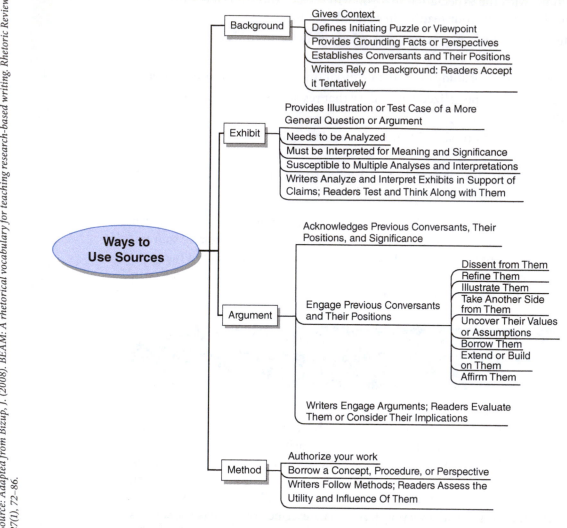

FIGURE 11.2 Joseph Bizup's BEAM. The BEAM method of employing sources.

A writer *relies* on background sources to provide context and to help delineate an initiating puzzle or question. Writers expect readers to *accept* them as authoritative.

THE "B" IN BEAM: BACKGROUND SOURCES

Because you will not be the first researcher working on your topic, you will need sources that enable you to formulate your research questions against a background of significant facts and previous ideas on the subject. According to Bizup, **background sources** provide "materials whose claims a writer accepts as fact, whether these 'facts' are taken as general information or deployed as evidence to support the writer's own assertions" (p. 75). Background sources enable you to provide context, show how other researchers and public commentators have seen the problem or issue under study, and summarize the current state of research on your topic.

They also enable you to prepare your reader to understand where your specific line of inquiry fits in the larger research conversation. By demonstrating that you have read and understood the existing literature, they also help you establish your qualifications for writing about your topic. In the following passage from her research project description, Emma is deploying her sources as background. In just two sentences, she establishes the scholarly foundation on which her research stands:

> Recent work by sociologists of technology argues that teens' use of social network sites such as Facebook has much more to do with their developmental needs as emerging adults. According to researchers such as Boyd (2008) and Livingstone (2008), teens use social network sites to seek status, experiment with identities, and separate from parental influence.

At this point in her essay, Emma expects readers simply to accept the views of these researchers as authoritative. That is why she provides their credentials ("sociologists of technology") and references to their scholarly papers.

THE "E" IN BEAM: EXHIBITS

Because readers of research essays expect your claims to be supported with evidence, you will need to illustrate your ideas and judgments using concrete data, cases, or examples. Bizup calls these materials "exhibits" (p. 75). The term "exhibit" is most often heard in the world of courtrooms. In criminal courts, prosecutors offer exhibits (evidence) to a jury in order to make a case that a particular perpetrator is guilty. In order to persuade the jury to see the exhibit as evidence of guilt, the prosecutor will need to analyze and interpret the exhibit to help the jury understand its larger significance, or to enable them to see it as suggestive of motivations.

Writers *analyze* and *interpret* exhibits to make them significant and meaningful to readers. Writers expect readers to *think* along with their analysis and interpretation, with the understanding that readers will think *critically* and *skeptically* about the writer's analysis and interpretation.

Like prosecutors, research writers offer exhibits to readers as suggestive objects to think with and about on their way to drawing a conclusion. Because exhibits do not speak for themselves, and different viewers might see them differently, writers must analyze, explain, and interpret them for their readers.

To help you better understand what an exhibit is and how researchers use them in their writing, consider an example from a piece of research Emma found on how young adults relate to their mobile phones. Researcher Gitte Stald (2008) asked 16-year-old students to write essays called "My Mobile and Me." Then she analyzed the essays as exhibits in support of her thesis that mobile phones are more than just communications tools—they are also personal development tools. Here is the passage with Stald's thesis italicized, her exhibit marked in bold, and her analysis and interpretation underlined:

> *We should consider the meaning of "mobile" as… being ready for change, ready to go in new directions.* **One of the sixteen-year-old participants… had been considering the ontological meaning of "mobile" and looked it up in her mother's dictionary… She found that it said: "Movable, agile, able to be moved or transported easily and fast; ready to march, ready for battle." She was somewhat surprised by the last two translations of "mobile," and concluded that in fact that is exactly what she is with her mobile [phone] at hand: "I am easily accessed and I am movable; I am agile and transport myself easily and quite fast; I am always ready to receive a message or a call; but best of all I am ready to march, ready for battle!…"** <u>This girl interprets mobile as more than a matter of physical movement between locations, she thinks of herself as physically on the move, supported by her mobile [phone], but at the same time she applies the military terminology to her own situation</u>

and her interest in moving forward in life and battling for herself in more than physical terms. The mobile [phone] facilitates her social mobility and readiness to communicate. Exchange between friends is an important part of the development of identity…. In this context, being movable, agile and ready to march means being ready to move as a person, too. (Stald, 2008, pp. 145–146)

Stald's exhibit is presented in enough detail so that a reader can quickly see its relevance to her thesis. Notice also that she does not assume that the girl's essay speaks for itself. Stald follows her exhibit with analysis and interpretation, calling readers' attention to the keywords and significant aspects of the exhibit.

THE "A" IN BEAM: ARGUMENT SOURCES

Writers *engage* the arguments (claims, support, and reasoning) of other writers. Readers *test*, *evaluate*, and *consider* the implications of a writer's argument.

Throughout this book, we have asked you to see research as a conversation. When you read and write research, you are in dialogue with other researchers, with whom you must agree or disagree, and on whose work you build or refute. So when you look for sources, you need to look for sources that offer you a perspective on the topic. Such sources are called **argument sources**. Argument sources provide you with "claims… [to] affirm, dispute, refine, or extend" (Bizup, 2008, p. 76). Commenting on the usefulness and limits of other researchers' claims (instead of just borrowing their data) not only helps you refine your own view as you account for the views of others who may disagree with you, it also helps you anticipate potential criticisms of your interpretation, and to develop the sophistication of your claims.

In the following passage from Emma's emerging essay, she wants to criticize and refine the ideas of John Palfrey, a writer who believes that today's technologically connected teens are categorically different from the teens of previous generations. Emma starts by conveying Palfrey's idea in a fair and balanced manner, and at the same time signals her disagreement, which is highlighted in bold:

> Even John Palfrey (2008) admits that teens today "establish and communicate their identities simultaneously in the physical and digital worlds" (p. 20). **Unfortunately in boiling things down, Palfrey misplaces the emphasis,** writing "the net effect of the digital age—paradoxically—is to decrease [a girl's] ability to control her social identity and how others perceive her" (pp. 19–20). **However, while the Internet has made the adolescent maturation process more public, it has done little to change how much control adolescents have over the essential process of how they establish and manage their identities. Teens have always had to negotiate their identities in a dynamic social environment where how they are viewed by others shapes their sense of self.**

By using transition tags, such as "unfortunately" and "however," Emma alerts her reader to see her perspective as an argument that counters Palfrey's view.

THE "M" IN BEAM: METHOD SOURCES

Some of the persuasiveness of a research essay rests on the assurance that the researcher has followed a reasonable method of finding, analyzing, and interpreting exhibits. Researchers develop reliable ways of working with data and cases to draw reasonable conclusions. According to Bizup, **method sources** "can offer a set of key terms, lay out a particular procedure, or furnish a general model or perspective"

(p. 76). They ensure that the researcher's general approach and foundational concepts are sound. When you want to know whether another researcher's claim is statistically significant, you are asking about his or her methods. When you analyze a researcher's survey to see which populations it represents, and which it does not, you are assessing his or her methods. As a researcher, you should not only adopt and follow a method for analyzing and interpreting data, but you should also reflect on the implications of your own methods, and assess the utility and influence of other researchers' methodological choices on their conclusions.

For the purposes of your research, your method is a systematic critical synthesis of previous research called a literature review.

As you use BEAM to choose a set of sources that will enable you to meet your needs as a writer, keep in mind that you may need multiple examples of all four kinds of sources, and that any single source likely provides you with more than one kind of material for your project.

"Writers follow methods" (Bizup, 2008, p. 76). Readers assess the utility and influence of methods.

FINDING SOURCES

In our experience, student researchers who struggle to find sources do so because of the following:

1. They are searching somewhat randomly for "general information" about a topic.

2. They are not aware of the important differences between searching web portals such as Google and searching the subscription databases found in most academic libraries.

© ESB Professional/Shutterstock.com

FIGURE 11.3 Sources can be found in various ways, such as searching for keywords online or using databases provided by an academic library.

In this section, you will learn how to overcome these problems and find the sources you need.

STARTING RESEARCH IN A NEW FIELD

Starting the research on a topic in an entirely new field presents researchers with a significant problem—namely, they do not know enough about the topic or field to know what they need to learn. In other words, they do not yet know the questions that other researchers have asked. They do not know the specialized vocabulary that has evolved. They do not yet know what aspect of the topic on which they want to work. It is very likely that as an undergraduate, you are facing the same problem with your current project. It seems natural that the first thing that you should do is to fire up your browser, log in to a database, and search away to find something, anything, to get your feet wet. But that is a counterproductive way to start acquiring the basic knowledge that you will need in order to find a useful set of sources and frame a set of questions.

Instead, you need to look for a *short overview of the topic* that will orient you to some of the driving concerns of the field. If you are conducting research for a college course, it is likely that some of your course materials can provide you with at least some of what you need. Course textbooks are especially good resources for surveying the breadth of a subject and acquiring the specialized language of the field. Mining them for concepts and exhibits can provide you both with search terms you can use right away and clues for developing others. Also consult lecture notes, handouts and slides, and assigned or recommended readings. If your readings are scholarly, review the sources listed on their references pages to locate the names of researchers working in your field and key concepts. Once you are searching the databases, try a few searches that include the term "review of the literature" with your topic to see if you can find an article that summarizes and evaluates recent research in the field.

Besides looking at course materials, you can also consult specialized encyclopedias, subject-specific dictionaries, and topic bibliographies. The reference sections of most academic libraries stock a wide range of these helpful orienting texts. Many libraries also provide librarian-prepared **subject guides** to often-used fields to help you identify the most useful orienting texts, bibliographic tools, and databases. Fields with subject guides include anthropology, company/industry research, criminal justice and law enforcement, early childhood education, healthcare administration, and literature. You can find these and more subject guides in tutorials on your university or local library websites. Often, you can also call, email, or chat online with a librarian for help deciding which ones might be of most use to you.

ASSESSING YOUR RESEARCH NEEDS

Once you have a basic overview of your topic, the first step in finding a coherent set of useful sources is to *assess your research needs*. With Bizup's BEAM mnemonic, you know that you will need (a) background sources, (b) exhibit sources, (c) argument sources, and (d) method sources. That is useful as far as it goes, but it does not go far enough to help you choose the right databases for your specific project or to search them effectively. If you have gathered an overview of your topic using course materials, subject-specific encyclopedias and dictionaries, and topic-specific bibliographies, you have already performed some of the preliminary steps necessary to assess your research needs. In particular, the initial set of questions you wrote will be a primary resource for your first targeted foray into the literature. If you are still in the design phase of your project, do not worry. This section will help you get your project started well.

DEVELOPING A SET OF RESEARCH QUESTIONS

The key to finding useful sources for your project is to approach a database session with good questions in hand. Research projects tend to have two different types of questions: essential questions that prompt you to investigate perplexing phenomena or solve complex problems, and supporting questions that guide you to find the material you need to answer your essential questions. You also learned that good questions should have a specific scope, which means they should clearly specify which populations, locations, time periods, subtopics, and theories are relevant to your question. If you have not written any essential or supporting research questions, you will need to do so before approaching the database.

CONSTRUCTING EFFECTIVE SEARCH QUERIES

Once you have good research questions, you must learn how to use them to query the database. If you have a lot of experience searching the Internet, you likely use **natural language**—language that looks and sounds like the language we use in everyday situations—to search for what you want to find. The following search queries are written in natural language:

- "What is the best Chinese restaurant in St. Paul?"
- "How can I catch more fish?"
- "What are some ways to help my child who does not like to read?"

On the Internet, natural language searches tend to work well enough to allow you to find what you want without too much effort. But if you query a research database using natural language, you will likely find that you get few or no results. What is more, the few results you get may be irrelevant because research databases are organized using the same categories and logic that organize the content of research libraries. As a result, databases "speak" a language that allows you to search and find more than just the specific title for which you were looking. It allows you to find clusters of related content as well. So in order to search academic library catalogs and academic databases well, you have to learn how to construct searches that the system can process.

Search construction involves analyzing your research question to identify potential search terms, refining the question by specifying the relationship between key terms, and finding synonyms for keywords that may be too imprecise to generate sources that are relevant to your project. To learn how to construct effective search queries, let us discuss each part of this process by analyzing the last research question on our list: "What are some ways to help my child who does not like to read?"

Step 1: Identify keywords or concepts in the research question.

Likely two keywords leap out at you: *child, read*. So you write them down on a research log form like the one shown in the *Sample Research Log*. While you could go directly to a multipurpose database and enter those two terms in a keyword search, you would likely get thousands of results. Only a few of them would be closely relevant to your question because there are many different possible relationships between your two keywords, and you have not yet specified the relationship between them. Without specifying the relationship between them, the database cannot tell if you are an elementary school teacher wanting sources on how to teach very young children to learn to read for the first time, a memoirist writing about the value of her time spent reading as a child, or a concerned parent wanting information on how to motivate your adolescent boy to enjoy reading more.

Step 2: Specify the relationship between keywords.

The first thing to do is to go back to the original question and see whether you can find additional keywords that better specify the relationship between the *child* and *read*. Here is the question again: "What are some ways to help my *child* who doesn't like to *read*?" A second look at the question reveals two additional key phrases that indicate a very specific relationship between the *child* and *read*: We have a *child* who *does not like* to *read*, and a parent who *wants ways to help* him or her. Notice how this reformulation of the question brings in a new keyword: *parent*. By finding the additional phrases that specify the relationship between our keywords, we have arrived at a better understanding of what it is we are looking for. Developing and refining your question is not only a key strategy for generating more productive search combinations, it also helps you better understand your research needs. If you are lucky, it can help you develop some other closely related research questions.

Step 3: Refine imprecise keywords by finding synonyms.

Adding new keywords and phrases to the search seems like it should help the database return sources that more specifically address your concerns, and to a degree it will. But you will not find everything written on the topic, and you may find nothing at all. This is because two of the primary keywords (*child* and *parent*) have multiple synonyms. Furthermore, two of the key phrases (*ways to help* and *does not like*) express relationships in everyday language that expert researchers would find too imprecise to use in their articles. Since researchers try to use language carefully and precisely to represent accurately the problems, data, and solutions on which they are working, you will need to produce a list of more precise synonyms that researchers might use for each of your keywords or phrases. Remember, different writers might choose different terms to convey the same idea. So you will need to develop and test several different combinations of search terms to locate all of the most relevant sources for your query.

Let us continue with our example by refining our imprecise terms—*ways to help* and *does not like*. You can use a dictionary or thesaurus to help find synonyms, but you may get better, more efficient results by using the materials you found earlier during your grounding research in specialized dictionaries and encyclopedias to guide your synonym development. Here is what a standard thesaurus suggests as potential synonyms for *ways: habits, conduct, customs, behavior, traditions*. None of these terms gets at what you want to find out. In everyday language, you are looking for *advice* or *techniques* to motivate your child. In your grounding research, researchers call teaching techniques *methods* or *pedagogies*. Here is the cluster of terms we have developed for *ways to help: advice, techniques, methods, pedagogies*. By stepping through a similar synonym development process, we can replace *does not like with reluctant, resistant, unenthusiastic, averse, unwilling.*

Child might seem like a specific enough term, but there are several others that researchers might use. *Youth, adolescent, teen, tween, juvenile,* and *kids* are just some of the possibilities. Considering that more boys than girls seem to become reluctant readers, your list should probably include gendered terms for the *child* as well: *boy, son, young man, male.*

SAMPLE RESEARCH LOG
Research Log
What are your research questions?

"What are some ways to help my child who doesn't like to read?"

What are the keywords and concepts in your questions?

child, read, ways to help, doesn't like, (parent)

What are some synonyms and related words for the keywords and concepts in your questions?

child: *youth, adolescent, teen, tween, juvenile, kids*
ways to help: *advice, techniques, methods, pedagogies*
doesn't like: *reluctant, resistant, unenthusiastic, averse, unwilling*

After all this question development, we can rewrite our original question in a much more specific way:

"What methods, techniques, or pedagogies can parents use to motivate teenage male reluctant readers?"

With such a specific question, you will find a reasonably small number of sources to review, and the majority of sources you locate should be relevant.

CHOOSING DATABASES

Once you have identified keywords and phrases and their variants, you are ready to approach a research database to do some searching. Before you can search, you need to decide which databases to choose to search (see Figure 11.4 for factors that can help you choose an appropriate database). Many libraries have made it simpler for you to know which ones to choose by listing databases by subject and describing contents. They have also provided subject guides to reliable resources for several disciplines, including anthropology, company and industry research, criminal justice and law enforcement, early childhood education, healthcare administration, and literature. These subject guides contain useful database recommendations as well as the names of useful subject-specific resources, including reference books, dictionaries, encyclopedias, and more.

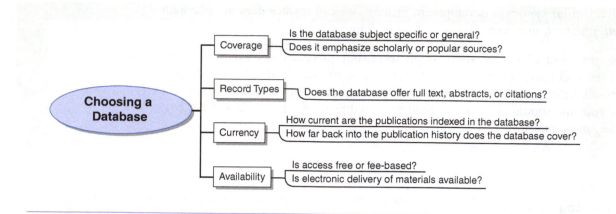

FIGURE 11.4 Choosing a database.

DATABASE CATEGORIES

For the purposes of your research project, you need to be able to distinguish between two major categories of the database. The first, known as a *general-purpose database* (or **multidisciplinary database**), is often a good place to start your research because it indexes many different fields or disciplines. But while this type of database offers breadth, it can sacrifice depth. In order to bring you a wide sample of research being done in so many fields, general-purpose databases tend to focus on the major journals in the field. EBSCOhost's Academic Search Premier and ProQuest are good examples of general-purpose databases widely used by college students.

On the other hand, **subject-specific databases** (also known as *field-specific databases*) aim to represent the full range of a particular field or a subject. If you do not find what you need in a general database, or if you suspect there is more to the topic than is covered in a general database, you should consult a subject-specific database such as Westlaw (law and business), Sage Journals Online (social sciences), PyschArticles (psychology), ERIC (education), PubMED (medicine and healthcare), or the MLA International Bibliography (literature). It is important to understand that no one database can serve all your research needs. You will need to try your searches in multiple databases to discover the best sources for your project. Be sure to record on your research log which databases provide you with the best results for each of your searches.

FURTHER CONSIDERATIONS WHEN CHOOSING A DATABASE

As you continue to consider which databases to choose for your research, the following questions could influence your choice:

1. *Does the database provide full-text access to sources or only abstracts or citations?* Full text is obviously best, but finding an abstract or citation can be useful. If you find a citation or abstract of a useful article, be sure to record the full citation information so you can search for the full text in another database.

2. *How current are the publications indexed in the database? How many years into the past does the database index?* The deeper and more recent the coverage the better.

3. *Is access to the contents of the database free or fee-based?* Remember, many fee-based databases that you find online are free to you when accessed through your university or local library.

4. *Does the database provide for electronic delivery of sources and citations?* If not, contact a librarian to learn how to request that an electronic copy of a source be sent to you.

SEARCHING DATABASES

Unlike search engines such as Google, Bing, or Yahoo!, which use keyword searches by default, academic databases work best when you specify the kind of search you want to conduct. There are three major kinds of database searches you can conduct: author/title searches, keyword searches, and subject searches. Which search you choose depends on (a) whether you are searching for unknown sources on a topic or a specific article or book written by a specific author, (b) what you know about what you're trying to find, (c) how specifically or broadly your topic is defined, and (d) how field- or discipline-specific your topic or research needs are. Table 11.2 is provided as a reference to help you determine what type of search you should conduct. Each search type is discussed in more detail in the following sections.

TABLE 11.2 *DATABASE SEARCH TYPES*

USE AUTHOR/TITLE SEARCH WHEN:
You know the name of the author you want to find.
You want to find additional articles by a known writer.
You know the title of an article or book you want to find.
You know the title of a journal, periodical, or book series that frequently contains sources relevant to your topic.

USE KEYWORD SEARCH WHEN:
You have a specific research question to answer.
Your topic has keywords that are distinctive, new, or field-specific.
Your topic can only be specified with multiple keywords (*methods* AND *motivate* AND *adolescent* AND *reluctant readers*).
You have multiple synonyms that you want to search simultaneously (*children* OR *kids* OR *teens* OR *adolescents*).
More than one field or discipline is relevant to your topic (*adolescent psychology* AND *reading instruction*).

USE SUBJECT SEARCH WHEN:
Your topic is broad, you are conducting grounding research, and you don't yet have specific research questions to answer.
You are looking for sources about a person rather than by a person.
A keyword in your topic has different meanings in different fields or disciplines, and you want to specify which fields or disciplines are relevant.

PERFORMING AUTHOR/TITLE SEARCHES

Author/title searches are used to acquire specific sources when you already know the author's name and title, or when you want to survey the work of a particular researcher in hopes of finding other relevant sources he or she has authored. Once you have one or two pieces in hand, consult their references pages for the names of other researchers working on your topic and the titles of their work. Also, since academic journals tend to specialize, take note of the titles of journals that show up repeatedly in your source list and search by title for those journals to find other relevant articles and researchers active in your field. In her research, Emma found multiple references to the *Journal of Computer-Mediated Communication* and *New Media & Society* in her results lists. When she searched for those journals by title and browsed their tables of contents, she found the names of several researchers working in her field and candidate sources for inclusion in her project.

PERFORMING KEYWORD SEARCHES

Although keyword searches can quickly supply you with lots of candidate sources to assess, they often return irrelevant results if not carefully constructed using a search term development process like the one we went through earlier in this chapter. So, in order to generate more relevant results, keyword searches are best used when you have a specific research question to answer or you are seeking sources on a topic that can be described with distinctive or field-specific keywords. They are particularly helpful when your research cuts across traditional disciplinary or field lines. You can use keyword sources for grounding research, but as noted above, you must monitor your search results for new keywords and new variants of keywords as you go. Otherwise, your search will return only the subset of articles that use everyday language to discuss the topic. In order for your source set to help you go beyond the obvious, you will have to conduct additional keyword searches using the more precise terms you collect as you browse through your results list.

Although truncation symbols vary by provider, typical truncation symbols include *, !, ?, #, and $.

Keyword searches return the most relevant results when you combine multiple keywords with the search term connector AND, which narrows your search, returning records that include *all* of your search terms. If you find that you need to broaden your search, use the search term connector OR to return records that include *any* of your search terms. While the specific look of a search interface will vary by provider, most search interfaces provide you with the opportunity to enter multiple keywords and to specify the relationship between them. You might have to find and click on the "Advanced Search" link to do so, but the increase in quality of results makes it well worth the effort.

The search shown in Figure 11.5 returns all the records that include the term *reading problems* AND either *adolescent* OR *teen*. Notice the asterisk in our search? It is a **truncation symbol**, which can be thought of as a "wild card" character that tells the database to return all results that include the characters up to the truncation symbol, no matter what other characters follow the last one.

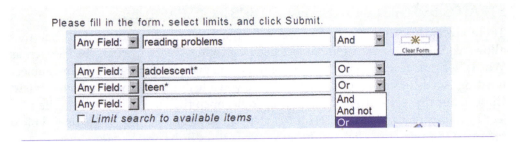

FIGURE 11.5 Using search term connectors.

Because we searched for *adolescent** or *teen**, the database returns records that include minor variations of my terms: *adolescent* and *adolescents, teen, teens, teenagers, teenaged*. Notice too that we might have selected "AND NOT" to omit results—say, on preschoolers—that are not relevant to our topic. Using these strategies helps ensure that our keyword search returns a reasonably small set of relevant results.

PERFORMING SUBJECT SEARCHES

Subject searches are useful when your topic is broad and has many dimensions. You can use subject searches both to survey the range of subtopics in a field and to narrow down your results to find only the results containing the subtopics you want. Unlike keyword searches, which return results based solely on the presence or absence of the word in any field in the record, subject searches search for your term only in the **subject headings** field of the record. Since subject headings are assigned by the Library of Congress, you need to formulate your search very precisely to match the assigned heading, or your search will return no results. For example, for our topic on how parents can motivate their adolescents to read, we could try a subject search for *reading* and *adolescent* (see Figure 11.6).

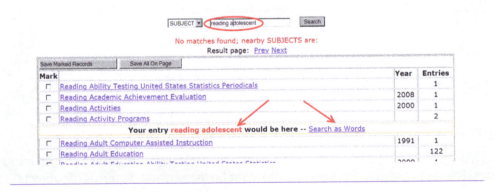

FIGURE 11.6 A failed subject search.

Our search returned no results because the Library of Congress has not assigned a heading that combines *reading* and *adolescent* in sequence. When you get a result like this, do not conclude that there are no sources on your topic. There are many resources available, but we cannot find them using a subject search without knowing some of the specific preassigned subject headings. It might seem at first glance that it would be much easier to use keyword searching. But once you find the Library of Congress subject headings specific to your topic, you will locate a treasure trove of sources, and most of them will be relevant.

STRATEGIES FOR HANDLING FAILED SUBJECT SEARCHES

There are two strategies you can use to turn a failed subject search into one that allows you to locate the right subject headings. One way is to click the "Search as Words" option (see Figure 11.7) to conduct a keyword search of only the subject headings fields of the records. That will give you a list of books or articles to review. Choose one that seems to be close to your topic, open the record, and look at the subject headings fields (see Figure 11.8 to locate the subject headings fields on a typical record). Often you can click on the subject headings links and be taken directly to a list of sources.

Another way to deal with a failed subject search is to start with a broader simpler description of the topic: in this case, *reading*. Doing a subject search on *reading* will result in a list of subject headings similar to the one shown in Figure 11.7.

FIGURE 11.7 Results of a broad subject search. Broad searches will result in many more subject headings, which must then be narrowed down to your specific topic.

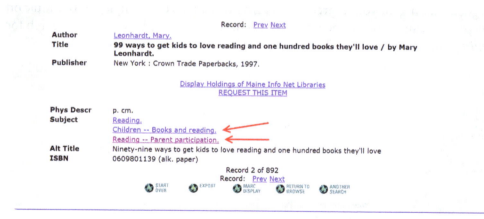

FIGURE 11.8 Subject headings on a typical record. It is important to keep in mind the different configurations that a title might be listed under in terms of subjects.

The number circled in blue tells us that there are 1,336 subject headings related to the word *reading* in this database. Of course not all of them have anything to do with the act of deciphering words on the page. Some have to do with places named "Reading" in England, Pennsylvania, Canada, and Australia. You could scroll through this list of 1,336 subject headings to find ones that are relevant to you. But that would take a long time, and you still would not be guaranteed of finding relevant subject headings that do not begin with the word *reading*. A faster and more reliable approach would be to click on the "Reading" subject heading and quickly browse some of the titles of the 892 sources on reading to find one that looks like it might be relevant. For this search, the very first page of results includes a book titled *99 Ways to Get Kids to Love Reading and One Hundred Books They'll Love*. When you pull up its record, you find two relevant subject headings you can select, including one, *Reading—Parent participation*, that seems spot on.

Clicking through both of the more specific subject headings leads you indirectly to hundreds of sources, many of which will lead you to other relevant subject headings. When you click through *Reading—Parent Participation*, you are directed to a list of related subject headings that provide you with access to relevant sources, as shown in Figure 11.9.

☑	**Reading Parent Participation**		142
☐	Reading Parent Participation Alaska	1999	1
☑	Reading Parent Participation Bibliography	1992	1
☐	Reading Parent Participation Case Studies	1994	1
☐	Reading Parent Participation Congresses	1994	1
☐	Reading Parent Participation Electronic Book		5
☐	Reading Parent Participation English Speaking Countries	c1999	1
☑	Reading Parent Participation Fiction		2
☐	Reading Parent Participation Great Britain	1998	1
☐	Reading Parent Participation Great Britain Electronic Book	c1996	1
☑	Reading Parent Participation Handbooks Manuals Etc		6
☐	Reading Parent Participation Juvenile Fiction	2006	1
☑	Reading Parent Participation United States		39
☑	Reading Parent Participation United States Case Studies		5
☐	Reading Parent Participation United States Electronic Book		6
☐	Reading Parent Participation United States Handbooks Manuals Etc		2
☐	Reading Parent Participation United States Handbooks Manuals Etc Electronic Book	2012	1
☐	Reading Parent Participation United States Statistics		4
☑	Reading Parental Participation		3

FIGURE 11.9 Search results: Reading—Parent Participation. Databases are organized to help maximize searches. In this instance, the specificity of subject headings for the search term "Reading—Parent Participation" will allow the researcher to quickly exclude irrelevant groupings and instead focus on those pertinent to his or her topic.

Notice how the subject headings list allows you to specify the kinds of sources you want to find (bibliographies, handbooks, case studies), geographic locations, reading genres, and more. You will want to select several of these related subject headings to produce a list of results to review. Clicking through the *Children—Reading* subject heading will produce another set of sources with additional subject headings to search. Since subject headings are uniform across databases, useful subject headings you discover in one database are likely to be useful in other databases. So be sure to record which of the subject headings you find are the most useful. And as always, be on the lookout for new search terms, new variants, and the jargon that expert researchers use to describe their topics and use those terms in future searches.

SEARCH NARROWING AND SEARCH BROADENING

One last note on searching: Use search-narrowing strategies when your searches return too many results to review or the results are not as relevant as you'd like them to be. Use search-broadening strategies when your search returns too few results or they are too specialized for your purposes. These strategies are encapsulated in Table 11.3.

TABLE 11.3 *SEARCH-NARROWING AND SEARCH-BROADENING STRATEGIES*

NARROWING STRATEGIES	BROADENING STRATEGIES
Using multiple search terms connected by "AND" or "AND NOT."	Searching for multiple terms connected by "OR."
Using more specific or specialized terms.	Using more common, less specific, or broader terms.
Using available limiters to set scope.	Using truncation to search for word variants.

We have already seen search-narrowing strategies at work earlier in this chapter when we looked for synonyms for our search term "child." We saw that more specific and specialized terms such as *adolescent, teen,* or *juvenile* return fewer but more relevant results. We also saw that combining multiple terms in a search (such as "parent" AND "reluctant reader" AND "techniques") significantly reduced the number of irrelevant sources we needed to sift through.

When searches return too few results, you need to expand your searches. Rewrite your search using fewer search terms, or by using "OR" as a connector instead of "AND," as in a search for "juvenile" OR "teen" OR "adolescent" AND "readers"). You can also try replacing technical or overly specific terms with more common or more general terms: "reading comprehension" might replace "semantic decoding," for example. Finally, try using truncation symbols to search for variations of a term: "read*" to search for "reading" and "readers."

SUMMARY

- As you review this chapter, pay particular attention to the concepts, strategies, and tools that enable you to see your sources as something more than containers of information. Being able to determine whether your source is "scholarly" or "popular" is a key determinant of the uses to which it may or may not be put. The BEAM mnemonic can help you see your sources as a writer does—as resources: to help you establish the background of your topic; to provide you with exhibits to analyze and interpret; to enable you to borrow, extend, or counter the arguments of other researchers; and to certify the rigor of your research by using reliable methods.

- It is vital to remember that success in searching for sources depends on what questions you ask and how well you ask them. If you are conducting research in a new field, be sure to use the strategies detailed in this chapter to learn the kinds of questions researchers working in the field ask and the specialized language they use. Once you have researchable questions, remember to analyze your questions to determine their keywords and the relationships among them. Do not forget to search for variants or synonyms of key concepts. Use your research log to keep track of successful searches so that you can use them in other databases.

- You should also experiment with Google Scholar and the databases available to you through your university or local library to become more familiar with database searching. Be sure to analyze your results list to discover the names of researchers working in your area, new terms or concepts, and subject headings that are relevant to your topic.

KEY TERMS

Argument source—a source that provides researchers with claims to affirm, dispute, refine, or extend.

Background source—a source that provides researchers with established facts and accepted ideas, which they use to establish a significant context for their own research.

BEAM—Joseph Bizup's memory aid to help researchers understand four common sense ways to use sources in research: background, exhibit, argument, or method.

Exhibit—a source that provides researchers with examples or cases to analyze and interpret in support or refutation of a claim.

Method—a source that provides researchers with a reliable process for gathering, analyzing, and interpreting exhibits.

Multidisciplinary database—also known as a "general-purpose database"; a database that indexes many different fields or disciplines.

Natural language—language used by human beings in the ordinary course of events, in contrast to computer, database, or machine languages and the systematic language of formal logic.

News source—a source written by journalists reporting on current issues or events.

Popular source—a source written primarily for entertainment or to earn money.

Scholarly source—a peer-reviewed source produced by credentialed experts seeking the truth and writing in their field of expertise.

Search construction—the analytical process by which researchers transform their questions into queries of a library database to find sources.

Subject guide—a research aid produced by librarians to provide researchers who are new to a field with guidance in locating appropriate databases, journals, and sources.

Subject heading—fields in a library database record that specify the topics and subtopics addressed in a text.

Subject-specific database—also known as a "field-specific database"; a database that aims to represent the full range of a particular field or a subject.

Trade source—a source written by a representative of a profession or an industry for the purpose of informing or advising.

Truncation symbol—a "wild card" character that tells a search database to return all results that include the characters up to the truncation symbol, no matter what other characters follow the last one.

Respond to the following questions **without** reviewing the text or your notes. These questions are provided to help you practice retrieving information and reflect on your reading.

A. What did you learn about finding good sources?

B. Did you agree or disagree with anything you read? Explain.

C. What did you learn that was new to you?

D. Was any information or advice helpful or useful to you? Explain your response.

Complete the Research Log below with your group's topic or subtopic in mind.

1. What are your research questions?

2. What are the keywords and concepts in your questions?

3. What are some synonyms and related words for the keywords and concepts in your questions?

WEBSITES FOR FURTHER REFERENCE

http://prezi.com/svjv-nfgka95/intro-to-library-databases/
This "Intro to Library Databases" Prezi by Nancy Bellafante explains the difference between the content available via Google and library databases, as well as how to analyze a research question and search a database.

http://www.schooltube.com/video/f42863cbb7cb4db6a3f4/Talking%20to%20Databases
This short video on "Talking to a Database" produced at Kent State University shows how to turn a research topic into a format that library databases will understand.

REFERENCES

Boyd, D. (2008). Can social network sites enable political action? *International Journal of Media & Cultural Politics, 4*(2), 241–244. https://doi-org.proxy.lib.ohio-state.edu/10.1386/macp.4.2.241_3

Livingstone, S. (2008). Taking risky opportunities in youthful content creation: teenagers' use of social networking sites for intimacy, privacy and self-expression. *New Media & Society, 10*(3), 393–411. https://doi-org.proxy.lib.ohio-state.edu/10.1177/1461444808089415

Palfrey, J. (2008). Enhancing child safety and online technologies. Internet Safety Technical Task Force.

CHAPTER 12

EVALUATING AND WORKING WITH SOURCES

BEFORE YOU READ

Respond to the following questions **before** you read the chapter.

1. What is your group's topic or your subtopic?

2. Briefly describe what you already know about your group's topic and/or your subtopic.

3. Have you begun searching for sources? Has the process been challenging or relatively easy? Why?

Research is to see what everybody else has seen, and to think what nobody else has thought.

—Albert Szent-Gyorgi

LEARNING OBJECTIVES

- EVALUATE AND CHOOSE SOURCES TO PRINT, READ, ANALYZE, AND INTERPRET.
- READ CRITICALLY, TAKE EFFECTIVE NOTES, AND UNDERSTAND HOW YOUR SOURCES RELATE TO ONE ANOTHER.
- EMPLOY SOURCES TO ANSWER YOUR RESEARCH QUESTIONS.
- UNDERSTAND THE COMPONENTS OF A THESIS PARAGRAPH.
- USE SOURCES RESPONSIBLY IN ORDER TO AVOID PLAGIARISM.

Now that you know how to search library catalogs and databases, you should have a few problems finding potential sources for use in your research project. In fact, it is likely that your searches have turned up far too many sources for you to read in the time allotted for your project. The next step in the research process, then, is to understand how to narrow down your sources. In this chapter, you will learn how to evaluate the sources you find, understand the criteria you will use to select sources from among the many you find, become familiar with effective strategies to read, analyze, and interpret your sources, and learn how to use sources both effectively and responsibly in writing your research essay.

EVALUATING AND CHOOSING SOURCES

As you begin to evaluate sources, keep in mind that you are looking for pieces of writing that will give you more than just facts or information. You are looking for sources that offer you ideas and perspectives that encourage you to think about your topic in a more nuanced manner. Sources that exclude other researchers' analysis and interpretation will make it very difficult for you to respond to the issues and questions driving research in your field. Remember, too, that your sources must provide you with each of the four elements of BEAM—background, exhibits, arguments, and methods.

EVALUATING SOURCES ACCORDING TO BASIC CRITERIA

Most systems for evaluating sources stress certain criteria. A source can be considered for inclusion in your source set when it is relevant, credible, timely, representative, motivated by the pursuit of truth, and bias-free. These criteria are useful because they establish a minimum threshold that sources must cross to be considered for inclusion in your source set. The *Basic Source Evaluation Tool* provides you with questions to guide your evaluation of sources.

Is This Source Relevant?

- To what degree does the subject of this source match my research needs as established in my Essential and Supporting Questions?
- Do keywords, concepts, and specialized jargon used in the source overlap with those used by other expert researchers in the field? Do they serve any of my research needs?
- Do the analytical methods used in the source overlap with those used by other expert researchers in the field? Do they serve any of my research needs?

Is This Source Credible?

- Is the writer certified expert writing in his or her field of expertise?
- Is the source peer-reviewed?
- Does the source offer reasons or evidence to support its claims?
- Does the source consider all available and relevant information as it makes its case?
- Are the data and arguments borrowed from other writers fairly and accurately rendered?

Is This Source Timely?

- Does the source represent a view or a position that is currently in the field, one that takes the latest available ideas and information into account?
- Does the source represents a significant earlier but still relevant view in the field?
- Does the source fill a gap in the history of the development of a line of thought you are tracking?

Is This Source Representative?

- Does the source illustrate a trend in thought in the field? Or is it an outlier or innovator?
- Are the data and examples and lines of thought applicable in a larger context?

Is This Source Motivated by Pursuit of Truth and Bias-Free?

- Is this source designed to sell a product or service?
- Is this source designed primarily to change your opinion?
- Does the source meet scholarly standards of fairness, accuracy, and open-mindedness?
- Does the source interpret data in light of a passionately held position, such that it distorts the truth or its reasonableness and open-mindedness may be questioned?

CHOOSING SOURCES THAT MEET YOUR RESEARCH NEEDS

Once you have determined whether your sources are fundamentally sound, it is important to evaluate your sources further in order to make sure that the time you spend reading them will be well spent. You will also need to ensure the coherence of your source set and make certain that your source set will meet your needs as a *writer* of a research paper. The advanced source evaluation tool (see the *Advanced Source Evaluation Tool*) can help you evaluate your sources for these purposes.

During this second level of source evaluation, you are trying to determine whether your sources are useful for more than the information they contain. Remember, when you sit down to write your research essay, you will need to establish the *background* or context of your topic, work with *exhibits* or illustrative material to give your reader samples to think with, bring forward or *counter-arguments* from other writers as well as make arguments of your own, and evaluate the *methods* that you and your sources have used to collect, analyze, and interpret data.

To do so, you will need to evaluate your sources both individually and as a set for how well they enable you to convey and discuss some coherent aspect of the conversation researchers are having on your topic. You will want your sources to serve multiple purposes and, at the same time, provide you with rich and sophisticated ways of thinking about your subject. That means you should prefer longer sources that treat their subjects with complexity rather than shorter ones that present answers as matters of fact. Sources that make it into your set should use the specialized language of expert researchers in the field who interact frequently with the ideas, arguments, and evidence of other researchers. If at all possible, look for a series of sources in which two or more researchers explicitly respond to one another's writing over a period of a few years. Doing so will allow you to observe the development of ideas and viewpoints over time and will also provide you with an example of how to respond to another writer's views.

Be sure that the sources you select do more than establishing a fact. You want sources to make an argument that attempts to account for multiple aspects of your topic, to consider alternative explanations, and to think through the implications of the exhibits they have presented. Since you will have to develop a perspective on your research and respond to the arguments of other writers, you should look for sources that take a different position than the one you hold and ones that inspire you to write back in response. If you can, find at least one strong source that approaches your topic in such an innovative way that it changes the conversation. Such a source might introduce new questions or complicating exhibits, develop a new explanatory concept, or dissent entirely from the usual ways of looking at your subject. Finally, try to find sources where the writer treats readers as fellow researchers, rather than as people who are being brought up to speed on a subject and need to be lectured to. You can tell that writers are treating readers as fellow researchers when they do the following:

- Invite readers to think along with them, by arguing for the significance and value of their ideas, rather than stating their views as foregone conclusions.
- Display the evidence and train of thought from which they draw conclusions.
- Present and consider sources whose evidence, arguments, and perspectives challenge and complicate their own.
- Admit that their own arguments and perspectives, however useful, are limited and subject to criticism and review.

WORKING WITH SOURCES— HOW TO REVIEW THE LITERATURE

As we move from *finding* sources to *working* with sources, it is important to understand what you are doing when you "review the literature" as well as get a better grasp on the structure and dynamics of research conversations. The most important thing to bear in mind when you are reviewing the literature is to remember that research articles and books are artifacts of living minds actively involved in a

ADVANCED SOURCE EVALUATION TOOL

1. **Are your sources long enough to treat subjects with complexity and sophistication?**
   Sources that present matter-of-fact answers in brief are likely oversimplifying the matter.

2. **Are your sources treating readers as partners-in-inquiry, or as mere decoders of information?**
   You're looking for sources that treat readers as partners-in-inquiry.

3. **Do your sources use specialized vocabulary, indicating that they are concept-rich? Or do they tend to present information in "everyday language"?**
   You should be looking for sources that use specialized language.

4. **Do your sources interact with the ideas of other writers and thinkers, defining their projects, forwarding and countering their ideas, and assessing the uses and limits of the sources they cite? Or do they present themselves as having all the answers, writing apart from other thinkers working on a similar topic?**
   You're looking for sources that take other writers' ideas into account.

5. **Do your sources seek merely to establish a fact or a casual/correlative relationship in the data? Or are they pursuing a line of inquiry to think through the implications or meaning of their observations?**
   You're looking for sources that pursue a line of inquiry.

6. **Does your source set accurately and fairly represent an existing conversation on your area of research, including both scholarly sources and sources of informed public commentary?**

7. **Does your source set include a "conversation changer," a source that rethinks something that one of your other sources takes for granted?**

8. **Can you imagine making your own use of each article in your source set? Can you see yourself having something to "say back" to the text?**

9. **Can you imagine putting your sources in conversation with each other? Do they "speak" to one another in ways that move the existing conversation forward? Can you identify or infer the issues that likely started the conversation? Is everyone in the conversation saying the same thing? Is anyone "listening" and "responding" to anyone else, or following a thread in the conversation? Or are your sources all speaking about different aspects of the problem without addressing themselves to the conversation going on around them?**

conversation with others. When you consult a research database to find information on a topic, you are actually seeking out **partners-in-inquiry**—people who are asking questions similar to your own and thinking about issues that concern you. You are looking both for more material (facts and concepts) to think with and for someone to think along with, someone who looks at things from a different perspective and who sees different aspects of the phenomenon or problem.

So when you start your review of the literature, remember to keep track of the names, disciplines, and areas of expertise of the researchers who wrote the articles you are reading. Over time, if you have located an active and coherent conversation, as Emma did, you should start recognizing names, be able to link them to positions and lines of thought, identify whose ideas and positions they use and whose they counter, and see the structure of the conversation emerge. In fact, creating this understanding of the structure and dynamics of the conversation is a significant part of the work you need to do in this phase of your research. If you do not understand how researchers are using the ideas, data, and analyses to make arguments, you risk cherry-picking data to support your own views and misunderstanding the positions of researchers. If you do not recognize how arguments are positioned with respect to one another, you also risk overestimating the certainty and consensus of the field, and underestimating the degree of reasoned controversy.

CRITICAL READING AND NOTE-TAKING STRATEGIES

During her earlier research, our student researcher, Emma, built a strong set of articles—ones she believes accurately represent the substance of the research conversations to which she has been listening. Now is the time to start to read the articles systematically so that she can construct a structural model of the relationships among the ideas she finds in the articles she is reading. Before we continue with Emma's research project, let us take some time to understand the differences between reading for information and reading to write about a topic. Along the way, we will collect some concrete strategies for reading more critically.

To get the most out of your time spent reading, you should set ambitious reading goals. Table 12.1 lays out some of the key differences between basic and advanced reading goals.

TABLE 12.1 BASIC AND ADVANCED READING GOALS

BASIC READING GOALS	ADVANCED READING GOALS
Read to store and retrieve information	Read to be conversant—to be able to speak about the details (and the relationships among them) and general effect of a text without referring to it
Read passively	Read actively—take notes, ask questions, make connections, paraphrase key points
Read to absorb	Read to explore, inquire, consider, question, criticize, analyze
Read to understand	Read to do something to/with the text—evaluate, synthesize, create, write
Read for the gist	Read to understand nuances and to assess views, to locate gaps in the conversation, to find places to comment and respond
Read each text in isolation	Read texts as part of an intertextual dialogue or field
Read impressionistically	Read systematically
Read to agree or disagree	Read to understand a position that is different from one's own

ANALYZING AND INTERPRETING

In order to read to fulfill these more advanced goals, you may need to alter your reading habits. In particular you will need to take an *analytical* approach to reading your sources in order to interpret them. By *interpretation*, we mean the process by which you have come to see the significance, meaning, or implications of the ideas, data, and questions with which you are working. Analysis and interpretation are notoriously fuzzy terms. But it is not hard to be concrete about the process used to do these activities. Let us begin by understanding what it means to read analytically. To read analytically is to attend to, understand, assess, and comment on the following:

1. The sequence of moves a writer uses to make an argument.
2. The relationship between claims made and the evidence and logic used to support them.
3. The significance and implications of specific keywords or phrases a writer chooses to convey his or her view.
4. Patterns in data, ideas, methods, or perspectives.
5. Anomalous data, ideas, methods, or perspective once a pattern has been established.
6. The explicit or tacit organizing binaries or oppositions in the piece.

Reading analytically also means the following:

7. To uncover and reveal the tacit values and assumptions that anchor a writer's perspective.
8. To understand the larger contexts in which specific data or phenomena are relevant.
9. To explore and reveal the implications of the data, ideas, or methods.

While it may seem that reading analytically requires you to pay attention to a lot, the following sections provide you with some strategies for a step-by-step reading and note-taking process that will maximize your chances of reading analytically.

APPROACHING THE TEXT WITH THE RIGHT MINDSET IN THE RIGHT ENVIRONMENT

It can be easy to check out if a reading that on first blush seems dull or irrelevant, is hard to follow, or is on the complex subject matter. Do not let yourself take the easy way out! It will make your life as a writer considerably more difficult if you do. So, try to focus hard, knowing that the work you put in upfront will pay off with time saved, less stress, and better results at the end of the project. Work actively to pay attention, understand, and respond to the material being presented. Concentrate on understanding what is being conveyed, whatever the deficiencies of the piece of writing. Try to connect what you are reading to what you already know (through personal experience or other reading you have done on the subject). Think about how what you are reading possibly changes what you think about the topic on which you are working. Assess the uses and limits of the ideas which you are reading for your own writing project.

USING PRE-READING STRATEGIES

Survey the reading and develop questions and interests to guide your reading. Activate what you already know about the topics, whether from other reading or life experiences. When you survey a text, you scan the table of contents, introduction, chapter introductions, headings, or summaries to pick up a shallow overview of the text. From your survey, develop a small set of initial questions or thoughts that you will to try to answer or think through as you read. Also, locate areas of particular interest (topics or subtopics, but also specific page ranges) to which you will give your best attention.

Before reading the text carefully, consider what you already know (or think you know) about the topic of the text. By creating expectations about what you are reading, you will notice when the writer's line of thought diverges from your expectations and see those moments as interesting, puzzling, troubling, ambiguous, or suggestive—as moments about which you will need to write.

MARKING UP YOUR TEXTS

The simple act of making marks on a reading focuses your attention and promotes an active and dynamic approach to your reading that is absolutely essential if you are to write effectively about what you read. Unless you have a late model tablet that accepts input from a stylus, and a good piece of "ink on PDF" software (such as PDFill's PDF Ink), it is best to mark up a reading using a pencil or a pen.

In the next paragraph, we will describe some basic marks and types of margin comments. But before we do, we want to prompt you to notice how they focus your attention more on the flow of the intellectual conversation, rather than on the specific pieces of information or materials the writers use to have the conversation. Remember, you are reading to further the conversation, not merely to acquire and retain information. To participate in the conversation, you have to be able to use the words on the page to map the *exchange* of ideas embedded in the text.

Use the following marks and margin comment types to help you make the conversation in your set of research texts come to life (see *Marked Up Text: Sam Anderson, "In Defense of Distraction"* for an example):

- Underline essential and supporting questions and label which supporting questions go with each essential question.
- Circle key concepts, and then define concepts and terms in your own words in the margin.
- Double-underline compelling passages and make margin notes about how you could use them in your own project.
- Draw a block around passages that are complicated, challenging, or hard to understand, and then on a separate sheet of paper, try to paraphrase them until you understand them.
- Jot down the ideas, examples, and lines of inquiry that occur to you as you read.
- Draw lines or make cross-references to forge connections and comparisons between sections of the reading, or between the current reading and others you have read previously.
- Make margin notes about the uses and limits of particular concepts or passages for your own work.

FIGURE 12.1 Marking up a source helps reinforce your engagement with it, regardless of which method you choose to make notes and annotations.

It is particularly important to track the **writerly moves** the writer is making. When you track a writer's moves, you are paying as much attention to the purpose of each paragraph as to the content of it. When you attend to the writer's purpose of a paragraph, you better understand how he or she wants you to synthesize the ideas, exhibits, and arguments he or she is presenting into a larger argument. When you understand how a writer is making his or her argument, you can better evaluate it. Table 12.2 below presents some common writerly moves for which to be on the lookout.

Keeping track of a writer's moves will enable you to better see the conversation in his or her text. By understanding how the author is making use of his or her sources, you can distinguish between what the sources say and what the author is saying in response. Then you can consider your response to all the voices in the text.

TABLE 12.2 *COMMON WRITERLY MOVES*

Offering background	Countering another writer's argument
Analyzing an exhibit	Making an argument
Interpreting an exhibit	Defining terms
Borrowing expert authority	Describing a method
Extending another writer's argument	Criticizing another writer's method
Presenting another writer's argument	Revealing tacit values or assumptions

Q – CAN DISTRACTION BE USEFUL?

SIMON, MEYER, GALLAGHER

PURPOSE: THEIR OWN EVIDENCE SHOWS THEY'VE MISSED SOMETHING VALUABLE ABOUT DISTRACTION

The prophets of total attention meltdown sometimes invoke, as an example of the great culture we are going to lose as we succumb to e-thinking, the canonical French juggernaut Marcel Proust. And indeed, at seven volumes, several thousand pages, and 1.5 million words, *Á la Recherche du Temps Perdu* is in many ways the anti-Twitter. (It would take, by the way, exactly 68,636 tweets to reproduce.) It's important to remember, however, that the most famous moment in all of Proust, the moment that launches the entire monumental project, is a moment of pure distraction: when the narrator, Marcel, eats a spoonful of teasoaked madeleine and finds himself instantly transported back to the world of his childhood: Proust makes it clear that conscious focus could never have yielded such profound magic. Marcel has to abandon the constraints of what he calls "voluntary memory," the kind of narrow, purpose-driven attention that Adderall, say, might have allowed him to harness in order to get to the deeper truths available by the distraction. That famous cookie is a kind of hyperlink: a little blip that launches an associative cascade of a million other subjects. This sort of free-associative wandering is essential to the creative process; one moment of judicious unmindfulness can inspire thousands of hours of mindfulness.

ANALYSIS

INTERRPRETATION

DISTRACTION CAN REVEAL TRUTH?

→ *I NEED TO TRY TO PARAPHRASE THIS*

EXHIBIT

DISTRACTION CAN BE A PRECURSOR TO CREATIVITY

My favorite focusing exercise comes from William James: Draw a dot on a piece of paper, then pay attention to it for as long as you can. (Sitting in my office one afternoon, with my monkey mind swinging busily across the lush rain forest of online distractions, I tried this with the closest dot in the vicinity: the bright-red mouse-nipple at the center of my laptop's keyboard. I managed to stare at it for 30 minutes, with mixed results.) James argued that the human mind can't actually focus on the dot, or any unchanging object, for more than a few seconds at a time: It's too hungry for variety, surprise, the adventure of the unknown. It has to refresh its attention by continually finding new aspects of the dot to focus on: subtleties of its shape, its relationship to the edges of the paper, metaphorical associations (a fly, an eye, a hole). The exercise becomes a question less of pure unwavering focus than of your ability to organize distractions around a central point. The dot, in all other words, becomes only the hub of your total dot-related distraction.

BORROWING a CONCEPT

PARADOX? NEED TO FIGURE THIS OUT

This is what the web-threatened punditry often fails to recognize: Focus is a paradox; it has distraction built into it. The two are symbiotic; they're the systole and diastole of consciousness. Attention comes from the Latin "to stretch out" or "reach toward", distraction from "to pull apart." We need both. In their extreme forms, focus and attention may even circle circle back around and bleed into one another. Meyer says there's a subset of Buddhists who believe that the most advanced monks become essentially "world-class multitaskers," that all those years of meditation might actually speed up their mental processes enough to handle the kind of information overload the rest of us find crippling.

ARGUMENT

The truly wise mind will harness, rather than abandon, the power of distraction. Unwavering focus the inability to be distracted can actually be just as problematic as ADHD. Trouble with "attentional shift" is a feature common to a handful of mental illnesses, including schizophrenia and OCD. Its been hypothesized the ADHD might even be an advantage in certain change-rich environments.

ARGUMENT

→ *ITS HARD TO SEE HOW. I SUPPOSE YOU MIGHT BE MORE AWARE OF DIVERSE STIMULI, BUT HOW WELL COULD YOU RESPOND TO IT?*

You should also keep track of your intellectual response to the reading: Are you skeptical of some of the ideas or arguments presented? Does some way of approaching a problem or object of analysis seem particularly interesting or puzzling? Is something confusing or suddenly particularly clear? Write it all down. Keep track of the questions, ideas, problems, potential forwards/counters, and personal experiences that percolate in your brain as you read. These will be the foundations on which you come to terms with the piece.

When you are finished reading, immediately write a healthy paragraph right on your printout (or on the first or last page of your chapter, right in the book if you own it) documenting both the basic substance of the writer's contribution to the conversation and your initial intellectual responses to it. Record the essential ideas, concepts, or claims that you want to forward or counter, and explain how and why. Describe how reading this text changed your thinking (furthered it? nuanced it? redirected it? complicated it? confused it?).

Transfer your margin notes to a word-processing program or note-taking program (such as Evernote) after reading. We recommend transferring notes only after you read, rather than as you go, because the act of transferring your notes from the page to the word processor helps solidify your encounter with the text. You will remember more of what you read and develop a deeper, more sophisticated response to the text by revisiting your margin notes in the act of transfer.

You do not need to transfer everything. In fact, you want to be selective to start winnowing important stuff from trivial (even if interesting) stuff. Start by transferring everything that went into your "healthy paragraph." When you wrote that paragraph, you started to develop your own response to the material. You began to integrate new ideas and information with old, and started to think about how your own project will be impacted by engaging this particular text in conversation. As you revisit your notes in light of other readings and further work on your own piece of writing, you will add to, revise, rethink, and respond to this initial response (so be sure to record the date of your initial reading, and each time you revisit your notes). By tracking the development of your thought as you revisit and rethink your response to a reading in light of further readings and thinking, you will have a history of your engagement with the ideas and lines of thought that are the substance of the conversation you and all the other writers are having. When you write your paper, you will rely on the history of your encounter with other conversationalists to formulate your own entry into the conversation.

After transferring that first "healthy paragraph," transfer only the most important concepts (especially ones named with specialized terms), conversation-changing insights, passages, examples, and lines of thought you might want to emulate or deploy in your own writing projects. Do not worry about capturing data or statistics—they are on paper and easily retrievable. If you need one or two specific pieces of information, go back and make a note on the first page of the reading indicating where exactly in the essay the data is (page number) and—here is the crucial step— explaining the meaning and implications of the data. Unless you write down what the data means to you, you will surely forget what you found interesting, useful, or troubling about the data.

This intensive approach to reading is necessary because you are not just reading to understand a fact, remember it, and select the right option on a multiple-choice exam. You are reading to respond to this text (and others) in writing. You need to cultivate and record a complex intellectual response to the text in order to write about it in an interesting and compelling way.

SYNTHESIZING

Once you implement this reading process and do some initial reading in your source set, you should start to see connections between your sources. Likely they will be pursuing some of the same questions, using similar kinds of exhibits or illustrations, and circling around a small set of explanations. When you read for research purposes, it is important not to treat each text in isolation. Instead, try to understand how the texts are talking back and forth to one another on a small set of issues.

In order to demonstrate one way to systematically represent the structural relationships in a conversation, let's review a visual representation of the research conversation represented in Sam Anderson's *New York* magazine piece "In Defense of Distraction" (2010). In it, Anderson reviews the scientific literature on distraction and multitasking with the purpose of challenging the notion that we are mired in a "crisis of attention." While Anderson admits that opportunities for distraction abound in our media-saturated society, he argues that mindful distraction can be a source of creativity and insight. Anderson's article discusses 10 different writers' views on the subject. That means he has condensed 10 or more different articles and books into several paragraphs of text to arrive at his own synthesis of their ideas. No researcher, not even a professional like Anderson, can hold the details of 10 complicated texts in mind. So as you learn more, it becomes important to develop some efficient means of representing a lot of material in a clear efficient way. One way to do this is to create a **synthesis table**, where the views of several different writers on a single topic are entered. Table 12.3 illustrates part of one Anderson might have made.

TABLE 12.3 *SYNTHESIS TABLE*

WRITER NAME	QUESTION: WHAT ARE THE CAUSES AND CHARACTERISTICS OF THE "ATTENTION CRISIS," AND WHAT CAN BE DONE ABOUT IT?
Herbert Simon	We live in a society where we have access to too much information. Too much information "consumes the attention of its recipients. Hence a wealth of information creates a poverty of attention, and a need to allocate that attention efficiently" (Anderson, 2010, para. 3).
David Meyer	Multitasking is a myth. Our brains process information across many different channels. When we "multitask" we're rapidly switching between channels. When a channel gets overloaded, our brains become "inefficient and mistake-prone" (Anderson, 2010, para. 12).
Linda Stone	The prevalence of networked mobile computing/communication devices means that we are frequently in a state of "continuous partial attention," which makes it hard to sustain focus (Anderson, 2010, para. 14).
Winifred Gallagher	While the world constantly intrudes on our attention, paying attention is an act of will. We should be able to choose to focus (Anderson, 2010, para. 15). Because the capacity of our attention is limited to 110 bits of information per second, we must choose to spend our attention on worthwhile things (para. 21). When we do not choose to spend our attention wisely, we should blame ourselves (para. 22).

While a synthesis table enables you to see the divergent views of the concept at a glance, it does not easily capture the relationships among the views. A **concept map** does a much better job. Figure 12.2 shows what a concept map based on Anderson's synthesis might look like:

Concept maps are designed to answer single questions—in this case, "What is the 'poverty of attention' thesis?" The thoughts of each writer are color-coded so that you can easily see which ideas belong to each writer, and where their ideas overlap.

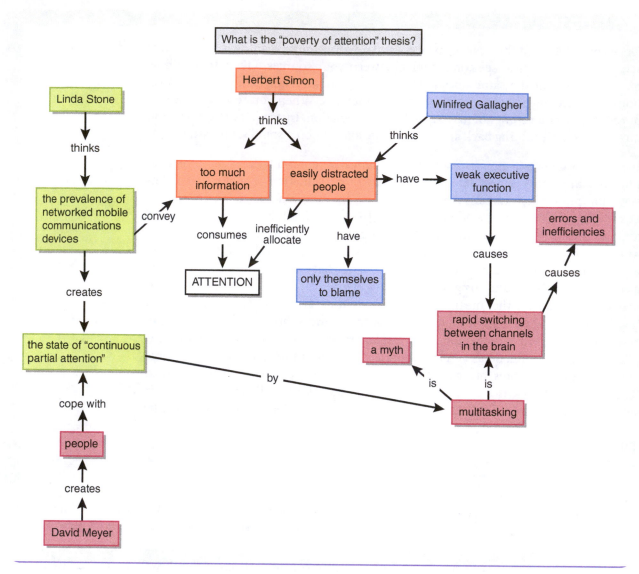

FIGURE 12.2 Concept map of Anderson's synthesis. Thinking creatively about concepts and questions—including using concept maps—helps to sort out your ideas and notes and synthesize the information in a useful way.

As you review the concept map, you will see how much detail it conveys, as well as gaining a sense of which writers agree with one another, and which dissent from the others.

To better understand how to create concept maps, visit the Institute for Human and Machine Cognition website at http://cmap.ihmc.us/docs/conceptmap.html. For now, remember this: However you decide to take notes on your reading, when it comes time to synthesize, be sure to capture areas of disagreement as well as agreement. Being able to acknowledge that there are alternative ways of thinking about your questions and responding to them fairly and thoughtfully is a prerequisite for joining the conversation of researchers in your essay.

Once you understand who is saying what in the conversation, you can use your synthesis table or concept map to write a sequence of paragraphs in which you synthesize what you have learned from the literature. Writers of syntheses weave together significant strands of previous research to create a bigger more useful picture of what the research community knows. More than summary, synthesis is an interpretive account of the literature. By "interpretive account," we mean that as you explain what other writers have written, you also explain what you think is the significance of the meaning of the literature. Here is an example of what a synthesis might look like in Emma's essay. Notice that while much of the first two paragraphs are the straightforward descriptions of other writers' ideas, the final two paragraphs evaluate the utility of the pieces of research discussed. Paragraph 3 explains what Emma thinks her sources have gotten right. Paragraph 4 details what she thinks they have gotten wrong.

Para. 1: There has been a lot of hand-wringing going on in the last 5 years about what "kids these days" are doing on the Internet, and what the Internet is doing to kids. Parents, teachers, clergy, and a host of commentators fear that the generation technology writer John Palfrey (2008) deems "born digital" is categorically different from previous generations because of how deeply their lives are intertwined with communications technologies. Tethered to one another via mobile phones, Facebook, and IM/texting, well-equipped teenagers are undeniably what linguist Naomi Baron (2008) calls "always-on," inseparable both from their gadgets and one another (p. 8).

Para. 2: For Baron, Palfrey, and Emory University English professor Mark Bauerlein, the fact that teens live at least partially in a virtual world is troubling. Baron worries that all this online writing that teens do is weakening their ability to use written language effectively. Palfrey (2008) is concerned that the sometimes risqué traces of Digital Natives' personal lives posted on Facebook, in forums, and other public places online expose them to both humiliation and danger (p. 7). Bauerlein (2008) thinks provocatively that today's online teens are "the dumbest generation" yet, precisely because their online connections to one another wrap them in a growth-stunting "generational cocoon" (p. 10).

Para. 3: It is undeniable that today's teens (well, those with the financial wherewithal to afford pricey smartphones and data plans) live in a media/technology–rich environment that is shaping who they are, how they think, and what they see as their purpose in life. Bauerlein is correct that teens' virtual activities reflect their powerfully absorbing interest in the dynamics and culture of teen life. John Palfrey gets it right when he writes that "new digital technologies—computers, cellphones, Sidekicks—are primary mediators of human-to-human connections. They have created a 24/7 network that blends the human with the technology to a degree we haven't experienced before, and it is transforming human relationships in fundamental ways" (Palfrey, 2008, pp. 4–5). What is more, their digital connectedness is transforming how knowledge is created and distributed, and how teaching and learning happen.

Para. 4: But Baron, Palfrey, and Bauerlein are wrong to view this moment of admittedly transformative change in human communications as a historic cusp, a moment threatening the collapse of reason, economy, and civic virtue. Despite what Palfrey (2008) writes, we are not "at a crossroads." There are more than "two possible paths before us—one in which we destroy what is great about the Internet, and one in which we make smart choices and head towards a bright future in a digital age" (p. 7). While Palfrey is almost right that the "choices we are making now will govern how our children and grandchildren live their lives in many important ways," it is important not to think about the transformations that come with our move into the digital world in the either/or terms of moral panic (p. 7).

When you write your synthesis, remember to attribute ideas to the researcher from whom you borrowed them. In the four paragraphs above, notice how many times the names Baron, Palfrey, and Bauerlein are repeated. Also, notice how the credentials of each researcher are presented at least once in the sequence. You will also want to use the specialized language that you find in texts you are synthesizing. Whenever possible, weave the quoted passages into sentences of your own, as Emma does throughout her synthesis. If you use these strategies, your reader should be able to easily distinguish between the views and ideas of other writers and yours.

USING RESEARCH TO ANSWER SUPPORTING AND ESSENTIAL QUESTIONS

With her project definition, well-designed set of sources, reading notes, and synthesis maps, Emma is ready to begin to try tentatively answering her supporting questions using the ideas, concepts, cases, and interpretive frameworks she finds in her sources. Her first step is to use these resources to formulate specific answers to her supporting questions. She should try to answer her questions as definitively as possible, presenting supporting data and analysis to be persuasive. She must also convey the full range of informed opinions represented in the conversation—including divergent points of view, alternative explanations, and areas of controversy, as well as the data and analysis supporting these alternative views. As she is answering her supporting questions, she should also start thinking about what these tentative answers suggest about elements of her essential question. Periodically, she should try to answer her essential question by writing a holistic account of her research and the conversation to which she has listened.

As Emma tries to explain what she thinks is happening when teen girls use Facebook within the context of their friendships and romantic relationships, she will develop ideas of her own and begin to recognize gaps in her research. For example, Emma has no peer-reviewed research explaining the developmental dynamics underpinning teen girls' formation of friendships and romantic relationships. While Emma has much research remaining, from here on out, the research work of Phase II is to repeat the process detailed above as her ideas evolve and gaps appear. Eventually, as she refines her stock of ideas, cases, and interpretive concepts; tests varying explanations; and develops her set of sources, she will arrive at a conviction that she knows why, in developmental terms, teen girls use the Internet to socialize with peers and romantic interests. She will be ready, that is, to formulate a thesis-driven argument. A thesis must do more than prove a point. It must be *formulated* as a response to one or more researchers' positions on issues driving the existing conversation.

FORMULATING A THESIS

In order for Emma's thesis to be responsive to the discussion, her work must be *situated* in the arguments of others. So far, Emma has decided that the "addiction" explanation of teen social network site usage obscures more than it reveals. She has also decided that a multidisciplinary explanation rooted in teen psychology and sociality and the affordances of social network sites reveals a lot about why and how teen girls use social network sites such as Facebook to seek status, try on identities, and mediate relationships. Her thesis paragraph would need to capture these elements of her thinking. Here is what the lead-in to her thesis might look like.

> Lead-In: While early researchers and popular articles understand teen use of the Internet in terms of addiction, recent studies by sociologists danah boyd [sic], Sonia Livingstone, and others have proposed an explanatory model that suggests that the affordances of social network sites such as Facebook are enabling teens to meet developmental needs. The value of this research is that, unlike previous research, it is based on surveys, interviews, and direct observation of teens.

Now that she has declared her dissent from the addiction model, and her consent for a developmental model, the next step is for Emma to establish how her own line of inquiry responds to an active question in the literature. It might look something like this:

> Line of Inquiry: Since empirical research on teen use of the Internet is relatively new, most studies treat both teen boys and girls. In order to better understand the specific nuances of teenage girls' use of social network sites, I will synthesize the current literature on teen girls' developmental imperatives and the affordances of social network sites to explain how girls use the affordances of social network sites to navigate the challenges of teen friendships and romantic relationships.

With this, Emma narrows her focus, establishes her method of research, and forges a key connection between technology and teen girls' developmental imperatives. Next is to issue her thesis statement:

> Thesis: Whereas parents and journalists explain teen girls' Internet use in terms of addiction, I argue that the multimedia affordances of Facebook (Timeline, status updates, links, photo posting, and tagging) feed into a gender-specific imperative for teen girls to "compose" an image of themselves that responds to their own needs and the expectations of their peers. Further, I argue that this image both reflects an ideal image of themselves and the way individual girls are seen by their peer group. Finally, I argue that parents who view their daughters' images misinterpret this online self-image, seeing them as documentary images instead of peer-negotiated projections.

The last part of the paragraph is to explain the significance of the thesis.

> Significance: If my arguments are correct, then we can better understand the gender-specific challenges teen girls face as they seek to

1. Establish the part of the conversation you want to work in with "lead-in" sentences.
2. Establish your own line of inquiry as a response to the conversation.
3. Articulate your thesis as a response to conventional wisdom and established research.
4. Explain the significance of your thesis—why does it matter if you are right?

establish an emerging adult identity for their peer group, and work to separate from the self rooted in the family setting. Moreover, we can better help parents interpret their daughters' Timelines in light of the developmental imperatives they express.

Having reviewed the literature well enough to formulate such a thesis, Emma is ready to begin using her project description; answers to essential and supporting questions; and her reading notes, synthesis tables or concept maps, to draft an essay.

By the end of this phase of the research project, you will have equipped yourself to be a knowledgeable participant in discussions on your topic. You should have well-formed questions, plenty of examples and cases to draw on as evidence, multiple partners-in-inquiry (including those who may disagree with you), and an interpretive framework to help you determine the significance and meaning of your analysis.

PLAGIARISM AND RESPONSIBLE USE OF SOURCES

Plagiarism is the unacknowledged use by a writer of words and ideas originating with other writers. In many ways, we live in a time when such use is easier than ever before. Previously written material about almost any subject is available with the click of a mouse. Unethical paper writing services prey on students who cheat themselves out of the benefits of their own education. To complicate matters, as the Council of Writing Program Administrators (2019) reminds us, "In some settings, using other people's words or ideas as [one's] own is an acceptable practice for writers of certain kinds of texts (for example, organizational documents)" ("Causes of Plagiarism" section).

It is no wonder that a majority of college students now view the Internet as a source of free information to be used without acknowledgment as they see fit. About 40 percent of 14,000 undergraduates admitted to copying a few sentences in written assignments. Perhaps more significant, the number who believed that copying from the Web constitutes "serious cheating" is declining to 29 percent on average in recent surveys from 34 percent earlier in the decade" (Gabriel, 2010, para. 10-11). As the Center for Academic Integrity found, Internet plagiarism is a growing concern on all campuses as students struggle to understand what constitutes acceptable use of the Internet. In the absence of clear direction from faculty, many students have concluded that "cut & paste" plagiarism—using a sentence or two (or more) from different sources on the Internet and weaving this information together into a paper without appropriate citation—is not a serious issue.

FIGURE 12.3 Today's technology makes it easier than ever to simply "copy and paste" data from your sources. However, be extremely careful to cite each source, as plagiarism can have very serious consequences.

According to academic integrity researchers Donald L. McCabe and Patrick Drinian, "[S]tudents blame the pressure to succeed—the need to meet the expectations of their families, graduate schools, and prospective employers" for cheating (1999, p. B7). But in college and university settings, such unacknowledged use is taken very seriously. Why? Because making false claims about authorship transgresses the scholarly values that make institutions of higher education able to do the important work of educating students and creating knowledge. Plagiarism by scholars at any level—whether students or faculty—undermines the standards of fairness, open-mindedness, and truth-seeking that academic endeavors require.

Plagiarism also undermines the value of your education. Students who submit the words and ideas of others as their own harm their education and the education of others. When you do not do your own work, you miss the opportunity to increase your knowledge and develop your skills. And when employers doubt the integrity of your college or university, your own knowledge, skills, and integrity will come into question.

Not all unacknowledged use of sources is intentional. As the Council of Writing Program Administrators (2003) argues, "[S]tudents may not know how to integrate the ideas of others and document the sources of those ideas appropriately in their texts or how to take careful and fully documented notes during their research" ("Causes of plagiarism" section). In this last section of this chapter, you will learn how to integrate your ideas with others and how to take careful and fully documented notes during research.

BEST NOTE-TAKING PRACTICES TO AVOID PLAGIARISM

One reason students get accused of plagiarism is that they do not always use note-taking practices appropriate for academic purposes. Whenever you take notes for an academic paper, you must ensure the following:

1. Record all bibliographic data for the source. Include author name, publication date, and title of the publication. For books, also write down the publisher of the book and the geographic location of the publishing company. For journals, record the journal title and volume and issue number.

2. Enclose all words taken directly from the source in quotation marks.

3. Record the page or pages on which the passage or idea appears.

4. Attribute all words and ideas to their correct author, taking into account that academic writers often quote other writers in their texts.

WAYS TO SIGNAL WHEN YOU ARE BORROWING WORDS AND IDEAS

To avoid plagiarizing, you must clearly signal when you are using words borrowed from another writer. First, be sure to enclose any words that you borrow from another writer in quotation marks. Second, use an **attributional phrase** to signal that the ideas and words you are conveying originate with another writer. Frequently encountered attributional phrases include ones like the following:

- According to _____, …
- As _____ claims, …
- _____ argues that …
- In an article titled "____," sociologist _____ examines …

Use attributional phrases even when you are summarizing or paraphrasing other writers' ideas, as well as when you are quoting them directly.

Besides acknowledging authorship, attributional phrases often give information about the writer's expertise and authority to write about her subject. Here's an example (the attributional phrase is in boldface):

> **According to pop culture analyst Liz Colville**, *"We give ourselves anxiety trying to decipher the tone of a text or the meaning of a tweet's punctuation"(Colville, 2009, para. 13).* Reference: Colville, L. (2009). Surfing alone: Is digital technology destroying relationships? *Pop Matters*. Retrieved from http://www.popmatters.com/pm/column/94800-surfing-alone-is-digital-technology-destroying-relationships/

In addition, do not allow quoted passages to stand alone as complete sentences. Instead, always embed quoted passages in sentences of your own composition, preferably ones that go beyond simple attribution to provide context to your readers:

> **In an article asking whether digital technology is undermining face-to-face relationships, pop culture writer Liz Colville (2009) explains that our devotion to digital communication may be eroding our**

willingness to invest in fully embodied relationships: "Technology has established it as a luxury, rather than a disorder, that we do not as often have to deal with the physicality of people" (para. 13).

Finally, provide readers with an in-text citation containing abbreviated publication information. All of our citation examples so far have included such a reference in parentheses at the end of the sentence containing the quoted passage. In APA style, parenthetical references include the author's last name (when not included in an attributional phrase), the year of publication, and the page or paragraph number where the passage appears. Do not forget that research papers require a reference page listing all of the sources you used in alphabetical order. Each style has unique procedures for references and other paper components.

SUMMARY

- It may take practice to implement the concepts, strategies, and tools presented in this chapter, but the benefits are well worth the effort. When your source set is well designed to support your research needs, you can spend your research time analyzing and interpreting sources, and making connections among ideas, rather than worrying about whether you have "enough" sources. Likewise, when you read critically to understand how researchers are conversing with each other, rather than to record information, you become aware of areas of disagreement, as well as consensus, enabling you to formulate your own reason-based judgments and advocate for them in your essay. When you see research articles and books as artifacts of human minds in pursuit of the truth, rather than repositories of information, you become motivated to use their ideas responsibly, avoiding the risk of plagiarism.

KEY TERMS

Attributional phrase—a phrase such as "according to Alvarez" or "as Johnson writes," which signals to readers that the words or ideas that follow have been borrowed from another writer.

Concept map—a visual representation of ideas, their components, and the relationships among them.

Partners-in-inquiry—researchers who are asking questions similar to your own and thinking about issues that concern you.

Plagiarism—the unacknowledged use by a writer of words and ideas originating with other writers.

Survey—while actively reading a text, the action of scanning content to pick up a shallow overview of the text.

Synthesis table—a means of representing the similar and contrasting views of a group of scholars in table form.

Writerly moves—the set of frequently used strategies that a writer uses to convey his or her argument.

QUESTIONS FOR REVIEW

Respond to the following questions **without** reviewing the text or your notes. These questions are provided to help you practice retrieving information and reflect on your reading.

A. What did you learn about using sources to develop an argument?

B. Did you agree or disagree with anything you read? Explain.

C. What did you learn that was new to you?

D. Was any information or advice helpful or useful to you? If yes, what was helpful and why? If no, why was it not helpful?

Complete the following steps. You may reference your text or notes to help you.

1. Using the suggestions for marking up a text, mark up one of the sources you intend to use in your first writing assignment. Submit a hard copy or an electronic copy of your marked-up text.

2. Using the same source, write a "healthy paragraph" immediately after you mark up your text. Do as the chapter suggests: document both the basic substance of the writer's contribution to the conversation and your initial intellectual responses to it. Record the essential ideas, concepts, or claims that you want to forward or counter, and explain how and why. Describe how reading this text changed your thinking (furthered it? nuanced it? redirected it? complicated it? confused it?).

3. Again using the same source, add information to your "healthy paragraph" as another paragraph, a bulleted list, or a concept map. Do as the chapter suggests: include only the most important concepts (especially ones named with specialized terms), conversation-changing insights, passages, examples, and lines of thought you might want to emulate or deploy in your own writing projects.

4. After you have completed the above steps for each required source, create either a Synthesis Table or a Concept Map to demonstrate connections between your sources.

WEBSITES FOR FURTHER REFERENCE

http://prezi.com/3bsfvefiq-ht/untitled-prezi/
This Prezi by Caroline Eichholz presents the mechanics of APA citation style in an appealing manner. Content derived from Temple University's Online Writing Lab.

http://cmapskm.ihmc.us/rid=1064009710027_1483270340_27090/CmapTools%20-%20Concept%20Map%20About%20Concept%20Maps.html .
This concept map by the Institute for Human Machine Cognition provides a step-by-step process for making concept maps. To better understand what concept maps are and how they work, see this concept map example.

http://wpacouncil.org/node/9
This article by the Council of Writing Program Administrators defines plagiarism and offers recommendations for avoiding it.

http://bcs.bedfordstmartins.com/resdoc5e/RES5e_ch09_o.html
Bedford/St. Martin's exhaustive online APA citation guide.

http://academic.ursinus.edu/writing/signal.html
This Ursinus College Writing Center web page offers a helpful list of verbs to enable you to construct signal phrases that provide "information about your source authors' attitudes or approaches" (para. 1).

REFERENCES

Anderson, S. (2009, May). In defense of distraction. *New York*. https://nymag.com/news/features/56793/

Baron, N. (2008). Always on: Language in an online and mobile world. 10.1093/acprof:oso/9780195313055.001.0001.

Bauerlein, M. (2008). The dumbest generation: How the digital age stupefies young Americans and jeopardizes our future. Los Angeles: Tarcher.

Colville, L. (2009, June 14). Surfing alone: Is digital technology destroying relationships? https://www.popmatters.com/94800-surfing-alone-is-digital-technology-destroying-relationships-2496034907.html

McCabe, D. L., & Drinan, P. (1999, October 15). Toward a culture of academic integrity. *The Chronicle of Higher Education*. https://www.chronicle.com/article/toward-a-culture-of-academic-integrity/

Council of Writing Program Administrators. (2019, December 30). *Defining and avoiding plagiarism: The WPA statement on best practices.* http://wpacouncil.org/aws/CWPA/pt/sd/news_article/272555/_PARENT/layout_details/false

Gabriel, T. (2010, August 1). Plagiarism lines blur for students in digital age. *The New York Times*. https://www.nytimes.com/2010/08/02/education/02cheat.html

PERSUASIVE PRESENTATIONS

This final section includes chapters about analyzing audiences, public speaking, listening, and critiquing speeches. You have crafted a strong persuasive message in your writing assignments, and now you need to decide how to use that information in your final presentation. The first chapter in this section emphasizes the importance of audience analysis and discusses attitude measurement. The next two chapters in this section discuss reasoning, fallacies, organizational patterns, and delivery skills. You will be able to plan and deliver an excellent persuasive presentation when you use the strategies in these chapters along with the knowledge you have acquired and skills you have developed throughout the course. The final chapter of the textbook discusses listening and critiquing speeches. You will apply these practical suggestions as you listen to the final presentations of your classmates.

CHAPTERS

CHAPTER 13

AUDIENCE-CENTERED PRESENTATIONS

BEFORE YOU READ

Respond to the following questions before you read the chapter.

1. Is it possible to measure someone's attitude? If so, how would you try to measure it?

2. What questions about your topic would you like to ask your audience? Why are those questions important to ask?

3. Do you think your audience is interested in hearing your presentation? Why or why not?

SPEAKING IN CONTEXT

When being audience-centered, it's important to speak with your audience in a way that they can recognize and relate to. For example, the way a politician delivers a speech in Texas could be drastically different from the same speech delivered to residents of New York. Radio host Jennifer Guerra identifies this type of public communication as "code-switching" (Guerra, 2014). Code-switching involves alternating between two or more languages (or language varieties) in the context of communication.

LEARNING OBJECTIVES

- KNOW HOW TO ANALYZE YOUR AUDIENCE AND TAILOR YOUR SPEECH TO THEIR WANTS, NEEDS, AND INTERESTS.
- UNDERSTAND THE BEST PRACTICES FOR OBTAINING AUDIENCE INFORMATION AND TAILORING YOUR PRESENTATION TO THEIR EXPECTATIONS.
- SPEAK WITH CONFIDENCE, USE HUMOR EFFECTIVELY (AND APPROPRIATELY), AND CREATE A PERSONALIZED EXPERIENCE FOR YOUR AUDIENCE.
- LEARN HOW TO ADJUST YOUR MESSAGE AS YOU PRESENT IT, AND ALSO ENCOURAGE PARTICIPATION FROM YOUR AUDIENCE.

Let's discuss a recent example of code-switching used in politics. During the first round of debates for the Democratic Presidential nomination, candidates Beto O'Rourke and Cory Booker exhibited code-switching by speaking in Spanish in an attempt to resonate with Lantinx viewers. There were mixed reviews on whether code-switching in this instance was effective or an attempt to haphazardly pander while answering questions.

Code-switching is a dynamic, constantly evolving skill; there is no empirically "correct" way to apply it. The ability to switch codes to adapt to your audience is something that comes with observation and practice. Alter your communication too strongly, and you risk coming off as insincere or even insulting to your audience. What is important is that you keep your own voice while still being able to relate to your audience.

As you study more about the importance of being audience-centered, remember to think reflexively about your presentation. Practice code-switching before your speech and then place yourself in the audience's shoes; would you perceive your speaking to be authentic and sincere? Also, remember the importance of ethics in public speaking. The goal is not to shamelessly pander to your audience, but to educate and motivate them to a course of action.

Whether in a large auditorium, a corporate boardroom, or a classroom, audiences are usually self-centered. Listeners want to know "What's in it for me?" That is, they want to understand what they can learn from a speech or how they can take action that will, in some way, enhance their lives. If you show your audience you understand their needs and help them achieve their goals, they will want to listen. Being audience-centered and adapting to their needs are critical factors in creating effective presentations. These two concepts are the focus of this chapter.

How do you prepare and deliver a speech that will mean enough to your audience to capture their attention and convince them to listen? Begin by learning as much as you can about your listeners, so you can identify and focus on their concerns.

AUDIENCE-CENTEREDNESS

Making your intended audience central in your message formation will result in a stronger, more tailored speech that resonates with your listeners. This is desirable because you can feel and respond positively to the energy and enthusiasm that a receptive and captivated audience exudes. In essence, if you are audience-centered, both you and your audience benefit greatly.

Spotify consistently uses consumer data to successfully create audience-centered advertising campaigns.

© Piotr Swat/Shutterstock.com

Spotify consistently uses consumer data to successfully create audience-centered advertising campaigns.

Early in your speech, telling your audience what's in it for them and letting them know they were front and center in your mind as you worked on your message is a great way to help establish your credibility, common ground, and build their interest in your topic. Knowing what your audience needs is the first step to being audience-centered.

AUDIENCE ANALYSIS

You need not be a presidential speechwriter to understand your audience. All speakers can create a sketch of their listeners by analyzing them in terms of key demographic and psychographic characteristics.

Demographics include age, gender, race and ethnicity, education/ knowledge, group affiliation, occupational group, socioeconomic status, religious background, political affiliation, and geographic identifiers. Depending on your general and specific purposes, certain demographics may be more important than others for any given speech.

DEMOGRAPHIC ANALYSIS

You need to craft a good fit between the various aspects of your speech, such as supporting material, thesis, and main points, and your audience's characteristics. Depending on the speaking situation, ascertaining demographics may or may not be easily accomplished. The following are 10 key demographics you should strive to identify.

1. **AGE.** Try to determine the age of your audience and if there is a large or a small variation in age. Examples and stories you provide need to relate to your audience. Think about how you might foster a feeling of inclusion among all ages present. If your audience is similar in age to you, you may be able to make more references to popular culture. Also, think about the language you use— you would likely speak differently to a group of high schoolers compared to an audience at a retirement community. Ask yourself, "How does my age potentially impact my audience's perceptions of me?" Perhaps certain stereotypes exist based solely on their assessment of your age. If you believe your age may influence their response to you, reflect on how you might make these assumptions work in your favor instead of against you.

   When taking into consideration your age and the age(s) of your audience, we suggest the following:

   - Avoid assumptions about the average age of your audience.
   - Focus on your speech, not your age.
   - Avoid dating yourself with references or language.

2. **GENDER.** Consider the composition of your next audience. Is it mixed or is there a majority of males or females? Also, while we do not identify sexual orientation as one of the 10 demographics, it is closely related. Every audience will likely contain members who are gay, lesbian, bisexual, or transgender. Maintaining this awareness by using sensitive and inclusive language and examples goes a long way toward fostering common ground, inclusiveness, and a more positive response to your message.

   Avoid unfairly categorizing or stereotyping members of the audience. For example, airlines no longer have "stewardesses," but "flight attendants." Departments on college and university campuses are no longer headed by a "chairman" but rather by a "chair" or a "chairperson." For the most part, speakers should avoid relying on the gendered pronouns and find ways to include men, women, and nonbinary individuals in their audiences.

3. **RACE AND ETHNICITY.** Long ago, the image of the United States as a melting pot gave way to the image of a rainbow of diversity—an image in which African Americans, Hispanics, Asians, Greeks, Arabs, and Rick Scott won the Florida Senator's race in large part because he appealed to Florida's Puerto Rican population by talking about issues they cared about without stereotyping the community.

Europeans define themselves by their racial and ethnic ties as well as by their ties to the United States. Within this diversity are cultural beliefs and traditions that may be different from your own (Wahl & Scholl, 2014).

Rick Scott won the Florida Senator's race in large part because he appealed to Florida's Puerto Rican population by talking about issues they cared about without stereotyping the community.

As you develop your speech, we ask that you avoid invoking **stereotypes** related to race, ethnicity, or nationality, even if these groups are not present in your audience. Even when couched in humor, such comments are deeply offensive and unethical. Appreciation of different people and ways can help you avoid several critical errors in your speech. Any of these gaffes will surely compromise the connection you are trying to create.

Understand also that **ethnocentrism**, which is the belief that one's own culture is superior to other cultures, comes into play when we express a bias for the way we do things. Unfortunately, some or many individuals who might be identified as ethnocentric have little experience with other cultures. Therefore, an accurate comparison is difficult to make. A speaker should try to avoid being offensive or unfair by examining his/her language usage as well as the examples, stories, and illustrations he/she is contemplating incorporating into a speech. A speaker can also exhibit ethnocentrism by passing of examples from their own life as the "norm." Remember, the societal "norm" may not be the norm for all audience members of varying backgrounds.

4. **EDUCATION/KNOWLEDGE.** Are the members of your audience high school or college graduates, experts with doctorates in the field, or freshmen taking their first course? Knowing the educational level of your audience will aid in the construction of your message. If you're speaking to elementary students about the *Challenger* explosion, you can safely assume they need to be provided with some historical background. But to an older group of adults who witnessed the tragedy on television such information would not be necessary.

   In addition to determining what type of background information or explanation is needed, another consideration is language. You want to speak to your audience, not over their heads or at such a basic level that you sound condescending. We have the following two suggestions that highlight how important it is to analyze your audience's needs::

   - **Do not assume that expertise in one area necessarily means expertise in others.** For example, if you are a stockbroker delivering a speech to a group of scientists about investment opportunities, you may have to define the rules that govern even simple stock trades. Although the more educated your audience, the more sophisticated these explanations can be, explanations must still be included for your speech to make sense.

   - **Be careful about assuming what your audience knows—and does not know—about technical topics.** Mention a server to people who know

© Everett Historical/Shutterstock.com

The *Challenger* explosion remains the worst space program disaster in U.S. history.

nothing about computers, and they may be baffled. Define it for a group of computer experts, and they will wonder why you were asked to speak to them. In both cases, you run the risk of losing your audience; people who are confused or who know much more about a subject may simply stop listening.

5. **GROUP AFFILIATION.** Listeners may identify themselves as members of formal and informal interest groups. An informal interest group generally doesn't require signing up or paying for a membership, or making any type of formal commitment. Examples include YouTube watchers, Starbucks customers, and residents of an inner-city neighborhood. A formal interest group usually requires an official commitment, such as signing a membership form or paying dues. Examples include members of Future Farmers of America, the Chamber of Commerce, or even a member of a Greek organization on a college campus.

If you are addressing members of the Sierra Club, you can be sure the group has a keen awareness of environmental issues. Similarly, if you are addressing an exercise class at the local Y, you can be sure that physical fitness is a priority of everyone in the room. It is important to know something about the group you are speaking to, so you can adapt your message to their interest.

Our main suggestion with regard to group affiliation is to *avoid assuming that all members of a group have similar attitudes.* All members of the International Students group on campus do not share the same set of values or beliefs. They represent different countries with different political and religious practices. Their one shared demographic is that they come from a country outside of the United States. While our two-party system in the United States classifies individuals as either Democratic or Republican, we know that there are conservatives and liberals in both parties. Knowing group affiliation may help us construct our main points and identify appropriate supporting material. We need to take caution, however, and avoid stereotyping the group.

6. **OCCUPATIONAL GROUPS.** You may find an occasion that involves speaking to a specific occupational group, such as teachers, students, doctors, lawyers, union representatives, miners, or factory workers. Occupational information can often tell you a great deal about listeners' attitudes. An audience of physicians may be unwilling to accept proposed legislation that would strengthen a patient's right to choose a personal physician if it also makes it easier for patients to sue for malpractice. A legislative speaker might need to find creative ways to convince the doctors that the new law would be in the best interests of both doctors and patients.

Knowledge of what your listeners do for a living may also tell you the type of vocabulary appropriate for the occasion. If you are addressing a group of newspaper editors, you can use terms common to the newspaper business without bothering to define them. Do not use job-related jargon indiscriminately; rather, use it to your advantage.

When conducting your audience analysis, try to determine what your listeners do for a living. The speaking occasion often makes this clear. You may be invited by a group of home builders to speak about the dangers of radon, or a group of insurance agents may ask you to talk about the weather conditions associated with hurricanes. Knowing the occupations of your audience may lead you to decide not only what type of information to include, but what specific statistics, examples, or illustrations would be most effective for the particular group.

Our suggestion regarding occupational groups is to *avoid too little analysis or too much analysis of the importance of occupational affiliation to your audience members.* When you ask people to describe themselves, what is the first thing they say? It might be "I'm a white female," "I'm a queer activist," "I'm the mother of four young children," or "I'm a lawyer." Some people define themselves by their occupation; others view their jobs as a way to feed a family and maintain a reasonable lifestyle. By determining how important the occupational group characteristic is to your audience, you can create an on-target message that meets their needs.

7. **SOCIOECONOMIC STATUS.** Depending on the situation, it may be difficult to determine whether members of your audience earn more than $100,000 a year or less than $30,000. However, this demographic characteristic may influence how you develop your speech and create common ground with your audience.

We suggest you to be *mindful of your audience's financial status while framing your message.* Giving a speech linking high credit card debt to filing for bankruptcy would need to be adapted to an audience that has no debt. However, those facing financial ruin do not need to hear a "holier-than-thou" lecture on the dangers of credit card debt. Additionally, be mindful of socioeconomic status when providing examples or humor in your speech. Joking about missing your morning Starbucks surely will not resonate with individuals in the audience who are concerned about living paycheck to paycheck.

8. **RELIGIOUS BACKGROUND.** Speakers seldom intend to offend their audiences. However, when it comes to religion, speakers can offend unwittingly. Please consider that *religious beliefs may also define moral attitudes.* When speaking on issues such as abortion, premarital sex, birth control, gay marriage, and the death penalty, we risk alienating our audience. By no means are we suggesting you avoid such topics. However, failing to acknowledge and address the religious beliefs of your listeners when your speech concerns a sensitive topic sets up barriers to communication that may be difficult to overcome.

So, what do you do if you are religious? What if your comments are framed in that specific moral attitude? Explaining your frame of reference and personal biases is ethical and builds rapport, even with those who don't share your convictions. Audiences expect and respect honesty. One student handled her religious frame of reference directly: "Now I am a Christian, and the in vitro procedure I received was in a Catholic hospital. I understand there are many other ways to look at the ethics of my decision, but I want to put that aside for now and focus only on the process." Where possible, remove stumbling blocks for your audience by being forthright and truthful about your own religious convictions while also communicating tolerance and open-mindedness to other perspectives.

9. **POLITICAL AFFILIATION.** In an election year, our interest in political affiliation is heightened. Whether you self-identify as a Libertarian, a mainstream Democrat or Republican, or an Independent, political affiliation may influence how you respond to a given speaker. If you are fundraising for the homeless,

you will probably give a different speech to a group with liberal beliefs than to a group of conservatives.

10. **GEOGRAPHIC IDENTIFIERS.** We have a variety of ways to discuss geographic identifiers. One is directional differences, such as north/ south or east/ west. Think how an audience composed largely of people from the Deep South might vary from an audience of individuals from the Northwest. A second geographic identifier is upstate versus downstate. For example, Illinois is divided into two general areas, Chicago and Downstate (everything south of Chicago). This also alludes to the geographic identifier of urban versus rural. You may have an audience that lives in the same community, or you may have an audience that represents a number of communities. A third geographic identifier relates to terrain, such as living near mountains, lakes, oceans, or, as one of your authors describes herself, living near corn and bean fields and being a "flatlander."

Your authors suggest that understanding geographical identifiers as well as *focusing your message as much as possible on geographical areas of concern will enhance your message's impact and your credibility with your audience.* You may need to adapt your message to accommodate not only differences in language, speech rate, and references, but also specific interests and issues.

ETHICS MATTER

Amy is a speechwriter for a politician running for state senator. The politician, Dan, has been polling fairly well, but does not have great backing with communities of color. Dan asks Amy to arrange a town hall in a community in the state that has a high population of black voters. Amy writes the speech as she normally would, but she does her research and includes points on some topics that are concerns for members of this community such as education.

When Dan looks over Amy's speech, he questions her on why she did not include more humor in the speech. He tells her that he wants to seem funny and approachable to these potential voters, so he wants her to pull some humor from the Black Entertainment Television (BET) channel so he can connect with the voters despite not being a person of color. Amy is now feeling uncomfortable about the whole speaking event.

QUESTIONS TO CONSIDER:

1. If you were Amy, what would you do in this situation about writing the speech?

2. How can you incorporate humor in a speech to appeal to an audience without it seeming fake, forced, or ingenuine?

3. What aspect of audience analysis is missing or not correct in this situation? How can this be fixed?

PSYCHOGRAPHIC ANALYSIS

Psychographics refers to the behaviors, attitudes, beliefs, and values of your listeners. Although an analysis of demographic characteristics will give you some clue as to how your listeners are likely to respond to your speech, it will not tell you anything about the speaking occasion, why people have come together as an audience, how they feel about your topic, or about you as a speaker. This information emerges from the second stage of analysis—psychographics—and centers on the speaking situation specifically.

BEHAVIORS. Your lifestyle choices say something about you. Do you walk, bike, drive, or take public transportation to work? Perhaps you avoid driving because walking and biking are "greener" and viewed as healthier. If you choose to be a city dweller who lives in a 22nd-story studio apartment, you probably have less inclination to experience nature than if you opt to live on a 50-acre farm in Vermont. If you put in 12-hour days at the office, your career is probably more important to you than if you choose to work part-time. Behavioral choices are linked to the attitudes, beliefs, and values of your listeners.

Attitudes, beliefs, and values. **Attitudes** are predispositions to act in a particular way that influences our response to objects, events, and situations. Attitudes tend to be long-lasting, but can change under pressure. They are often, but not always, related to behavior. If I like vegetables, I am likely to bring a vegetable tray to a party. If I don't like big business, I'm less likely to shop at Walmart. Someone who doesn't care about the environment is less likely to recycle.

Beliefs represent a mental and emotional acceptance of information. They are judgments about the truth or the probability that a statement is correct. Beliefs are formed from experience and learning; they are based on what we perceive to be accurate. To

© MinDof/Shutterstock.com Beliefs

People choose to buy food from farmer's markets based on different values—some may value eating local, whereas others may value cheaper prices.

be an effective speaker, you must analyze the beliefs of your audience in the context of your message. For example, if you are dealing with people who believe that working hard is the only way to get ahead, you will have trouble convincing them to take time off between semesters. Your best hope is to persuade them that time off will make them more productive and goal-directed when they return. By citing authorities and providing examples of other students who have successfully followed this course, you have a chance of changing their mindset.

Values are deep-seated abstract judgments about what is important to us. According to Rokeach's (1968) seminal work, we have both terminal and instrumental values. *Terminal values* are those we would like to achieve within our lifetime. These include national security, family security, equality, and freedom. *Instrumental values* help us achieve the terminal values, such as intellect, ambition, self-control, responsibility, and independence. Values separate the worthwhile from the worthless and determine what we consider moral, desirable, important, beautiful, and worth living or dying for.

An audience of concerned students that values the importance of education might express this value in the belief that "a college education should be available to all qualified students" and the attitude that "the state legislature should pass a tuition reduction plan for every state college." If you address this audience, you can use this attitude as the basis for your plea that students picket the state capitol in support of the tuition reduction plan. Understanding your listeners' attitudes, beliefs, and values helps you put your message in the most effective terms.

ADAPTING TO DIFFERENT AUDIENCES AND SITUATIONS

Throughout this chapter and this textbook, you will read the words "it may" or "it might," or "perhaps." We are equivocal because audiences behave differently and have different expectations depending on their characteristics *and* the context or situation. An effective speaker adapts their message based on audience characteristics, both demographic and psychographic, and the situation that brings the audience together. A politician may give a speech in New York City, then tweak it before appearing at a gathering in America's heartland. Adapting a speech may be easy or difficult. In your public speaking class, it is important to keep in mind that your teacher is part of the audience. As such, you might need to make a few minor changes to be inclusive.

At a funeral, we know the mood is somber, but depending on the person being remembered and the individuals congregated, there may also be smiles and laughter. The circumstances may call for a fond memory of a person's idiosyncrasies, or in case of a tragic death, laughter may be inappropriate. Also, if **seven** people are giving eulogies, then each one should be relatively brief, but if only **two** or **three** are speaking, more time can be allotted to each person. At a political rally, a speech given to an audience that has just seen its candidate soundly defeated would sound different than a speech given by someone on behalf of the winning candidate.

INTEREST LEVEL AND EXPECTATIONS

Discovering the interest level in your topic and your audience's expectations helps you adapt to your audience. Interest level often determines audience response. High school seniors are more likely than high school freshmen to listen when someone from the financial aid office at the local college discusses scholarships, grants, and financial aid possibilities. People who fly frequently are less likely to pay attention to the flight attendant's description of safety procedures than individuals who fly less often. We tend to pay attention to things that are timely and that we know will affect us.

Experienced and successful professionals who speak frequently to audiences around the country collect information that will tell them who their listeners are and what they want and expect from their presentations. Robert Waterman Jr., coauthor of the successful book *In Search of Excellence*, indicates he spends a day or two before a speech observing his corporate audience at work. What he learns helps him address the specific concerns of his listeners (Kiechel, 1987). Waterman achieved success as a professional speaker in part because he assumed little about the characteristics of his prospective audience. To analyze an audience, questionnaires, observation, and interviews are techniques that can be used successfully.

ACCESSING AUDIENCE INFORMATION

To adapt our message to a particular audience within a specific situation, we need to gather information. Three ways to access your audience's demographic and psychographic characteristics as well as their interest level and expectations include creating a questionnaire, observing, and interviewing.

© Rachael Warriner/Shutterstock.com

The Sunrise Movement relied heavily on online focus groups to show politicians that more Americans cared about the environment, leading to policy proposals such as the Green New Deal.

USING A QUESTIONNAIRE

Public opinion polls are an American tradition, especially around election time. Just about anything is up for analysis, from views on candidates to opinions on foreign policy to ice cream preferences and brand recognition.

A questionnaire can determine the specific demographic characteristics of your listeners as well as their perceptions of you and your topic. It can also tell you how much knowledge your listeners have about your topic and the focus they would prefer in your speech.

By surveying all your classmates, sampling every fourth person in your dorm, or emailing selected members of your audience to ask them questions, you can find out information about your audience in advance. These methods are simple and effective. In addition, and depending on the age of your intended audience, online survey creation and response tabulation companies like SurveyMonkey.com now make it easier to poll a group of people via the Internet.

The first step in using a questionnaire is to design specific questions that are likely to get you the information you need. Three basic types of questions are most helpful to public speakers: fixed-alternative questions, scale questions, and open-ended questions (Churchill, 1983).

Fixed-alternative questions limit responses to specific choices, yielding valuable information about such demographic factors as age, education, and income. Fixed-alternative questions can offer many responses, or they can offer only **two** alternatives, such as yes/no questions. The following is an example of a fixed-alternative question focusing on attitudes:

Do you think collegiate athletes should be paid? (Choose one)

Collegiate athletes should be paid in addition to receiving sports scholarships.

Collegiate athletes should only receive scholarships.

Collegiate athletes should be paid in addition to receiving merit/academic scholarships.

Collegiate athletes should not be paid or receive scholarships.

No opinion.

This type of question is easy to answer, tabulate, and analyze. These questions yield standardized responses. For example, it would be more difficult to ask people, "How many times a week do you eat out?" without supplying possible responses, because you may receive answers like "regularly," "rarely," "every day," and "twice a day." Interpreting these answers is more difficult.

Fixed-alternative questions avoid confusion. When asking for marital status, consider providing specific choices. Do not ask about marital status if it is irrelevant to your topic.

What is your marital status?

Single
Widowed
Married
Divorced

The disadvantage of using fixed-alternative questions is that it may force people to respond to a question when they are uncertain or have no opinion, especially if you fail to include "no opinion" as a possible response.

Scale questions are a type of fixed-alternative question that asks people to respond to questions set up along a continuum. For example:

How often do you vote?

Always   Regularly   Sometimes   Seldom   Never

If you develop a continuum that can be used repeatedly, several issues can be addressed quickly. For example, you can ask people to use the same scale to tell you how frequently they vote in presidential elections, congressional elections, state elections, and local elections. The disadvantage of the scale question is that it is difficult to get in-depth information about a topic.

In an open-ended question, audience members can respond however they wish. For example:

How do you feel about a 12-month school year for K-12 students?

In response to this question about extending the school year, one person may write, "Keep the school year as it is," whereas another may suggest a workable plan for extending the year. Because the responses to open-ended questions are so different, they can be difficult to analyze. The advantage to these questions is that they allow you to probe for details and you give respondents the opportunity to tell you what is on their minds. Here are some guidelines for constructing usable questions.

GUIDELINES FOR SURVEY QUESTIONS

Avoid leading questions. Try not to lead people to the response you desire through the wording of your question. Here are two examples of leading questions:

> Do you feel stricter handgun legislation would stop the wanton *killing* of innocent people?

> Do you believe able-bodied men who are *too lazy* to work should be eligible for welfare?

These questions should be reworded. For example, "Do you support stricter handgun legislation?" is no longer a leading question.

Avoid ambiguity. When you use words that can be interpreted in different ways, you reduce the value of a question. For example:

How often do you drink alcohol?

Frequently   Occasionally   Sometimes   Never

In this case, one person's "sometimes" may be another person's "occasionally." To avoid ambiguity, rephrase the possible responses to more useful fixed-alternatives:

How often do you drink alcohol?

More than once a week
At least once a month
Less than twice every 6 months
Never

Ask everyone the same questions. Because variations in the wording of questions can change responses, always ask questions in the same way. Do not ask one person, "Under what circumstances would you consider enlisting in the Army?" and another, "If the United States were attacked by a foreign nation, would you consider joining the Army?" Both of these questions relate to enlisting in the military. The first one is an open question whereas the second is a closed question. The answers you receive to the first question have much more information value than the second, which could be answered "yes" or "no." If you do not ask people the same questions, your results may be inaccurate.

Be aware of time constraints. Although questionnaires can help you determine interest, attitudes, and knowledge level, they also take time. If your instructor allows you to pass out a questionnaire in class, make sure it takes only a few minutes to complete. Make it brief and clear. Ask only what is necessary and make sure the format fits your purpose. Even if there is no structured time in class for a survey, you can still catch students between classes, during group work in class, and by email. Any time spent getting to know your audience helps ensure you are audience-centered.

OBSERVE AND INTERVIEW

You may find that the best way to gather information about a prospective audience is to assume the role of an observer. If you want to inform your audience about the effects of technology on communication, you could observe how phone usage affects conversations in the student union at your university. Share your observations during the speech: Did people on their cell phones and laptops seem less engaged with the people they were sitting with?

If you want to persuade your audience to get more involved with issues on campus, you might attend a student government meeting to see how many students attend (other than those *in* student government), and what types of issues are brought forth. Then you could interview members of the group as well as audience members to find their perceptions of student involvement on campus.

The information you gather from observing and interviewing is likely to be richer if you adopt a less formal style than you used in a traditional audience analysis questionnaire to gather information about your speech topic.

CREATING THE SPEAKER–AUDIENCE CONNECTION

It takes only seconds for listeners to tune out your message. Convince your audience your message has value by centering your message on your listeners and adapting your message to that specific audience and situation. The following suggestions will help you build the type of audience connection that leads to the message being understood and well received.

GET TO THE POINT QUICKLY

First impressions count. What you say in the first few minutes is critical. Tell your listeners how you can help them first, not last. If you save your suggestions to the end, it may be that no one is listening. Experienced speakers try to make connections with their listeners as they open their speeches. For example, here is how one CEO addressed falling sales to his employees, "Good afternoon. Sales are down. Profits are gone. What's next? Jobs. I want to see all of you here again next month, but that may not happen. Let me explain how we got here and what we can do." With an opening like that, you can bet the CEO had the full attention of all employees present.

HAVE CONFIDENCE: THEY WANT TO HEAR YOUR SPEECH

It happens frequently: Speakers with relatively little knowledge about a subject are asked to speak to a group of experts on that subject. An educator may talk to a group of athletes about intercollegiate sports. A lawyer may talk to a group of doctors about the doctor–patient relationship. When you feel your listeners know more than you do about your topic, realize they have invited you for a reason. In most cases, they want your opinion. Despite their knowledge, you have a perspective they find interesting. Athletes may want to learn how the college sports program is viewed by a professor, and doctors want to hear a lawyer's opinion about malpractice. Simply acknowledging your audience's education or intelligence and mentioning your contribution may be a unique approach, and also may help create a bond of mutual respect.

USE HUMOR

Humor can help you connect with your audience and help them think of you as approachable rather than remote. Opening your speech with something that makes people smile or laugh can put both you and your listeners at ease. Subject and self-deprecating humor play well; insulting your audience does not. Effective humor should be related in some way to the subject of your speech, your audience, or the occasion. So, starting with a joke that is wholly unrelated to your topic is inappropriate. Also, remember that some of us have difficulty being funny. Others of us do not gauge the audience well. In either of these cases, attempts at humor may end up falling flat or offending. So be careful: Useless or ineffective humor can damage your credibility and hurt your connection with your audience. Yet, when well executed, humor is a powerful tool in your speaker arsenal.

SPEAKING EXCELLENCE IN YOUR CAREER

Being audience-centered can be challenging for new communication professionals. With hurdles such as speaking anxiety, audience apathy, and general lack of experience, it can be difficult for speakers to connect with their audience in a meaningful way. It has been well established that humor is an effective tool for gaining rapport with an audience, but many students have issues with using humor effectively (and appropriately). Researchers Dick Carpenter, Marjory Webster, and Chad Bowman discuss how humor can be used appropriately in public speaking and formal situations in the workplace—even for the most powerful individuals in the United States.

The researchers studied U.S. presidents from Franklin Roosevelt to George W. Bush, specifically looking at how these individuals used humor as a leadership tool. Presidents may use humor to lighten the mood when talking to the press, and some have even gone as far as to hire specific speech writers to focus on humor (Carpenter, Webster, & Bowman, 2019). The researchers note how humor can help create a speaker–audience connection, which can make the listeners more in tune to the actual content of the speech in addition to the humor. Now, you may consider how adding humor may relate to audience members or draw that back in mid-speech if you are nervous about their audience drifting. Humor can also be used in your career field to add some dynamism to mundane office presentations.

GET PERSONAL

Connections can be made by linking yourself directly to the group you are addressing and by referring to your audience with the pronoun "you" rather than the third person "they." The word "you" inserts your listeners into the middle of your presentation and makes it clear that you are focusing attention on them.

Content is another way to make it personal. Stories, anecdotes, and examples from your own experience are generally appreciated. But keep in mind, there is too much of a good thing where self-disclosure is concerned. Abide by this rule: If you are not comfortable with it being put in the headlines of the local paper, leave it out of your speech.

ENCOURAGE PARTICIPATION

When you invite the listeners to participate in your speech, they become partners in the event. One of the author's friends, a first-degree black belt in karate, gave a motivational speech to a group of college women at a state university in Michigan. At the beginning of her speech, and to the excitement of the crowd, she broke several boards. She talked about her childhood, her lack of self-esteem, and her struggle to become a well-adjusted businesswoman. She used the phrase "I can succeed" several times during her speech and encouraged her audience to join in with her. By the end of her speech, the group, standing, invigorated, and excited, shouted with her, "I can succeed!"

Another way to involve your listeners is to choose a member of your audience to take part in your talk—have the volunteer help you with a demonstration, do some role-playing—and the rest of the group will feel like one of their own is up there at the podium. Involve the entire audience and they will hang onto your every word. Although adding participation takes time away from your speaking, it is well worth the investment. And, like using humor, you will find it also lightens the mood and sets a favorable tone.

EXAMINE OTHER SITUATIONAL CHARACTERISTICS

When planning your speech, other situational characteristics need to be considered, including time of day, size of the audience, and size of the room.

Room size is important because it influences how loudly you must speak and determines whether you need a microphone. As a student, you will probably be speaking in a classroom. But in other speaking situations, you may find yourself in a convention hall, a small office, or an outdoor setting where only the lineup of chairs determines the size of the speaking space.

If you are delivering an after-dinner speech in your own dining room to 10 members of your reading group, you do not have to worry about projecting your voice to the back row of a large room. If, in contrast, you are delivering a commencement address in your college auditorium to a thousand graduates, you will need to use a microphone. And keep in mind, proper microphone technique takes practice, preferably in the auditorium in which you will speak.

LEARN AS YOU GO

Discovering what your audience thought of your speech can help you give a better speech next time. Realizing the importance of feedback, some professional speakers hand out post-speech questionnaires designed to find out where they succeeded and where they failed to meet audience needs. At workshops, feedback is often provided through questionnaires that can be turned in at the end or at any time during the event. When you are the speaker, you may choose to interview someone, distribute questionnaires randomly to a dozen people, or even ask the entire audience to provide feedback.

Valuable information often emerges from audience feedback, which enables speakers to adjust their presentations for the next occasion. For example, let's assume you delivered a speech to a civic organization on the increasing problem of drunk boating. You handed out questionnaires to the entire audience after your message. Results indicated that your audience would have preferred fewer statistics and more concrete suggestions for combating the problem. In addition, one listener offered a good way to make current laws more easily understood, a suggestion you may incorporate into your next presentation.

Finding out what your audience thought may be simple. In your public speaking class, your fellow classmates may give you immediate, written feedback. In other situations, especially if you are running a workshop or seminar, you may want to hand out a written questionnaire at the end of your speech and ask listeners to return it at a later time. Online survey tools (e.g., SurveyMonkey) are free and can provide rich feedback for you after your speech. Here are four questions you might ask:

1. Did the speech answer your questions about the topic? If not, what questions remain?
2. How can you apply the information you learned in the presentation to your own situation?
3. What part of the presentation was most helpful? Least helpful?
4. How could the presentation have better met your needs?

To encourage an honest and complete response, indicate in the instructions that people do not have to offer their names in the questionnaire. Remember that the goal of feedback is an improvement, not ego gratification. Focus on positive feedback as much as possible and take negative comments as areas for growth.

Your ability to create and maintain a strong connection with your audience is helped by a clear understanding of their demographics and psychographics. Using this information will set you on track for an exceptional experience, for you and your audience.

DIGITAL CITIZENSHIP

Many upcoming activists are taking to Twitter in order to connect with people who share a similar vision. One such activist is the Swedish schoolgirl Greta Thunberg. Greta is passionate about putting a stop to climate change, and has gained support on Twitter from over 700 thousand followers (Thunberg, 2019). Her Twitter popularity led to the Youth Strike for Climate movement, where Greta has helped organize climate strikes in over 105 countries (Carrington, 2019). Greta continues to be active on and off of Twitter, resulting in her nomination for the Nobel peace prize.

© photocosmos1/Shutterstock.com

1. What might be some common demographics of Greta's Twitter followers?

2. If you were to advise Greta on how to start a climate strike in your area, what would be some characteristics of people in your community that she should know?

3. Practice writing a Tweet compelling people in your community to hold their own climate strike. Remember you have a maximum character limit of 280 characters, but most successful Tweets are much shorter.

Carrington, D. (2019, March 14). Greta Thunberg nominated for Nobel peace prize. *The Guardian.*

Thunberg, G. [Twitter page]. Available at https://twitter.com/GretaThunberg?s=17. Accessed 29 June 2019..

SUMMARY

- Being audience-centered and adapting to the audience's needs are critical factors in creating effective presentations.

- Your ability to create and maintain a strong connection with your audience is helped by a clear understanding of their demographics and psychographics. Using this information will set you on track for an exceptional experience, for you and your audience.

- A questionnaire can determine the specific demographic characteristics of your listeners as well as their perceptions of you and your topic. It can also tell you how much knowledge your listeners have about your topic and the focus they would prefer in your speech.

- The information you gather from observing and interviewing is likely to be richer if you adopt a less formal style than you used in a traditional audience analysis questionnaire to gather information about your speech topic.

- One of the best ways to gather information about a prospective audience is to assume the role of an observer. Watch the actions and mannerisms of your audience, and learn what their motivations and expectations are.

- You can create a personalized experience for your audience by speaking with confidence, using humor effectively and appropriately, making content personal, and encouraging participation.

KEY TERMS

Adapting—making your speech fit the audience's needs.

Attitudes—predispositions to act in a particular way that influences our response to objects, events, and situations.

Audience-centered—showing your audience you understand their needs and want to help them achieve their goals.

Beliefs—represent a mental and emotional acceptance of information. They are judgments about the truth or the probability that a statement is correct.

Demographics—age, gender, race and ethnicity, education/ knowledge, group affiliation, occupational group, socioeconomic status, religious background, political affiliation, and geographic identifiers of listeners.

Ethnocentrism—the belief that one's own culture is superior to other cultures.

Fixed-alternative questions—limit responses to several choices, yielding valuable information about such demographic factors as age, education, and income.

Open-ended questions—audience members can respond however they wish.

Psychographics—refer to the behaviors, attitudes, beliefs, and values of your listeners.

Scale questions—a type of fixed-alternative question that asks people to respond to questions set up along a continuum.

Stereotypes—avoid generalizations related to race, ethnicity, or nationality, even if these groups are not present in your audience.

Values—socially shared ideas about what is good, right, and desirable; deep-seated abstract judgments about what is important to us.

Respond to the following questions without reviewing the text or your notes. These questions are provided to help you practice retrieving information and reflect on your reading.

A. How would you define audience analysis?

B. Did you agree or disagree with anything you read?

C. What did you learn that was new to you?

D. What concepts, if any, were confusing to you?

Respond to the following questions. You may reference your text or notes to help you.

1. What does it mean to be audience-centered?

2. What are 10 key demographics?

3. What are psychographics?

4. What is a type of fixed-alternative question that asks people to respond to questions set up along a continuum?

5. What are some guidelines for survey questions?

1. Why will a speech fail in the absence of audience analysis? What speeches have you seen that didn't consider the audience?

2. What demographic characteristics does this class have in common? Where does this class differ in terms of demographic characteristics? Why are some demographic characteristics important to the success of your speech in one situation but not so important in another situation?

3. With your group, brainstorm a few items that would help you measure the attitudes and beliefs of your audience about your group's topic. When you are finished, discuss the process. What items were relatively easy to develop and what items were more difficult? Why were they easy or difficult?

4. We talked about humor in Chapter 5 and again in this chapter. How do you feel about using humor in your presentation? What would make you feel more or less comfortable about using humor?

5. Discuss the ethical questions provided at the end of the first chapter. What ethical considerations are relevant to information about reasoning, fallacies, and persuasive speaking in general?

- Are there guidelines (e.g., don't lie) that would be appropriate for every situation, or are ethics relative?

- Do the ends (e.g., a good outcome) justify any means?

- Is deceiving the receiver ever appropriate?

- Should the source of the message bear primary responsibility for ethics, or should the receiver share that responsibility (e.g., buyer beware)?

REFERENCES

Churchill, G. A., Jr. (1983). *Marketing research: Methodological foundations*, (3rd Ed.) Chicago: The Dryden Press.

Griffin, J. D. (1989, July 16). To snare the feet of greatness: The American dream is alive (Speech). Reprinted in *Vital Speeches of the Day, September 15, 1989, 735–736.*

Guerra, J. (2014, July 16). Teaching students how to switch between black English and standard English can help them get ahead. *State of Opportunity.* Retrieved from http://stateofopportunity.michiganradio.org/post/teaching-students-how-switch-between-black-english-and-standard-english-can-help-them-get-ahead

Holland, J. (1988). Whose children are these? The family connection (Speech). Reprinted in *Vital Speeches of the Day, July 1, 1988, 559.*

Kiechel, W., III. (1987, June 8). How to give a speech. *Fortune*, 179.

Kushner, Harold S. (2002). *When all you've ever wanted isn't enough: the search for a life that matters.* New York: Random House.

Mazur, M. (2015, January 29). 5 ways to make the audience the star of your presentation. *Fast Company.* Retrieved from http://www.fastcompany.com/3041558/5-ways-to-make-the-audience-the-star-of-your-presentation

Melendez, S. (2016, April 27). What it's like to use a chatbot to apply for jobs. *Fast Company.* Retrieved from http://www.fastcompany.com/3059265/the-future-of-work/what-its-like-to-use-a-chatbot-to-apply-for-jobs

Noonan, P. (1989, October 15). Confessions of a White House speechwriter, *New York Times*, 72.

Pilkington, E. (2009, January 29). Barack Obama inauguration speech. *The Guardian*. Accessed August 4, 2011 from www.guardian.co.uk/world/2009/jan/20/barack-obama-inauguration-us-speech.

Rackleff, R. B. (1987, September 26). The art of speechwriting: A dramatic event (speech). Reprinted in *Vital Speeches of the Day, March 1, 1988*.

Rokeach, M. (1968). The role of values in public opinion research. *Public Opinion Quarterly, 32*(4), 547–559.

Sharples, A. J. (2014). "Do you know why that's funny?" Connecting the scholarship of humor to the practice of after-dinner speaking. *National Forensic Journal, 32*(1), 4-20.

The Y, Share the Day. (2010, July 12). A Brand New Day: The YMCA Unveils New Brand Strategy to Further Community Impact. Retrieved August 4, 2011 from www.ymca.net/news-releases/20100712-brand- new-day.html.

Wahl, S.T., & Scholl, J. (2014). *Communication and culture in your life*. Dubuque, IA: Kendall Hunt

Wrege, L. (2016, April 25). Overcoming cerebral palsy. *The Herald Palladium*. Retrieved from http://www.heraldpalladium.com/news/local/overcoming-cerebral-palsy/article_47073098-4f76-5713-87a7-16464f4f1b8e.html

CHAPTER 14

PERSUASIVE SPEAKING IN THEORY AND PRACTICE

BEFORE YOU READ

Respond to the following questions before you read the chapter.

1. Do you have a story to tell your audience about your topic? If not, brainstorm some ideas or search for a source that includes a story.

2. How do you plan to use ethos in your final presentation? How will you use pathos? How will you use logos?

3. Will you have a balance of ethos, pathos, and logos for your final presentation? If not, what is lacking? What information do you need to add or remove?

SPEAKING IN CONTEXT

On June 23, 2016, the United Kingdom (UK) voted to leave the European Union (EU), becoming the first nation to leave the European Union since its creation in 1993. Known as "Brexit," the move was heavily

LEARNING OBJECTIVES

- IDENTIFY THE THREE DIFFERENT LEVELS ON WHICH PERSUASIVE COMMUNICATION TAKES PLACE.
- DEFINE THE FIVE LEVELS OF MASLOW'S HIERARCHY OF NEEDS.
- RECOGNIZE THE DIFFERENT TYPES OF ARGUMENT FALLACIES.
- UNDERSTAND THE FOUR PERSUASIVE AIMS OF SPEAKING.
- DEFINE THE THREE TYPES OF PERSUASIVE CLAIMS.
- IDENTITY ORGANIZATIONAL PATTERNS FOR PERSUASIVE SPEECHES AND ANALYZE WHICH MAY BE THE BEST FIT FOR YOUR SPEECH.
- RECOGNIZE AND DEVELOP THE FIVE STEPS OF MONROE'S MOTIVATED SEQUENCE.

divisive; more than 30 million British citizens (71.8% of voters) voted in the referendum, with the leave position winning 52% to 48% of the vote. Although the referendum was passed, many questions and issues were presented to both the United Kingdom and the European Union. Would British citizens still be able to move and work freely in European Union countries? What will happen to EU nationals currently working in the United Kingdom? While many of these questions await answers, many individuals expressed surprise that the measure passed in the first place. Writers for the British Broadcasting organization examined the persuasive tactics of Boris Johnson, one of the leaders of the Vote Leave campaign.

Boris Johnson, a senior member of the Conservative Party and now the Prime Minister of the United Kingdom, often argued that the European Union was holding Great Britain back by imposing too many rules on British businesses and charging billions of pounds a year in membership fees (Wheeler & Hunt, 2016). Johnson also criticized the "free movement" of European Union members, which allowed many non-British citizens to enter and work freely in the United Kingdom. Johnson appealed to citizens to take back full control of their borders and reduce the number of foreigners coming to live and work in the United Kingdom. In the end, Johnson was successful in persuading a majority of British voters to end the economic partnership with the European Union.

As you learn the skills needed to become a successful persuasive speaker, remember the importance of appealing to your audience's needs. Many voters in the United Kingdom were initially skeptical of the plan to leave the European Union, but Johnson and his fellow Vote Leave supporters succeeded in changing public opinion by catering to the concerns and needs of their audience. Whether you agree or disagree with the Brexit vote, analyzing the persuasive tactics employed by both sides can help you become a more effective persuader.

THE AUDIENCE IN PERSUASIVE SPEAKING

Imagine the following situations:

- You talk to a student group on campus about the benefits of spending a semester with the Disney College Program in Orlando, Florida.
- You speak before your city council, urging them to implement a curbside recycling program.
- You speak before a group of parents of the high school musical cast to get them to volunteer to help make tickets, sell tickets, sell concessions, monitor students during rehearsal, work on the set, work backstage, sell advertisements, work with costume rental, and design and sell T-shirts.

Your success or failure to get your audience to act in the situations above is determined by a number of factors. Knowing who your listeners are is important. But, in a persuasive speech, knowing *the attitude of your audience* is crucial, and trying to *determine the needs* of the audience is important to your success.

In general, we can classify audience attitudes into three categories: (1) they agree, (2) they don't agree, and (3) they are undecided. When you are clear on which category your audience rests in, you will be able to craft a more targeted, effective message. Here is a closer examination of each category.

The **supportive audience**, the audience that agrees with you, poses the least difficulty. This type of audience is friendly; its members like you, and they are interested in hearing what you have to say. Your main objective is to reinforce what they already accept. You want to strengthen their resolve or use it to encourage behavioral change. You also want to keep them enthused about your point of view or action plan. A candidate for state's attorney who has invited a group of friends and colleagues to an ice cream social will use that time to restate their strengths and urge attendees to help him/her with the campaign.

The audience that agrees with you will welcome *new* information, but does not need a rehashing of information already known and accepted. The speaker should work to strengthen the audience's resistance to counter persuasion. For example, the candidate for state's attorney who is running against an incumbent can talk about how change is necessary, and how their experience or background will bring a fresh perspective to the office.

With the **opposed audience**, the speaker runs the risk of having members in the audience who may be hostile. This audience does not agree with you, it is not friendly or sympathetic, and most likely, will search for flaws in your argument. Your objective in this case is to get a fair hearing. A persuasive speaker facing a group that does not agree with him/her needs to set reasonable goals. Also, developing arguments carefully by using fair and respected evidence may help persuade an audience that disagrees with you.

One thing to consider when facing an audience opposed to you is the nature of their opposition. Is it to you? Your cause? A specific statement you made or information made available to them? If you can determine why they are opposed, your effort can be spent on addressing the nature of the opposition.

Seeking common ground is a good strategy when people do not agree with you. Find a place where you and your audience can stand without disagreeing. For example, hospital employees who smoke may not be willing to quit, but they may recognize the need to have smoking banned on hospital property, so they may still smoke on break if they go off-site.

Acknowledging differences is also a helpful strategy for the opposed audience. Making sure you do not set your attitudes, beliefs, or values to be "right" and the audience's to be "wrong" is essential if any movement toward your point of view is likely. Avoid needless confrontation.

Speaking before an **uncommitted audience** can be difficult because you don't know whether they are uninformed, indifferent, or are adamantly neutral. This audience is neither friendly nor hostile, but most likely, they are not sympathetic.

The uninformed audience is the easiest to persuade, because they need information. A scholarship committee trying to determine which of the five candidates will receive $2,000 needs sufficient information about the candidates to make an informed choice.

The indifferent audience member doesn't really care about the issue or topic. These audience members can be found in most "mandatory" meetings held at work, school, and sometimes training. In this case, it is important that the speaker gets the attention of the audience members and gives them a reason to care. Making the message relate to their lives is important, and providing audience members with relevant, persuasive material helps move audience members out of the uncommitted category. However, it may be difficult to sway most or all audience members.

The neutral audience member has the tendency to not take either side of an issue. The person may be well-informed on the subject, but does not want to make a definitive choice.

MASLOW'S HIERARCHY OF NEEDS

Knowing the audience's disposition toward you helps you structure a more effective persuasive speech. Speakers should also consider the needs of the audience. The persuader can develop lines of reasoning that relate to pertinent needs. Human needs can be described in terms of logic or what makes sense to a listener, but needs are immersed in emotions of the individual as well.

Psychologist Abraham Maslow (1943) classified human needs according to the hierarchy pictured in Figure 14.1. Maslow believed that our most basic needs—those at the foundation of the hierarchy—must be satisfied before we can consider those on the next levels. In effect, these higher-level needs are put on "hold," and have little effect on our actions, until the lower-level needs are met. Maslow's hierarchy provides a catalog of targets for emotional appeals, including the following:

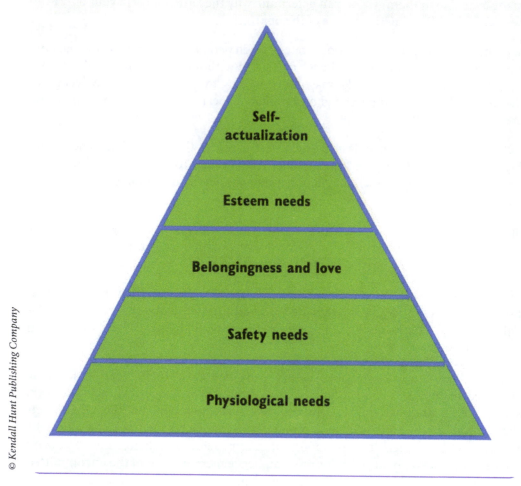

FIGURE 14.1 Maslow's hierarchy of needs.

PHYSIOLOGICAL NEEDS. At the foundation of the hierarchy are our biological needs for food, water, oxygen, procreation, and rest. If you were delivering a speech in favor of a proposed new reservoir to a community experiencing problems with its water supply, it would be appropriate to appeal to our very basic need for safe and abundant water, without which our lives would be in danger.

SAFETY NEEDS. Safety needs include the need for security, freedom from fear and attack, a home that offers tranquility and comfort, and a means of earning a living. If you are delivering the same speech to a group of unemployed construction workers, you might link the reservoir project to safe, well-paying jobs.

BELONGINGNESS AND LOVE NEEDS. These needs refer to our drive for affiliation, friendship, and love. When appealing to the need for social belonging, you may choose to emphasize the unity and cohesiveness that will emerge from the community effort to bring the reservoir to completion.

ESTEEM NEEDS. Esteem needs include the need to be seen as worthy and competent and to have the respect of others. In this case, an effective approach would be to praise community members for their initiative in helping to make the reservoir project a reality.

SELF-ACTUALIZATION NEEDS. People who reach the top of the hierarchy seek to fulfill their highest potential through personal growth, creativity, self-awareness and knowledge, social responsibility, and responsiveness to challenge. Addressing this audience, you might emphasize the long-range environmental and ecological implications of the reservoir. Your appeal to your audience's sense of social responsibility would stress the need to safeguard the water supply for future generations.

Maslow's Hierarchy of Needs can guide you in preparing a persuasive speech. Think about the needs of your audience and how you can reach them. Understanding the basis for Maslow's hierarchy is helpful when developing a persuasive speech, for if you approach your listeners at an inappropriate level of need, you will find them unable or unwilling to respond.

ELEMENTS OF PERSUASION

As we discussed in Chapter 2, critical building blocks of persuasion have been studied by generations of rhetorical scholars, starting with Aristotle. Persuasion is intended to influence choice through what Aristotle termed ethos, pathos, and logos. More recent scholarly work has provided the addition of mythos. These four elements provide the underpinnings of our modern study of persuasion.

To illustrate these, let's consider the speech given days after the deadly earthquake, tsunami, and nuclear disaster struck Japan. Here is how Emperor Akihito addressed a stunned nation on March 16, 2011:

> The 9.0 earthquake that struck the Tohoku-Pacific region was an extraordinarily large earthquake. I have been deeply hurt by the miserable situation in the affected areas. The number of deaths from earthquakes and tsunamis has increased day by day, and we do not know yet how many victims we will eventually have. I pray for the survival of as many people as possible. (Emperor Akihito, 2011)

© thele y/Shutterstock.com

Emperor Akihito relied heavily on ethos in his speech, as we will see later with other excerpts.

ETHOS AND THE POWER OF THE SPEAKER'S CREDIBILITY

As a speaker, you must decide not only what to tell your audience, but also what you should avoid saying. In a persuasive speech, you ask listeners to think or act in ways needed to achieve the desired response. Aristotle believed that **ethos**, which refers to speaker credibility, makes speakers worthy of belief. Audiences trust speakers they perceive as honest. Ethics provide standards for conduct

In Western society, Aristotle is considered one of the founders of persuasive rhetoric.

that guide us. Persuasive speaking requires asking others to accept and act on ideas we believe to be accurate and true.

We see the Japanese emperor standing on the firm ground of the credibility of his office. In Japanese culture, the emperor has typically been recognized as both statesman-ruler and messenger from God. When the emperor spoke, everyone listened, due in large part to his inherent credibility. Let's take a closer look at what makes up an impression of ethos or speaker credibility.

DIMENSIONS OF SPEAKER CREDIBILITY

What your audience knows about you before you speak and what they learn about your position during your speech may influence your ability to persuade them. As we discussed in Chapters 2 and 4, credibility is a multidimensional concept. Here, we'll consider again the dimensions of intelligence and good character and we'll introduce dynamism.

INTELLIGENCE. In many cases, your audience will decide your message's value based on perceived speaker intelligence or expertise. Your listeners will first ask themselves whether you have the background to speak. If the topic is a crime, an audience is more likely to be persuaded by the Atlanta chief of police than by a postal worker delivering her personal opinions. Second, your audience will consider whether the content of your speech has firm support. When it is clear that speakers have not researched their topic, their ability to persuade diminishes. Finally, audiences will determine whether you communicate confidence and control of your subject matter through your delivery.

© Attila JANDI/Shutterstock.com

Akihito wields enormous persuasive power.

In our example above, Emperor Akihito makes clear that he is abreast of all the relevant information. He relays the strength of the earthquake, the results of the tsunami, and the seriousness of the nuclear disaster. Listeners quickly understood that he was well informed in this emergency. His display of expertise by demonstrating an understanding of the facts increases his credibility even further.

GOOD CHARACTER. When someone is trying to persuade us to think or act a certain way, trusting that person is important. And although intelligence is important, research has shown that the trustworthy communicator is more influential than the untrustworthy one, regardless of their level of expertise (Wahl, 2013; Wahl & Maresh-Fuehrer, 2016).

Audience perceptions of good character are based largely on your perceived respect for them, your ethical standards, and your ability to establish common ground. Audiences gauge a speaker's respect for them by analyzing the actions a speaker has taken before the speech. If a group is listening to a political candidate running for office in their community, they will have more respect for someone who has demonstrated concern for their community through past actions.

Good character is also influenced by the audience's perception of your ethical standards. Telling the truth is paramount for the persuasive speaker. If your message is biased and you make little attempt to be fair or to concede the strength of your opponent's point of view, your listeners may question your integrity.

Your credibility and your ability to persuade increase if you convince your audience that you share "common ground." In the popular movie 300, Queen Gorgo addresses a reluctant Spartan Council, pleading with them to send the Spartan army into battle. Rather than appealing to the council as queen, she appeals to common ground in the opening: "Councilmen, I stand before you today not only as your Queen: I come to you as a mother; I come to you as a wife; I come to you as a Spartan woman; I come to you with great humility" (American Rhetoric: Movie speeches, 2007).

While few can identify with being a queen, most feel a sense of identification with a humble mother, wife, woman, or citizen. With this common ground appeal in place, the stage is set for the queen to persuade the council to side with her. In this instance, Queen Gorgo establishes common ground by identifying with her audience and provoking them to identify with her.

DYNAMISM. Your credibility and, therefore, your ability to persuade are influenced by the audience's perception of you as a dynamic spokesperson. Dynamic speakers tend to be vibrant, confident, vigorous, attractive, and skilled in public speaking. Your listeners will make critical decisions about how dynamic you are as they form a first impression. This impression will be reinforced or altered as they listen for an energetic style that communicates a commitment to your point of view, and for ideas that build on one another in a convincing, logical way. While charisma plays a part in being dynamic, it is not enough. Dynamic public speakers tend to be well-practiced presenters.

Does credibility make a difference in your ability to persuade? Pornpitakpan (2004), who examined five decades of research on the persuasiveness of speaker credibility, found that "a high-credibility source is more persuasive than is a low-credibility source in both changing attitudes and gaining behavioral compliance" (p. 266).

Lifelong learning in the art of persuasion involves building and enhancing your speaker ethos.

PATHOS AND THE POWER OF EMOTION

Aristotle argued that **pathos**, which is the "consideration of the emotions of people in the audience" is an integral part of persuasion (Kennedy, 2007, p. 15).

Emperor Akihito makes use of emotion in his message. Although stoic by American standards, he acknowledges the suffering of victims:

> [U]nder the severe cold weather, many evacuees have been placed in an unavoidable situation where they are subject to extreme suffering due to the lack of food, drinking water, fuel, and so on. I truly hope that, by making the greatest effort possible to rescue the victims promptly, we can improve their lives as much as possible" (Emperor Akihito, 2011).

Akihito's reference to extreme suffering adds an emotional appeal to support the need for continued rescue efforts.

Emotional appeals have the power to elicit happiness, joy, pride, patriotism, fear, hate, anger, guilt, despair, hope, hopelessness, bitterness, and other feelings. Some subjects are more emotionally powerful than others and lend themselves to emotional appeals. Look at the list of topics that follow:

- The homeless
- Abused children
- Cruelty to animals
- Death penalty
- Sex education in school
- Teaching evolution in school
- Gun control
- Terrorist attacks

Many of these topics cause listeners to have emotional responses. Emotional appeals are often the most persuasive type of appeal because they provide the motivation listeners need to change their minds or take action. For example, instead of simply listing the reasons sugary foods are unhealthy, a more effective approach is to tie these foods to frightening consequences:

> Jim thought nothing could ever happen to him. He was healthy as an ox—or so he thought. His world fell apart one sunny May morning when he suffered a massive heart attack. He survived, but his doctors told him that his coronary arteries were blocked and that he needed bypass surgery. "Why me?" he asked. "I'm only 42 years old." The answer, he was told, had a lot to do with the sugar-heavy diet he had eaten since childhood.

This illustration appeals to the listener's emotional state, and is ultimately more persuasive than a list of facts.

We must not forget that emotional appeals are powerful, and as such, can be tools of manipulation in the hands of unscrupulous speakers who attempt to arouse audiences through emotion rather than logic. For example, in an effort to lose weight, individuals may buy pills or exercise equipment that may be useless, or worse, a true health risk. Those selling the products accept the emotional message ("lose weight, look beautiful, gain friends, have a great life").

The speaker has an ethical responsibility when using emotional appeals. The ethically responsible speaker does not distort, delete, or exaggerate information for the sole purpose of emotionally charging an audience to manipulate their feelings for self-centered ends.

ENGAGING IN COMMUNITY

For Colonel Christopher Holshek, the value of community service can be defined quite simply: when people serve their community, they help create a better country. Holshek, who has been active in the community spanning a 30-year career in the army, plans to bring home the principles he learned from an unusual career he describes as working "the many spaces in between" a citizen and a soldier (Shen, 2016). By participating in a cross-country motorcycle ride, Holshek plans to share his message of community service and citizenship.

The cross-country motorcycle journey will be known as the National Service Ride. Holshek's goal is to generate a more positive narrative about community service by stopping at schools and community events to teach the value of "service learning," the idea that valuable skills can be gained by volunteering at a local level. Anyone is allowed to join in his motorcycle journey, which Holshek believes links the motorcycle's appeal for personal freedom and mobility with the idea of connecting people around the country. The Ride has support from several advocacy organizations, including the Service Year Alliance, United Nations Association, Alliance for Peacebuilding, and several others (Shen, 2016). For anyone else who wants to help, Holshek encourages them to spread the word through social media links and by serving in their own communities.

"Too many of us are looking around and blaming the government or someone other than ourselves for what we think is wrong today," said Holshek. "But if you want to see things get better, start by looking in the mirror and asking yourself, 'how can I contribute?' The more you do that the more you see what's right and good in people and things."

LOGOS AND THE POWER OF LOGICAL APPEALS AND ARGUMENTS

Logos, or logical appeals and arguments, refers to the "rational, factual basis that supports the speaker's position" (Walker, 2005, p. 3). For example, if a friend tried to convince you not to buy a new car by pointing out that you are in college, have no savings account, and are currently unemployed, that friend would be making a logical argument.

ANATOMY OF AN ARGUMENT: CLAIM, DATA, WARRANT

Logical, critical thinking increases your ability to assess, analyze, and advocate ideas. Decades ago, Stephen Toulmin (1958), a British philosopher, developed a model of practical reasoning that consists of three basic elements: claim, data, and warrant. To construct a sound, reasonable argument, you need to use three essential parts:

1. The **claim** is a statement or a contention the audience is urged to accept. The claim answers the question, "So what is your point?

    Example: It's your turn to do the dishes; I did them last time.

    Example: You need to call your sister this week; she called you last week.

2. The **data** are evidence in support of an idea you advocate. Data provide the answer to "So what is your proof?" or "Why?"

    Example: It looks like rain. Dark clouds are forming.

    Example: When I stop at McDonald's on the road, they seem to have clean bathrooms.

3. The **warrant** is an inference that links the evidence with the claim.

    It answers the question, "Why does that data mean your claim is true?"

    Example: Augie is running a fever. I bet he has an ear infection.

    Example: Sarah will be on time. There isn't any traffic right now.

To put the three elements of an argument together, let's consider another example. At a restaurant, you take a bite of a steak sandwich and say, "This is the worst sandwich I have ever tried." With this announcement you are making a *claim* that you *infer* from tasting the meat.

The evidence (*data*) is the food before you. The *warrant* is the link between data and claim and is the inference, which may be an *unstated belief* that the food is spoiled, old, or poorly prepared, and will taste bad.

When you reason with your audience it is important to craft claims, warrants, and data your audience will understand and accept. Sound reasoning is especially important when your audience is skeptical. Faced with the task of trying to convince people to change their minds or do something they might not otherwise be inclined to do, your arguments must be impressive.

We persuade others that a claim or a conclusion is highly probable by **inductive** and **deductive reasoning**. Strong evidence shows that you have carefully analyzed the support of your points. Only when a strong probability is established you can ask your listeners to make the *inductive* leap from specific cases to a general conclusion, or to take the *deductive* move from statements as premises to a conclusion you want them to accept. We now look more closely at inductive and deductive reasoning.

INDUCTIVE REASONING

Through inductive reasoning, we generalize from specific examples to draw conclusions from what we observe. Inductive reasoning moves us from the specific to the general in an orderly, logical fashion. The inference step in the argument holds that what is true of specific cases can be generalized to other cases of the same class, or of the class as a whole. Suppose you are trying to persuade your audience that the decline of downtown merchants in your town is a problem that can be solved with an effective plan you are about to present. You may infer that what has worked to solve a similar problem in a number of similar towns is likely to work in this case as well.

One problem with inductive reasoning is that individual cases do not always add up to a correct conclusion. Sometimes a speaker's list of examples is too small, leading to an incorrect conclusion based on limited information. With inductive reasoning, you can never be sure that your conclusions are absolutely accurate. Because you are only looking at a sample of all the possible cases, you must persuade your audience to accept a conclusion that is probable, or maybe even just possible. The three most common strategies for inductive reasoning involve analogy, cause, and sign.

REASONING BY ANALOGY

Analogies establish common links between similar and not-so-similar concepts. They are effective tools of persuasion when your audience is convinced that the characteristics of one case are similar enough to the characteristics of the second case that your argument about the first also applies to the second.

As noted in the chapter on language, a *figurative analogy* draws a comparison between things that are distinctly different, such as "Eating fresh marshmallows is like floating on a cloud." Figurative analogies can be used to persuade, but they must be supported with relevant facts, statistics, and testimony that link the dissimilar concepts you are comparing.

Whereas a figurative analogy compares things that are distinctly different and supplies useful illustrations, a *literal analogy* compares things with similar characteristics and, therefore, requires less explanatory support. One speaker compared the addictive power of tobacco products, especially cigarettes, with the power of alcoholic beverages consumed on a regular basis. His line of reasoning was that both are consumed for pleasure, relaxation, and often as relief for stress. While his use of logical argument was obvious, the listener ultimately assesses whether or not these two things—alcohol and tobacco—are sufficiently similar.

The distinction between literal and figurative analogies is important because only literal analogies are sufficient to establish logical proof. Your analogy should meet the following characteristics:

- There are significant points of similarity.
- Similarities are tied to critical points of the comparison.

- Differences need to be relatively small.
- You have a better chance of convincing people if you can point to other successful cases (Freeley, 1993, pp. 119–120).

REASONING FROM CAUSE

When you reason from a cause, you infer that an event of one kind contributes to or brings about an event of another kind. The presence of a cat in a room when you are allergic to cats is likely to bring about a series of sneezes until the cat is removed. As the following example demonstrates, causal reasoning focuses on the cause-and-effect relationship between ideas.

CAUSE: An inaccurate and low census count of the homeless in Detroit

EFFECT: Fewer federal dollars will be sent to Detroit to aid the homeless

An advocate for the homeless delivered the following message to a group of supporters:

> We all know that money is allocated by the federal government, in part, according to the numbers of people in need. The census, conducted every 10 years, is supposed to tell us how many farmers we have, how many urban dwellers, and how many homeless.
>
> Unfortunately, in the 2010 census, many of the homeless were not counted in Detroit. The government told us census takers would go into the streets, into bus and train station waiting rooms, and into the shelters to count every homeless person. As advocates for the homeless, people in my organization know this was not done. Shelters were never visited. Hundreds and maybe thousands of homeless were ignored in this city alone. A serious undercount is inevitable. This undercount will cause fewer federal dollars to be spent in Detroit aiding those who need our help the most.

When used correctly, causal reasoning can be an effective persuasive tool. You must be sure that the cause-and-effect relationship is sound enough to stand up to scrutiny and criticism. To be valid, your reasoning should exhibit the following characteristics:

- The cause and effect you describe should be connected.
- The cause should be acting alone.
- The effect should not be the effect of another cause.
- The claim and evidence must be accurate (Sprague & Stuart, 1988, pp. 165–166).

To be effective, causal reasoning should never overstate. By using phrases like "This is one of several causes" or "The evidence suggests there is a cause-and-effect link," you are giving your audience a reasonable picture of a complex situation. More often than not, researchers indicate that cause-and-effect relationships are not always clear, and links may not be as simple as they seem.

REASONING FROM SIGN

With the argument from a sign, the inference step is that the presence of an attribute can be taken as the presence of some larger condition or situation of which the attribute is a part. As you step outside in the early morning to begin jogging, the gray clouds and moist air can be interpreted as signs that the weather conditions are likely to result in a rainy day.

The public speaker who reasons from sign must do so with caution. Certainly there are signs all around us to interpret in making sense of the world, but signs are easy to misinterpret. For example, saying, "Where there's fire, there's smoke" is a strong sign relationship, but saying, "Where there's smoke, there's fire," is not so strong. Therefore, the responsible speaker must carefully test an argument before using it to persuade an audience.

DEDUCTIVE REASONING

Through deductive reasoning, we draw conclusions based on the connections between statements that serve as premises. Rather than introducing new facts, deductions enable us to rearrange the facts we already know, putting them in a form that will make our point. Deductive reasoning is the basis of police work and scientific research, enabling investigators to draw relationships between seemingly unrelated pieces of information.

At the heart of deductive reasoning is the syllogism, a pattern of reasoning involving a major premise, a minor premise, and a conclusion. When deductive reasoning is explicitly stated as a complete syllogism, it leads us down an inescapable logical path. The interrelationships in a syllogism can be established in a series of deductive steps:

1. **STEP 1:** Define the relationship between two terms.

    Major premise: Plagiarism is a form of ethical abuse.

2. **STEP 2:** Define a condition or special characteristic of one of the terms.

    Minor premise: Plagiarism involves using the words of another without quotations or footnotes as well as improper footnoting.

3. **STEP 3:** Show how a conclusion about the other term necessarily follows.

    Conclusion: Students who use the words of another, but fail to use quotations or footnotes to indicate this or who intentionally use incorrect footnotes, are guilty of an ethical abuse.

Your ability to convince your listeners depends on their acceptance of your original premises and the conclusion you draw from them. The burden of proof rests with your evidence. You must convince listeners through the strength of your supporting material to accept your premises and, by extension, your conclusion.

© PBMW/Shutterstock.com

Founder of the Virgin Group, Richard Branson uses stories to create a sense of mythos, making his personal brand and Virgin's brand necessarily interconnected.

Sound and reasonable statements that employ inductive and deductive reasoning are the foundation for effective persuasion. More recently, scholars have recognized the story or narrative as a powerful persuasive appeal they call mythos.

MYTHOS AND THE POWER OF NARRATIVES

Humans are storytellers by nature. Long before the written word people used narratives to capture, preserve, and pass on their cultural identity. Within the last several decades, scholars have begun to recognize the power of stories, folklore, anecdotes, legends, and myths to persuade (Wahl, 2013). **Mythos** is the term given when content supports a claim by reminding an audience how the claim is consistent with cultural identity.

The strength of the mythos depends on how accurately it ties into preexisting attitudes, values, histories, norms, and behaviors for a cultural, a national, a familial, or other collectives. For example, when you were a child, you may have been told stories of the boy who cried wolf. Every culture has similar myths and stories that define what is unique and important to that culture. In the case of the boy who cried wolf, the cultural value is honesty and the intent is to teach children that bad things happen when we lie.

When speakers use mythos effectively, they create common ground with their listeners. If you were addressing an American audience and chided them to not listen to "that little boy who cries wolf" when refuting claims of an impending economic crises, your audience will likely be receptive to your position because of the common ground you invoked through their understanding of the myth.

Mythos may not work as well when the argument is inconsistent with other, stronger cultural myths, however. So, if you offered the same retort of the boy crying wolf in response to allegations that you have engaged in illegal, illicit activities, including collusion, embezzlement, and racketeering, the audience will be less likely to agree with your claim of innocence. They are more likely instead to reject the comparison you are drawing to the myth of the boy crying wolf, and instead decide "sometimes cries are warranted, you crook."

Recall the example of Japan's emperor addressing his people following their calamity. Notice how mythos is employed in the following statement that ties the perceived virtues of a disciplined, collectivist orientation to the need for order and calm solidarity:

> I have been informed that there are many people abroad discussing how calm the Japanese have remained—helping one another, and showing disciplined conduct, even though they are in deep grief. I hope from the bottom of my heart that we can continue getting together and helping and being considerate of one another to overcome this unfortunate time.

The extent to which Emperor Akihito's audience embraces these collectivist ideals reflects a cultural value that becomes a reason for pride in their actions that are consistent with these values.

Aristotle offers the advice of employing all available means when crafting persuasive messages. Availing yourself of ethos, pathos, logos, and mythos brings a balanced, well-received message much of the time. Critical thinking is essential for both persuasive speakers and effective listeners if strong, reasonable arguments are the goal. Recognizing fallacies is an important aspect of critical thinking and can prevent poor arguments from leading us astray.

ARGUMENT FALLACIES

Sometimes speakers develop arguments either intentionally or unintentionally that contain faulty logic of some kind. A **fallacy** is traditionally regarded as an argument that seems plausible but turns out on close examination to be misleading (Wahl, 2013). So whether the speaker intended to misuse evidence or reasoning to complete their persuasive goal, the result is that the audience is led to believe something that is not true.

GLITTERING GENERALITIES. Glittering generalities rely on the audience's emotional responses to values such as home, country, and freedom. Suppose the real issues of a campaign are problems associated with the growing budget deficit, illegal immigration, and dependence on foreign oil. If a candidate avoids these issues and argues for keeping the Ten Commandments in front of courthouses, reciting the pledge of allegiance more often, and amending the Constitution to prevent flag-burning, that particular candidate is likely relying considerably on glittering generalities. Although it is acceptable to talk about these latter concerns, manipulating the audience's response so that critical judgments about major issues are clouded in other areas is unethical.

BANDWAGONING. Bandwagoning is another unethical method of deception. Often listeners are uncomfortable taking a position no one else supports. Realizing this reluctance, unethical speakers may convince their listeners to support their point of view by telling them that "everyone else" is already involved. As a speaker, try to convince others of the weight of your evidence—not the popularity of your opinion. In the case above, the speaker should not be asking everyone to jump on the bandwagon, but should be explaining to people why a certain course of action is a positive thing.

AD HOMINEM. Ad hominem ("to the man"), also known as attacking or name-calling, occurs when a speaker attacks the person rather than the substance of the person's argument. A personal attack is often a cover-up for lack of evidence or solid reasoning. Name-calling and labeling are common with this fallacy, and the public is exposed to the ad hominem fallacy regularly through political shenanigans. While fallacies do not meet ethical standards, politicians have been elected based on attacks on their opponents rather than refuting stances on issues.

RED HERRING. A red herring occurs when a speaker attempts to divert the attention of the audience from the matter at hand. Going off on a tangent, changing the focus of the argument, engaging in personal attacks, or appealing to popular prejudice are all examples of the red herring fallacy.

The red herring fallacy appears regularly in interpersonal communication. A son might be told to "take your shoes off the table," and retort with, "these are boots, not shoes," thus changing the focus of the argument from the issue to the object. In a public speaking environment, red herrings are relatively common. For example, suppose an audience member asks a candidate at a political debate the following: "Do you realize your proposal to bring in a new megastore will result in the loss of livelihood for owners of smaller businesses in town who are active, contributing members to this community? A red herring response might be: "I think everyone likes to shop for bargains!"

HASTY GENERALIZATION. A hasty generalization is a fallacy based on the quantity of data. A faulty argument occurs because the sample chosen is too small or is in some way not representative. Therefore, any conclusion based on this information is flawed. Stereotypes about people are common examples of this fallacy. Imagine getting a B on a test, then and asking the students on your right and left what grade they received. Finding out they also received a B on the test, you tell your roommates that "everybody received a B on the test."

FALSE CAUSE. A false cause is also known as *post hoc ergo propter hoc* ("after this, therefore, because of this"). The speaker using this fallacy points out that because one event happened before another event, the first event caused the second event. For example, a speaker might say that, "Germs are more likely to spread outside of the work environment, because more people call in sick on Mondays than on any other day of the week."

FALSE ANALOGY. A false analogy compares two things that are not really comparable. You may have heard someone say, "You're comparing apples and oranges," or worse, "You're comparing apples to footballs." In the first case, you may be making a faulty comparison because apples and oranges, while both fruits, are different.

In the second case, the listener believes you are comparing two things with nothing in common.

SLIPPERY SLOPE. A speaker using this fallacy claims that if we take even one step onto the slippery slope, we will end up sliding all the way to the bottom; that we can't stop. In other words, there will be a chain reaction that will end in some dire consequence.

DIGITAL CITIZENSHIP

At the time of this writing, Portuguese football star Cristiano Ronaldo has the second-most popular Instagram account and sixth-most popular Twitter account on each platform. This large following allows Cristiano to portray himself as more than simply a football player. He creates his personal brand by developing a mythos around himself. His pictures and videos create stories of Cristiano as a father, a boy-friend, and a teammate.

1. Find the latest photo on Cristiano Ronaldo's Instagram account. Does it make a pathos, a logos, a ethos, and/or a mythos appeal? Why?

2. Find the latest post on Cristiano's Twitter account. Does it make a pathos, logos, ethos, and/or a mythos appeal? Why?

3. Which post did you find more persuasive? Use key terms and ideas from the chapter to back up why you found that post more persuasive.

© Chip Somodevilla /Getty Images

Parkland shooting survivor Emma Gonzalez utilized dynamic language to persuade her audience to take again against gun violence.

SPEAKING IN CONTEXT

On March 24, 2018, Marjory Stoneman High School senior and Parkland shooting survivor, Emma Gonzalez gave an impactful and memorable speech at the March for Our Lives rally in Washington D.C. Gonzalez's speech included many important elements discussed in Chapter 8 (Language) and Chapter 9 (Delivery) that contributed to the effectiveness of the speech. The speech was full of parallelism, imagery, vivid word choice, and pathos. Gonzalez memorialized her deceased classmates while making a persuasive appeal to pathos when saying:

For those who still can't comprehend, because they refuse to, I'll tell you where it went. https://www.youtube.com/watch?v=u46HzTGVQhg

The use of dynamic language captures audience members attention while making a persuasive appeal. Consider how a carefully and meticulously crafted speech can help persuade audience members of varying behaviors, attitudes, beliefs, and values.

FOCUSING PERSUASIVE MESSAGES: GOALS, AIMS, AND CLAIMS

Since Aristotle, some researchers have emphasized the outcomes or the results of persuasion. The definition of persuasion we prefer emphasizes the process of attempting to change or reinforce attitudes, values, beliefs, or behavior (Wahl, 2013). We are not talking about coercion, bribes, or pressure to conform. Persuasion is accomplished through ethical communication. Careful consideration of the goals of persuasion, the aims of your speech, and the type of proposition you are making helps focus your persuasive message.

GOALS OF PERSUASION

Critical to the success of any persuasive effort is a clear sense of what you are trying to accomplish. As a speaker, you must define for yourself your overall persuasive goal and the narrower persuasive aim. The two overall goals of persuasion are to *address attitudes* and to *move an audience to action*.

SPEECHES THAT FOCUS ON ATTITUDES. In this type of speech, your goal is to convince an audience to share your views on a topic (e.g., "The tuition at this college is too high" or "Too few Americans bother to vote"). The way you approach your goal depends on the nature of your audience.

When dealing with a negative audience, you face the challenge of trying to change your listeners' opinions. The more change you hope to achieve, the harder your persuasive task is. In other words, asking listeners to agree that U.S. automakers need the support of U.S. consumers to survive in the world market is easier than asking the same audience to agree that every American who buys a foreign car should be penalized through a special tax.

President Obama successfully persuaded lawmakers to bail out the failing U.S. automotive industry.

By contrast, when you address an audience that shares your point of view, your job is to reinforce existing attitudes (e.g., "U.S. automakers deserve our support"). When your audience has not yet formed an opinion, your message must be geared to presenting persuasive evidence. You may want to explain to your audience, for example, the economic necessity of buying U.S. products.

SPEAKING WELL USING TECHNOLOGY IS ESSENTIAL FOR EXCELLENCE

In deeply historical cities like Florence, Italy, officials are heavily challenged to keep graffiti off the many national landmarks, especially those from the Italian Renaissance period. Both locals and tourists alike seem motivated to leave their own mark on invaluable monuments. To combat this trend, many institutions in Florence are trying a new persuasive tactic to discourage graffiti: smartphone apps that allow anyone to create and share "digital" graffiti.

"It's actually working beyond our wildest expectations," says Pietro Polsinelli, a member of the technical team at the Opera di Santa Maria del Fiore (Leveille, 2016).

The new app, called Autography, gives visitors to monuments the ability to post graffiti online instead of the centuries-old marble walls. Users of the app can snap a picture of any monument and create personalized digital graffiti to superimpose over the image. Polsinelli notes that the number of graffiti on the monument walls has been decreasing dramatically as of late. The desire to "leave a mark" permanently is satisfied by the app's ability to publish users' graffiti in an online gallery (barring ones that contain insults or inappropriate material). According to Polsinelli, the context of the technology is what makes it so effective.

Although this chapter generally focuses on the speaking dimensions of persuasive techniques, you should be aware of the ways technology can persuade us to certain actions or ways of thinking. How often have you used your smartphone to "check-in" to events, businesses, or landmarks? As the global community continues to adapt and expand upon communication technology, it falls on communication professionals

SPEECHES THAT REQUIRE ACTION. Here your goal is to bring about actual change. You ask your listeners to make a purchase, sign a petition, attend a rally, write to Congress, attend a lecture, and so on. The effectiveness of your message is defined by the actions your audience takes.

Motivating your listeners to act is perhaps the hardest goal you face as a speaker, since it requires attention to the connection between attitudes and behavior. Studies have shown that what people feel is not necessarily what they do. Ahmad may be favorably inclined to purchase a BMW but still not buy it. Jill may have a negative attitude toward birth control pills, but still use them.

Once you establish your overall persuasive goals you must then decide on your persuasive aim.

PERSUASIVE AIMS

Determining your persuasive goal is a critical first step. Next, you must define the narrower persuasive aim or the type and direction of the change you seek. Four persuasive aims define the nature of your overall persuasive goal.

ADOPTION. When you want your audience to start doing something, your persuasive aim is to urge the audience to adopt a particular idea or a plan. As a spokesperson for the American Cancer Society, you may deliver the following message: "I urge every woman over the age of 40 to get a regular mammogram."

CONTINUANCE. Sometimes your listeners are already doing the thing you want them to do. In this case, your goal is to reinforce this action. For example, the same spokesperson might say:

> I am delighted to be speaking to this organization because of the commitment of every member to stop smoking. I urge all of you to maintain your commitment to be smoke-free for the rest of your life.

Speeches that urge continuance are necessary when the group is under pressure to change. In this case, the spokesperson realized that many reformed smokers constantly fight the urge to begin smoking again.

DISCONTINUANCE. You attempt to persuade your listeners to stop doing something you disagree with.

> I can tell by looking around that many people in this room spend hours sitting in the sun. I want to share with you a grim fact. The evidence is unmistakable that there is a direct connection between exposure to the sun and the deadliest of all skin cancers—malignant melanoma.

DETERRENCE. In this case, your goal is avoidance. You want to convince your listeners not to start something, as in the following example:

> We have found that exposure to asbestos can cause cancer 20 or 30 years later. If you have flaking asbestos insulation in your home, don't remove it yourself. Call in experts who have the knowledge and equipment to remove the insulation, protecting themselves as well as you and your family. Be sure you are not going to deal with an unscrupulous contractor who will probably send in unqualified and unprotected workers likely to do a shoddy job.

Speeches that focus on deterrence respond to problems that can be avoided. These messages are delivered when a persuasive speaker determines something is highly threatening or likely to result in disaster. The speaker may try to bring about some sort of effective block or barrier to minimize, if not eliminate, the threat or danger. New homeowners, for example, may find themselves listening to persuasive presentations about the purchase of a home security system. The thrust of such a persuasive speech is the need to prevent burglary through the use of an effective and economical security system.

MONROE'S MOTIVATED SEQUENCE

As emphasized throughout this text, effective communication requires connecting with your audience. Audience awareness is particularly important in speeches to persuade, for without taking into account the mental stages your audience passes through, your persuasion may not succeed. The *motivated sequence*, a widely used method for organizing persuasive speeches developed by Monroe (1965), is rooted in traditional rhetoric and shaped by modern psychology.

Monroe's motivated sequence focuses on five steps to motivate your audience that follows the normal pattern of human thought from attention to action. If you want only to persuade your audience that a problem exists, then only the first two steps are necessary. If your audience is keenly aware of a problem, then you may focus only on the last three steps. Most of the time, however, all five steps are necessary, and they should be followed in order.

STEP 1: ATTENTION. Persuasion is impossible without attention. Your first step is to capture the minds of your listeners and convince them that you have something important to say. Many possibilities were discussed in Chapter 7. For example, addressing the United Nations regarding prospects for peace in the Middle East, Israeli Prime Minister Benjamin Netanyahu (2009) began his speech by saying:

> ...Netanyahu (2009) began his speech by saying that he was speaking on behalf of the Jewish state. He lashed out against the President of Iran, whom he said was insisting that the Holocaust was a lie.

The prime minister's keen use of irony and strong language surely engaged all who were listening. His opening also establishes his credibility and introduces his topic. In your attention step, you must catch your audience's attention, introduce and make your topic relevant, and establish your credibility.

© yakub88/Shutterstock.com

Israeli Prime Minister Benjamin Netanyahu often must motivate the people of his country in times of crisis.

STEP 2: NEED. In the need step, you describe the problem you will address in your speech. You hint at or suggest a need in your introduction, then state it in a way that accurately reflects your specific purpose. You motivate listeners to care about the problem by making clear a problem exists, it is significant, and it affects them. You illustrate need by using examples, intensifying it through the use of carefully selected additional supporting material, and linking it directly to the audience. Too often the inexperienced speaker who uses the motivated sequence will pass through the need step in haste to get to the third step, the satisfaction step.

The need step has four parts. It (1) establishes there is a problem, (2) explains the problem, (3) proves that the problem is serious, and (4) connects the problem to specific needs the audience holds dear.

STEP 3: SATISFACTION. The satisfaction step presents a solution to the problem you have just described. You offer a proposition you want your audience to adopt and act on. A clear explanation as well as statistics, testimony, examples, and other types of support ensure that your audience understands what you propose. Show your audience how your proposal meets the needs you presented earlier in your speech. You may use several forms of support accompanied by visuals or audiovisual aids.

An audience is usually impressed if you can show where and how a similar proposal has worked elsewhere. Before you move to the fourth step, meet objections that you predict some listeners may hold. We are all familiar with the persuader who attempts to sell us a product or service and wants us to believe it is well worth the price and within our budget. In fact, a considerable amount of sales appeal today aims at selling us a payment we can afford as a means to purchasing the product, whether it is an automobile, a vacation, or some other attractive item. If we can afford the monthly payment, a major objection has been met.

Here is how a citizen and mother suggested solving the problem of head injuries in Little League baseball:

> Well, "some sort" of protection has been developed. American Health reports that Home Safe, Inc. has found an all-star solution. Teams like the Atlee Little Leaguers in Mechanicsville, Virginia, have solved many of their safety problems by wearing face shields like this one [shown].

> This molded plastic shield snaps onto the earflaps of the standard batter's helmet. Most youth teams require the use of a batter's helmet, but with this shield they could add complete facial protection, including the eyes, for a cost of under $15 per shield. Some might say that is expensive, but former Little Leaguer Daniel Schwartz's head injuries have cost his family $23,000 so far.

In sum, a strong satisfaction step involves clearly stating an acceptable solution, offering strong evidence supporting the solution, demonstrating how the solution solves the problem, proving that it is a workable solution, and clarifying how the solution will satisfy the audience's unresolved needs.

STEP 4: VISUALIZATION. The visualization step compels listeners to picture themselves either benefiting or suffering from adopting or rejecting your proposal. It focuses on powerful imagery to create a vision of the future if your proposal is adopted or, just as important, if it is rejected. It may also contrast these two visions, strengthening the attractiveness of your proposal by showing what will happen if no action is taken.

Positive visualization is specific and concrete. Your goal is to help listeners see themselves under the conditions you describe. You want them to experience enjoyment and satisfaction. In contrast, negative visualization focuses on what will happen without your plan. Here you describe the discomfort with conditions that would exist. Whichever method you choose, make your listeners feel part of the future. For example, here would be an appropriate visualization step:

> Imagine yourself on a quiet and lazy summer afternoon watching your own child, a niece, a nephew, a cousin, or a neighborhood friend up at bat in an exciting youth league baseball game. Think about the comfort you will experience when you see that they have the proper safety equipment on so that there is no possibility that a speeding baseball will take their life, or result in any permanent disability. See for a moment the face and the form of a child enthusiastically awaiting the pitch and see as well this child effectively shielded from the impact that could come from a missed pitch.

The visualization step can be enhanced with powerful visuals. Movie clips, soundtracks, interviews, and memorable photos have all been used successfully to help listeners fully engage their imagination in the future scenario.

STEP 5: ACTION. The action step acts as the conclusion of your speech. Here you tell your listeners what you want them to do or, if action is unnecessary, the point of view you want them to share. You may have to explain the specific actions you want and the timing for these actions. This step is most effective when immediate action is sought.

Many students find the call to action a difficult part of the persuasive speech. They are reluctant to make an explicit request for action. Can you imagine a politician failing to ask people for their vote? Such a candidate would surely lose an election. When sales representatives have difficulty in closing a deal because they are unable to ask consumers to buy their products, they do not last long in sales. Persuasion is more likely to result when the direction is clear and action is the goal. Here is how we might conclude our Little League example:

> We must realize, however, that it may be a while before this equipment scores a home run, so now it is your turn up at bat. If you are personally interested in protecting these young ballplayers, spread the word about these injuries, especially to businesses that sponsor youth teams. Encourage them to purchase safety equipment for the teams and then to sponsor them only on the condition that the equipment is used. Additionally, I ask for your signature on the petition I am circulating. This will send a loud message to our representatives in Congress.

To create closure and reinforce the need to act, our final comment might be:

> Now that we have discovered how children are being seriously injured and even killed while playing baseball, I know you agree that, given the children's lack of skill, we need to mandate the use of face shields. So take them out to the ball game, but make it one that children can play safely, because children may be dying to play baseball, but they should never die because of it. (Spurling, 1992)

From *Winning Orations of the Interstate Oratorical Association* by C. Spurling. Copyright © 1992 by Interstate Oratorical Association. Reprinted by permission.

In review, remember the five-step sequence if you want to lead your audience from attention to action. The motivated sequence is effective but, like all tools of persuasion, can be misused. The line between the use and abuse of persuasive tools warrants further examination.

ETHICS AND PERSUASIVE SPEAKING

The importance of ethics is stressed both implicitly and explicitly throughout this textbook. Ethics provide standards of conduct that guide us. The ethics of persuasion call for honesty, care, thoroughness, openness, and concern for the audience without manipulative intent. The end does not justify the means at all costs. In a world as complex as ours, marked in part by unethical as well as ethical persuaders, the moral imperative is to speak ethically.

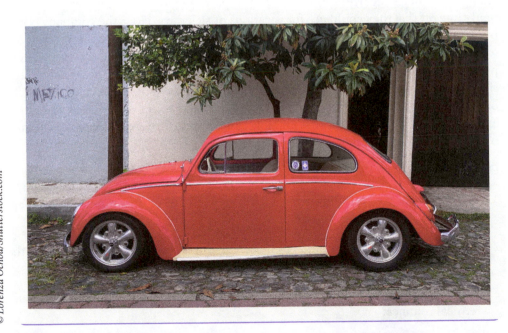

© Lorenza Ochoa/Shutterstock.com

Volkswagen markets their cars to consumers by appealing to nostalgia and a sense of adventure. However, when investigators found that Volkswagen was actually lying on emission reports for their cars, audiences were less persuaded to buy their product.

The choice between right and wrong is not simple. Informing people about a particular topic assumes providing knowledge to an audience that, in turn, learns more about the topic. In a persuasive speech, however, you are asking listeners to think or act in ways called for to achieve your specific purpose.

As members of an audience, many of the choices we make are inconsequential, such as which soft drink to buy at a convenience store or which magazine to read in a doctor's waiting room. Far more important, however, is the decision to reject our religious, social, or political beliefs in order to embrace new ones. Even the purchase of an expensive automobile is a considerable decision for us when weighed against the selection of a soft drink.

As a speaker, you must decide not only what to tell your audience but what you should avoid saying. Be mindful of your audience's needs and values, and weigh the benefits of successful persuasion against possible risks or harms. If a doctor, for example, prescribes a medication for a patient that results in the patient having to fight addiction to the medication, was that an appropriate act on the part of the doctor? Depending upon the circumstances, it may be unethical.

As you prepare for any persuasive speech, respect your audience. Be informed, truthful, and clear about your motives, use various appeals ethically, avoid misleading your audience through faulty arguments, and work to create your most effective, honest persuasive message.

ETHICS MATTER

Aaron is in charge of internal communications at his company. The company is changing policies regarding time off. In the past, employees would have a pool of paid-time off that they could use for vacations or sick days. Now, the company is giving employees a certain number of sick days and vacation days for the year. Aaron wants the transition to be stress-free and well received by the employees, so he is very positive in his presentation of the policy. Aaron does not mention that vacation and sick days no longer roll over to the next year (unlike the old policy for paid-time off), but he didn't want to include this policy with a negative impact in his presentation and assumes that it is fine because employees are expected to read the policy on their own and be familiar with it.

QUESTIONS TO CONSIDER:

1. What ethical concern did Aaron breach in persuading the employees to accept the new vacation and sick time policy?

2. What possible backlash could Aaron face if employees started talking about the new policy's no rollover rule?

3. What are some other ways Aaron could have presented the new policy in a more ethical manner?

DIGITAL CITIZENSHIP

Makeup artist and entrepreneur Jaclyn Hill had to respond to fans about a controversy surrounding her lipsticks. After launching the lipstick line, numerous fans posted videos to YouTube claiming hair, mold, glass shards, and other foreign objects in their lipstick upon opening the package for the first time. In order to recover her product line and her YouTube fans, Jaclyn had to make a video addressing the claims, which was titled, "My Lipsticks." Fans were still upset, however, so Jaclyn took a month off from social media so that she could focus on relaunching the product and hiring better quality control staff. After returning to social media, Jaclyn posted her video, "Where I've Been."

1. Watch Jaclyn's videos and one customer complaint video of your choice. Make sure to notice when the customer uploaded their video. Do you feel like Jaclyn adequately responded to the client's complaint?

2. What is Jaclyn's organizational pattern in her "Where I've Been" video?

3. On YouTube, do you think it is easier or harder for a speaker to get their audience to visualize a scenario than if that speaker were face-to-face? Why or why not?

4. How might you structure Jaclyn's apology video in order to persuade fans to buy her new lipstick?

© Lorenza Ochoa/Shutterstock.com

ESSENTIALS FOR EXCELLENCE

In this chapter, we have examined the elements of persuasive speech as well as the foundations of creating effective persuasive messages. We have learned about the hierarchy of needs that people want to be fulfilled, as well as sequences needed to motivate an audience toward your persuasive message. To conclude this chapter, it is necessary to offer practical advice that can enhance your persuasive presentations. Adam Frankel, a Senior Speechwriter to President Barack Obama, offers several tips to writing a persuasive speech on any topic.

Write like you talk.

A speech is meant to be spoken, not read (Frankel, 2015). Use short words and write short sentences. Try to avoid awkward speech constructions that might cause you to stumble over your words.

Structure matters.

The order of the points you wish to make is as important as the words themselves. Order of points matters because arguments that are clear and logical are more likely to be persuasive. Lists (like this one) are one way to create the structure of a speech.

Be authentic.

Think about the moment you are in, and speak something that feels true. Don't rely on soundbites and generic language; simply say something you believe in as simply as you can. Sharing personal stories can help you find your voice and create a connection with the audience (Frankel, 2015).

SUMMARY

- Adoption, continuance, discontinuance, and deterrence are the four persuasive aims of speaking.
- Persuasion takes place on an interpersonal, professional, and societal level.
- The five levels of Maslow's Hierarchy of Needs include physiological needs, safety needs, belongingness and love needs, esteem needs, and self-actualization needs.
- Different types of argument fallacies include glittering generalities, bandwagoning, ad hominem, red herring, hasty generalization, false cause, false analogy, and slippery slope.
- The five steps of Monroe's Motivated Sequence are attention, need, satisfaction, visualization, and action.

KEY TERMS

Ad hominem—occurs when a speaker attacks the person rather than the substance of the person's argument.

Adoption—when you want your audience to start doing something.

Bandwagoning—unethical speakers may convince listeners to support their point of view by telling them that "everyone else" is already involved.

Claim—a statement or contention the audience is urged to accept.

Continuance—when your listeners are already doing the thing you want them to do.

Data—evidence in support of an idea you advocate.

Deductive reasoning—drawing conclusions based on the connections between statements that serve as premises.

Deterrence—your goal is to convince your listeners not to start something.

Discontinuance—an attempt to persuade your listeners to stop doing something.

Ethos—speaker credibility.

Fallacies—appealing to audience emotions to disguise the deficit of the speaker's logic not holding up under scrutiny.

False analogy—compares two things that are not really comparable.

False cause—when a speaker uses a fallacy to point out that because one event happened before another event, the first event caused the second event.

Glittering generalities—rely on the audience's emotional responses to values such as home, country, and freedom.

Hasty generalization—a fallacy based on the quantity of data.

Inductive reasoning—generalizing from specific examples and drawing conclusions from what we observe.

Logos—an appeal that is rational and reasonable based on the evidence provided.

Mythos—a term given when content supports a claim by reminding an audience how the claim is consistent with cultural identity.

Opposed audience—this audience does not agree with you, is not friendly or sympathetic, and will search for flaws in your argument.

Pathos—persuading through emotional appeals.

Red herring—occurs when a speaker attempts to divert the attention of the audience from the matter at hand.

Slippery slope—this fallacy claims there will be a chain reaction that will end in some dire consequence.

Supportive audience—an audience that agrees with you.

Uncommitted continuance—an audience that is neither friendly nor hostile, but most likely not sympathetic.

Warrant—an inference that links the evidence with the claim.

Respond to the following questions without reviewing the text or your notes. These questions are provided to help you practice retrieving information and reflect on your reading.

A. What are some key ideas about persuasive speaking?

B. Did you agree or disagree with anything you read? Explain.

C. What did you learn that was new to you?

D. What concepts, if any, were confusing to you?

Respond to the following questions. You may use your text or notes to help you.

1. What are ethical, logical, emotional, and mythic appeals? How are these appeals distinct, yet interrelated?

2. How can you avoid fallacies in your speech? How can you identify fallacies as an audience member?

3. Is your audience supportive, opposed, or uncommitted? What does this mean for your presentation?

4. Why is the motivated sequence audience-centered? How does the motivated sequence relate to Maslow's Hierarchy of Needs?

5. Consider again: How important is evidence in a persuasive speech? How important are ethics in persuasive speaking? Does the importance depend on the audience and its shared needs and expectations?

QUESTIONS FOR DISCUSSION

1. In your small group, discuss whether you will use inductive or deductive reasoning in your final presentations. How will you avoid argument fallacies? (You should discuss as a group, but make individual decisions about your presentations.)

2. What have you learned about your topic since you began your research? How did you plan to approach your topic at the beginning of the course? Has that approach changed based on what you've learned and/or what you now know about your audience? Why or why not?

3. How does this chapter connect with what you've learned about persuasion in Chapters 1-9? Does this chapter illuminate ideas from those chapters? Explain.

4. How can you use Monroe's Motivated Sequence to organize your group and individual presentations? Is one step weaker than the others? How can you strengthen that step?

5. Discuss the ethical questions provided at the end of the first chapter. What ethical considerations are relevant to information about reasoning, fallacies, and persuasive speaking in general?

   • Are there guidelines (e.g., don't lie) that would be appropriate for every situation, or are ethics relative?

- Do the ends (e.g., a good outcome) justify any means?

- Is deceiving the receiver ever appropriate?

- Should the source of the message bear primary responsibility for ethics, or should the receiver share that responsibility (e.g., buyer beware)?

REFERENCES

American Rhetoric Movie Speeches. (2007). *300*. https://www.americanrhetoric.com/MovieSpeeches/moviespeech300battleatplataea.html

Emperor Akihito. (2011, March 16). *Speech to the Nation on disaster relief and hope*. Retrieved July 8, 2011 from www.americanrhetoric.com/speeches/emperorakitodisasterspeech.htm.

Frankel, A. (2015, January 12). 6 tips for writing a persuasive speech (on any topic). *Time*. Retrieved from http://time.com/3664739/6-tips-for-writing-a-persuasive-speech-on-any-topic/

Freeley, A. J. (1993). *Argumentation and debate: critical thinking for reasonable decision-making*, (8th Ed.). Belmont, CA: Wadsworth Publishing.

Hirsen, J. (2011, April 13). Tina Fey voices Palin parody pangs; "Idol" voting needs reboot. Retrieved July 8, 2011 from www.newsmax.com/Hirsen/Tina-Fay-Palin-Parody/2011/04/13/id/392760.

Kennedy, G. A. (2007). Aristotle's 'On Rhetoric': A theory of civic discourse. (2nd Ed.). (G. A. Kennedy, Trans.). New York: Oxford University Press. (Original work published 350 BCE.)

Kupor, D., & Tormala, Z. (2015). Persuasion, interrupted: The effect of momentary interruptions on message processing and persuasion. *Journal of Consumer Research*, *42*(2), 300-315.

Leveille, D. (2016, March 28). Florence tackles the problem of graffiti with 'playful, persuasive' technology. *Public Radio International*. Retrieved from http://www.pri.org/stories/2016-03-28/florence-tackles-problem-grafitti-playful-persuasive-technology

Maslow, A. H. (1943). A theory of human motivation. *Psychological Review*, *50*(4), 370–396.

Monroe, A. H. (1965). *The psychology of speech* (Seminar). Purdue University.

Netanyahu, Benjamin. (2009, September 24). *Speech delivered before the United Nations.* Retrieved July 8, 2011 from www.washingtontimes.com/news/2009/sep/transcript-Israeli-Prime-Minister-Benjamin-Netanya.

Osborn, M. (1990). In defense of broad mythic criticism—A reply to Rowland. *Communication Studies, 41,* 121–127.

Pearson, J. C., Child, J. T., Mattern, J. L., & Kahl, D. H., Jr. (2006). What are students being taught about ethics in public speaking textbooks? *Communication Quarterly, 54*(4), 507–521.

Pornpitakpan, C. (2004). The persuasiveness of source credibility: A critical review of five decades' evidence. *Journal of Applied Social Psychology, 34*(2), 243–281.

Regan, D. T., & Fazio, R. (1977). On the consistency between attitudes and behavior: look to the method of attitude formation. *Journal of Experimental Social Psychology, 13,* 28–45 (Cited in Zimbardo, p. 618.)

Shen, A. (2016, July 7). Community and contribution: National Service Ride promotes a life of service. *Huffington Post.* Retrieved from http://www.huffingtonpost.com/anna-shen/a-veteran-takes-his-messa_b_10743090.html

Simons, H. (2001). *Persuasion in society.* Thousand Oaks, CA: Sage Publications.

Sprague, J., & Stuart, D. (1988). *Speaker's handbook,* (2nd Ed.). San Diego: Harcourt Brace Jovanovich.

Spurling, C. (1992). Batter up-batter down. *Winning Orations of the Interstate Oratorical Association.* Mankato State University: The Interstate Oratorical Association.

Toulmin, S. (1958). *The uses of argument.* Cambridge, UK: Cambridge University Press.

Vancil, D. L. (1993). *Rhetoric and argumentation.* Boston: Allyn and Bacon.

Wahl, S. T. (2013). *Persuasion in your life.* Boston, MA: Pearson.

Wahl, S. T., & Maresh-Fuehrer, M. M. (2016). *Public relations principles: Strategies for professional success.* Dubuque, IA: Kendall Hunt.

Wheeler, B. & Hunt, A. (2016, June 24). The UK's EU referendum: all you need to know. *BBC News.* Retrieved from http://www.bbc.com/news/uk-politics-32810887

Wicker, A. W. (1969). Attitudes versus actions. The relationship of verbal and overt behavioral responses to attitude objects. *Journal of Social Sciences, 25*(4), 41–78.

Walker, F. R. (2005). The rhetoric of mock trial debate: Using logos, pathos and ethos in undergraduate competition. *College Student Journal, 39*(2), 277–286.

Zimbardo, P. G. (1988). *Psychology and life,* (12th Ed.). Glenview, IL: Scott, Foresman and Company.

CHAPTER 15

PRACTICING AND DELIVERING PUBLIC SPEECHES

BEFORE YOU READ

Respond to the following questions **before** you read the chapter.

1. How do you feel about public speaking? When have you had an opportunity to speak in front of a group? What was that experience like for you?

2. What are two of your strengths as a speaker? What are two of your weaknesses?

3. What do you hope your audience notices or remembers about your speech?

PERSONAL

You have been asked to pay tribute to your undergraduate academic advisor who is retiring at the end of the school year. Since your graduation several years ago, you have remained close. Many of the professors in the department who taught you will also be there. You have been successful in your career, and yet you are nervous about speaking at this retirement party for two reasons. First, you want to do a great job expressing what this person has meant to you and many other students like you. In addition, you find it rather daunting to speak in front of many of your former professors. As you prepare your speech, you reflect on your advisor's

LEARNING OBJECTIVES

- IDENTIFY THE VARIOUS METHODS OF SPEECH DELIVERY.
- RECOGNIZE THE IMPORTANCE OF BOTH VERBAL AND NONVERBAL DELIVERY IN PUBLIC SPEECHES.
- EFFECTIVELY INTEGRATE PRESENTATIONAL AIDS INTO YOUR SPEECHES.
- EFFECTIVELY MANAGE QUESTION-AND-ANSWER PERIODS.
- INCORPORATE REFLECTION INTO YOUR PUBLIC SPEECHES.

characteristics and how these personally helped you over the years. You identify several examples and humorous stories that support your advisor's traits; organize and outline your ideas; and spend a great deal of time practicing this relatively brief and important tribute. Despite your nervousness, you are honored to speak on your advisor's behalf. Will you be able to convey how much this person means to you?

PROFESSIONAL

As your organization's chief financial officer (CFO), it is your responsibility to address all of its members at the end of the fiscal year. Each year, you present a summary and a review of the company's financials. You will be speaking not only to those who are familiar with the financial aspects of the company, but also to those who may not have a strong understanding about the financial side of a business. Since you are only one speaker on a rather large agenda, you have been allocated 15 minutes to present your summary. Over the past few weeks, hours have been devoted to creating visual aids that highlight various aspects of the company's financial picture and you have tried to put the information in terms that everyone at the meeting will be able to understand. You have reviewed everything you want to say several times over and have even practiced in front of key members of your staff. Are you ready to go public?

PUBLIC

For the last 3 years, you and a committee of seven other community members have worked tirelessly to raise funds, recruit volunteers, solicit donated materials, and rebuild a playground in your town. It has been a labor of love for you and the other members. Finally, the project has come to fruition and the formal dedication of the new space is being held. Everyone who donated money, time, or materials as well as the entire community has been invited to the dedication. An estimated 500 people will attend the event. You have been asked as chair to make the formal dedication of the playground. In your brief remarks, you plan to thank those who have helped make this dream a reality and you will speak about the importance of the new playground to the families in your town as well as how the community came together to create something significant for the town. The speech is well organized and you have practiced it countless times, but are you ready to speak in front of such a large group?

CHAPTER OVERVIEW

Careful preparation and practice are essential elements of effective public speaking. This chapter focuses on the concepts that will help you effectively present your speeches. There are many delivery elements that can help you when you "go public." As you will learn in the following pages, speakers present speeches using a variety of methods ranging from a full manuscript, to an outline, brief notes, or from memory. In this chapter we examine each of these delivery strategies. In addition, we discuss both verbal and nonverbal elements of delivery and how these influence the effectiveness of presentations. Finally, we identify strategies for managing question-and-answer sessions and discuss how the use of reflection before, during, and after a speech can be utilized to help you improve as a public speaker.

METHODS OF SPEECH DELIVERY

There are four basic methods of speech delivery that are frequently used in public speaking: manuscript, memorized, impromptu, and extemporaneous delivery (Figure 15.1). Selection of one method over another depends on the circumstances of the speaking engagement. Factors impacting the choice of delivery method may depend on the audience, the speech purpose, and the speaker's own preferences.

Manuscript	Memorization	Impromptu	Extemporaneous
• Written word for word • Usually in complete sentence and paragraph form • Used when the wording needs to be precise or there is a concern about being misunderstood • Can cause speakers to read rather than speak to their audience • Speakers may not pick up on audience feedback as effectively	• Worded exactly as the speaker would like to present it to the audience • Speaker commits the speech to memory • May come across as "scripted" rather than conversational while speaking • If the speech is very brief and the occasion warrants it, this may be a possible method of delivery	• Preparation time is limited • Comes across as spontaneous and natural • Word choice, organization, and fluency may not be optimal • Because remarks are not written down, speakers may actually wind up saying something they hadn't intended to say	• Speakers research, organize, and practice their speeches • An outline is used • The speech isn't written word for word and speakers haven't tried to memorize it • Speakers come across as well prepared yet spontaneous in their delivery • Wording may not be as precise and may actually change during practice and delivery

FIGURE 15.1 Methods of speech delivery.

SPEAKING FROM A MANUSCRIPT

Manuscript delivery involves writing a speech word for word in complete-sentence and paragraph format. This allows the speaker to carefully craft what will be said and how it will be said, ensuring accuracy and predictability. Manuscript speeches are often utilized in formal speaking situations or in settings where a transcript of the speech will be placed on record. Examples of situations where a manuscript speech may be used include the inauguration of the president of the United States, or perhaps when a corporate spokesperson is asked to share their comments with the media. Speakers use this format if the wording needs to be precise or there is a concern they will be misunderstood. Thus, the advantage of this method is that it provides speakers with a script of exactly what they want to say. As long as the speaker does not go off script, the wording will be just as the speaker intended it.

This format, however, has several disadvantages that limit its use. First, it can cause speakers to read rather than speak to their audiences. Audiences indicate a preference for speakers who are engaging and appear to be speaking to them—not reading to them. Reading a speech may also cause a lack of facial expression or inflection in the speaker's voice. Another disadvantage of this method is that it does not allow speakers to respond to the nonverbal feedback the audience may be giving them. Thus, for example, if you are using a manuscript and you notice your audience seems to be confused about something in your speech, you would be much less likely to provide a different example or an explanation of that point and much more likely to simply stick to the "script" you have in front of you.

If you choose to use a manuscript, you would write the speech exactly how you would speak it. This enhances your ability to come across as more conversational

© Matej Kastelic/Shutterstock.com

FIGURE 15.2 With the manuscript delivery format, the speaker can ensure accuracy.

and less strategic. Also, you will need to spend a great deal of time preparing, editing, and revising what you plan to say as well as practicing it so that it comes across as natural. While this method may be useful in certain situations and for certain speakers because it ensures accuracy and predictability, given the importance of building a connection with your audience through eye contact and using feedback from the audience to adjust your message while you are speaking, this method is not a preferred method in most public speaking settings.

SPEAKING FROM MEMORY

Memorized delivery is the second method of delivery. Similar to the manuscript method, speakers are able to craft the wording of the speech exactly as it will be presented to the audience. Once the speech is constructed word for word, practice sessions consist of committing the speech to memory. A wedding toast is one example of when a memorized delivery would be appropriate. This type of delivery might also be used when accepting an award since the recipient wants to appear surprised and spontaneous. Recall award shows such as the Oscars or the Grammy Awards. Nominees don't know until the moment when the winner's name is revealed that they have won. Prior to the show, many actors and musicians may find that preparing a memorized acceptance speech is more appropriate than bringing notes to the podium. If used properly, this method can come across as unplanned and natural, even if it has been very carefully planned. This can be the primary advantage to this type of delivery.

On the other hand, there are actually very few times when one would need to memorize a speech. Audiences don't mind if a speaker occasionally glances at an outline or

© Monkey Business Images/Shutterstock.com

FIGURE 15.3 As much as you might prepare for job interview questions, your responses are still impromptu.

notes as long as they feel you are speaking—not reading—to them. However, there are some potential disadvantages to consider with this method. First, memorizing a speech of any significant length would be difficult. Second, you may come across as "scripted" rather than conversational as you speak. Also, if you forget one piece of your speech, you may not be able to think quickly on your feet, smoothly recover, and move to the next part of your speech. Finally, at times when speakers use this method, even though they are not looking at their speech, they may still appear to be reading it. Instead of the speech being on the podium, they may visualize an imaginary speech somewhere in the space in front of them or the back wall of the room and their eyes may still give the impression of reading, lacking a direct connection with the audience.

If you do use this method, as indicated in the manuscript method, be sure to write your speech in a conversational way. Try to make it seem less formal and spontaneous. In general, if the speech is very brief and the occasion warrants it, this may be a possible method of delivery.

IMPROMPTU DELIVERY

The third method of delivery is **impromptu delivery**, which involves little to no advance preparation by the speaker. Suppose you are at a school board meeting as a concerned parent and, based on the discussion, you want to share your opinion about a proposal currently being considered. You would most likely use this method of delivery. Certainly, the advantage of this type of delivery is that you come across as spontaneous and natural. On the other hand, it is more difficult to be as prepared, organized, and well thought out. You may actually wind up saying something you didn't intend to say, and this is one primary reason why public speakers state that they do not prefer to use this particular method of delivery.

If you do find yourself in this situation, quickly try to organize your thoughts so that you identify the key points you want to discuss. For example, if you are the spokesperson for a company and, at a media event, you are asked about what immediate challenges the company will face as a result of a recent merger, you would quickly think of two or three points you want to make. Once you have those in mind, indicate each challenge and provide specific examples or facts you have that support each one. Your ability to collect your thoughts and provide an appropriate and well-organized response will help you when you are called upon to speak using the impromptu method of delivery.

EXTEMPORANEOUS DELIVERY

Extemporaneous delivery is the final delivery type. With this method, speakers have advance notice of their speaking engagement and are able to research, organize, and practice their speeches. An outline of key ideas and support for those ideas is constructed. In essence, extemporaneous speech provides you with the best of all possibilities. You have the organizational strategy mapped out, the ability to research support for your main ideas, and an outline to use when practicing your speech. The disadvantage of this method is that the precise wording of the speech may not be as carefully structured as with the manuscript or memorized methods. The wording may also change somewhat each time you practice the speech as well as during your actual presentation to the audience.

When using this method, as you prepare your outline and practice your speech, you will become more comfortable with the wording and more familiar with each of your main points and the support for each idea. The more you practice using your outline, the less you will need to depend on it. Since you don't have the speech written word for word and haven't tried to memorize it, you will come across as well prepared yet spontaneous in your delivery.

Overall, with any delivery method, it is important to consider the audience, the occasion, and the amount of time you have been given to speak. Knowledge of your audience's familiarity, attitudes, and interest level regarding your topic will help you select the supporting material and **word choice** to clearly develop and organize your ideas. In addition, knowing if the audience consists of colleagues, friends or family, members of the media, or the general public will help you determine what method of delivery will be appropriate. Analyzing the occasion will help you make the right choice with regard to the delivery method you will use. Is the occasion an informal gathering or will it be broadcast on live television? Are you speaking at a monthly business meeting or addressing Congress? Finally, your choice of delivery method should take into account the amount of time you have been allocated to speak. If your speech is brief, memorized delivery may be appropriate to use. On the other hand, if you have been asked to give a 10-minute speech at graduation, you may want to choose the manuscript or extemporaneous method. Knowing the advantages and disadvantages of each method as well as considering the factors mentioned above, you will be more effective in selecting the appropriate method to use in any given speaking situation.

EFFECTIVE VOCAL AND NONVERBAL DELIVERY

Regardless of the delivery method you select, attention should be given to your vocal and nonverbal delivery. In this section, we concentrate on both elements of delivery. Recall the example of the tribute speech for your former academic advisor at the start of this chapter. What if you begin your presentation at his retirement party and your nerves cause you to speak softly, avoid eye contact, and speak at a rapid pace? While you may have wonderful things to say about your advisor, will the message be as effective if the vocal or nonverbal elements of delivery are lacking? Some speakers may use appropriate volume and rate of delivery, but may lack eye contact or facial expression. There are several vocal and nonverbal considerations to help speakers deliver speeches effectively. Vocal delivery elements include the speaker's volume, rate of delivery, pitch, and vocal variety. Nonverbal elements include eye contact, facial expression, gestures, posture, and movement.

VOCAL ELEMENTS OF DELIVERY

There are several elements of your vocal delivery that can make a difference to your effectiveness as a public speaker (Figure 15.4). These include volume, speaking rate, pitch, and vocal variety.

Volume refers to the loudness or softness of your voice. You may need to adjust your vocal volume according to the environment in which you are speaking. Every member of the audience must be able to hear you without straining to do so. Just as you would naturally adjust your voice if you were whispering confidential information to

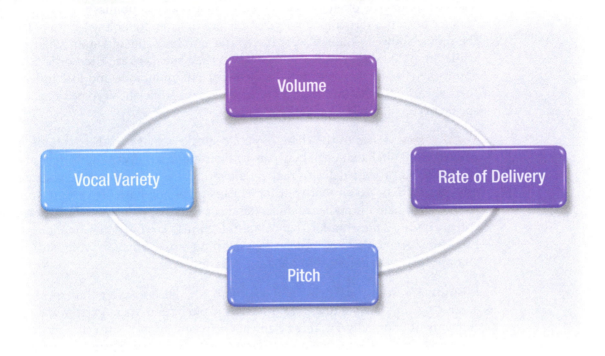

FIGURE 15.4 Vocal elements of delivery.

a friend, public speakers need to adjust their volume when speaking to a large room filled with people. The goal is to identify the correct volume for the size of the room. It is difficult and annoying for an audience to listen to a speaker whose volume is too soft. In some speaking situations, a microphone may be available to assist the speaker. If a microphone is used, speakers must learn not to speak too loudly into the microphone or stand too close to it.

Just as finding the right volume is important for public speakers, so is finding the appropriate rate of delivery. **Rate** is the speed at which someone speaks. Some speakers tend to speak very quickly. This may be the result of nerves or excitement. When speakers present their information too quickly, it doesn't allow the audience time to process the message. Speaking too slowly is not as common, but it does happen. When speakers speak too slowly, it draws out their message and audiences may become distracted and unable to focus on the message. In addition, speakers who speak slowly may be perceived as less credible. In a study examining speaking rate and perceptions of credibility (Simonds, Meyer, Quinlan, & Hunt, 2006), speakers with slower speech rates were perceived as less credible compared to those with moderate speech rates. Finding the right rate of delivery is important to maintain the audience's interest and help maintain the perception of credibility. If you know you tend to speak too quickly, some techniques to assist you in your delivery include visualizing yourself separating each word or writing notes such as "slow down" or "breathe" on your outline as a reminder.

Pitch is another element of vocal delivery that refers to the highness or lowness of your voice. When public speakers are nervous, their pitch may become higher than their normal speaking voice. Speakers who do not incorporate any variety in their pitch are considered to be monotone. In the movie Ferris Bueller's Day Off, Ben Stein's character is often described as the monotone economics teacher. This type of voice becomes very difficult for an audience to listen to for any length of time. As the movie showed, students were inattentive and had difficulty even staying awake while Stein's character spoke to the class. When speakers are tired or lack passion about their topic, they are more likely to become monotone and lose inflection in their voices. Through careful practice and perhaps sufficient sleep before you speak, speakers can add inflection to their voices.

Vocal variety refers to the changes public speakers make in their volume, rate of delivery, and pitch that help them convey their message effectively. The volume, rate, and/or pitch of your delivery may be altered to help communicate your enthusiasm, concern, or passion for your topic. Pausing or emphasizing certain words and phrases will help the audience understand the intent of your words. For example, if you are giving a presentation that contains technical jargon, it may be appropriate to pause or slow your rate of speech when defining terms. This way, your audience has an opportunity to digest what you are discussing.

In summary, your vocal delivery is critical to your success as a public speaker. Concentrating on your volume, rate of delivery, pitch, and vocal variety are essential elements of your delivery. These elements help convey your sincerity, concern, passion, confidence, and other emotional elements. Always try to listen to yourself while speaking, so that you know your audience can easily hear you, that you are speaking at a rate that allows your audience to capture what you are saying, that your voice has inflection, and that your vocal variety reinforces your message (Figure 15.5).

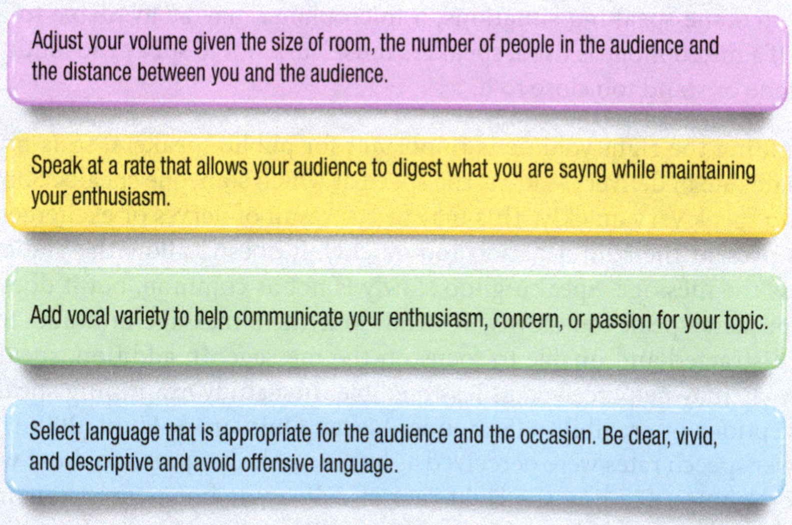

Adjust your volume given the size of room, the number of people in the audience and the distance between you and the audience.

Speak at a rate that allows your audience to digest what you are sayng while maintaining your enthusiasm.

Add vocal variety to help communicate your enthusiasm, concern, or passion for your topic.

Select language that is appropriate for the audience and the occasion. Be clear, vivid, and descriptive and avoid offensive language.

FIGURE 15.5 Suggestions for vocal delivery.

NONVERBAL ELEMENTS OF DELIVERY

The elements of volume, rate of delivery, pitch, and vocal variety influence how your message is received. Another important factor in your delivery is how you communicate nonverbally. Simply put, it isn't just the words you say but also how you say them and how you communicate nonverbally that can make the difference in effective speech delivery. Consider the importance of the nonverbal delivery in the following example. As the president of the student government at her college, Tanya was asked to speak to the college's board of trustees to present student concerns about the possible elimination of some majors. When she attended the meeting, she wore a suit, walked into the room in a confident manner, and smiled at the board members. Although she had an outline of what she planned to say, she looked directly at the members of the board and her tone of voice was professional and self-assured. The board members were impressed with Tanya not only because she made many valid points but also because her nonverbal communication was positive and professional. Eye contact, facial expression, gestures, posture, and movement are important nonverbal elements to consider when preparing to deliver your speech (Figure 15.6).

As stated earlier, audiences prefer speakers who speak to them, not those who read to them. **Eye contact** refers to the degree to which you establish and maintain a visual connection with your audience. It is the primary way public speakers connect with their audiences and engage them in the topic. Not only do speakers use eye contact to build and maintain rapport with an audience, but it also enables them to pay attention to the nonverbal feedback from the audience. When looking down at written speech notes while presenting, it is difficult to tell if an audience understands or is interested in what you are saying. Later in this chapter, we identify strategies that you can consider if an audience seems confused by what you are saying, but it is essential to maintain eye contact to remain connected to the audience and to receive feedback from them.

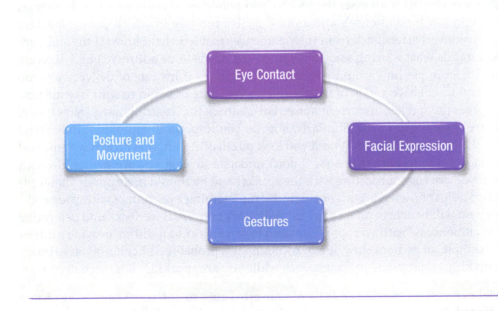

FIGURE 15.6 Nonverbal elements of delivery.

FIGURE 15.7 Eye contact connects you with your audience.

Establishing and maintaining eye contact is not an easy task for many public speakers. It takes a great deal of practice and confidence. Using the impromptu or extemporaneous method of delivery provides the best chance for public speakers to stay connected with their audiences. It stands to reason that, if you are speaking from an outline or notes, you will not try to remember the exact wording as you might if using a manuscript.

Just as eye contact is an essential tool to help public speakers connect with, engage, and maintain the audience's attention, it is also the way in which public speakers receive nonverbal feedback from their audiences that lets them know if the audience understands what is being said or if something needs to be addressed in a different way. For example, how would you let a speaker know if his rate of delivery was too fast? You might have a look of frustration on your face or begin to shift in your seat. This gives the speaker important nonverbal feedback that basically says, "Slow down, you are speaking too fast." Similarly, how do you respond if you didn't understand what the speaker is saying? Would you look puzzled? Again, this provides nonverbal feedback to the speaker that says, "I don't understand what you are saying." In both cases, you are communicating with the speaker and he should incorporate that feedback to adjust his message accordingly. By maintaining eye contact with your audience, you will be able to pick up on the audience's nonverbal feedback and determine if the audience is "with you" or if you need to re-explain something, provide a different example, or perhaps slow down. Although it is probably difficult for you to imagine making adjustments to your speech while you are speaking, it is often necessary.

Facial expressions provide additional nonverbal cues to enhance the message being presented. **Facial expressions** are the changes a speaker makes to express emotions and reinforce what is being said. Your facial expressions add feeling to your speech.

For example, if you are selected to give a toast at your best friend's wedding, it is natural to communicate excitement through the use of a smile or extended eye contact with your friend. A wide range of emotions are communicated via facial expressions. They let the audience know if your speech is serious, sad, frightening, or perhaps humorous. As discussed in the previous section, when a speaker possesses a monotone speaking voice, it is difficult to maintain the audience's attention. Similarly, a presentation that lacks facial expressiveness may result in the loss of the audience's attention. It's important to incorporate facial expressions that are appropriate for the topic and the tone of the speech. After all, you wouldn't want to grin from ear to ear when speaking about a serious subject. The facial expressions you use must reinforce what you are saying, yet they must also seem natural and unrehearsed. Practice helps most public speakers identify the appropriate facial expressions to enhance the effectiveness of their speech delivery.

Gestures are another form of nonverbal communication that can help speakers deliver their message effectively. **Gestures** are movements of the speaker's arms or hands used appropriately and purposefully to emphasize or reinforce what the speaker is saying verbally.

Gestures may also be used to visually demonstrate something to the audience. Effective gestures would include pointing to a specific area of a chart or a graph, widening your hands or narrowing them to demonstrate the size of something, or holding up three fingers as you say, "There are three main areas I want to speak with you about today." As a public speaker, it is important to avoid gestures that serve no purpose in your speech. For example, fidgeting with jewelry, adjusting your hair, or wringing your hands would be distracting gestures. In fact, your audience may interpret these movements as speaking anxiety or that you failed to prepare for the presentation.

© Monkey Business Images/Shutterstock.com

FIGURE 15.8 Gestures can help emphasize what the speaker is saying verbally.

These may also lessen the audience's perception of your credibility. Practicing your speech and becoming aware of the gestures you tend to use will help you eliminate ones that detract from your delivery.

Posture and movements are nonverbal elements of delivery that can enhance or detract from your speech as well. **Posture** refers to how the speaker stands or the position of the speaker's body. It is the way in which you carry yourself, and it can convey confidence or reticence. Slouching over the podium or leaning against the wall conveys a negative impression. Your posture should appear natural and comfortable to convey confidence and help boost your credibility. Standing tall and strong even when you may be feeling somewhat nervous will enhance perceptions of your credibility as a speaker.

Movements are another aspect of nonverbal delivery to consider when presenting your speech and refer to any physical shift the speaker makes. Moving around the room or changing position while speaking is fine as long as you maintain the audience's attention and their focus is on you rather than what you are doing. Movements should be done with a purpose. They may help you transition to a new topic or communicate the importance of something you just said. Movements to avoid include actions such as swaying back and forth, crossing one leg over the other, or pacing rapidly. If you are using presentational aids, avoid turning your back toward the audience as you refer to them. Overall, your goal is to have your audience focus on listening to what you are saying rather than watching what you are doing.

Nonverbal communication is an important consideration in speech delivery. Be sure to establish and maintain eye contact; incorporate facial expressions that help convey your message; and use gestures that are purposeful and help emphasize or reinforce what you say. Also, be aware of your posture and movements (Figure 15.9). Concentrating on these elements will help you become an effective public speaker. Working on nonverbal elements of delivery will enhance your chances of being a successful public speaker whether you are in a classroom or an organizational setting, at a community meeting, or giving a toast at a friend's wedding.

PRACTICING YOUR SPEECH DELIVERY

Now that you understand the various delivery options available and the vocal and nonverbal characteristics that make speech delivery effective, let's turn our attention to the importance of rehearsing or practicing your speech. Even though you have completed the process of researching the topic, organizing the speech, and identifying effective methods of delivery, practicing speech delivery will further enhance your public speaking confidence. When you practice the speech, you will gain comfort with the sequence of ideas, word choice, and supporting material you plan to present. Practice will also aid your nonverbal delivery.

While many of us have the tendency to procrastinate, waiting until the last minute to prepare a speech can sabotage your ability to deliver a quality presentation. Completing all of the steps in the speech process far in advance of when you will be delivering your speech will enable you to devote the time you need to practice your delivery. There are many things you can accomplish by practicing your speech ahead of time. The following suggestions should help make your practice time more effective.

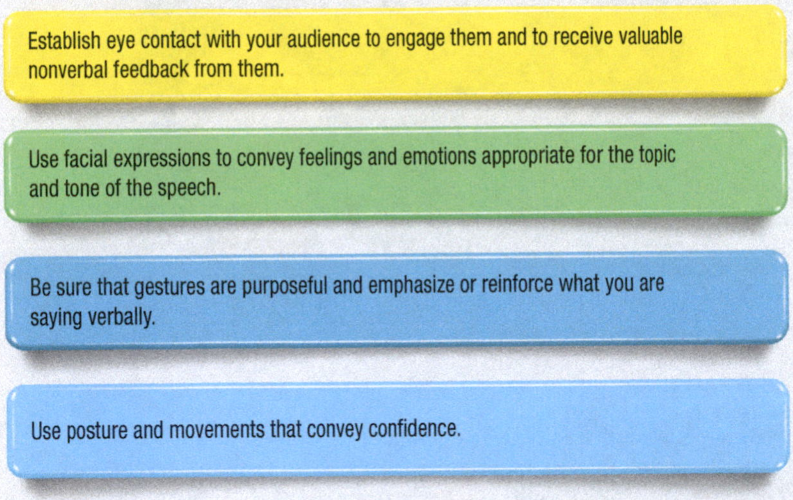

Establish eye contact with your audience to engage them and to receive valuable nonverbal feedback from them.

Use facial expressions to convey feelings and emotions appropriate for the topic and tone of the speech.

Be sure that gestures are purposeful and emphasize or reinforce what you are saying verbally.

Use posture and movements that convey confidence.

FIGURE 15.9 Nonverbal elements of delivery.

PRACTICE YOUR SPEECH OUT LOUD

Be sure to practice your speech out loud. This provides several advantages. Practicing out loud will help you simulate the real speaking situation and help you identify any issues with your speech before you make your actual presentation. For example, because the spoken language is different than the written language, speaking out loud will allow you to actually hear the word choice and sentence structure you plan to use and make any necessary adjustments to it before you present the speech.

As you practice out loud, you may realize you need a stronger attention-getter or that you have not clearly previewed the key points of your speech. You may realize that transitions move too abruptly from one main idea to the next or that an additional transition is needed to help guide your listeners from one main point to the next. While rehearsing your speech, you may discover that a supporting idea that you have associated with one main idea truly belongs with a different one. While you could pick up on these issues by carefully reading the speech to yourself, practicing it out loud enables you to identify issues because you have the opportunity to hear what your audience will hear when you actually deliver the presentation. Consider video recording your speech so that you can review how you look and sound when you are speaking.

Another advantage of practicing out loud ahead of time is that it enhances your ability to be more extemporaneous in your speech delivery. As mentioned previously, increased familiarity with the wording of your speech and the flow of your ideas will enable you to sound more conversational and possess a more natural delivery style.

FIGURE 15.10 Practicing your speech out loud can improve your nonverbal delivery.

Finally, practicing your speech out loud can potentially improve your vocal and non-verbal delivery. As you practice, you will be able to identify the tone, rate, volume, and word emphasis that should be used in order to convey your ideas effectively. In addition, practicing increases your ability to maintain eye contact with your audience. As you rehearse, you will become more familiar with the wording and the sequence of your ideas and less reliant on the written speech. You will become more comfortable with the appropriate facial expressions and gestures that can enhance your speech, thus eliminating any nonverbal elements that may detract from your message.

PRACTICE IN FRONT OF OTHERS

While it might feel awkward to practice your speech in front of others, it will help you speak more effectively. Recruit friends or classmates to help you. Practicing in front of others will help you become aware of any issues you might not notice when you rehearse by yourself. Getting feedback from others on any areas that need to be corrected before you deliver your speech will help you strengthen the actual speech when you deliver it to the intended audience (Menzel & Carrell, 1994). Smith and Frymier (2006) also found that students who practiced their speeches in front of an audience prior to their delivery were more effective during their actual presentations. In their study, they found that students who practiced in front of an audience of four or more people scored an average of three points higher on their graded speech presentations. Over the course of the semester, practicing in front of others can have a significant impact on your grade. Overall, a volunteer audience can offer constructive feedback that will enable you to make improvements to your speech or delivery. At the very least, practicing in front of an audience should help boost your confidence.

TIME YOUR SPEECH EACH TIME YOU PRACTICE

Just about every speaker is provided with a time limit for their presentations. Your time frame will be either given to you specifically, as is the case in a classroom situation, or it will be implicit in the speaking situation because of common practice, as is the case for speakers at a commencement ceremony. Similarly, business meetings and civic organizations often use agendas to keep meetings on track. In these situations, speakers need to be mindful and respectful of the agenda and monitor the length of their presentation to meet the guidelines or parameters provided by the agenda. When speakers run too short or too long in a classroom, it can have an impact on their grades. Both inside the classroom and beyond, if you give your audience too little information, you may lose credibility. If your speech runs too long, you may lose the attention of the audience. Timing your speech several times will help ensure you meet the explicit or implicit guidelines of the speaking situation.

GIVE EXTRA ATTENTION TO YOUR INTRODUCTION AND CONCLUSION

One thing you can do to help you present your speech effectively is to spend additional time practicing your introduction and conclusion. This will help you start and end your speech on a strong note. For example, if you know exactly what you want to say in your introduction, you will be able to increase your level of eye contact as you start to speak and immediately begin to develop a rapport with your audience. As speakers first begin their presentations, they often feel nervous, but become more comfortable after the first few minutes of speaking. Knowing your introduction well will help you conquer the initial nervousness you might feel. Likewise, knowing your conclusion well will allow you to end strongly. Again, this will allow you to maintain direct eye contact with your audience. Since you do not want your audience to "guess" when you are done, providing your audience with a clear sense of completion to your speech is important. Knowing both the introduction and conclusion well will help your delivery overall.

EDIT YOUR SPEECH IF NEEDED

Throughout the development and practice phases of speech preparation, it is important to continually refine your speech. Each time you practice your speech, try to evaluate what worked and what did not. Consider how you can improve both what you have written and how you deliver it. If you think a sentence is unclear or your word choice is vague, now is the time to change it. Many speakers make changes right up until the time they actually deliver their speeches. For example, on December 23, 1960, Ted Sorensen, on behalf of then President-elect John F. Kennedy, sent a telegram to several individuals including Adlai Stevenson, Dean Rusk, and John Kenneth Galbraith asking them for any suggestions they had for his inaugural address. Their suggestions and Kennedy's other revisions were given to Sorensen's secretary on January 18, 1961, who typed the final version that Kennedy delivered to the nation on January 20, 1961 (www.jfklibrary.org). Your own evaluation of what needs to be changed, as well as the feedback you receive when you practice in front of an audience, will help you strengthen your speech before you deliver it to the actual audience.

PRACTICE TO INCREASE CONFIDENCE

As alluded to previously, practicing ahead of time will increase your confidence and, hopefully, you will feel less apprehensive about speaking in front of an audience. Although some level of anxiety is normal for most speakers, as you rehearse, you will likely increase your chances of transforming potential perceptions of your nervousness into enthusiasm and excitement for your topic. This may be compared to an athlete getting energized for a game. In addition, many speakers focus on practicing **positive visualization** when they rehearse. In other words, envision yourself succeeding in your speech delivery. As you rehearse your speech, try to imagine the audience engaged in what you are saying and envision their nonverbal reactions as they give you positive feedback. Do this during your speech as well. In the practice phase of your speech preparation, positive visualization can help replace potential negative thoughts with positive ones. Instead of telling yourself you can't do something or that you aren't good at something, this strategy will help boost your confidence level.

Practicing your speech has many advantages. These include your ability to recognize areas that need to be strengthened before you deliver your speech to an audience, improve the likelihood that your delivery will seem extemporaneous, increase the effectiveness of your vocal and nonverbal delivery, and increase your confidence and decrease any level of apprehension (Figure 15.11). To make the most out of your practice, prepare your speech well in advance in order to allow sufficient time to practice, rehearse out loud in front of others, and time your speech each time you practice. Be sure to devote extra attention to practicing your introduction and conclusion and edit your speech as needed. As you practice, pay attention to your eye contact, gestures, and body movements. Are there words you want to emphasize?

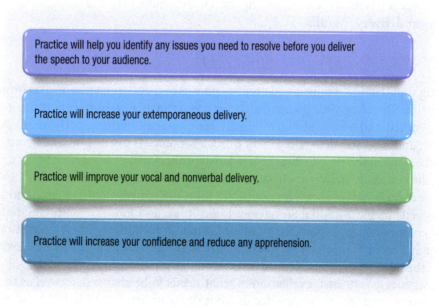

FIGURE 15.11 Advantages of practicing your speech.

FIGURE 15.12 Tips for practicing your speech.

What nonverbal gestures will help you emphasize that point? Familiarizing yourself with the nonverbal aspects of delivery during your rehearsal will help you gain the confidence you need to be perceived as an effective public speaker (Figure 15.12).

All of the suggestions above will help you deliver a more effective speech. By rehearsing your speech delivery and focusing on what you want to convey to your audience, the time devoted to preparing and practicing your speech will be well worth it. In the next sections, we discuss two other dimensions of public speaking that can help you enhance your effectiveness. These include managing the question-and-answer period and the ability to reflect before, during, and after you speak to an audience.

THE QUESTION-AND-ANSWER PERIOD

A question-and-answer (Q&A) period often occurs after a speech is presented. While it is not always easy to know what an audience may ask, it is important to consider how to approach the question-and-answer period and what potential topics may be brought up. Your audience may ask questions to solicit more information on a specific area, to get your opinion on a particular aspect of your presentation, or to clear up a point of confusion they may have about something you said. Usually, the questions asked are presented in a positive manner and provide an opportunity for the speaker to interact with the audience. Public speakers also need to be prepared, however, for an audience member who asks a confrontational question. There are some common strategies that will help you successfully manage a Q&A.

One of the best suggestions for responding to a question is to *repeat* the question the audience member has asked as part of your answer. This is beneficial for many

FIGURE 15.13 It's beneficial to repeat a question in your response to it.

reasons. First, this will help ensure the entire audience has heard the question. If you are in a large room and the person asking the question happens to be sitting toward the front, you may hear the question because of your proximity. It can be very frustrating for people if they are sitting behind the person asking the question, can't hear the question, or only hear the speaker's response. Second, repeating the question helps speakers know that the question the audience member asked is the one that has been received. This will allow for any clarification that needs to occur before the question is answered. Finally, repeating the question gives speakers that extra moment to consider how to respond and to organize their responses.

When you respond to questions, *be brief* and to the point. Lengthy answers may become confusing to the audience and if there are time constraints, they may also prevent other members of the audience from asking questions. Needless to say, some questions may naturally be answered briefly. For example, an audience member may ask a simple question such as "Can you repeat what you said the project will cost to complete?" Some questions, however, may take more time to respond, such as a question that asks, "Can you explain the major challenges of completing the project successfully and the cost of not meeting those challenges?" When speakers feel it would take too long to respond to the question, they may provide a brief response, thank the audience member for asking the question, and indicate their willingness to speak with the audience member at more length after the presentation or to correspond with them in some way.

When asked a question, it is important to be *honest*. If you do not know the answer to a question, admit it. Audiences don't expect speakers to know everything about a subject. In the long run, providing the audience with a false or misleading response will damage a speaker's credibility and is considered unethical. If you do not know the answer to a question, respond with a statement such as, "I don't know the answer to that but I would be happy to research that and let you know."

Speakers should *be careful* about what they say and how they say it. Many politicians and public figures have said something they wished they had never said. When responding to questions, it is best to take a moment and consider what you should say and how the message may be perceived. For example, the mayor of Boston publicly stated that if he lived in Detroit he would "blow up the place and start all over." Needless to say, this statement insulted many people. While his intent was to convey that Detroit should reevaluate some of its policies and consider reforms, his poor choice of words communicated another meaning. Because public speaking is public, speakers must always be mindful of what they plan to say and how they plan to say it, especially during a question-and-answer period.

The last suggestion is to *check* to make sure that the question asked by the audience member was answered successfully. Speakers can simply ask, "Have I answered your question?" If the audience member indicates you have, you may move on to the next question. If not, the audience member may need to ask a second question or request clarification. While this is important, avoid focusing only on one audience member's question since this eliminates the opportunity for other audience members to ask their questions. If this occurs, you can ask the audience member to meet briefly after the Q&A session is complete and move on to other questions.

The question-and-answer period is an important part of public speaking and can help clarify any questions audience members have and enhance what the speaker has said. To be successful during this time, speakers need to remember to restate each question, try to answer questions briefly and honestly, and carefully consider what they say and how they say it. Just as you might try to anticipate questions an interviewer might ask you on a job interview, it is also important to consider what potential questions an audience may ask. In doing so, you will be more prepared to respond effectively.

THE IMPORTANCE OF REFLECTION

Thus far, we have spoken about the methods of delivery public speakers use, the vocal and nonverbal elements of speech delivery, the importance of practicing your speech, and the question-and-answer period that typically follows public speeches. Your ability to speak effectively may also be enhanced through reflection. Reflection means giving something serious thought or consideration. This should occur before you speak, while you are delivering your speech, and once you have completed your speech.

Before you speak, reflection should guide your speech preparation. First, you should analyze your audience. Having a deeper understanding about the audience to whom you will be speaking is a reflective activity that will help you research and organize your speech effectively, select the best methods of support for your ideas, and even choose the best way to word your ideas and support. Reflecting on the type of

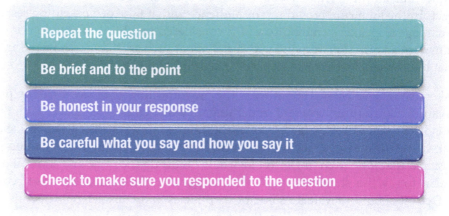

FIGURE 15.14 Strategies for speakers.

audience, the occasion at which you will be speaking, and even the time of day the speech will be given will assist you in preparing an effective speech and this, in turn, will help you deliver your speech successfully.

Reflecting during your presentation will also help you deliver a more effective speech. Schön (1983, 1987) highlighted the need for reflection-in-action as a way to improve one's level of performance. According to Schön, when individuals use **reflection-in-action**, they isolate and name a problem that needs attention; frame the problem to help organize and clarify how they will solve it; and reframe the problem in such a way that it provides a new understanding of it and possible alternative ways of acting to resolve it. Schön underscored the need for reflection-in-action, which he believed helps people consider what and how they are doing while they are doing it. In turn, this can be used to improve their performance. He notes that musicians and athletes, for example, do this constantly and often make needed changes in a split second to improve their performance.

What does all of this mean for public speakers? Reflection-in-action can help public speakers improve their delivery. Again, it is thinking about what you are doing *while* you are doing it and making any necessary "*on-the-spot*" changes "*in action*" to improve your speech. While you might think this is impossible to do while you are speaking in public, developing the ability to reflect-in-action will help make you a more effective public speaker. When you reflect-in-action, you carefully listen to yourself as well as observe the nonverbal feedback you are receiving from the audience while you are presenting your speech. For example, if you are speaking too fast, your ability to reflect-in-action will let you know you need to slow down. If your voice has lost its inflection or your volume seems to trail off at the ends of sentences, your ability to reflect-in-action will let you know you need to make the necessary adjustments to your pitch and/or volume. If you pick up from the audience's nonverbal feedback that they don't understand something you have said, again, if you are reflecting-in-action, you know you need to adjust your message to make your ideas clear to your listeners.

Similarly, having the ability to reflect-in-action will allow you to edit your speech while speaking if necessary. Perhaps because you repeated something or provided a different example of something, you are almost out of the time you have been given to speak. Through your ability to reflect-in-action, you could give two forms of support for an idea rather than three or paraphrase a quote rather than providing the entire quote for the audience. If you can train yourself to reflect-in-action, you can improve your speech delivery and make those types of "on-the-spot" adjustments that musicians and athletes make in order to improve.

The last type of reflection comes after your speech has concluded. Schön (1983, 1987) called this **reflection-on-action**. Once you have delivered your speech, analyze your strengths, what areas need improvement, and any elements you would change if you were to deliver that same speech again. By reflecting on what you did and how you could do it better, you will help yourself be more effective during your next presentation. In a classroom situation, you may be evaluated by your instructor and perhaps even your classmates. While this feedback is intended to provide the constructive steps you need to take to improve for the next time, what happens after the course is complete and you are not receiving their feedback? If you can learn to reflect on what things worked well and what things needed to be improved each time you deliver a speech, you will continue to improve as a speaker long after the course ends. If you can learn to self-reflect each time you speak in public, you will analyze what you could have done to make your speech even better.

Overall, learning how to reflect before you speak, while you are speaking, and after you have spoken will help you become a more effective public speaker. Reflection before you speak will help you construct an effective presentation, which, in turn, will help your delivery. Reflecting while you are speaking will also help your delivery because you will make any necessary adjustments to help you improve during your presentation. Finally, reflecting on your speech and on its delivery after you have presented it will help you analyze what strengths you brought to the public speaking situation and what areas should be strengthened for the next time.

SUMMARY

In this chapter, we discussed the four types of delivery methods commonly used by public speakers and the advantages and disadvantages of each type. Public speakers need to determine which type of delivery method is best given a particular speaking situation. This chapter also focused on the vocal and nonverbal elements of your delivery. The vocal elements of volume, rate, pitch, and vocal variety as well as the nonverbal elements of eye contact, facial expression, gestures, posture, and movement are critical components of a public speaker's delivery. Furthermore, this chapter focused on the various reasons why practice is important, and some things to keep in mind when practicing your speech. Managing a question-and-answer period was also discussed as part of a speaker's delivery. Finally, the chapter examined the use of reflection to help you improve as a public speaker before, during, and after you speak. Keeping all of this in mind as you research, organize, prepare, practice, and deliver any type of speech is important to becoming an effective public speaker.

KEY TERMS

Extemporaneous delivery—type of delivery where the speaker researches, organizes, and practices the speech but uses only an outline while delivering the speech to the audience.

Eye contact—degree to which you establish and maintain a visual connection with your audience.

Facial expression—changes a speaker makes to express emotion and to reinforce what the speaker is saying.

Gestures—movements of the speaker's arms or hands used appropriately and purposefully to emphasize or reinforce what the speaker is saying verbally.

Impromptu delivery—type of delivery that is characterized by limited preparation time; often not as organized or carefully worded as other speech delivery types but does come across as spontaneous.

Manuscript delivery—type of delivery method where the speech is written word for word as it will be delivered; commonly used when the wording must be precise.

Memorized delivery—type of delivery method where the speech is written word for word and the speaker commits it to memory; may be useful if the speech is brief and the occasion warrants it.

Movement—any physical shifts the speaker makes.

Pitch—highness or lowness of a person's voice.

Positive visualization—when a speaker envisions succeeding in his or her speech delivery.

Posture—how the speaker stands or the position of the speaker's body.

Rate—speed at which a person speaks.

Reflection—giving serious thought or consideration to something.

Reflection-in-action—thinking about what you are doing while you are doing it and making any necessary adjustments immediately.

Reflection-on-action—thinking about what you did and how well you did it and what you would do differently the next time.

Vocal variety—changes the speaker makes in volume, rate, and/or pitch to add meaning to the speech.

Volume—loudness or softness of the speaker's voice.

Word choice—carefully selecting words to convey your message clearly, vividly, and ethically.

Respond to the following questions **without** reviewing the text or your notes. These questions are provided to help you practice retrieving information and reflect on your reading.

A. What are some key ideas about speech delivery?

B. Did you agree or disagree with anything you read? Explain.

C. What did you learn that was new to you?

D. What concepts, if any, were confusing to you?

Respond to the following questions. You may reference your text or notes to help you.

1. Identify and explain the four methods of delivery. What method are you expected to use when you deliver your final presentation? Why?

2. Before you read the chapter, you were asked to identify your strengths and weaknesses as a speaker. Which vocal and nonverbal elements of delivery need more practice before you present? What suggestions were helpful for you?

3. What suggestions are provided to help make your speech practice time more effective? Which suggestions have you used in the past, and which suggestions do you plan to follow before your presentation?

4. What strategies can help you successfully manage a Q&A session?

5. Describe the process of reflection before, during, and after your speech.

QUESTIONS FOR DISCUSSION

1. In your small group, develop a plan to help each member practice his or her speech before the presentation. Use the suggestions that were provided to help make speech practice time more effective.

2. In your small group, designate a time for all members to practice their speeches. Be prepared to ask questions of each speaker, and then participate in a practice Q&A session.

3. Search online for an example of a speaker who uses effective vocal or non-verbal delivery skills. Review the speech and discuss each skill. How does a speaker's effective delivery connect with other ideas and concepts you have discussed in this class?

4. Search online for an example of a speaker who does not use effective vocal or nonverbal delivery skills. Review the speech and discuss each skill. How does a speaker's ineffective delivery connect with other ideas and concepts you have discussed in this class?

5. Discuss the ethical questions provided at the end of the first chapter. What ethical considerations are relevant to the information in this chapter about delivery, Q&A sessions, reflection, and public speaking in general?

- Are there guidelines (e.g., don't lie) that would be appropriate for every situation, or are ethics relative?

- Do the ends (e.g., a good outcome) justify any means?

- Is deceiving the receiver ever appropriate?

- Should the source of the message bear primary responsibility for ethics, or should the receiver share that responsibility (e.g., buyer beware)?

REFERENCES

Menzel, K. E., & Carrell, L. J. (1994). The relationship between preparation and performance in public speaking. *Communication Education, 43*(1), 17–26.

Schön, D. A. (1983). *The reflective practitioner: How professionals think in action.* New York: Basic Books.

Schön, D. A. (1987). *Educating the reflective practitioner: Toward a new design for teaching and learning in the professions.* San Francisco: Jossey-Bass.

Simonds, B. K., Meyer, K. R., Quinlan, M. M., & Hunt, S. K. (2006). Effects of instructor speech rate on student affective learning, recall, and perceptions of nonverbal immediacy, credibility, and clarity. *Communication Research Reports, 23*(3), 187–197.

Smith, T. E., & Frymier, A. B. (2006). Get "real": Does practicing speeches before an audience improve performance? *Communication Quarterly, 54*(1), 111–125.

CHAPTER 16

LISTENING AND CRITIQUING SPEECHES

BEFORE YOU READ

Respond to the following questions **before** you read the chapter.

1. Would other people describe you as a good listener? Why or why not?

2. Think of someone in your life who is a good listener. Why did you choose this person? What makes him or her a good listener?

3. Do you feel comfortable providing peer feedback to other speakers? Why or why not?

LISTENING AND PUBLIC SPEAKING

Two of the first researchers to study listening, Thomas Lewis and Ralph Nichols (1965), wrote that "effective listening and effective speaking are so closely woven together as to be inseparable" (p. 7). In other words, to discuss speaking without a concurrent discussion of listening is not productive. Our communication model identifies the Sender/Receiver and the Receiver/Sender elements of the model, noting that sending and receiving are simultaneous activities.

LEARNING OBJECTIVES

- UNDERSTAND THE DIFFERENCE BETWEEN LISTENING AND HEARING.
- KNOW AND PRACTICE THE FOUR STAGES OF LISTENING.
- USE THE FIVE CRITERIA FOR EVALUATING SPEECHES TO CRITIQUE YOUR CLASS-MATES' SPEECHES.

One way to improve your chances of success-ful public speaking is to approach the pro-cess from the listening side—that is, to work at developing better listening skills. These skills are essential for two different but com-plementary reasons. First, by understanding the needs of your listening audience, you are able to develop and deliver speeches that have the greatest chance of communicating your intended meaning. Second, by understanding the factors affecting listening, you are able to monitor your own listening habits, and more effectively evaluate and criticize the speeches of others, including your classmates. A direct relationship exists between the quality of your listening and the quality of your speaking.

© wavebreakmedia ltd, 2012. Under license from Shutterstock, Inc.

This chapter focuses on listening in the context of public speaking. First we discuss ⌈the foundations of listening. Then we discuss listening barriers and the listening process. We end the chapter by discussing how to evaluate and critique speeches.⌋

SPEAKING IN CONTEXT

Julian Treasure is a top-rated international speaker and leading TED (Technology, Entertainment, Design) speaker who specializes in listening. His five TED talks have been viewed an estimated 30 million times, and his recent book, *How to be Heard: Secrets for Powerful Speaking and Listening*, won the 2019 Audie Award for Best Audio Book in Business and Personal Development, as well as other awards.

A recurring theme in Treasure's work is the idea of conscious listening.

> I believe that every human being needs to listen consciously in order to
> live fully—connected in space and in time to the physical world around

us, connected in understanding to each other, not to mention spiritually connected, because every spiritual path I know of has listening and contemplation at its heart. (Treasure, 2017)

But Treasure is concerned that "we are losing our listening." Because of our technology-addiction and our self-absorption, we are often focused anywhere other than the here and now. This is especially true in an academic public speaking context. Imagine: it's speech day, but nobody is listening to anybody's speech because everybody is worried about their own speech! Add to this our collective, compulsive phone-checking, and it's unclear why we're here at all.

Don't let this happen to you! The art of public speaking and the art of listening are inextricably linked. Remember that for each speech assignment you encounter, you only have to give one speech, but you get to listen to many more speeches, depending on how many people are in your class. A listening audience is inherent in the very definition of public speaking. This chapter will help you examine your listening obligations and understand how to discharge them responsibly.

From *Communicating in Your Personal, Professional and Public Lives* by Sara Chudnovsky Weintraub, Candice Thomas-Maddox and Kerry Byrnes-Loinette. Copyright © 2016 by Kendall Hunt Publishing Company. Reprinted by permission.

TYPES OF LISTENING

Lisa Downs, training and development specialist, identifies four primary types of listening: informational, critical, appreciative, and empathic.

- The goal of informational listening is to accurately receive information from another person. It does not involve judgment or criticism.
- When engaging in appreciative listening, the goal is to listen for enjoyment or entertainment. It does not involve analyzing or evaluating information.
- The goal of empathic listening is to understand what the speaker is saying and feeling. This involves making an effort to look at the world through someone else's view.
- Finally, critical listening involves considering ideas heard from a speaker to decide if the message makes sense. A person using critical listening makes decisions about the message based on logic and evidence, rather than on emotion. An effective listener in a public speaking situation engages in critical listening. The following are four brief tips to help the critical listener:
  - Look for evidence to support ideas.
  - Consider the source of the evidence.
  - Check for logical reasoning.
  - Make a special effort to understand what the speaker is saying.

For more information on the types of listening and other listening topics, visit the American Society for Training and Development website at www.astd.org/content/publications/ASTDPress/ListeningSkillsTraining.htm.

FIGURE 16.1

LISTENING AND OTHER COMMUNICATION ACTIVITIES

Listening and hearing are not synonymous. **Hearing** is the physical ability to receive sounds. The Hearing Loss Association of America reports that, according to recent statistics from the National Center for Health, 36 million Americans, or 17%, have some hearing loss. This places hearing loss third in a line of public health issues behind heart disease and arthritis (www.hearingloss.org). So, we shouldn't assume our entire audience will hear us.

Listening is an active process that includes hearing. Many definitions of listening exist, but the International Listening Association defines **listening** as ⌐"the process of receiving, constructing meaning from, and responding to spoken and/or nonverbal messages" (International Listening Association, 2012).⌐ This is a complex process with multiple elements, and *responding* is part of the listening process. We discuss the four stages of listening later in the chapter. But before we discuss listening in further depth, it makes sense to see what role listening plays in our everyday communication. (For more information, see Figure 16.1.)

THE IMPORTANCE OF GOOD LISTENING SKILLS

We listen for entertainment (watching movies, listening to music), and we listen to our professors to understand and retain the material. We also listen to friends so we may develop and maintain relationships. ⌐But more than this, listening can help us in nearly all areas of life, including school (Bommelje, Houston, & Smither, 2003), work (AICPA, 2005), and leadership (Johnson & Bechler, 1998). Poor listening, in contrast, may result in negative consequences, including missing a message, not understanding a message, taking extra time for repetition or clarification, creating a negative impression by appearing disinterested, and being unable to participate fully in conversations.⌐

Each of these short-term effects may not seem terribly problematic, but in the long term, damage to personal and professional relationships can occur. For example, when we perceive someone is not listening to us or seems disinterested, it may hurt our feelings or we may feel defensive. We may choose not to communicate with that person again.

On a professional level, we want to make sure the messages we send are interpreted correctly. Having to clarify, repeat, or rephrase takes time away from the task at hand. Poor listeners at the organizational level may get chastised for their ineffective behavior, or colleagues may start to avoid working with someone who does not listen well.

So far, we have shown that listening is an important activity that consumes a large portion of our waking hours. We also know that good listeners are valued in the professional world, and poor listening leads to a variety of negative personal and professional consequences. Next, we provide an opportunity for you to think about your own listening habits.

REFLECT ON HOW YOU LISTEN

Many people think of listening as a simple task that involves sitting back and giving the speaker your attention. As public speakers, we hope our message and meaning will be understood. As audience members, we may have other things on our minds—distractions, prejudices, and stress—and the message we receive may be much different from the message sent. As the following interchange suggests in Table 16.1, listening is more complicated than it appears. The speaker (left column) is an elderly activist from the 1960s. The listener (right column) is a 24-year-old student.

TABLE 16.1

SPEAKER	LISTENER
Around 40 years ago, at about this time of year, I—and a whole lot of other committed students—spent a solid week—day and night—in the offices of our college president. Needless to say, we hadn't been invited.	*Here I am again—listening to another speaker who says he stormed his college administration building in the 60s. This must be a popular topic on the college speaking circuit. Maybe this guy will be different from the other three middle-aged radicals I heard, but I doubt it ... The least they could do is turn up the air conditioning. It's so hot I can hardly breathe.*
We were protesters and proud of it. We were there because we believed the Vietnam War was wrong. We were there because we believed racism was wrong. We were there because we believed that women should be given the same opportunities as men.	*These guys keep talking about how they know the way and how we're all wrong ... I wonder what he does for a living. I'll bet he hasn't saved any lives lately or helped the poor. He probably earns big bucks giving speeches on campus telling us how horrible we are ... He looks like he spends a lot of time cultivating his hippie look.*
Were we victorious? For about 10 years, I thought so. Then something happened. The signs were subtle at first. Haircuts got shorter. The preppie look replaced torn jeans. Business became the major of choice.	*He's harping on the same old issues. Doesn't he know the Vietnam War is ancient history; that women have more opportunities than they ever had—I wish I could earn as much as Zendaya ... I guess I'll have a pizza for dinner. I should have eaten before I came.*
In a flash—it happened that quickly—these subtle changes became a way of life. Campus life, as I knew it, disappeared. Revolution and concern for the oppressed were out, and conservatism and concern for the self were in.	*Of course we're interested in business. Maybe he had a rich father who paid his tuition, but I don't. I need to earn money when I graduate so I can pay back my student loans.*
From the point of view of someone who has seen both sides—the radical, tumultuous 60s and the calm, money-oriented 80s, 90s, and the new century—students of today are really 40-year-olds in 20-year-old bodie, conservative to the core at the only time of life when they can choose to live free. I am here to help you see how wrong you are.	*Who does he think he is—calling us conservatives? I'm not a bigot. When I believe something is wrong, I fight to change it—like when I protested against ethnic cleansing overseas and flag burning right here. I wonder when he'll finish. I've got to study for my marketing exam. He just goes on and on about the same old things.*

LISTENING BARRIERS

You may see a bit of yourself in the speaker–listener above. Most of us experience this kind of internal dialogue occasionally. It is clear that listening is important, and research has shown that we do not retain much of what a speaker says. So, the question remains, why do we stop listening? There is no single answer to this question, but the following things can cause us to stop listening.

1. **When our attention drifts.** Listeners drift in and out of a speech, thinking about the heat, their next meal, or an impending exam. Studies have shown that few of us are able to pay attention to a single stimulus for more than 20 seconds without focusing, at least momentarily, on something else.

2. **When we are distracted.** Our environment determines how well we can listen. In the speaker–listener example, the heat made it difficult to pay attention. Internal stresses—hunger, unresolved conflict, and concern about exams—are also distractions. With people leaving cell phones on, checking messages, and texting or checking social media during a speech, listeners can be distracted, either because they're creating the distraction or they are near the distraction.

3. **When we have preconceived notions.** Before the speaker in the example above opened his mouth, the listener had already decided what the speaker stood for based on the speaker's appearance and on a stereotype of what 60s radicals stood for. Although in this case the listener was right—the speaker's views conformed to the listener's preconceived notions—he/she may be wrong about other speakers.

4. **When we disagree.** Although the speaker identified continuing social ills, the listener did not share his concerns. From the listener's point of view, much more was right with the world than the speaker admitted—a perspective that reduced the listener's willingness and ability to consider the speaker's message.

5. **When we are prejudiced or inflexible.** Very few women earn as much as Zendaya. Yet the listener based their reaction to the speaker's message on the

Named by Harvard Law School as one of history's best negotiators, Nelson Mandela challenged South African leaders to listen to the plight of non-white South Africans (Mnookin, 2011).

premise that if one member of a group can succeed, all can. His prejudice prevented him from seeing the truth in the speaker's words.

6. **When we are faced with abstractions and form our own opinions.** The speaker never defined the term "conservative." As a result, the listener brought his/her own meaning to the term, equating it with bigotry. This meaning may or may not have coincided with the speaker's intent.

As audience members, we know our purpose is to listen, think critically, and retain the central idea of the message. But think about what you do as you listen and why you stop listening. You may consciously or unconsciously tune the speaker out. You may focus on minor details at the expense of the main point. You may prejudge the speaker based on appearance. You may allow your own emotional needs and responses to distort the message. In this chapter, we provide specific tips for improving your listening skills, but first, we discuss the four stages of listening.

ENGAGING IN COMMUNITY

Kuwame Kinsel did not begin his multimedia career in the safest of environments. Growing up in Pittsburgh's Hill District at a time when gang activity was surging, Kinsel would find himself attending six funerals before his senior year in high school. However, rather than let his unfortunate experiences bring him down, Kinsel found himself moved toward mentorship to the members of his community.

"It's mentorship that makes a difference in people's lives," Kinsel says (Aldrich, 2016).

Kinsel engages in many community outreach programs for his neighborhood. He is a head cyclist for Bike Pittsburgh (a program designed to give young people a healthy outlet to explore their city) and a supervising intern at BOOM Concepts, a community arts space where artists and musicians are able to showcase their work. Kinsel acknowledges his skill in listening to others as a crucial part of his work; he admits that being a good listener helped him overcome some of his own misconceptions and prejudices.

"Interacting with various artists has caused me to change my entire perspective about women—my sensitivities are heightened around the prevailing sexism in our culture," Kinsel says (Aldrich, 2016).

As you continue to hone your active listening skills, reflect over Kinsel's story and how it stands as a testament to the power of having an open mind.

From *Communicating in Your Personal, Professional and Public Lives* by Sara Chudnovsky Weintraub, Candice Thomas-Maddox and Kerry Byrnes-Loinette. Copyright © 2016 by Kendall Hunt Publishing Company. Reprinted by permission.

THE FOUR STAGES OF LISTENING

Think back to a time when, in an argument with a family member or a friend, you responded with "I hear you!" True, you may have *heard* them. It is possible, however, that you did not *listen* to them. Although listening appears to be instinctual and instantaneous, as noted earlier, it consists of four identifiable stages (see Figure 16.2). We move through these stages every time we ⌐listen; if we do not, then listening can't

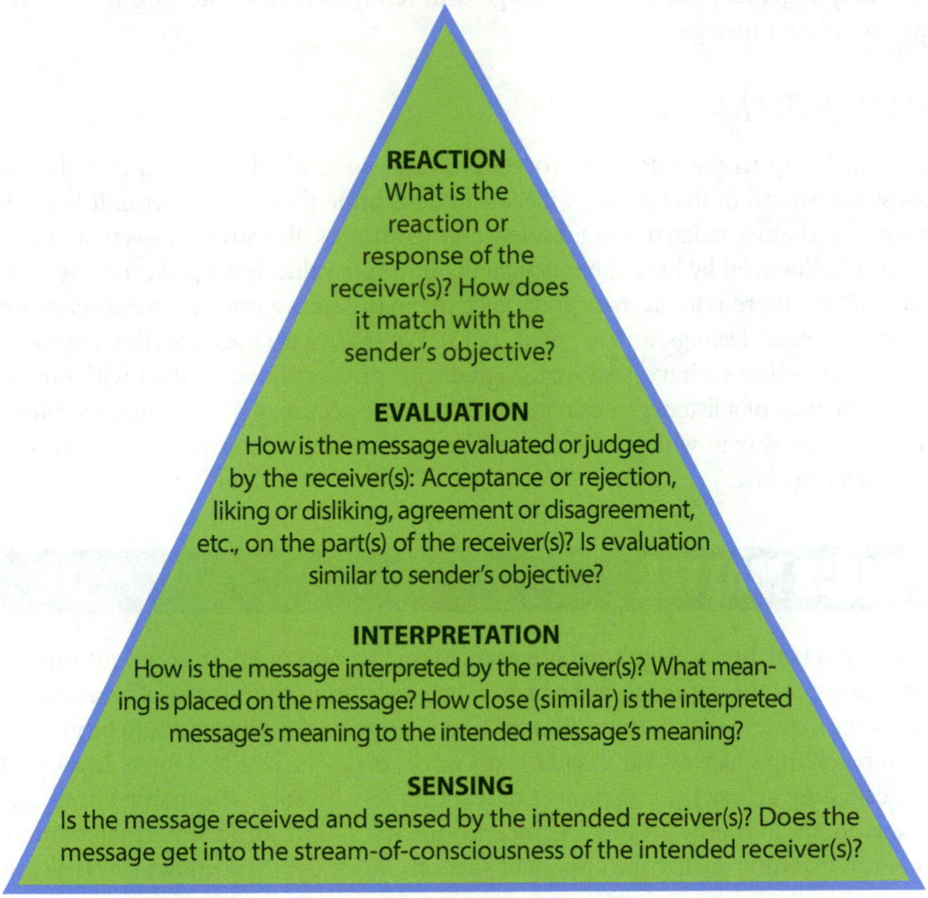

REACTION
What is the reaction or response of the receiver(s)? How does it match with the sender's objective?

EVALUATION
How is the message evaluated or judged by the receiver(s): Acceptance or rejection, liking or disliking, agreement or disagreement, etc., on the part(s) of the receiver(s)? Is evaluation similar to sender's objective?

INTERPRETATION
How is the message interpreted by the receiver(s)? What meaning is placed on the message? How close (similar) is the interpreted message's meaning to the intended message's meaning?

SENSING
Is the message received and sensed by the intended receiver(s)? Does the message get into the stream-of-consciousness of the intended receiver(s)?

FIGURE 16.2 Four-stage communication model.

be truly said to have occurred. (This is true whether we are part of a formal audience listening to a paid speaker, engaged in conversation with a friend, or at home alone, or listening to a political debate on television.) The following is an elaboration of the four stages of listening.

SENSING

Listening starts when you sense information from its source, which requires the ability to hear what is said. For a variety of reasons, sometimes we don't "sense" that someone is talking to us, so we miss part or all of the message. Sight is also a factor with sensing, because the speaker's gestures, facial expressions, and the use of presentational aids also communicate intent.

INTERPRETING

Interpreting messages, which involves attaching meaning to the speaker's words, is also part of listening. Both as a speaker and as a listener, keep in mind that words have different meanings to different people. Individual audience members may interpret words differently based on subjective experiences. Our ability to interpret what we hear may be influenced by the listening barriers discussed earlier.

Sign language, just like vocal language, still requires active listening skills to receive the complete message.

EVALUATING

The third step in the listening process is **evaluation**, which requires that the listener assess the worth of the speaker's ideas and determine their importance. It is a mistake to assume that we judge messages solely on their merits. Research shows that our assessment is influenced by how the message fits into our value system. According to Friedman (1986), there is a "human preference for maintaining internal consistency among personal beliefs, feelings, and actions" (p. 13). We agree with messages that are consistent with other beliefs we have, and we disagree with messages that conflict with our beliefs. ⌈The accuracy of a listener's evaluation rests on the accuracy of the listener's interpretation, and the way in which a listener evaluates a message determines the nature of the listener's response.⌟

ETHICS MATTER

Mia is part of her college's debate team. During one of their competitions with a rival campus, the opposing team began their debate on the subject of financial aid. In their argument, the other team asserted that low-income students should be given priority in receiving financial aid. As her team works on their rebuttal, one of Mia's partners suggests they accuse their opponent of wanting to withhold scholarships from middle-class students altogether. A quick glance around the auditorium reveals that many people were not listening during the opponent's speech. Although Mia knows this is clearly not

© fizkes/Shutterstock.com

FIGURE 16.3 Sign language, just like vocal language, still requires active listening skills to receive the complete message.

what the other team meant, she is almost certain the insinuation will turn the audience unfairly against her opponents.

Questions to consider:

1. Is there an ethical breach in taking advantage of an audience of passive listeners?

2. Is it immoral to use audience misconceptions to strengthen Mia's arguments?

3. What (if any) ethical obligations does the audience have in a debate scenario such as this one?

REACTING/RESPONDING

Listening involves **reacting/responding** to the speaker's message. Feedback is also part of the listening process. In a conversation, the roles of listener and speaker change regularly. As the listener, you can interrupt the speaker, ask questions, and provide nonverbal cues such as eye contact, touching, or hugging. (For tips on asking questions of a speaker, see Figure 16.4.)

Listeners in a public speaking setting provide feedback in a variety of ways: laughing, smiling, nodding in agreement, cheering or booing, clapping, or questioning the speaker after the presentation. Listeners also provide feedback on a less conscious level, such as yawning, texting, looking around the room, or whispering to the person next to them.

⌈As a listener, do not underestimate the impact your nonverbal feedback has on a speaker. When you are in a live audience, you are not watching a YouTube video: *the speaker can see you.* This is true whether you are smiling and nodding or picking your nose and checking your phone.

Speakers rely heavily on and encourage feedback from their audience. They watch carefully for messages of approval or disapproval and adjust their presentations accordingly.⌋

EIGHT STEPS FOR FINE-TUNING YOUR LISTENING SKILLS

As a skill, listening is notoriously undervalued. Philosopher Mortimer Adler (1983) uses the following sports analogy to describe why the act of listening is as important as the act of speaking: "Catching is as much an activity as throwing and requires as much skill, though it is a skill of a different kind. Without the complementary efforts of both players, properly attuned to each other, the play cannot be completed." The players involved in the act of communication are speakers and listeners, all of whom have a role in the interaction. In this section, we explain how you can improve your listening skills—and, therefore, the chances of meaningful communication—by becoming conscious of your habits and, when necessary, redirecting your efforts.

FIGURE 16.4

1. GET READY TO LISTEN

Preparation is critical, especially when you have other things on your mind. Plan to make the effort to listen even before the speech begins, deliberately clearing your mind of distractions so you are able to concentrate on the speech. This also means turning off your cell phone. In some cases, it may involve having proper "tools" with you, such as pen and paper or a tablet and stylus.

2. MINIMIZE PERSONAL BARRIERS TO LISTENING

This step is more difficult than it sounds, for it involves overcoming emotional and intellectual barriers to listening that we identified in preceding passages. Often, we need help in recognizing our listening "blind spots." Most people take it for granted that the message they heard from a speaker was the same message the speaker intended. But sometimes, an entire audience misses the point. If a question-and-answer period follows the speech, you can question the speaker directly to make sure you have the right meaning.

3. LEAVE DISTRACTIONS BEHIND

Some distractions are more easily dealt with than others. You can change your seat to get away from the smell of perfume but you cannot make a head cold disappear. You can close the door to your classroom, but you cannot stop the speaker from rattling change in his pocket. Although dealing with distractions is never easy, try putting them aside so you can focus on the speaker and the speech. This task becomes easier when you view listening as a responsibility—and as work. By considering listening to be work which requires serious effort, you are more likely to hear the message being sent.

4. DO NOT RUSH TO JUDGMENT

It is important to resist the temptation to *prejudge* speakers. Listeners may prejudge topics as well as speakers. ⌈We demonstrate prejudgment of a speaker when we find ourselves dismissing someone because "she's old" or "he's conservative." As a listener, you have the responsibility to evaluate the content of the speech and not jump to conclusions based on surface speaker characteristics.⌋ You may yawn at the thought of listening to one of your classmates deliver an informative speech about the "pickling process" or "stage make-up" until you realize that the topic is more interesting than you expected. You may not have an inherent interest in the topic, but that does not mean the speaker cannot be interesting or thought-provoking. Some speakers save their best for last. They may start slowly and build a momentum of ideas and language. Your job is to listen and be patient.

5. LISTEN FOR CONTENT FIRST, DELIVERY SECOND

Confronted with poor delivery, it is difficult to separate content from presentation. The natural tendency is simply to stop listening when speakers drone on in a monotone, deliver speeches with their heads in their notes, or sway back and forth. However, delivery often has little to do with the quality of the speaker's ideas. Many of the speakers you will hear over the years will be in the position to address you because of their accomplishments, not their speaking ability. While a Nobel Prize–winning scientist may be able to explain a breakthrough in cancer therapy, he or she may have no idea how to make eye contact with an audience. In some situations, it is helpful to outline the main ideas as the speaker presents them so that you focus on the ideas instead of the delivery.

6. BECOME AN EFFECTIVE NOTE TAKER

Each time a professor lectures or conducts a class discussion, you and your fellow students are expected to take notes. Even if you do take notes in school, this skill often disappears at graduation. Most people do not pull out a pad and a pen when listening to a speech in the world outside the classroom. But note-taking is as appropriate and necessary for nonstudents as it is for students.

⌈In a world full of search engines and online content, taking personal notes is a lost art. Nevertheless, when you listen to a speech at a public event, a political rally, or on TV, taking notes helps you listen more effectively. The following suggestions will help you improve your note-taking—and listening—skills:⌋

- **Create two columns for your notes.** Write "Facts" at the top of the left column and "Personal reactions/questions" at the top of the right column. If the speaker does not answer your questions during the course of the speech, ask for clarification at the end.
- **Use a keyword outline instead of full sentences to document the speaker's essential points.** If you get bogged down trying to write full sentences, you may miss a huge chunk of the message. At the end of the speech, the keyword outline gives you a quick picture of the speaker's main points.
- **Use your own abbreviations or shorthand symbols to save time.** If you know that "comm" means communication, then use that. If you are not sure whether it means "communication," "communism," or "community," then the

FIGURE 16.5 By viewing listening as a responsibility, you will be more likely to hear the message being sent.

abbreviation is not working for you. We have seen students use up and down arrows instead of writing "increase" or "decrease." Develop a system that works for you.

- **Use a numbering system to get down procedural, directional, or structural units of information.** Numbering helps organize information, especially if the speaker did not organize the units of information for you.

7. BE AN ACTIVE LISTENER

As listeners, we can process information at the rate of about 400 words per minute. However, as most people talk at only about 150 words per minute, we have a considerable amount of unused thinking time to spare (Wolf et al., 1983, p. 154). This "extra time" often gets in the way of listening because we tend to take mental excursions away from the speaker's topic. It is natural to take brief trips ("I wonder what's for lunch?") but it can be problematic when we take major vacations. To minimize the potential for taking a lengthy vacation while listening, we suggest trying a few active listening techniques:

- **Before the speech begins, write down questions you have about the topic.** As the speech progresses, determine whether the speaker has answered them.
- **Take notes to keep your focus on the speech.**
- **Apply the speaker's comments to your own experience and knowledge.** This makes the message more memorable.

© VladKol, 2012. Under license from Shutterstock, Inc.

FIGURE 16.6 Taking notes helps you listen more effectively.

- **Identify the thesis statement.** This will help keep you focused as you listen.
- **Decide whether you agree with the speaker's point of view and evaluate the general performance.** This keeps you engaged by focusing on the message and the speaker.

8. PROVIDE FEEDBACK

Let speakers know what you think. You may be able to provide feedback through the use of questions during or after the speech, and there may be an opportunity to give feedback to the speaker later on a personal level.

Even in a large lecture hall, the speaker is aware of the audience and will establish eye contact with audience members. As a listener, you can provide nonverbal feedback by leaning forward in your chair, nodding your head, smiling, and frowning when the occasion or your emotions call for it. This kind of participation forces you to focus your attention on the speaker and the speech. Providing feedback at the various stages of a speech is hard work that requires total involvement and a commitment to fighting distractions.

FIGURE 16.7 How can you provide feedback to a speaker?

CRITIQUING SPEECHES

As an audience member in a public speaking situation, you listen to be informed on some topic, to be persuaded to change an attitude, or to engage in some specific behavior. Whatever your reason, several options exist for providing feedback on the speech. Clapping, laughing, asking questions at the end of the speech, giving a standing ovation, and talking to the speaker afterward are all forms of feedback. You may also be asked to provide written and/or oral feedback for a speaker.

When you evaluate speeches, you are engaging in a feedback process that makes you a speech critic. As you consider the elements included in a speech and note the speaker's strengths and weaknesses, you are taking part in a formal process of analysis and appraisal. ⌜Criteria are always applied each time someone in an audience thinks about a speech, whether you are delivering a graded classroom speech or speaking in some other nonacademic context. As a participant in a public speaking course, you are expected to criticize your classmate's speeches constructively.⌟

FIVE KEY CRITERIA FOR EVALUATING SPEECHES

As you criticize the strengths and weaknesses of speakers, keep in mind that your comments help your classmates develop as speakers. Your remarks help focus their attention on areas that work effectively as well as areas that need improvement. All speakers need this feedback to improve the quality of their performance.

SPEAKING EXCELLENCE IN YOUR CAREER

More and more often, companies are challenged to increase their branding by using social media platforms to better listen to their audience. This is often a difficult task; social media is notorious for changing drastically in a very short period of time. However, the investigation into the relationship between social media and advertising is critical for the success of contemporary businesses. Researcher Joseph Rosendale examines the connection between communication technologies in organization communications and branding.

Of all the technologies available for business organizations, social media currently attracts the most attention. Not only is social media a revolutionary tool for communicating and organizing information, but these benefits are also practically free of charge (Rosendale, 2015). However, Rosendale notes that businesses cannot simply send an old message through a new medium and expect results; communication must be two-way in social media. The way that consumers and businesses communicate and engage with one another in a turn-taking format is crucial to create and maintain interest. As marketing officer Tim Leberecht notes, an organization's brand quality can be measured by paying attention to what people say when they do not think the company is listening (Leberecht, 2012). Social media now allows companies to be listening and active in that conversation at all times. An organization's success, performance, and overall valuation can be tied to its brand-communication strategy (Argenti, 2013). Clearly, social media savvy underscores the importance of social media integration in creating a profitable bottom line for companies in the present and future.

From *Communicating in Your Personal, Professional and Public Lives* by Sara Chudnovsky Weintraub, Candice Thomas-Maddox and Kerry Byrnes-Loinette. Copyright © 2016 by Kendall Hunt Publishing Company. Reprinted by permission.

Five general criteria can be applied to a special occasion speech, an informative speech, or a persuasive speech. We present these with guiding questions that allow the critic to examine both content and delivery. These are not presented in order of importance.

1. **Organization**
   - Was the speech effectively organized?
   - Were the general and specific purposes clear and relevant to the assignment?
   - Were the functions of the introduction and conclusion clear (such as gaining attention and previewing)?
   - Were main points clear?
   - Did the speaker use appropriate transitions and internal summaries?
   - Was an organizational pattern clear?

2. **Research/Supporting Material**
   - Did the speaker use effective and relevant material to support the thesis statement?
   - Was there evidence of sufficient research?
   - Was supporting material timely?

- Did the speaker include a variety of supporting material?
- Was supporting material relevant, helpful, and credible?
- Were sources integrated into the speech appropriately and cited correctly?

3. **Analysis**
   - Was the topic appropriate for the assignment/audience?
   - Was the structure of the speech consistent with the specific purpose?
   - Did the speaker make an effort to analyze the audience and adapt the speech to their needs?
   - Was all evidence presented made relevant and concrete?
   - If used, did presentational aids contribute to the effectiveness of the speech?

4. **Language**
   - Did the speaker use clear and accurate language?
   - Did the speaker use various language techniques to engage the listener?
   - Were unfamiliar terms defined?
   - Was language appropriate to the situation and the audience?

5. **Verbal and Nonverbal Delivery**
   - Did the speaker appear confident and self-controlled?
   - Did the speaker establish and maintain appropriate eye contact?
   - Were movements and gestures meaningful?
   - Was the quality of the speaker's voice acceptable?
   - Did the speaker pronounce words correctly and articulate effectively?
   - Did the speaker look for and respond to feedback?
   - Did the speaker include relevant emphasis and pauses?
   - Was the speech relatively free of fillers (such as um, er, like, etc.)?
   - Did the speaker use notes effectively?

Use these five criteria as a guide to evaluate your classmates' speeches. Often instructors ask students to use a speech evaluation form similar to the one provided in Figure 16.8. This gives feedback to the speaker on a sliding scale and also gives listeners the opportunity to provide constructive comments. No matter what criteria are used, the goal of evaluating speeches is to provide each speaker with valuable feedback.

A FINAL NOTE ABOUT SELF-EVALUATION

Just as editing your own writing can be tedious and difficult, so is evaluating your own speech. Often lacking in objectivity, we tend to be hypercritical at times and completely unaware of our errors at other times. This is why critiques from your classmates are so helpful. As you process comments you receive from your listeners, focus on the content, not how it was said or written. Even severe feedback may hold helpful information if you look closely. Try to recognize the important aspects of any criticism, but do not feel you need to attend to every comment.

Public Speaking Evaluation Form

Speaker: _____ Evaluator: _____ Date: _____

Topic: _____

5 — excellent   4 — very good   3 — satisfactory   2 — fair   1 — unsatisfactory

Rating

Organization

Was the speech effectively organized?   1 2 3 4 5

(effective introduction and conclusion; clear main points; used transitions and internal summaries; pattern related to specific purpose)

Comments:

Research/Supporting Material

Did the speaker use effective and relevant material to support the thesis statement? 1 2 3 4 5

(Evidence of sufficient research; supporting material time, varied, relevant, helpful, credible; sufficient sources; integrated appropriately and cited correctly)

Comments:

Analysis

Were the topic and structure appropriate for the assignment/audience?   1 2 3 4 5

(Clear audience analysis, evidence relevant and concrete; presentational aides contributed to effectiveness)

Comments:

Language

Did the speaker use clear and accurate language?   1 2 3 4 5

(Varied language technique; defined unfamiliar terms; appropriate to the situation)

Comments:

Verbal and Nonverbal Delivery

Did verbal and nonverbal delivery enhance the effectiveness of the speech?   1 2 3 4 5

(Appeared confident, effective eye contact; appropriate gestures and movement; relatively free of nonfluencies; solid pronunciation and diction; good vocal quality; responded to feedback

Comments:

FIGURE 16.8 Using a public speaking evaluation form like this one helps you give a speaker constructive and valuable criticism.

FIGURE 16.9 As a public figure and the Duchess of Sussex, Meghan Markle had her speeches evaluated not only by citizens of the U.K., but also by the world at large.

While our first reaction after giving a speech might be to look at the comments others wrote, we encourage you to first reflect on how *you* think you did. What *do you believe* were your strengths and weaknesses? Did you think you had appropriate organization, adequate research, and effective delivery? Were you fluent? Enthusiastic? What positive aspects of your speech should you keep in mind for the next speech, and what should you try to avoid? Set a few goals for yourself, and view each speech as a learning experience.

SUMMARY

- ⌈Listening is defined as attending, receiving, interpreting, and responding to messages aurally.
- Hearing is the physical ability to receive sound.
- Listening is a complex activity that involves four stages: sensing, interpreting, evaluating, and reacting/responding.
- Sensing: Listening starts when you sense information from its source, which requires the ability to hear what is said. · Interpreting: Interpreting involves attaching meaning to a speaker's words. · Evaluating: Evaluation requires that you assess the worth of the speaker's ideas and determine their importance

to you. · Reacting/responding: Both reacting and responding ask you to offer feedback, which is a crucial part of the listening process.

- The five criteria for evaluating speeches are organization, research/supporting material, analysis, language, and verbal and nonverbal delivery.

KEY TERMS

Evaluation—assessing the worth of the speaker's ideas and determining their importance to you.

Hearing—the physical ability to receive sounds.

Interpreting—attaching meaning to a speaker's words.

Listening—the attending, receiving, interpreting, and responding to messages presented aurally.

Reacting/responding—providing feedback to the speaker's message.

Sensing—to become aware of or to perceive.

QUESTIONS FOR REVIEW

Respond to the following questions **without** reviewing the text or your notes. These questions are provided to help you practice retrieving information and reflect on your reading.

A. What did you learn about listening?

B. Did you agree or disagree with anything you read? Explain.

C. What did you learn that was new to you?

D. What concepts, if any, were confusing to you?

Respond to the following questions. You may reference your text or notes to help you.

1. Why are good listening skills important?

2. The chapter discusses six barriers that can cause us to stop listening.

3. Identify and describe the four stages of listening.

4. What are the eight steps to improve your listening skills? Which one are you most likely to try? Which one would be difficult for you? Why?

5. What are the five criteria for critiquing speeches?

QUESTIONS FOR DISCUSSION

1. In your small group, review the barriers that may cause an audience may stop listening. Which of these barriers may be a concern during your presentations? What can you do to counter these concerns and encourage better listening?

2. How do you tend to respond to critiques of your speech? Why do you think you respond this way? Does anything in the text encourage you to be more open to feedback and evaluation? Why or why not?

3. How does information about the four stages of listening connect with other ideas and concepts we have discussed in this class?

4. In your small group, designate a time for all members to practice their speeches. Use the Public Speaking Evaluation Form to provide feedback to each member. Review the feedback you receive and make necessary adjustments before your final presentation.

5. Discuss the ethical questions provided at the end of the chapter. What ethical considerations are relevant to the information in this chapter about listening and critiquing speeches?

- Are there guidelines (e.g., don't lie) that would be appropriate for every situation, or are ethics relative?

- Do the ends (e.g., a good outcome) justify any means?

- Is deceiving the receiver ever appropriate?

- Should the source of the message bear primary responsibility for ethics, or should the receiver share that responsibility (e.g., buyer beware)?

REFERENCES

Adler, M. J. (1983). *How to speak, how to listen.* New York: Macmillan.

AICPA. (2005). *Highlighted responses from the Association for Accounting Marketing Survey. Creating the future agenda for the profession—Managing partner perspective.* Retrieved April 8, 2005 from www.aicpa.org/pubs/tpcpa/feb2001/hilight.htm

Aldrich, R. (2016, May 9). Generation NEXT: Multimedia artist, advocate has a heart for community. *The New Pittsburgh Courier.* Retrieved from http:// newpittsburghcourieronline.com/2016/05/09/generation-next-multimedia-artist-advocate-has-a-heart-for-community/

Argenti, P. A. (2013). *Corporate communication* (6th ed.). New York, NY: McGraw-Hill/Irwin.

Bommelje, R., Houston, J. M., & Smither, R. (2003). Personality characteristics of effective listeners: A five-factor perspective. *International Journal of Listening, 17,* 32–46.

Friedman, P. G. (1986). *Listening processes: Attention, understanding, evaluation* (2nd Ed., pp. 6–15). Washington, DC: National Education Association.

International Listening Association. (2021). https://www.listen.org/

Johnson, S. D., & Bechler, C. (1998). Examining the relationship between listening effectiveness and leadership emergence: Perceptions, behaviors, and recall. *Small Group Research, 29*(4), 452–471.

Leberecht, T. (2012). 3 ways to (usefully) lose control of your brand [video file]. Retrieved from http://www.youtube.com/watch?v=_xM-WqUe8FdU

Lewis, T. R., & Nichols, R. (1965). *Speaking and listening: a guide to effective oral-aural communication.* Dubuque, IA: W. C. Brown.

Mnookin, R. (2011). *Bargaining with the devil: When to negotiate, when to fight.* New York City: Simon & Schuster.

Naistadt, I. (2004). *Speak without fear.* New York: HarperCollins.

Rosendale, J. A. (2015). New communication technologies in organization communications and branding: The integral role social media now play. *Florida Communication Journal, 43*(2), 49-59.

Wolf, F. L., Marsnik, N. C., Taceuy, W. S., & Nichols, R. G. (1983). *Perceptive listening.* New York: Holt, Rinehart and Winston.

SIA information can be obtained
www.ICGtesting.com
nted in the USA
HW060635290122
09086LV00008B/2

9 781792 472626